UNGODLY RAGE

THE HIDDEN FACE OF CATHOLIC FEMINISM

DONNA STEICHEN

Ungodly Rage

The Hidden Face of Catholic Feminism

IGNATIUS PRESS SAN FRANCISCO

Cover by Roxanne Mei Lum

With ecclesiastical approval

ISBN 0-89870-348-4
Library of Congress catalogue number 90-84593
Printed in the United States of America

Contents

There shall be no strange god among you
nor shall you worship any alien god.
I, the Lord, am your God
who led you forth from the land of Egypt.
But my people heard not my voice,
and Israel obeyed me not;
So I gave them up to the hardness of their hearts;
they walked according to their own counsels.

Psalm 81

The life we joined in 1960 is like the old Motherhouse: gone without a trace. Maybe it was all a dream.

Catherine Victory

Foreword

Mother Teresa of Calcutta has said, “Words which do not give the light of Christ increase the darkness.” This book is about darkness. Its pages document one of the most devastating religious epidemics of our, or any other, time—an infectious and communicable disease of the human spirit for which there is no easy cure, and which afflicts not only the “carriers”, but nearly all religious believers—including our children, the future of the human race and the future of the Church. The book should be read attentively by all who are concerned about or responsible for the religious welfare and spiritual development of others.

This disease, the source of the “ungodly rage” of the title, has a name: “feminism”. The evidence contained in these pages may cause a few sleepless nights for some bishops and clergy who have regarded the feminist influence in the Church and feminist issues (like “inclusive” language and female altar servers) as of little real importance, or who have convinced themselves that radical religious feminism is so loony it will burn itself out in due course with little damage done to the Church. Donna Steichen's penetrating account, based on hours of personal interviews and attendance at feminist gatherings, sounds a necessary alarm.

Among the phenomena Mrs. Steichen's diligent reporting reveals is the relentless iconoclasm of religious feminism (the “rage”) coexistent with a calculated effort to “remythologize” Christianity—to substitute a concocted changeling myth for perennial religious truth. Feminism's iconoclasm and mythmaking result from profound spiritual malaise, a predictable consequence of the erosion of confidence in human reason during a century fraught with cataclysmic wars and social upheavals, compounded by the manifest weakening of nearly every established social institution, including the Church. Traditional forms of piety have virtually disappeared during the past twenty years, and the transcendent dimension of religion has been, for a variety of reasons, obscured. But the effects of religious feminism have been to produce further anguish and confusion and to deepen divisions rather than to accomplish healing and restoration and unity.

In direct proportion to waning confidence in the rational faculty, feminists desire to affix blame for our predicament, to find a scapegoat and immolate him and to create an oxymoronic "new tradition", a new "prevailing myth" and a means whereby we can construct with our own wills and "liberated" imaginations a radically new social and cultural "structure"—a new "Tower of Babel", stripped of the original's flaws, purged of the stink of the past and rising from a foundation swept clean of all the rubble of former allegiances and ties and beliefs. This objective has become a compulsion for feminist social reformers and professional religious.

The principal targets of feminist "re-formation" are the Catholic Church and women, for the very good reason that both provide strong links with the past and both are primary transmitters to future generations of received culture and perennial religious beliefs. The Catholic Church uniquely represents and embodies all of Christianity, which has provided the moral and ethical foundation of our civilization. Women, who literally bear within their bodies the future of humanity, are essential to the establishment of families, the fundamental unit of any society. The economy of the re-formers' strategy thus entails an assault on the faith of the Church *through* the women of the Church—an ingenious strategy, assuredly, and so far it is working very well.

Recent events in eastern Europe which have effectively discredited Marxist revolutionary social theories have had little or no effect on feminist and other "liberationist" theologians. The reason for this may be (although I have never seen it stated in their works) that classic Marxism viewed religion *per se* as a defect of man's imagination to be overcome, whereas religion is, of course, the theologians' stock-in-trade—in fact, their livelihood. (Is it cynical to suggest that people who "do" theology must endlessly invent "new" material in order to justify their salaries or simply to stave off boredom?) Perhaps some "revolutionary" theologians perceive that social theories which attempt to base themselves on human reason alone must eventually fail, precisely because the rational faculty itself is unreliable. Marxist theories may have failed in part because they neglected to integrate the subjective, the personal, the sensual —intuitive impulses, emotions, individual experience, "feelings", etc.—which are integral to human experience and which form an essential part of religious experience. Feminist theologians, in fact, define "dualism" as the subordination of subjective, intuitive experience (often identified as "feminine") to objective, rational intellectual perception (often identified as "masculine").

But if feminist and other liberationist theologians perceive the defect inherent in systems and social structures that do not take full account of the subjective, that element within human consciousness that is hidden, interior, "dark"; if they are reacting to the dimming of the Enlightenment and its ideas of the perfectibility of humanity and society through human reason and if they correctly see the need to integrate the "religious impulse" into the structures of society; their critique also involves denial of objective truth, which transcends the limitations of a particular culture or individual perception or experience of it. They also reject most traditional manifestations of the religious impulse, especially authentic Christianity.

Feminist theologians have given themselves license to create a New Mythology for a New Age, freed from the "oppressive" inherited "myth" they believe was imposed on them by "the patriarchy". In "claiming their power" they feel compelled to reject authority (though they are quite willing to exercise power over others). They seek to impose their "new morality" on the rest of the world, to manipulate and politicize language, to deconstruct texts of Scripture and re-construct them according to the feminist "hermeneutic of suspicion" and to inhabit and use the established structures of Christianity (i.e., the churches) in order to effect a collapse from within. One of the most dishonest of the New Myths is the claim of feminist zealots to speak in the name of *all* women—including those who are "not yet aware" of "oppression by the patriarchal Church".

Other examples abound. The new "Spirit" invoked by feminist theologians gives them power "to smash the idols of Church and culture"; and the "God" of feminism, as Monika Hellwig writes in *The Role of the Theologian in Today's Church*,

> creates human persons in the divine image by awakening them into freedom, self-determination and creativity in which they discover that they are essentially relational . . . in this they are fulfilling and realizing the creativity of God; when they shape communities which offer liberation, happiness and fulfilling relationships to all, they fulfill the purpose of creation; then all creation is drawn into a great harmony and returns to the Creator in peace, and God is glorified.[1]

The implications of such a "theology" are stunning.

According to the New Mythology of feminist fundamentalists, we are all "cosmic Christs"; Jesus (who is not the *only* "Christ") "never intended to found a Church", was "culturally conditioned" to be incarnate as a male and to choose only men as his apostles, although he was "counter-cultural" in his dealings with women; Mary was a proto-feminist revolutionary; traditional Christianity is a creation of male domination; the Church, to be valid, must make herself "credible"(!) even to those who reject her most essential teachings; hierarchy is of its very nature self-evidently evil; ancient "goddess religions" offer "promising insights" for the construction of the New Myth of religious feminism.

Whatever else this New Mythology is, it is "Christian" or "Catholic" only insofar as these concepts are also re-defined by feminists. Despite this, the feminist movement has been astonishingly successful in occupying the official structures of the national churches in the West—notably in northern Europe, Canada and the United States—like so many hermit crabs (even more like jays, who destroy the eggs and young of other birds in order to inhabit nests they did not build).

[1] Monika Hellwig, *The Role of the Theologian in Today's Church* (St. Louis, Mo.: Sheed and Ward, 1987), 13.

Feminist women (and men) occupy prominent chairs in theology at Catholic and secular universities; they are members of seminary faculties; they hold powerful diocesan offices; they are writers and editors for Catholic journals and Catholic publishing houses that produce catechetical materials used throughout the Catholic school system; they have access to financial resources and often official ecclesiastical support for endless conferences and workshops involving many thousands of Catholic teachers, retreat leaders, directors of religious education, etc. They are liturgists, chaplains of Catholic hospitals and sit on boards of abortion clinics. "Catholic" feminists also have instant access to the communications media, Catholic and secular, which they do not hesitate to use at every opportunity to bludgeon the Catholic Church, discredit Church leaders and ridicule Catholic believers.

Although feminist women complain endlessly that they are prohibited from access to power in the Church, it is hard to imagine any elitist revolutionary group having greater real power in any institution than do Catholic feminists and their sympathizers. From ordinary parish Sunday liturgies to the very machinery of governance of the Church itself (notably in national bureaucracies), their influence—and the damage they do—is incalculable.

Donna Steichen documents with chilling accuracy the progressive takeover of a substantial portion of the Church in the United States by an ideology which is not only alien to authentic Catholicism, but inimical to the most essential Christian beliefs. Her investigation unmasks the "ungodly rage" which will not abate until every vestige of the "patriarchy", embodied, for them, in the Catholic Church, disappears from view and until every Catholic woman has had her "consciousness" of "oppression by the patriarchy" "raised" to their own fevered pitch.

Male Church leaders who are not feminist converts, though vilified at every opportunity, are not the only "enemy" for feminist "sexists". An even greater threat, in fact, are women who dare to contradict feminist nostrums, whose faith transcends the *Zeitgeist* and whose lives and witness confirm the validity of the perennial teachings of the Church. One thinks, of course, of the open secret that Catholic women are both the leaders and foot soldiers of the anti-abortion movement. Such women are even more victimized by feminists, if possible, than non-feminist men. Women of conviction and action, like the author of this book herself and thousands of other faithful Catholic women—mothers, teachers, religious sisters, professional women, academics and even theologians—who refuse to serve the Enraged Goddess of the New Myth and her angry minions, are recognized as a central obstacle, a sign of contradiction, to feminist orthodoxy; and they are treated (or ignored) accordingly. Women who cannot be enlisted in the feminist "struggle" against the "patriarchy" are non-persons to feminists. Many Catholic women have experienced this at the "listening sessions" held in connection with the U.S. bishops' proposed pastoral letter on "women's concerns".

A ray of light for the future is the unprecedented response, during the past five years, of tens of thousands of Catholic women to the statement of fidelity to the Church and her teachings called the "Affirmation for Catholic Women". Clearly, women are recognizing the need for their active witness in the present crisis. Other hopeful signs are that young women are increasingly critical of feminist orthodoxy (although there are strong indications that a majority of their generation have already been lost to the Church) and militant secular feminism is apparently in a state of decline. While there is evidence that some of these factors are beginning to have an effect on the Church, even the most optimistic analysis would concede that it is likely to be a very long time before visible signs of recovery can be expected—although dramatic improvement could take place if the bishops were willing to take a leading role in what must now be termed a restoration of authentic faith. The diocesan "women's commissions" demanded by feminists and proposed by the draft pastoral on "women's concerns" will certainly be the locus of much controversy in the near future.

Orthodox Catholics, whether bishops, religious or laity, now find their vocation to authentic evangelization impeded by the necessary struggle merely to *defend* the Faith—and their families

—from continuous assault. This can be both exhausting and discouraging. Yet we might well view these troubled times—times which truly "try men's souls"—as affording all believers almost unlimited opportunities for strengthening their own faith and for heroic Christian action in service to the Church and to others. This obligation, if it is oppressive, if it is a burden, is also Christ's burden, which we are, through his grace, privileged to bear.

Our battle, being Christ's battle, means also that we have to fight it differently than his persecutors. We must not err, as feminists do, by calling rage and anger "love", and corrosive hatred "loyalty". Nor can we ignore God's call to us—to every believer—to "give the light of Christ" and to spread his truth throughout the world with courage and wisdom and with every other gift the Holy Spirit has given us. For not only our earthly lives, but also the eternal lives of our children and our children's children and the future of the Church are at stake.

Helen Hull Hitchcock
Women for Faith & Family
St. Louis, Missouri
January 1991

Introduction

Agents of Catastrophe

American Catholicism could not be called triumphalist today. In March of 1989, at a historic Vatican meeting between American archbishops and curial officials, John Cardinal O'Connor spoke for multitudes of laymen when he described the unintended side effects of the Second Vatican Council as catastrophic. "We are still trying to recover from the chaos of misunderstanding and deliberate distortions", he said. "Suddenly all the old certainties seemed to be in question. Many Catholics felt betrayed. They felt the rug had been pulled out from under their most sacred and certain beliefs."

The public face of Catholicism is more altered than anyone would have predicted in 1960. Holy Mother Church, long regarded as unchanging and unchangeable, seemed all at once to repudiate her certitude, cast away her ancient Tradition, and plunge into chaos, like an empress seized with a mysterious madness. That an organization claiming divine origin could be so quickly and drastically transformed has been all the more bewildering because it did not follow a defeat by external forces or mass defection among the laity. Instead, it arose from a *trahison des clercs*, a betrayal of the intent of the Council by midlevel Church professionals, who should have had a strong natural interest in maintaining and enhancing the status of the institution they served. Instead they adopted a new, adversarial orientation: obedience to the Church was seen no longer as a service owed to Christ but as an obstacle to a higher call. Determined to accept no further magisterial direction toward the Kingdom of God, they listened instead to dissident theologians and leftist politicians, who announced that the Kingdom would be an earthly utopia. To observers, the transformation seemed to occur in a blinding flash, like St. Paul's experience in reverse. But in reality, beneath an apparently serene surface, neo-modernism had been eroding traditional theology, liturgy and catechetics for some years prior to the Council.

To examine the prevailing American Catholic disorder is to uncover a tangle of irony, credulity and perversity. Foreign missionaries today are apt to be so respectful of indigenous cultures that they fail to evangelize, yet the once-vital culture of Western Catholicism has been dismantled with brutally callous disrespect for the sensitivities of the American laity. At Mass, with the "greeting of peace" and hand-holding during the recitation of the Our Father, liturgical innovators seek to compel "horizontal" expressions of reverence for Christ's presence in the community. Yet, having effectively deprived the faithful of the privilege of kneeling to receive Holy Communion, they are now striving to do away with other "vertical" expressions of reverence for the incomparably glorious Presence of Christ in the Eucharist, such as genuflections before the tabernacle and even kneeling during the Consecration.

Restiveness under Vatican authority is epidemic among the Church's elite class, though, as George Weigel has observed, "the very same people who press the case for an 'American Church' seem . . . to have precious little use for America as a culture, society or polity".[1] In pursuit of "peace and justice", clerics and bureaucrats without diplomatic or political qualifications pontificate against American foreign and domestic policies. Yet it is so rare as to make headlines for one of them to speak forthrightly against moral evils about which they are presumably better qualified to judge, such as the complicity of Catholic jurists and legislators in the hideous injustice of abortion.

Theologians silent or shamefully equivocal before the mounting evils of abortion, state-subsidized contraception, homosexuality,

[1] George Weigel, *Catholicism and the Renewal of American Democracy* (New York: Paulist Press, 1989), 69.

laboratory experimentation on human embryos and euthanasia often wax disproportionately vehement about ecological concerns that, however valid, are certainly less urgent. And far from decrying heresy, they are likely to teach it. Scholars who pruned the supernatural from scriptural interpretation on the grounds that "modern man" could not believe it give no sign of having second thoughts as modern men and women flood into fundamentalist churches or pay thousands of dollars to seek advice from New Age mediums.

The sacrament of Penance, in which the penitent privately admits his own sins, is so widely neglected that many parishes no longer set regular hours for Confession. But in Catholic "feminist spirituality" groups, it is considered essential for members to "tell their stories"—in which they publicly accuse those who have sinned against them—in order to raise their consciousness of oppression.

Most of the mistaken or mutinous theories that brought American Catholicism to its present state originated with male theologians. Nevertheless, male revolutionaries tend to retain in their rhetoric some semblance of Catholic doctrine. Even when they reject discipline and morality and distort doctrine to rationalize a personal agenda, they rarely discard the entire substance of the Faith as female revolutionaries are apt to do. And women are prominent among today's religious rebels, notably professionals in religious orders, academia and the bureaucratic positions that proliferated as religious communities dwindled.

Some had valid grievances, of course. In every relationship, fallen human beings sin against God and each other. Nuns, like wives and mothers, were often too little appreciated in the days of unquestioning service, and their good judgment too little regarded. Indeed, only God can sufficiently appreciate a holy, selfless, heroic nun, truly conformed to Christ. But far greater harm has been inflicted on them by those who seduced them into the smouldering resentment that poisoned their lives, drew them from their commitments and drained away their faith. Their last condition is infinitely worse than their first.

Ironically, it was adversarial feminist theologians bent on manipulation who succeeded in overcoming the inattention with which male clerics do, as charged, tend to regard women. Instead of responding to their complaints according to the mind of the Church, however, some of the bishops who engaged in dialogue were converted to feminism, while others mistakenly supposed those implacable revolutionaries could be placated with sympathy and token concessions. Meanwhile, the judgments of docile daughters of the Church—particularly of married women, but also of lay employees and nuns—were given as little weight as ever. "The good ladies" are still dismissed without serious consideration.

Nevertheless, the intellectual and spiritual defection of Church career women was utterly unexpected. During the wholesome years between Maria Monk and the National Coalition of American Nuns, the image of nuns as consecrated virgins, sweet and self-sacrificing, had been so firmly etched in the minds of Catholics that most laymen could not comprehend their transmutation when it happened, and even the hierarchy apparently misunderstood or minimized it. Reeling under successive waves of liturgical, disciplinary and catechetical innovation, shocked by the defection of some ten thousand priests and fifty thousand nuns between 1966 and 1976, Catholics assumed that religious who remained at their posts, at least, were faithful, sane and trustworthy. Most excused the puzzling actions of the religious professionals in their parishes and schools as sincere, if mistaken, efforts at "updating" to fit the contemporary Church. Malevolent intent was rarely suspected, and the possibility of a neo-pagan or witchcraft revival was unimaginable. Like their secular contemporaries, American Catholics were sure, not only that witchcraft was outmoded, but that it had never existed at all outside the imaginations of misogynist clergymen and superstitious peasants. But as feminist extremists seized and maintained control of religious houses, the unimaginable became reality.

Early rumors of excesses among nuns were dismissed as distasteful and flatly incredible except by the few who encountered them firsthand. At my own first exposure to witchcraft, I thought I had stumbled into a uniquely lunatic social cul-de-sac. I didn't know it was part of a movement and didn't guess how closely it was entangled with general theological dissent, broader political feminism and epidemic neo-gnosticism. Later investigation revealed that witchcraft is one particularly bizarre manifestation of a widely disseminated decay. Most of the old Catholic culture has been devoured by spiritual termites, leaving behind a structure that looks solid to the eye but crumbles at a touch.

The post-conciliar metamorphosis has been more profound among female religious professionals than any other group, and more instrumental to the misapplication of "the spirit of Vatican II". Many such women, especially those in positions of ascending power, having ceased to believe in the central doctrines of the Catholic Faith, internalized the heretical premises of revived modernism and all the rebellious secular notions of the 1960s, and poured them with vocational passion into the service of religious feminism. For spiritual sustenance, as this book will document, they turned to sources alien and eclectic in the extreme.

Not only eccentric individuals but entire religious communities from motherhouse down adopted policies adversarial toward the Church. As Catherine Victory, a former Dominican, has reported,[2] the old structured convent life changed beyond recognition, and some of those who departed did so not because they had lost their vocations but because there no longer seemed to be a community in which to live it. One former sister of the order of the Humility of Mary told me, "I left the convent because I couldn't find anyone to pray with anymore."

The nuns' abandonment of identifying religious garb, their demands for autonomy in place of hierarchical obedience, for altar service as eucharistic ministers, lectors or acolytes, for ordination

[2] Catherine Victory, "Reflections of a Former Nun", *Catholic Twin Circle*, Nov. 1, 1987, 3.

as deaconesses and even as priestesses turned out to be merely prefatory. When they encountered appeasement in some of those areas,[3] they pressed more astonishing moral and dogmatic claims. Realizing that ordination would entail admission that the Church has power to ordain, feminist theoreticians anathematized all subordination, every trace of cultural, pastoral, episcopal or papal patriarchy, including the episcopally ordained priesthood, and called for a "reconstituted" priesthood of self- or community-identified pastoral and ritual leaders of either sex. They began to insist that non-marital sexual relations, contraception, abortion and homosexuality must be declared licit, even among women vowed to chastity. Politically, they moved toward the kind of illusionary leftism that, George Orwell observed in *The Road to Wigan Pier*, once attracted "with magnetic force every fruit-juice drinker, nudist, sandal-wearer, sex-maniac, Quaker, 'Nature Cure' quack, pacifist and feminist in England". Their enthusiasm for Third World revolutions of the left and their parallel opposition to democratic Third World rebel forces were unquenched by either mass uprisings against collectivist tyrannies in Eastern Europe or election results in Central America.

Leading feminist theologians distinguish two camps, moderate "reformers" and separatist "revolutionaries", within their movement. But traffic between them is so heavy that the distinction is only a matter of variable emphasis in a single plague of immanentism, which repudiates faith, reason and common sense. Nuns

[3] The formal two-year "dialogue" (1979–81) between a small committee from the National Conference of Catholic Bishops and representatives of Women's Ordination Conference (reported in *Origins*, vol. 11, no. 6, 81, and vol. 12, no. 1, 1) was a feminist victory before a shot was fired, because the 1976 "Declaration on the Question of the Admission of Women to the Ministerial Priesthood" (Vatican City: Sacred Congregation for the Doctrine of the Faith, 1976) had specifically prohibited episcopal discussion of the question. As matters developed, no shot ever *was* fired. The participating bishops, apparently overwhelmed by culture shock, were converted to feminism, though the conference took no action as a result, and some bishops disapproved. The NCCB pastoral on women's concerns was to a great extent a gesture intended to placate feminists.

who in the early 1960s had warned students not to view the sacraments as "magical", came to embrace occult practices, implicitly if not explicitly demonic. Out of the human instinct to express faith in physical gestures, many of those who ceased to kneel for prayer began to substitute yoga postures, T'ai Chi, "New Age" spiritualism or circle dances, widdershins, around a smoking cauldron. They sought "empowerment" in the "ancient wisdom" of Eastern monism, "goddess" paganism, dubious "Native American traditions", voodoo, witchcraft or the animist "spirits" of newly invented earth religions. Some who denied the existence of angels found New Age "channeling" and "spirit guides" credible. From disparate shreds of mythology, politics and imagination, religious feminists have cobbled together neo-pagan and neo-gnostic rituals to offer as appropriate expressions of "women's spirituality". The situation of Church career women has in fact become the stuff of anti-Catholic farce. Yet it is tragic, because those engaged in it are immortal beings of flesh and spirit, and because they exploit their positions within the Church to subvert trusting innocents.

The truth is that feminists don't like women, and they don't want to be women. Like Gloria Steinem, a few may wish to become the men they once wanted to marry. But most, including the statistically significant proportion who are lesbians, disapprove of gender entirely. Viewing existence through the distorting lens of self-pity, they are enraged with the limitations of incarnational reality. Probably because few of them are tied to the concrete necessities of family life, they exceed secular feminists in ideological zeal and perseverance and exceed Prometheus in presumption. Their ultimate rebellion, against God the Father and his Son, the male Savior Jesus Christ, has been disguised for public consumption as a campaign for "inclusive" liturgical language. On its face, it is a child's complaint against grammatical convention, to be addressed in an introductory course on the structure of the English language. But in private, and in their own publications, feminist theologians reveal, behind that mask, naked denial of the objectively existent, transcendent Father God. They hope to replace him with a gnostic deity, androgynous, immanent and worshipped in themselves. Chesterton's prediction "that Jones shall worship the god within him turns out ultimately to mean that Jones shall worship Jones", is as true of Catholic feminists as of other gnostics.

"Feminist theology" is not the study of what can be known about the true God but justification for the invention of a symbolic deity better suited to their ideological purposes. Its formula is drawn from comparative religion: *first the god, then the dance and finally the story*; that is, first the subjective emotional experience —interpreted in collective encounters—then the ritual and finally the new religion. Feminist ritual is not intended as worship but as psychological manipulation and political theater. The drive for feminist "liberty" very slightly conceals an intent to impose universal submission to its own rigid orthodoxy. As Brigitte Berger has observed, feminism has become a new imperialism.

This book is a report on the subterranean phenomena of religious feminism as observed over more than a dozen years. My journalistic investigation began, roughly, in 1977, when Rosemary Ruether, in a keynote address to Minnesota's International Women's Year (IWY) meeting, identified feminist theology as a species of liberation theology.[4] Catholic laywomen, protesting the exclusion of pro-life viewpoints from the IWY sessions, were further startled to discover nuns, in good standing with their communities, among the IWY participants and even among delegate slates elected to the national meeting.

As Catholic institutions continued to disintegrate, later reportorial assignments took me deeper into the underworld of religious feminism. Most of the chapters in the book originally appeared in other publications. They have been revised and expanded, and new chapters have been added, to acquaint a wider audience with the agents of catastrophe who have done incalculable damage within

[4] At that time Dr. Ruether also provided an early glimpse of the ethics of religious feminism when, to reporters, she vehemently denied any connection with Catholics for a Free Choice, while a CFFC spokeswoman, contacted by telephone, readily admitted that Ruether chaired one of its committees.

Church institutions over the past generation. It is necessary that these distressing facts be put on record. The Church has always been identified as feminine: Holy Mother, Bride of Christ. Today she appears as a battered woman, outrageously abused by many of her own children, religious professionals she has loved and nurtured. Adult Catholics, empowered by the sacrament of Confirmation, are obliged by faith and honor to defend her. They must be armed against prevalent error, so that they can recognize it and the sources from which it proceeds, and must insist on the authentic teaching that canon law guarantees as their right.[5] Most of a generation of young Catholics have been lost to the Faith *because* their trusting parents sacrificed to send them to Catholic catechetical programs, schools and colleges. Unless the aberrant activities of Catholic feminists are critically examined, their goals recognized, their rationale understood and their assault on the truth challenged, they will continue to destroy the faith of children exposed to their corrosive teaching. Nor are children the only victims. Inauthentic teaching pervades North American Catholicism from parish to press to academia, even to the convents of contemplative nuns and the advisory councils of national conferences of Catholic bishops.

It is not my contention that all women religious have betrayed the Faith. United under the banners of the Institute on Religious Life and Consortium Perfectae Caritatis, sound and admirable orders exist, and although most are new and small, some are thriving, including Mother Teresa's Missionaries of Charity and the Nashville Dominican Sisters of St. Cecilia. Even within decadent major orders devoted to feminism instead of the Catholic Faith, not all are equally conscious or equally extreme, and many faithful nuns remain, powerless, suffering personal Calvaries as their religious families shrivel toward extinction. Nor does all blame for the present disorder in the American Church rest on women; the ideas that led to their collapse originated among masculine dissenters, who have been numerous, influential and rarely disci-

[5] See canons 212, no. 2, no. 3; 213; 226, no. 2; 229, no. 1; 217.

plined. Ultimately it is those who hold but fail properly to exercise hierarchical authority who bear the heaviest responsibility.

But among contemporary assailants of the Church, the female of the species is more spiteful, irrational, unscrupulous and destructive than the male. Unlike most men who cease to believe in the truth of Catholic teaching, religious feminists will not, by choice, move on to a different way of life. They are tenaciously committed to their careers, frequently unqualified for secular employment of equal prestige, usually unmarried and often unattracted to marriage and intent on building a new feminist religion in the ruins of the Church. Even those who leave their religious orders tend to remain in Church employment and organizations. Authentic Catholic teachings will not get a hearing while they remain at the control centers of Catholic institutions.

Of course, I cannot cite every feminist challenge to Catholic authority, but this book describes some of the most extraordinary. As far as possible, it traces the origins and development of religious feminism within established Catholic communities and organizations. Many of the movement's leaders are not nuns. Several of the most important, like Rosemary Radford Ruether and Elisabeth Schussler Fiorenza, are married women with children. An influential percentage, concentrated in the political wing, are only putatively "Catholic", and claim that identity merely to draw attention to their positions; Catholics for a Free Choice is a salient example. Ironically, some prominent figures, including Father Matthew Fox, O.P., and Daniel Maguire, are males, though Fox's manner approximates the androgynous ideal. Yet nuns still affiliated with their orders, however tenuously, and former nuns still employed by the Church seem to make up the bulk of the membership. This book attempts to diagnose the puzzling susceptibility of consecrated women religious to the feminist virus. It explores the interlocking coalition, ranging from the consummately extreme Women-Church Convergence to the reputedly mainline National Catholic Education Association, through which feminists are attempting, with much success, to carve a position in the respectable "middle ground" of American Catholicism.

Throughout the book, for stylistic reasons, I have used the terms *American Church* and *progressive* without quotation marks. Readers will know, as I do, that revolutionaries use them as code words and will, I trust, read them in the sense of "so-called".

Finally, the book examines the movement's evolving rhetoric, assessing its ideology and overt and covert goals. It contrasts those errors with Catholic philosophical, theological and social teachings that illuminate the truth about the nature of reality, the human condition, the complementary roles and the equal dignity of men and women. Those teachings, which God has entrusted to his Church, constitute the truth for which the world is starving and, now as always, offer the only hope of securing for women a position of appropriate honor, establishing harmony between the sexes, restoring the family and achieving peace and justice in society. Full-blown feminism is not a transient fad but a rival belief system pitted against those truths. It is not a schism, for schism retains the Church's doctrine while denying her authority. It is not a heresy, for heresy discards only a part of the truth. It is an apostasy to an alien religion. Until its subversives are removed from the influential posts they currently hold, there will be no Catholic restoration in North America.

Chapter One

From Convent to Coven

Except among religious career women, American society entered a post-feminist period during the 1980s. Feminist presumptions about sexual permissiveness, contraception, abortion and paid employment for women still reigned in media and in educational institutions, but only veterans of the failed Equal Rights Amendment drive talked about "women's liberation" anymore. Disillusionment and resurgent normalcy had deprived militant feminism of its charm for the general public. Geraldine Ferraro had proved to be a political disaster; witty liberal essayist Nora Ephron had ruefully admitted that women got nothing from the women's movement but the Dutch lunch; young couples had started having babies again; *Ms* magazine was lurching toward bankruptcy. When asked what the feminist movement could hope to accomplish in the future, Betty Friedan told reporters, "I can't tell you that now. You wouldn't believe it anyway. It's theological."

On October 25, 1985, Ms. Friedan was complaining to an audience at Ball State University in Muncie, Indiana, that "young urban professional women" no longer appreciated the movement's labors on their behalf. Illustrative of her hope for the future, however, religious feminism was thriving. The Women's Ordination Conference opened a national meeting in St. Louis. And at Mankato State University (MSU) in Minnesota, some five hundred women gathered for a fourth annual conference on "Women and Spirituality". Its chaotic agenda combined demands for priestly ordination and "inclusive" liturgical language with neo-pagan ritual magic, absurd historical claims and radical politics.

Jesus was rarely mentioned except, by keynote speaker Rosemary Radford Ruether, as a "symbol" some might want to retain. Sin was adverted to only in ridicule, except for the "original sin" of "sexism". The conference theme, "Language and Imagery", was interpreted in speeches and workshops as calling for the use of feminine pronouns and maternal images for God, and a vehement *non serviam* to all patriarchy, from the local pastor through the Fathers of the Church to Jesus the God-Man and to God the Father. Speakers varied in degree in their rejection of revelation. Some claimed only that, as Spirit, God cannot be "imaged" as male or must be imaged as both male and female. Others rejected any God "out there" in favor of a "goddess within", sometimes identified as the "Divinity in each of us", sometimes as the goddess of "ancient matriarchal religion". As in previous years, the conference was held on the weekend closest to Halloween, a date celebrated by many participants as Samhain, the festival of the dead in the "old religion" of witchcraft. At least in embryo, the event incorporated virtually every element of neo-pagan feminism, though I was not yet familiar enough with the movement to recognize them as typical. In net effect, as opposed to intent, the weekend made the most persuasive argument I have ever encountered for the superiority of patriarchy.

The Women and Spirituality meeting was an official activity of Mankato State University, offered for optional academic credit. University president Margaret Preska, chairwoman of the Governor's Council on Youth (and just five weeks short of election as national president of Camp Fire, Incorporated),[1] warmly welcomed the group back again. Dean Jane Earley of the College of Arts and Humanities introduced Dr. Ruether with reverence. The weekend event was co-sponsored by MSU's women's studies and religious studies departments and the United Christian Campus

[1] Diane Mundt, "President of Mankato State Heads Camp Fire, Inc.", *Minneapolis Star and Tribune*, Dec. 5, 1985, 1B. On that occasion, Dr. Preska said the organization "has been one of the least sexist programs for young people in the country", and revealed that 31 percent of the nation's 393,000 Camp Fire girls are boys.

Center, a collaborative ministry of the American Baptist, Disciples of Christ, United Church of Christ, United Methodist, Presbyterian and Moravian churches. The Campus Newman Center did not participate "officially", said conference co-chair Patti Lather, an associate professor of women's studies, but the School Sisters of Notre Dame, headquartered in Mankato, were deeply involved. "Lots and lots" of S.S.N.D. nuns helped with preparations, presented workshops or registered to attend, according to Lather. Conference housing was available at low cost at Good Counsel Educational Center, site of the now-defunct S.S.N.D. girl's residential high school.

Supporters described the conference as "an ecumenical endeavor", and it certainly was heterogeneous, at least. The program offered sixteen speakers identified as Catholic in background: nuns, former nuns and Catholic laywomen. A few speakers represented Protestant denominations. One or two were Jews. A Hindu spoke about the "benevolent and malevolent" faces of the goddess Kali. There were teachers of hatha yoga and Himalayan raja yoga, the latter a former Catholic nun. There were professedly Christian lesbians and a profusion of professing witches. On Sunday morning, in the tax-supported student union building, three worship services were held: an ecumenical communion service conducted by a woman minister, a feminist liturgy and a Wiccan (witchcraft) ritual conducted by two priestesses, Patti Lather and Antiga, a professional witch from Minneapolis. What they all had in common was a determination to worship a female deity.

A startling majority of the women in attendance appeared to be Catholics: nuns, ex-nuns, students and faculty members from Catholic women's colleges, parochial school teachers, staff members of Catholic bureaus and counseling agencies, parish administrators, campus ministers, laywomen from Catholic Newman Centers, even hospital chaplains. They looked, on the whole, entirely normal; few would have attracted special notice at a Council of Catholic Women convention. But none appeared to take offense at the bitter bias displayed against their Church; instead, they initiated the criticism. And none indicated alarm about participating in frankly pagan rituals. Still, they seemed unwilling or unable to make an honest break with the Church; most described themselves as practicing Catholics.

Defining the Ground

An insight into that apparent contradiction came in Dr. Ruether's keynote address. Ruether is a professor of applied theology at Garrett-Evangelical Seminary in Evanston, Illinois, and a featured columnist for *National Catholic Reporter*. Her name would be prominent on any list of contemporary women theologians; her books can be found in most Catholic libraries; reporters frequently consult her opinion on Catholic matters. Yet she rejected Catholic belief at the outset of her academic career. According to an autobiographical essay published in 1975,[2] she discarded "the doctrine of the personal immortality of the soul . . . the very nub upon which all discipline and doctrine are hinged", during her freshman year at Scripps College. Having "crossed over" to "autonomous selfhood", she came to view dogmas not as statements of ontological truth but as useful symbols, and the Church "not as a repository of truth . . . but as a terrible example of what we all are". In that new light, Ruether found paganism more attractive than Catholicism. "A lot of evil had been done in the name of Christ", she wrote, but "no crusades or pogroms had been sent in the name of Ba'al, Isis or Apollo." Over the years she has from time to time recommended the worship of pagan goddesses as more beneficial for women than Christianity. Nevertheless, she decided not to leave the Church but to stay on in the hope that she could "help" it toward "a new future". Implausible as it would seem, her efforts in that direction have had enormous effect. She did not invent religious feminism alone, but she can justly be called the mother of Women-Church, an organization deeply hostile to

[2] Rosemary Radford Ruether, "Beginnings: An Intellectual Autobiography", in *Journeys: The Impact of Personal Experience on Religious Thought*, ed. Gregory Baum (New York: Paulist Press, 1975), 34.

Catholic spirituality and Tradition, and a major tributary to the spiritual stream flowing through the Mankato conference.

"Any church that makes you feel depressed Sunday after Sunday should be regarded as an occasion of sin", Dr. Ruether declared in her keynote address, titled "Emerging Women-Church: The Challenge of Feminist Liturgical Communities". She called on conferees to "exorcise from the self the deep layers of compliance with patriarchal subordination", and to establish female "base communities", "Women-Church groups" or "covens" for the celebration of their own rituals. Such groups can serve in place of the "patriarchal Church", she advised, or, for those with reason to retain Church affiliation, as a retreat in which to "speak their feelings".

Dr. Ruether offered an instant summary of human history as unremittingly oppressive of women. "The God of Exodus is not the source and sacralizer of repression and patriarchy," she said, "but we have to say that a funny thing happened to the idea of *ecclesia* on the way to Sinai." From the Greek city-states through Exodus, from "1 Timothy through Jerry Falwell", from the American Revolution even through Marxism and socialism, century after century, she said, "Women have participated enthusiastically in movements of liberation, only to find themselves excluded in the new society."

Women-Church is "the ultimate Exodus", she said, "from the powers and principalities of oppression . . . into a spirituality of social emancipation". It is essential that feminist spiritual communities be formed for "liturgy, for mutual support and spiritual growth". But while "the development of feminist liturgies is the central function of such groups", there must also be "interaction between feminist spirituality and social praxis . . . to work toward the new social order". The group may combine several traditions, such as Christian, Jewish, Wiccan and shamanistic, but if it grows too large, it should be subdivided into smaller "circles". The "optimal number" for a circle is thirteen, "the size of a proper coven".

In one model community in Portland, Maine, she reported, "Ecumenism has quickly developed to include even males."

Ruether told the audience to watch for her forthcoming book of feminist liturgies[3] for celebrating "the cycles of the day and night, the cycles of the seasons, the cycles of our own bodies month by month, our own life cycles. . . . Nature recreates itself through cycles, and that means we have to be as positive about the death side of the cycle as we are about the resurrection side." One chapter, she promised, would contain "liturgies for healing" from painful experiences, such as "coming out as a lesbian. Not that *being* a lesbian is unnatural, but that the way we've been oppressed by homophobia *is* unnatural." Rituals, she said, can incorporate observances of social oppression, such as a Halloween ceremony in remembrance of the persecution of witches. "A Hallow-mass liturgy for the burning of witches . . . will be done next week in our seminary", she said. "The Catholic bishops have no business writing a pastoral on women until they repent the slaughter of women."

Judaism and Christianity are "linear" religions, Ruether continued. They see history as moving from past to future, "over against the nature and fertility religions, pagan religions", which view life as cyclic. She scoffed at any notion of paganism as satanic, explaining that "pagans" originally meant "country people". It was the arrogance of newly dominant Christianity that transformed the word "into the negative antithesis", she explained; when a new religion becomes dominant, it typically "turns the old gods into devils". That defense, one notes, was not a denial that contemporary witches worship some being other than God, only a denial that the being they worship is Satan.

In conclusion, Ruether praised the conference schedule as evidence of "the blossoming of feminist spirituality in a very short time". Her presence at the event raised questions about the extent to which its growth may have modified her earlier attitude toward

[3] Ruether, *Women-Church: Theology and Practice of Feminist Liturgical Communities* (San Francisco: Harper & Row, 1985).

feminist witchcraft. In a widely noted 1980 essay,[4] Dr. Ruether had punctured several of the balloons of that "counter-cultural spirituality". First of all, she said then, its "tendentious use of historical material reduces everything to one drama: the story of original female power and goodness, and the evil male conquest and suppression of the same". In reality, those ancient Near Eastern cultures with female deities did not create "a feminist religion or one concerned with liberating the oppressed" but "a religion fundamentally interested in keeping Middle Eastern male kings on the thrones of their city-states". Ruether said she had not seen "the slightest evidence" in medieval records that either opponents or proponents regarded witchcraft as "centered in a female deity". Women were "never the sole targets" of witch-hunts, she went on, and "responsible scholarship" sets the total number executed at "several hundreds of thousands". The figure of "'nine million women burned', which is continually cited in feminist literature on the issue, appears to be completely unsubstantiated." Further, she wrote, "The concept of goddess worship as nature religion is a fantasy of European Christianity. . . . The romantic nature-civilization split seems to me to be an essentially escapist notion rather than the basis for a genuine social ethic". What the creation of a liberated feminist spirituality requires, she concluded, is not such "separatism and rejection" but "synthesis and transformation" utilizing "many of the elements of earlier traditions".

While Ruether's Mankato address mercifully did not assert the existence of a lost golden age of global matriarchy, it was not otherwise incompatible with the prevailing fantasies. Her attitude toward goddess feminism had softened during those five years. "It is possible that we are witnessing in this movement the first stirrings of what may become a new stage of human religious consciousness", she wrote of feminist witchcraft in 1981.[5] In

[4] Ruether, "Goddesses and Witches: Liberation and Counter-cultural Feminism", *Christian Century*, Sept. 10–17, 1980, 842.

[5] Ruether, "The Female Nature of God: A Problem in Contemporary Religious Life", in eds. Johannes-Baptist Metz and Edward Schillebeeckx, *Concilium* 143 (Mar. 1981): 64.

Women-Church: Theology and Practice, the book she announced at Mankato, she communicates the gnostic view that contemporary feminists constitute a radical "spirit-filled" millennialist community in direct encounter with the divine, prophetically empowered to construct "a church liberated from patriarchy". It must be "open to authentic spirit wherever it is found", even among those who "legitimately seek new religions generated from hints of ancient times and their own experience".[6]

A theologian who does not believe in life after death must be concerned with the history, anthropology, psychology or sociology of religion; presumably she would see no Christian truth to examine. If she were a revolutionary who regarded religion as a strategic vehicle, she might adapt her rhetoric to manipulate a "blossoming", potentially useful political force. Dr. Ruether is, indeed, openly and consistently revolutionary. In a 1980 essay, she called for "the equivalent of a French revolution" to overthrow the authority of the hierarchy, so that "the academy" could become "the teaching magisterium of the Church". To achieve that end, she said, it would be essential for the "liberal wing" of Catholicism to retain both "autonomy" and the appearance of legitimate "Catholicity" in its "institutional power bases".[7] Less than a month after the Mankato conference, she advised Chicago Call to Action members to maintain Church membership as camouflage while revolutionizing from within.[8]

In her autobiographical essay, Ruether recalled her "great excitement" when an introductory course on comparative religion gave her a "new orientation" toward religion as a "metaphor for inner transformation" rather than as a body of revealed truth. That excitement has "shaped much of my intellectual elan ever since", she said:

[6] Ruether, *Women-Church*, pt. I. See esp. 21–23, 31–40, 61.

[7] Ruether, *Journal of Ecumenical Studies* (Winter 1980): 65–67.

[8] Ruether, "Crises and Challenges of Catholicism Today", *America*, Mar. 1, 1986, 152. See also chap. 2, below.

> We learned the formula, "first the God, then the dance, and finally the story." Every religion begins with the concrete expression of the god; not the "one God," but of a particular god. . . . [T]hrough the seers and poets, it is given form, so that the people can dance it, and relive the experience . . . in ritual and drama. Out of the liturgy arises the story, the *mythos*, from which comes, as the last stage, formulated creed and doctrine.[9]

The Mankato conference was my first glimpse of the megalomaniacal feminist attempt to follow that formula in the construction of a depraved new goddess religion, by "synthesis and transformation", out of myth, recurrent heresy and imagination.

Feminist Culture

Between workshops, conferees could browse at a variety of booths and displays. There were tee shirts and bumper stickers bearing the slogans "I (love) the Goddess" and "Ankh If You Love Isis". There were sample copies of *Of a Like Mind*, a newspaper published by a Wiccan network based in Madison, Wisconsin. Prominent among the books it recommended as "must" reading were Starhawk's *Dreaming the Dark* and *The Spiral Dance*. There were *Circle Network News*, an eclectic occult publication from Mount Horeb, Wisconsin, and an accompanying *Circle Catalogue* advertising buttons with such messages as "NOT Saved" and "Nothin' Says Lovin' Like Somethin' From the Coven." Despite the unanimous denial of any association between witchcraft and satanism, an advertisement for a series of five "altar posters" included two depicting "The God", a horned and bearded male figure indistinguishable from traditional images of Satan.

Another booth offered information about homosexual organizations, most of it from Wingspan, a "ministry to gay and lesbian people" by Reformation Lutheran Church of St. Paul, Minnesota. Of special interest was a leaflet titled, "What the Bible Seems to Say . . . but Does It?" by Joseph C. Weber of Wesley Theological

[9] Ruether, "Beginnings", 40–42.

Seminary, in which the author claimed that Deuteronomy 23:17 and 1 Kings 14:24, 15:12 and 22:46 have been misinterpreted. These passages do *not* condemn homosexuality, Weber wrote, but "sacral male prostitution", because it was "an expression of the cultic worship of foreign gods" that denied "the unique claim of the One God over His people". I wondered what Weber would have made of the complaisant Christians at the Wiccan worship service.

As is common at conferences, a political notice was circulated. It was as unusual as the conference itself. Headlined "Pagan Action Alert: ACT NOW!" it called for the defeat of Amendment 805 to HR 3036, the 1986 Treasury, Postal Service and General Government Appropriations Bill. The amendment, which denied tax-exempt status "to any cult, organization or other group" involved in promoting "satanism or witchcraft", had been introduced by Senator Jesse Helms, unanimously passed by the Senate on September 26, and was under consideration by a Joint Senate-House Conference Committee. The action alert, prepared by Circle Network, listed the name and address of each committee member and legislative aide. It advised witches and pagans to contact them, alert pagan friends in other states, send donations to the Pagan Rights Fund and "to work magick".

Workshop offerings included "Spirituality and the Web of Life", by Sister Dorothy Olinger, S.S.N.D., and "Spirituality and Mother Earth", by Sister Delmarie Gibney, F.S.P.A. Both women were described as staff members at Global Education Associates' Minneapolis center. Christina Potyondy, who talked about "Women's Experience of the Divine", holds a master's degree in religious studies from United Theological Seminary and apparently unites conflicting theologies in her own life; she claimed affiliation with both the esoteric Aquarian Light church and St. Joan of Arc Catholic Church. Sister Rose Tillemans, C.S.J., presented a workshop titled "Women Who Are Poor" and distributed reprints of her own writings in the display area. A vocal advocate of women's ordination, Sister Rose had left teaching and was running a Minneapolis walk-in center called Peace House.

Indira Junghare, an associate professor of Indian languages and literature at the University of Minnesota, conducted a workshop, "The Many Faces of the Goddess", on the importance of goddess worship in Hinduism. Lynn Levy, editor of *Of a Like Mind* and a founder of the Re-formed Congregation of the Goddess, spoke on "reframing reality". Mary Gail Sovik, manager of the Center for Higher Consciousness in Minneapolis and a former nun with a master's degree in educational psychology from the University of Notre Dame, said in a talk entitled "Meditation and the Feminist Experience" that meditation "evokes the energy of the Divine Mother". Sister Lucille Matousek, S.S.N.D., director of Good Counsel Education Center, offered a workshop on "God the Mother of Scripture". Jade River, another founder of the Re-formed Congregation of the Goddess, talked about "The Emerging Vocabulary of Women's Spiritual and Psychic Information". In the presentation "Sexuality and Spirituality", Wiccan priestess Antiga invited women to "visit a time when the Goddess was worshipped and sexuality was sacred. Discover what you want your own sexuality to be if you could let go of the rules and the definition of sexuality as evil." Last-minute cancellations deprived conferees of the opportunity to hear Jan Bodin's "Spiritual Preference/Sexual Preference" ("based on my experience as a lesbian Christian") or Anita Hill of Wingspan on "Homophobia: Impact on Spirituality and Gay/Lesbian Liberation".

In a lobby between workshops I met Chrystal, an engaging young wife and mother of three from St. Cloud, my own hometown. She was thrilled to be present and eager to be interviewed. "I love it!" she chirped about the conference. "I wish it could last a lot longer." When her friend Susan first showed her the conference program, she said, "I went, 'Oh, wow! Can I go, too?'" Although Chrystal said she was new to Wicca, she wore a pentacle on a chain around her neck, and her comments later, during the Wiccan rites, indicated some previous involvement.

Susan too was a wife and mother and a "non-traditional student" at St. Cloud State University, majoring in sociology because she wanted to work with troubled adolescents. "We have a women's spirituality group in St. Cloud", Susan told me. "We meet on the first and third Tuesdays. . . . On the third, we usually do a ritual. On the first, we discuss, oh, whatever the members want to: play or sexuality or whatever." None of the members are regular students, she said. "Except for me and another nontraditional student, they're all older: 25 to 55, I'd say. . . . I've only been going for a few months. . . . We meet sometimes at members' homes and sometimes at Newman Center." How had Susan found the group? "I knew one of them, and she mentioned it", she said. "And it was mentioned once in the Newman Center bulletin and in the newsletter from Jean Donovan House [a Catholic Worker center in St. Cloud]. I really enjoy it."

The Catholic Feminist Viewpoint

Four of the presentations deserve special attention for the light they cast on the initial attraction, ideological base and eventual consequences of Catholic involvement in the feminist spirituality movement. Feminism appears to be the bait, moral disintegration the hook and the occult the dark and treacherous sea into which the deluded are towed.

The Bait

"Women and the Catholic Church: A Discussion for Ambivalent and Alienated Women" was the title of a workshop conducted by Barbara Keating, an MSU associate professor of women's studies. She had been educated in Catholic schools "through a college B.A." and later, at graduate school in Nebraska, had attended "an alternative parish". Married and a mother, she described herself as "currently on leave of absence from institutional religion". Pope John Paul II, she said, exemplifies the attitudes she found intolerable in the Church. "Every time the Pope got media coverage, it was a crisis of faith. . . . And then came his Canadian trip. This man does not see women as full human beings. We're breeders; we're servants; we're cheap labor."

Other women in the group were asked to identify themselves and tell their reasons for attending. A nun "on leave of absence" from her religious order in Milwaukee said, "I participate when it's life giving and forget the rest." During her sabbatical, she was deciding whether or not to leave the order. Shirley, employed "in a professional capacity in the St. Paul archdiocese", said, "I feel that I'm in a different Catholic Church than I was twenty years ago. I'm very angry with the present Pope . . . but at the same time, I do have opportunities to work within the Church . . . opportunities to work with alienated men and women. I'm in a position to be heard." Shirley said her job involved confirmation programs.

Another woman indicated that at least one Minnesota bishop was not without redeeming qualities; Bishop Raymond Lucker of New Ulm had condemned sexism as sin, she observed. But Sister Kay, a Notre Dame nun who was pastoral administrator of a small town parish in his diocese, said she was angry that she was not permitted to celebrate Mass as male pastors do, simply "because of the shape of my skin".

The workshop was reminiscent of the feminist consciousness-raising sessions popular in the late 1960s, designed to stir up rage against male "oppression", even in women who had not previously felt oppressed. In such settings, lack of anger is interpreted as proof that the subject is too thoroughly conditioned to recognize her victimization. The practice, nearly extinct in secular circles, still flourishes among religious feminists.

The Hook

A similarly dated attitude toward "sexual expression" was evident in "A Theological Approach to Teaching Human Sexuality", a workshop presented by Joan Timmerman, Ph.D., and Patricia Bartscher, M.S. Intended as a model for other sex educators, it epitomized the moral desolation of the feminist search for unrestricted ecstasy. "Spiritual feminists" have apparently failed to learn what even secular hedonists have learned—from herpes, from AIDS, from anomie—over the past twenty years. Like aging flower children, Dr. Timmerman and Ms. Bartscher proffered a utopian vision of the therapeutic benefits of sexual expression unlimited by any rule but mutual choice. Their cheerful description of strategies and tactics for the corruption of their students reeked more of the diabolic than anything their Wiccan colleagues proposed all weekend.

Ms. Bartscher, an associate professor in nursing at the College of St. Catherine in St. Paul, said she and Dr. Timmerman developed the course because "I saw a tremendous number of people out there that hadn't any idea about their own anatomy or how the young women were getting pregnant", and "Joan saw a lot of guilt marring the real beauty potential she saw in sexual relationships . . . some of the negative attitudes that have come to us about sexuality from our religion." Timmerman is an associate professor of theology at St. Catherine's.

At first they taught the course in general college presentations, but when parental objections to their sponsorship of Sol Gordon and Mary Calderone forced cancellation of the speakers' contracts, they decided to teach it as a regular semester course instead. That "turned out to be a very good thing", chuckled Bartscher, because "academic freedom protects you against all kinds of things that you might not otherwise be protected from".

"Teaching the course as a theology course removes limits that would be prevalent . . . if the course were offered only in nursing, say, in regard to abortion", Dr. Timmerman added. Since theology is speculative, she explained, they can safely introduce "new ideas"; students are "*doing* theology, rather than learning someone else's theology". This kind of course should be required "as the central humanistic core of the liberal arts, and belonging at every level of college education", she said, because "once we, with our vision, bring in the New Order, where are the sexual relationships within that New Order going?" She insists that the class be mixed, so that men too will acquire "feminist assumptions".

At the beginning of each term, Bartscher said, they introduce their "central assumptions":

"Sexuality has been harmed by the belief that it should not be talked about." They want their students to "be comfortable" in discussing their sexuality openly.

"Guilt need not be associated with sexuality; it was intended to be celebrated."

Not only sexual feelings but sexual fantasies are "natural, healthy and normal"; such fantasies may be "an adaptive way to deal with stress". (There was general laughter as Bartscher reminded the audience how "we were taught in our Catholic grade school never to have impure thoughts".)

"You have the right to know the full range of human sexual behavior and to be acquainted with current information. . . . You have the right to know the dimensions of the variations in sexual expression. You don't have to partake of them, but you have a right to know."

"We need to be acceptant of the whole variety of sexual expression. We need to be concerned with another person's needs. . . . We all have different value systems, and none of those value systems is right or wrong."

"Every person has a right to their own beliefs and convictions." By exploring your attitudes, "you can come to your own truth."

"Sex is an integral part of everyone's personality and is expressed in a multitude of ways. Understanding and taking responsibility for your sexuality can be a real positive force in your life."

To deal with the attitudes students bring with them, Timmerman explained, "One of our early exercises is asking them to read, not biblical texts, but . . . scholarly commentaries on certain biblical texts. Many students from a Catholic tradition . . . come in with a sense that the Bible has already decided all the moral questions . . . a naïve fundamentalist position." She went on,

> It's usually eye opening when they begin to see that not only is there dispute about these issues, but in many cases the claims that have been built on them are superstructures built on sand. If they want to make claims for a particular morality in regard to sexuality . . . they have to leave the Bible out of it. So . . . the Bible cannot be used by our students against each other,

each other's sexuality. I think that's a great accomplishment in a theology program.

Students are required to keep journals, which are not returned to them at the end of the course. Timmerman and Bartscher find the journals fascinating. "One of my estimates of success in the course, and this very often comes off in the journals," Timmerman said, "is if we've succeeded by the end . . . in redefining both theology and sexuality. Usually they have redefined theology from morality, first of all."

"It's very interesting to see the development in the journals, away from the legalistic kind of thinking", Bartscher agreed.

"I question the assumption that there is no right or wrong", a woman in the audience objected.

Bartscher replied, "There are very few absolutes in terms of right and wrong."

"Right and wrong are relative to one's system", said Timmerman.

"It sounded as though you meant there are no moral limits on sexual conduct", another woman protested. "You have to make the limit that incest and sex abuse and battering and rape are *not* okay."

"At the risk of bringing the roof down, I have to say that there might be a situation where incest is okay," Bartscher said. "I can only say that I try very hard not to be closed to anything. . . . There are people who are into extremely erotic, very fulfilling sadomasochistic relationships . . . and it isn't my business to say that it's right or wrong."

"What differentiates something from being moral or immoral cannot be the class of acts", Timmerman said. "It cannot be that there's a class of acts that in themselves are immoral."

Sister Brenda Penning, S.S.N.D., a secretary at Good Counsel Education Center, told me later that she thought the workshop was "beautifully presented".

"Didn't you find some of it at least surprising?" I asked. "What about its moral perspective?"

"The material was not unusual for me", Sister Brenda answered. "I thought it was presented within the Catholic perspective."

When I asked Dorothy Rollins, associate campus minister at St. Benedict's College, St. Joseph, Minnesota, how she liked the Timmerman-Bartscher workshop, she described it as "excellent in presentation, reflecting an excellent value system".

The effects of the sexuality course could be glimpsed in a memorable workshop "Compassion: Weaving Our Sexuality and Spirituality", or "how religion and sexism can leave one depressed, empty and without a soul", jointly presented by Peggy Kavaney and Janet Bucher. "Reclaiming one's soulness and integrating sexuality and spirituality, one is provided with the basis and climate to take risks and go beyond boundaries of fear, shame and oppression", the program notes promised. In an oblique way, it made a case against promiscuity—at least, against indiscriminate, submissive promiscuity.

A pretty ex-nun, petite, gray haired and clad in improbable 1960s hippy attire, Ms. Bucher revealed previously unsuspected aspects to the life of a hospital chaplain when she recounted a lurid "herstory" in soap-operatic detail. Formative influences (i.e., her mother and the Church) had damaged her attitude toward her body, she said. As a first example, she recalled that the "wonderful feeling of exploration and excitement" she experienced as a child in "mutual discovery of our bodies" with her cousin Jimmy was dampened when her mother found them mutually discovering and told her that sex was to be reserved for someone you loved and preferably married. Next, she learned as a Catholic schoolgirl that if you were good, you wouldn't have sex except in marriage, and "if you were *really really* good, you would remain a virgin in the convent". She wanted "to be really good and go to heaven", she said, so for a time she became a nun. "When I left after sixteen years in the convent, after sixteen years of saying 'no' to my body, I decided to say 'yes' to my body", she went on. "And I did, in many appropriate and inappropriate ways." Eventually, she came to "the emptiness that can follow when sexuality and spirituality are separated". When "an impressively gentle doctor" asked her to meet for a drink, other workers at the hospital where she served as chaplain warned her that he was not only married but also a Don Juan who "had been through every nurse in the hospital who said 'yes' ". The time had come to say "no" again, she decided. She met him and "within five minutes felt sexual vibes". So she told him, "I want you to know that I'd like to be your friend, but I'm not going to have sex with you", and she went home "feeling real good about myself". Her peak moment of triumph came later, when he invited her to dinner with his wife. Having finished her tale, Ms. Bucher instructed her Mankato audience to divide into groups of three and share "*your* moment of triumph when spirituality and sexuality came together, when *you* felt blended and strong".

At the time, in addition to her chaplaincy duties, Bucher was a "consultant" at Sycamore, an archdiocesan "Ministry to Parishes" directed by Mark Scannell, an ex-priest with ties to Matthew Fox,[10] and ex-nun Elaine Gaston. The agency offers assistance on "spiritual and organizational development".

The second speaker was Peggy Kavaney, a sturdy, middle-aged pastoral minister at St. Luke's parish in St. Paul, a job for which she was prepared in St. Catherine's pastoral ministry program. She expressed a profound debt of gratitude to Dr. Timmerman for the liberating effects of her teaching. In the course of her own ministry, Kavaney said, she led days of recollection, gave "talks and homilies" and "ministered to men and women in search of their soulness". Her role in the workshop seemed to be chiefly interpretive, but nevertheless she opened in standard feminist style with "herstory", which, she said, went "upward" from "sex and religion" to "sexuality and spirituality". Coming as she did from "an alcoholic and Catholic background", she was raised "with a

[10] In the 1983 edition of the *Minnesota Catholic Directory*, Scannell was identified as a Dominican priest and Gaston as a Dominican nun. By 1985, the directory had dropped their religious titles. Also in 1985, Scannell was listed in the *Resources in Creation Spirituality* catalogue from Matthew Fox's Institute for Culture and Creation Spirituality (ICCS) as a member of its "National Speakers' Circle".

chasm between public and private"; her family taught her to be concerned only with how things looked from the outside, she said. They sat in the same pew at church on Sunday and even said the Rosary together on the radio. "You can imagine that was not much help with my sexuality", she said, provoking audience laughter. Women "have been taught in a very sick way to be caretakers, to be nurturers", not to care for themselves, but Dr. Timmerman helped her to "discover blending. It's my center, and I'm in love with it." Now, her definition of spirituality is "I am loved. I am a small part of the energy that goes beyond me into the god or goddess." Sexuality, she said, means "affirming my body and being with it".

Kavaney advised her audience to examine the historical position of women and "do away with much of it. Cross out the Fall-Redemption; it hasn't worked for us. . . . I think that's not where we're at today." It produced "tons and tons of dualisms", such as "boy/girl" and "soul/body", leading to a "shame-faced system" full of "no-nos and taboos, relations that totally go against intimacy". In the patriarchal 1950s, she said, women had only two possible roles: "the Marilyn Monroe image—you have a sexy body and no mind so we'll use you", or "Mom with chocolate-chip cookies and an apron". With the emergence of the women's movement in the 1960s and 1970s, "We began looking at our stories", she said. Now, in the 1980s, "There's a lot happening. Addictions are being discussed: sexual, chemical, cleaning . . ."

The old dualism left a residue of "sterile images, empty rituals and bad jokes", she continued. "When we come out of a sick religion or a sick relationship, we don't know our boundaries." Rigidity, fear, violence, powerlessness, submissiveness and co-dependency follow. But when "we can combine sexuality and spirituality", we can go "from being a victim to being the actor in my own story". Love is only possible between equals, and "its expression must be optional. Don't let anyone hug you against your will." Even in the 1980s, society remains patriarchal, she mourned. "I'm sure that each of us could name a time within the past week when we received different treatment because we are women."

Kavaney later moved from St. Luke's parish to a new job at Archdiocesan Catholic Charities. Bucher left Sycamore and apparently gave up hospital chaplaincy. At last report, she was among the speakers scheduled for a 1990 "Autumn Gathering" at St. Timothy's Church, in Blaine, Minnesota. The brochure describes her as "a spiritual director in private practice".

The Dark Waters

Joan Keller-Maresh, ex-nun, feminist activist, wife, mother of two, organizer of a coven that meets in her home, called her workshop "From Convent to Coven: A Journey to the Old Religion of the Goddess". She opened it by saying, "Perhaps I should ask how many in here are ex-nuns, but I won't. I was in one of these once where almost everyone was a nun."

Before telling "herstory", Keller-Maresh led workshop participants in an extended Wiccan circle ritual drawn from Starhawk's book *Dreaming the Dark.* Then she recounted in painful detail her journey from a Catholic faith so intense that she vowed to live for God alone, to the antithesis of that faith, in which she worships the "goddess" in herself. Of her thirteen years as a member of the Sisters of St. Joseph in Concordia, Kansas, she said sadly, "I loved the life. . . . I still miss it. I still miss the quiet, the time for study." But it was, she said, a "sheltered garden", lacking "a sense of reality".

Her story is worth examining for the elements it has in common with those of many other demoralized religious who fled their vows only to find themselves blown about on the winds of fad and impulse, the search for "a sense of reality" abandoned along with an intellectually coherent faith. Today, she said, she still goes to Mass and still serves as a parish song leader, though "I struggle with myself every day" to understand why. "The words of the Consecration make me sick", she said in an interview later.

Her faith began to decay, she said, when she was introduced to the reinterpretation of Scripture as "myth" containing a "kernel of truth". The doubts born then "had a domino effect", though she still loved "living with good women", where she found it "easy to be good, easy to pray". As her work in nursing and her associations in "social justice groups" brought her into closer contact with those "people of God" who were *not* living in sheltered gardens but "struggling with the birds, the moles and the weeds", her doubts continued to grow.

Living away from her community while attending graduate school, Keller-Maresh said she was encouraged to try "the third way", a practice fleetingly fashionable during the turbulent early years of Vatican II, when religious of both sexes attempted to "relate to others in close friendships that were still supposed to be celibate. . . . But the richness of the relationships" and the relative anonymity of a foreign convent soon "made the vow of celibacy a struggle", she said. "Many followed their hearts in relationships." Keller-Maresh said she remained celibate but struggled even harder with doubts about God. Next came the abandonment of religious dress and a move into "small-group living". Soon she began to wonder, "What am I doing now that I couldn't be doing outside?" Her close friendship, "now grown to love, demanded changes in my life", and she left the order "to be with him".

"For a very short time", her subsequent marriage "seemed very right and good", she continued. But it proved to be harder than she expected. "After several years of nurturing, and feeling defined not as a separate person, not as an empowered person", she was again struggling with resentment and confusion. In a supermarket, she picked up *The Cinderella Complex*,[11] and reading it propelled her into conscious feminism. She went on to read all the books in the bibliography and found most compelling those by "women who challenged established religion. The exclusion of women from the Deity hit me: he was a man, and I was a woman! My image of God was male! I was furious with the Church, with my family, with the order. . . . I looked at my life in despair. It was all patriarchy,

[11] Colette Dowling, *The Cinderella Complex: Women's Hidden Fear of Independence* (New York: Summit Books, 1981).

from top to bottom." Now in her forties, Keller-Maresh began "pursuing certification in women's studies" at the University of Wisconsin in LaCrosse.

As parish song leader, she tried to introduce the use of "female terms for the Deity", explaining that "it was only by analogy, since God is Spirit, not gender". Cautioned that "God language was not to be altered", she moved deeper into rebellion. Finally, "Starhawk's *Dreaming the Dark* spoke to me", she recalled. There she read, "Power from within can be called 'spirit', but that implies the separate, the dualist. I have called it 'immanence' and I have called it 'goddess'." Keller-Maresh was exultant at last to see God "not as a being outside myself. Here was a woman, a proclaimed witch, saying things that were a part of me! After reading this, 'power-over' seemed an absurdity. . . . For a woman to worship a male God is to deify her oppressor." Seeing herself as goddess "was indeed liberating. It gave meaning to all my experience."

She gathered women who shared her views, and her coven was born. "The first 'coming together' was in my home. The energy of that first gathering still lingers in the room." In the beginning, she said, she was fearful "of naming the directions, of calling on the goddess. The rituals seemed hokey at first. But in experience, it was awesome." To other women planning to start a coven, she recommended, "It is of utmost importance always to have the centering ritual and to hold the gathering outside of any church facilities." Summing up, she said, "Because I am and you are the goddess, she is here right now. She's alive; she's reinvented; she's changing and growing with us."

Someone in the group asked, "Are you still going to Mass?"

"Yes. There's something there I would miss. . . . Many are still hanging in because of ties in the community. Certainly not for the theology."

"We can at least hope to create change in our own parishes", a woman said. "We are powerful people."

One of the younger women asked, "Where do morality and ethics fit into Women-Church?"

"Trust the goddess within you", Keller-Maresh answered.

"*I* can follow the good in me, but what about those who don't?" the young woman asked.

"Female morality is circumstantial", another woman replied.

In contrast to the revolutionary content of her address and to her frequent references to "energy", Keller-Maresh's manner was conspicuously sad and listless. While her case history is certainly a cautionary tale of temptations succumbed to, she can also be seen as a victim of the death of a culture. When the sense and structure of convent life were dismantled, many religious discovered that their vocations had depended on them. Displaced, naïve for their years, often rootless, they may well have looked back on the past with wistful affection from the bruising world outside.

The Harassment of Witches

At most workshops, there seemed to be a deliberate attempt to draw participants into ritual activities. No one asked me to leave when I declined, but I began to suspect a concerted effort to enlist everyone present in the conspiracy against the "patriarchal" Church through group dynamics. All the rituals I witnessed, and most of the "language and imagery" discussed, were drawn from Starhawk's books. Clearly, she had become a matriarch of feminist spirituality. As further evidence of her status, she was invited to appear as keynote speaker for the even larger 1986 Women and Spirituality Conference.

Born Miriam Simos in St. Paul, Minnesota, Starhawk was given dubious respectability, and introduced into many Catholic settings, by Rev. Matthew Fox, O.P., the founder and director of the Institute for Culture and Creation Spirituality (ICCS). Starhawk began teaching in his program on a regular basis in 1983; earlier she had been a visiting lecturer. She has often accompanied Fox as a "ritual teacher" in his seminars on the Catholic lecture circuit. During the summer of 1985, they had presented one at the College of St. Thomas in St. Paul. Fox had been back in Minnesota again in late August as keynote speaker at the Upper Midwest Catholic Education Congress. His own views resemble Starhawk's, as well as those generally espoused at MSU's Women and Spirituality gathering, and strikingly parallel the ancient and recurrent religion of gnosticism. Fox rejects the "fall-redemption theology" of original sin and exalts the pursuit of "ecstasy". In an appendix to *Original Blessing*, he contrasts good (i.e., "creation-centered") beliefs with bad (i.e., "fall-redemption") beliefs: "ecstasy" is good, "control of passions" bad; "death as a natural event, prelude to recycling and rebirth" is good, "death as wages for sin" bad; "God as Mother, God as Child, as well as Father" is good, "God as Father" bad. It was to *Original Blessing* that Dr. Ruether referred when she wrote,

> One place to start dismantling clericalism is by theologically reenvisioning the relationship between nature and grace, creation and redemption. Women-Church is rooted in what has been defined recently as "creation-based spirituality."[12]

At the time of the 1985 MSU conference, Father Fox was under investigation by the Vatican Congregation for the Doctrine of the Faith. As though to simplify the Congregation's task, Fox that year chose the November/ December issue of his bi-monthly magazine *Creation* to launch a furious attack on critics of his collaboration with Starhawk. He claimed "Native European mother goddess religions" prevailed for twenty-five thousand years of peace, "until the Indo-European invasions around 4500 B.C." The invaders' intrusive heirs are still making trouble for peace-loving pagans, he complained. "One of the most vicious words that repressed Christians speak when they attack me . . . is the word *pagan*. They are always pitting Christ against the *pagans*. . . . Was Jesus Christ hostile to rural life and rural ways?" Indignant, he warned, "The harassment of witches is to cease if one wishes to be a Roman Catholic. So states Vatican II. . . . Those righteous Catholics who wish to burn witches . . . ought to . . . get a confessor to help them be healed. Otherwise they are effectively outside the doctrine of the Catholic Church as enunciated at the Vatican Council."

[12] Ruether, *Women-Church*, 86.

The document to which he referred is the "Declaration on Non-Christian Religions", which does not mention the anomaly of trying to be pagan and Catholic at the same time. Fox's pomposity would have been comic if it hadn't been in demand in so many Catholic environments. Adherents of his "creation-centered spirituality" make up a pernicious network inside the "official" Church, and the spread of his infectious errors was not detectably diminished by the year of public silence his Dominican superiors imposed on him late in 1989.

Going into the Dark

By Sunday morning, the Mankato conference crowd had declined to about three hundred. While two other feminist services were held down a hallway, some 150 women gathered for the Wiccan rite described in the program as combining "both ancient matriarchal concepts and contemporary feminist issues". The large room was unfurnished except for a table altar, decorated with corn and gourds, four unlighted candles, a conch shell and a small brass cauldron. Priestesses Patti Lather and Antiga said the service would be conducted in the "Dianic Wiccan tradition". The women formed a loose circle and followed Antiga and Lather in a vigorous opening chant:

> We are strong and loving women;
> We will do what must be done,
> Changing, feeling, loving, growing,
> We will do what must be done.

It was repeated, in accelerating tempo, half a dozen times. Next came a song in a quick folk-blues rhythm. The women sang eagerly, clapping in time, some singing the harmony:

> Woman am I, Spirit am I,
> I am the infinite within my soul;
> I have no beginning and I have no end,
> All this I am.

Antiga presided. "The theme for our celebration today is 'Going into the Dark' ", she said, because Wiccans celebrate the cycles of the year, and from Halloween until the spring equinox is the dark time of the year. She offered to answer questions later, "since many of you are probably attending for the first time". (As a veteran of hymn introductions at Sunday Mass, I doubt the accuracy of her assumption; I can recognize a congregation familiar with the music.) "One of the things witchcraft is very much about is changing energy", Antiga continued. The first ritual activity was to be "casting the circle" to create a "sacred space", a kind of energy field. Later, she promised, there would be "an actual energy-raising activity . . . raising energy to send to Washington, where Senator Jesse Helms is trying to, uh . . ."

"Burn the witches!" the group shouted.

"Yeah", Antiga agreed. "We're going to start now by invoking the directions", she said. Because the group was so large, it would be divided into four separate circles for the four directions. East, she explained, stands for air, birds, wind, clouds, all airy things. West stands for water, rain, ponds, oceans. South, for fire and anything related to fire. North symbolizes earth, the dark and all dark things. "We're trying to get in touch with the elements out there in the world. Go to the group you feel drawn to." Each circle was to plan its invocation of the spirits, then present it before the whole group.

"Will we have a center, too?" Lather asked.

"Yes", Antiga replied formally. "I think I would like to invoke my goddess as our center."

Two young women left the room, and a third followed a moment later. A few in the congregation were barefoot; one carried a teddy-bear hand puppet. The older women were neatly groomed in tailored skirts and blouses, their dignified appearance in startling contrast to the nature of the ritual. When the four smaller groups had planned their invocations, Antiga called the large circle together again with a blast from her conch shell. The women stood with hands linked, eyes closed, while she led them in the hypnotic "centering meditation", a "Tree of Life ritual", largely taken from Starhawk's *Dreaming the Dark*"[13] and almost identical to the one used earlier in Joan Keller-Maresh's workshop.

> Begin by breathing . . . breathing in, relaxation, breathing out, tension. . . . Imagine you are a tree, standing in the beautiful fall day. Feel your roots going down, down, to the very center of the earth. When you reach the center, attach your root down there so you feel really well grounded. With your root attached to the center of the earth, begin to send down anything that you don't want: fear, anger, resentment, send that down with a sound.

There were sighs and groans.

"In the center of the earth, fire and earth combine to make molten lava. Fire is the most transforming of all the elements", Antiga continued.

> So feel that healing, transforming fire in the center of the earth and allow that energy you don't want to be transformed into an energy you can love. That loves you. It's an energy of self-love. . . . Trust in yourself, believe in yourself. Bring that energy up, up, through your roots, into your body. Let it come in through the soles of your feet, rise up your body, all the way to your fingertips. That energy can handle whatever comes to you. All you need to do is call it up. Feel the power of that energy. Now allow that energy to spiral around your spinal column, rising . . . and then allow the energy to sprout out your head as branches. . . . Feel your connection with the other women in the circle. . . . Be aware that this circle is not complete without your energy. . . .
>
> Now allow your heads to fall forward on your chests. . . . Feel your head getting heavier and heavier and allow your head to pull your body down, until you are bending over with your head pointing to the ground.

Around the room, bodies obediently swung forward, heads hanging down, like a circle of rag dolls.

[13] Starhawk, *Dreaming the Dark: Magic, Sex and Politics* (Boston: Beacon Press, 1982); 30.

> Feel yourself solidly rooted in the earth, with your own center very secure. Begin to move to the right and then gently to the left. . . . Feel yourself a part of the tribe, the tribe of women who are trusting in their own spiritual expression. Feel yourself being pulled by your sister as you sway from right to left. . . . Again, be aware of your connection to the center of the earth . . . drawing up just the energy you need for right now. . . . Begin to be ready to open your eyes. I'll count from five to one. As I do, your alertness and awakeness will return. Five—four—three—two—one.

She paused. "Open your eyes, and we'll begin casting the circle of the east."

The circle of the east lay on the floor like spokes of a wheel, toes together. Crooning, the women rose slowly, waving their arms, then joined hands and moved in and out from the center, like children dancing around a maypole. They made windy, whistling sounds.

"Welcome, spirit of the east", said Antiga, lighting the first candle. "Blessed be."

"Blessed be", the congregation responded.

The circle of the south knelt with foreheads touching the floor, then rose and raised their arms. "Blessed fire", they intoned. "Fire is transformation, is passion, is beauty, is eternity. . . . Come join our fire."

"Welcome, spirit of the south. Blessed be." Antiga lit the second candle.

"Blessed be", the group replied.

The circle of the west stood, alternately lifting their arms, then folding them in. "Hear me, Aphrodite . . . sunset . . . intuition . . . life giving . . . deep waters, dark waters", they crooned, swaying.

"Welcome, spirit of the west. Blessed be." The third candle was lighted.

"Blessed be."

The circle of the north knelt, foreheads pressed to the floor. As they began to sway from side to side, they lifted their heads and droned, "Oooom, oooom." Rising, arms linked, they called out, "North star. Cold. Cold moon dying. Ice. Northern lights. Blackness. Nothingness." They howled wordlessly. Then they knelt, pressed their heads to the floor again, raised them and, swaying, chanted over and over, "O mah-to-qui-ah-sen, o mah-to-qui-ah-sen."

"Welcome, spirit of the north. Blessed be", said Antiga.

"Blessed be." The last candle was lighted, the large circle re-formed.

Antiga lit incense in the small brass cauldron and invoked the goddess "under her three aspects of maiden, mother and crone". All joined in the chant:

> Holy Virgin Huntress, Artemis, Artemis,
> Maiden, come to us.
> Silver shining wheel of radiance, radiance,
> Mother, come to us.
> Ancient queen of wisdom, Hecate, Hecate,
> Old one, come to us.

"The circle is cast. The ritual is beginning", Antiga proclaimed. Holding hands, the women began the "spiral dance", winding around the inside of the circle, following each other in a line that coiled toward the center, then wove outward again, while they chanted musically, over and over:

> We all come from the goddess,
> And to her we shall return,
> Like drops of rain,
> Flowing to the ocean.

At last the chant ended, and the circle formed again. Nadia, a storyteller, moved to the center to retell the story of Persephone and Demeter from a feminist perspective. "We all know the story, we who live in this year of 'our Lord' 1985. But as *I* live in the year 9985, in the year of my goddess, I tell you, it was different. She *chose*! And I'll tell you why she chose to go to the underworld." According to Nadia, it was to bring comfort and guidance to the dead souls. "We have much to gain from Persephone and Demeter", she said. "Demeter is the conduit between us and that dead person we love and also to the dead parts of ourselves: the little girl we had to stuff away, the little boy in us we could never allow to grow . . . the racial memories . . . the animal.

"Persephone shall reach the netherworld in five days, on Halloween. That is the time when the veil between the worlds rips open", she went on. "It is the most fortuitous time to contact the dead souls and the dead parts of ourselves."

"Blessed be", the congregation intoned as Nadia left the circle.

Now the group broke into small groups of five or six "to share why we're here, what you want to change while you're growing in the dark". Near my feet, as I sat with tape recorder and open notebook, young women from a "women's spirituality" group in my hometown of St. Cloud discussed their feelings about witchcraft.

"I like this because we can look at everything, not just what's been presented to us as 'truth'", said Chrystal, the recent convert. "And not feel guilty about it. . . . But setting up the altar seems just too silly. You know, that 'dirty magazine' feeling." The others murmured their understanding.

Susan, who had introduced Chrystal to goddess religion, said, "I just tell my husband that I'm going to my space." But she waits until her children are in bed, she admitted, and sometimes she thinks, "Maybe I don't have to light the candles. Maybe I can cast my own circle."

"It's hard for me even to get those things together", another woman said. "But I feel okay about the prayers I can make by myself in the dark."

"I had a guilt trip last week when I watched *Jesus Christ Superstar*", Chrystal said with a giggle.

"I know!" another woman groaned. "Just now I thought, 'God! If my mother came in that doorway!'"

"But I really felt good during the ritual", Chrystal said.

In a few minutes, Antiga moved the smoking cauldron to the center of the circle. Everyone was invited to "cast into the cauldron all that you want to let go of". Voices called out, "Patriarchy!"

"Anger!" "Fear!" "Oppression!" "Lack of time!" "Military mindset!"

To close the service, Antiga said, the group would now

> raise all your wonderful energy from the conference. . . . Probably you have seen the witch's hat that goes in a cone. Well, that has a very specific significance in witchcraft, and it is the image of the way that energy is raised. It goes around the circle in a spiral, getting smaller and smaller until it reaches the peak, and the energy is released. . . . A lot of energy raising is making noise. . . . But first I want to talk a little bit about this process of sending energy. With all these women here, the amount of energy we can raise is considerable. Today we're going to do a specific thing. For background on this, three women are going to talk about what's going on in Congress right now.

"We are three witches from different places", one of the trio said. "But we all have a fear." She explained the dangers of Amendment 805, as detailed in the Pagan Action Alert.

> I *resent* being classified with satanism! . . . The things they related [in hearings] were all about satanism. *Satanism has nothing whatever to do with women's religion! Satanism is a perversion of the white male Catholic religion!* What Hugh Downs says on "20–20" is not necessarily the truth about witches! So we would like to create *power*! Make noise! And she will help us to *block the bill*!

"Freedom! Freedom!" Kneeling in a circle, the congregation shouted. They pounded on the floor. The shouts became screams, and then a rising roar. The energy was sent to Washington.

Finally it was time to "ground the energy". The circle of women stood, dangling their hands toward the floor as instructed. "Imagine it flowing back into the earth", Antiga said. Then, again and again, they sang together, clapping in time:

> The earth, the water, the fire, the air,
> Returns, returns, returns, returns.

"The circle is open. The circle is never broken", Antiga proclaimed.

"Merry meet and merry part and merry meet again", the group responded.

"May the blessings of the goddess go with you", Antiga said. The service was over.

Connecting with God

As the Wiccan worshippers left the room, I stopped one middle-aged participant to ask whether she was a nun. "No, I'm not. Never was. I'm a peer counselor at a women's crisis center in Central Minnesota", she said amiably. "But I always see a lot of nuns at these things. The nuns are on the move. That's where the action is in the Catholic Church."

Gentle, smiling, silver-haired Sister Dorothy Olinger, S.S.N.D., who told me she had helped to organize the first Women and Spirituality Conference in 1982, defended the word *pagan*. "The whole word is taking on new meaning, being redeemed", she said. "It is not the belief we condemned in the past. . . . I believe that was where Jesus was coming from. . . . We *are* part of the earth, and we must work out our evolution into the beings we must become, in harmony with the earth."

Sandra Bot-Miller, a staff member in the student development program at St. Benedict's Catholic women's college in St. Joseph, Minnesota, and a leader in the St. Cloud "women's spirituality" group, was less at ease about answering my questions. I asked whether she was still a Catholic and, if so, whether she recognized a contradiction in taking part in such a ritual. She said tersely that she is a Catholic and sees no conflict. The Wiccan ritual is "different", she said. "I think there are many different ways of connecting with God."

"But do you believe Wicca is true? Is Catholicism true?" I asked.

"I don't use the word *truth*", Sandy said, edging toward the stairs. "I don't think there's one true religion that you're going to be saved by. I don't know what you mean by *truth*."

Later I asked Father George Wertin, St. Benedict's campus minister, what he thought about Catholics taking part in pagan rites. He hastened to assure me that "witchery" doesn't deserve its bad name. "There's a lot of misunderstanding about what Wicca involves. It has nothing to do with satanic worship. . . . It has to do with women reclaiming their role as prophets. . . . It helps them to get in touch with themselves." He said it might involve "getting in touch with the right side of the brain". Father Wertin said "practical considerations" had made it impossible for him to attend the conference, but he had published a notice recommending it in his campus bulletin, *Good News*, and had offered to arrange transportation for those who wanted to go. Ten women from St. Benedict's attended, both faculty and students among them, he said. One was his assistant, Dorothy Rollins.

"Were you aware of the nature of the conference?" I asked.

"Yes", he said, he had "studied the content of the program and definitely saw value in it".

Dorothy Rollins, too, defended both the conference and the Wiccan "tradition", which she said, "pre-dates Christianity" but "has been overlooked by the major organized religions". Today, she said, "enlightened women" are finally able "to take a look at this ancient tradition and culture", so long silenced by the established religions. Echoing Ruether, Fox and Sister Dorothy Olinger, Rollins told me that the word *pagan* means "country people". The "negative connotations" that have come to be associated with it reflect "citified" prejudice, she said.

Misguided Martyrs

In interviews with those variously involved in the Women and Spirituality conference, I asked two questions: "Do you recognize a conflict of conscience for Catholic women who participate in pagan rites? Were the early Christian martyrs mistaken when they chose to be put to death rather than worship pagan gods?"

Father Wertin saw no conflict. "The context today is considerably different", he said. "Today people are searching." But he emphasized his belief that participation certainly ought to be optional.

"Was lack of choice the deciding factor for the martyrs, then?" I asked.

He said he thought it was and repeated that he saw "no problem of conscience for those who are exploring".

Dorothy Rollins, too, saw no conflict. "I am open to other traditions", she said. When I asked whether she thought the martyrs were in error, she replied, "I couldn't say. I wouldn't want to say."

Sister Dorothy Olinger said she does not participate in Wiccan worship herself, because "I come from a Catholic tradition", but she sees "a lot of beauty and goodness coming out of that. . . . I'm not in the kind of Catholic tradition that says only Catholicism is true."

I asked her about the contrast between the acts of the martyrs and those of the Catholic women at the conference.

"Well," she said, "I wonder what similarity there really is. I think the Romans saw the state as God. The acknowledgment of the goddess goes way, way back, far earlier than the Roman gods, so your question does not seem to relate to the situation today."

One of the St. Benedict's College students at the conference, a senior theology major preparing for a career in "the peace and justice ministry", told me she believes "there are real powers, real forces in nature". Did she see a contradiction between her Catholicism and her participation in Wicca? She said she did not. "I still accept parts of the Creed," she volunteered, "but I don't believe in the Virgin Birth. . . . I believe that Mary was a free woman, that she belonged to no man. I think that's what it means." She said she believes that Jesus had a special relationship with God, just as we all can have.

Among those attending the conference were ten young women seminarians from the Church of God Seminary in Anderson, Indiana. Retha Brechmacher, a senior, said the seminary was paying their expenses. "We had *no* idea what we were getting into", she said. "I thought, you know, that it would be about women and *Christian* spirituality." Of Wicca, she said, "It disturbs me, in part, because confusion scares me. I don't believe that God the Creator is a God of confusion." She had attended Antiga's workshop, where, she said, they were led in much the same ritual as that used at the Wiccan worship service. "Some of it made me uncomfortable, and yet I acknowledge that there is something there. But I draw the line at calling that power God. Or goddess. . . . It has been quite an experience. I'm going to be processing this for a long time." Her companions' responses were mixed, she said. "One said flat out, 'This is not for me; they aren't straight.' But some of the others are saying, 'Yeah, this all makes sense.'"

To Bend or Shape

Wicca, according to initiates, is an Anglo-Saxon word meaning "to bend or shape"; witchcraft is a way of bending or shaping reality to their will by means of "magick". Jade River, in her address to the conference's closing assembly, said there are different "traditions" in witchcraft, just as there are different denominations in Christianity. She mentioned the Gardnerian, but said her own group was Dianic. Male Wiccans are not generally Dianic, she said, because "about 90 percent of Dianic witches are lesbians".

"Harm no one" is the one rule of Wicca, River said. "Personal responsibility is supreme. But two different decisions may both be right. It all depends on your own truth." There is a cyclic pattern to the universe, she believes, "so there need be no fear of death". Some Wiccans believe in reincarnation, while others see the death of the individual as "just the end of a cycle".

"A severe ethic" governs the use of Wicca, she said. "Most Wiccans would consider it unethical to send out energy to get *that* job. Instead they would ask to get the *right* job." River said Wiccans believe in the goddess as immanent in each person, not as an external deity, but as "a life force energy that some of us call the goddess, a part of ourselves". Thus they need no hierarchy "between the deity and us. We are not in a supplicative relationship." Like other Wiccans, she emphasized that Wiccans are not satanists. "I don't even believe there is a Satan", she said. "And not necessarily a true good and evil."

Wicca, as defined at Mankato, seems to mean different and contradictory things. How can they know what will harm another if there is no good or evil? In a system where all is relative, isn't one's perceived good apt to weigh heavily in the scales of judgment? If the goddess is simply a divine spark within each person, why do witches call on spirits and goddesses? Isn't it "supplicative" to ask for the *right* job? From whom do they ask it? What power works their "magick"? Are they worshiping themselves? Or are they worshiping something—or someone—whose existence they deny?

Startling as it was, the Women and Spirituality meeting was far from unique in its incorporation of witchcraft. Over the previous decade, journalists writing about neo-paganism as a minor manifestation of sociopathology had no need to engage in witchhunts; the witches declared themselves. Perhaps because of the presence of Llewellyn Press, an occult publishing company headed by "Craft priest" Carl Weschke, Minnesota was reportedly a center for the outbreak. That a period of Catholic decline should also see a pagan revival is more than coincidental. Unless the living truth about God's love for man is proclaimed in liturgy, sacraments and teaching, with the jubilant certainty that it is the greatest of all romances, the pearl above price, the summit and source of all power and beauty, the Church can neither stir the hearts of her own children nor attract others hungry for transcendent meaning in their lives. Tepid souls tend to drift into secularist apathy. Those with greater zeal are attracted by the fiery conviction of fundamentalism. But the more imaginative, immature, unstable or antagonistic may be drawn to the occult in a search for meaning, power and beauty or by a resentful desire to shock the respectable. What was astonishing at the Mankato event was the discovery that Catholic professional women, even consecrated religious, were among them. That conference proved to be only an introduction to a hidden subculture bubbling toward the surface of American Catholicism.

Strange Gods

At least for those who were originally Christians, goddess spirituality is more directed to destroying traditional religion than to seeking new sources of truth. It is unlikely that anyone believes the wisps of fairy tale that practitioners call "goddess traditions". In reality, ancient pagan deities were not benign; historic witchcraft was not the pretty enchantment of a movie Merlin. Present-day understandings of primitive goddess religions and of archaic witchcraft are based on scattered and uncertain sources in mythology, legend and superstition and on trial records of less-than-absolute objectivity. The Old Testament condemns the worship of "strange gods" as an abomination hateful to Yahweh, involving ritual prostitution and human sacrifice,[14] but clinical detail is not provided, nor is its interior logic explicated. Temple prostitution, which feminist art historian Merlin Stone admiringly calls "sacred sexual custom",[15] was practiced in the Middle East as worship honoring the goddess as patron of sexual love. Some authorities believe that children

[14] See, among many examples, Jer 7:16–34, condemning such idolatrous abuses as offering "cakes for the queen of heaven" (Ishtar, Assyro-Babylonian goddess of fertility, in v. 18) and the sacrificial immolation of children at Topheth (v. 31). Jer 19:5 and 32:35, 2 Chr 28:3 and 2 Kings 17:16–23 also condemn child sacrifice and threaten God's punishment. Hos 2:7–15, 1 Kings 14:24, 2 Kings 23:7 and Dt 23:18 mention sexual practices honoring Ba'al as male principle of reproduction and goddess Asherah (Astarte, Ashtaroth) as his mate. 1 Kings 18:26–28 describes pagan ritual. Nb 25:1–9 refers to the early seduction of the Israelites from worship of Yahweh to worship of the golden calf, referred to also in Hos 9:10 and Ps 106:19–23. References to later apostasies appear in Jg 2:11, 13 and 6:25, 31; 1 Kings 16:31–32; 18:19; 19:10, 14, 18; 22:54; and 2 Kings 3:2–3; 10:18–28, among others, until Yahweh said, "Even Judah will I put out of my sight as I did Israel. I will reject this city, Jerusalem", and permitted the Babylonian captivity (2 Kings 23:27).

[15] Merlin Stone, *When God Was a Woman* (New York: Dial Press, 1976), passim.

born to temple prostitutes were commonly killed in sacrifice. The faithless wife of Hosea left him to live as a ritual prostitute.

There were goddess cults with common characteristics in many primitive cultures—those of Tiamet in Babylon, Isis in Egypt, Ishtar in Akkadia, Inanna in Sumeria, Astarte in Syria, Aphrodite, Diana and Koré (Persephone) in Greece—all figures in dualist fertility cults, of which, some claim, European witchcraft may have been a folk-level corruption. Consistent in the old myths is the Great Goddess or Great Mother as female life force, representative of fertility and appearing in the "triple aspect" of maiden-mother-crone. In the annual religious cycle, she bore a son (in winter, usually at the solstice) who became her lover (May Day), impregnated her, then died or was sacrificially killed by the goddess at the firstfruits festival, to be reborn as her son. In primitive cults, the high priestess as an earthly incarnation of the goddess annually took a young consort, symbolic of the son/lover (the Horned God), who was ritually sacrificed (in later times he was castrated or an animal substituted) at the end of the year. The goddess was one of many deities, all of them forces to be placated. The term *grim reaper*, for example, originated in pagan England, where according to English scholar Joanna Bogle, the last harvester in the field was ritually killed as a blood offering to the earth as Mother Goddess so that she would bear again the next season. In a more colloquial description, feminist Robin Morgan has said, "Witches were the first Friendly Heads and Dealers, the first birth-control practitioners and abortionists".[16]

How closely contemporary witchcraft may resemble that of the past and to what extent there is today a defined "thealogy"[17] interpreting it for an "inner circle" of the enlightened are not entirely clear. Margot Adler, a "participant-observer" whose book *Drawing Down the Moon* is the most authoritative internal report on the neo-pagan movement, says that many "revivalist Witches"

[16] Robin Morgan, "WITCH Documents: New York Covens", *Sisterhood Is Powerful* (New York: Random House, 1970), 539.

[17] Because they refer to a goddess rather than to God, feminists put the word in feminine form, i.e., *thealogy*.

invent their own mythic stories, unconcerned about authenticity or logical consistency because they assume that psychic experiences are natural phenomena not yet understood; they "do not believe in a supernatural".[18] Others follow esoteric theories originated over the past century by enthusiasts whose opinions, if they were ever taken seriously by scholars, have been discredited.

Radically anti-male "Dianic" groups—and Matthew Fox—draw on the theories of nineteenth-century anthropologist J. J. Bachofen, who held that Stone Age European societies centered on the worship of Mother Earth lived in matriarchal harmony until patriarchal males seized power some five thousand years before Christ.[19] Elizabeth Gould Davis popularized much the same views in *The First Sex* in 1971.[20]

Charles Leland, a nineteenth-century American folklorist, occultist and political radical, claimed his *Aradia, or the Gospel of the Witches*[21] was a sacred book of myths and rituals given to him by a surviving practitioner from an ancient Italian witch family. Aradia is identified as a daughter of the goddess Diana (or Tana) by Lucifer (the sun), sent to earth to teach radical equality and the pursuit of ecstasy. Its view that women are the superior sex in witchcraft makes it a more popular ritual source among neo-pagan feminists now than it was when first published. Contemporary priestess Zsuzsanna Budapest also claims to be a "hereditary witch". While the gaudily extravagant "wimmin's religion" she preaches would seem to render belief a feat of blindest faith, Naomi Goldenberg mentions her with respect, and it was she who taught the "Craft" to the more socially accepted Starhawk.[22]

Theosophy, the enormously influential strand of nineteenth-

[18] Margot Adler, *Drawing Down the Moon* (Boston: Beacon Press, 1986), 41.

[19] Johannes J. Bachofen, *Religion, Myth and Mother Right* (Princeton: Princeton University Press, Bollingen Series 84, 1967 [1854]).

[20] Elizabeth Gould Davis, *The First Sex* (New York: Putnam, 1971).

[21] Charles Godfrey Leland, *Aradia, or the Gospel of the Witches* (London: David Nutt, 1899; reprinted New York: Samuel Weiser, 1974).

[22] Z. Budapest, "Letter to the editor", *Christian Century*, Nov. 26, 1980, 1162.

century occultism founded by Helena Petrovana Blavatsky,[23] not only survives but flourishes today in the strange but widely popular blend of gnosticism, spiritualism and scientism called the New Age movement. While New Age involvement is considered less bizarre than witchcraft, little in fact separates the two, and devotees often dabble in both simultaneously. Occult author Isaac Bonewits, who claims to be a Druid priest, explains that traditional witches always concealed their beliefs under "more respectable" coloration ("Freemasonry and Rosicrucianism in the 18th century, Spiritualism and Theosophy in the 19th"), while continuing to practice the same "occult arts".[24] Starhawk calls the goddess movement "a New Age revival" of witchcraft; at Matthew Fox's Institute, where she teaches, witchcraft blends easily into a predominantly New Age curriculum. According to neo-pagan priestess Adler:

> There is a funny saying in the Pagan movement: "The difference between Pagan and 'new age' is one decimal point." In other words, a two-day workshop in meditation by a "new age" practitioner might cost $300, while the same course given by a Pagan might cost $30.[25]

British anthropologist Margaret Murray,[26] writing in the first half of the twentieth century, argued that witchcraft was Europe's pre-Christian religion, a cyclic fertility cult of the two-faced, horned god Janus or Dianus, which survived in secret covens, still celebrating its sabbats and fertility rites. The Inquisition correctly described its practices, she said, but erred in concluding that its god was evil.

In the 1950s, retired British civil servant Gerald Gardner

[23] James Webb, *The Occult Underground* (La Salle, Ill.: Open Court, 1974), 80ff., *The Occult Establishment* (La Salle, Ind.: La Salle, 1976), passim.

[24] Isaac Bonewits, "Witchcraft", Part III, *Green Egg* 9, no. 79 (June 21, 1976): 5–6.

[25] Adler, *Drawing Down the Moon*, 420.

[26] Margaret A. Murray, *The Witch-Cult in Western Europe* (Oxford: Oxford University Press, 1921); *The God of the Witches* (London: Sampson Low, Marston, 1933); *The Divine King in England* (London: Faber & Faber, 1954).

claimed in several books[27] to be an initiate of a surviving coven of "the Old Religion", which he painted as a peaceful and sensual cult of the triple goddess of fertility. He incorporated elaborately detailed and poetic rituals borrowed from authors ancient and modern, and some 162 "craft laws", including ritual nudity and the "Great Rite" of sexual intercourse between priestess and priest. So influential have his writings been that he is the closest approximation to a witch-traditional authority. Many Wiccan groups call themselves "Gardnerian", although, according to Adler, they may not follow all his laws.

The most monstrous of the neo-pagan innovators was Aleister Crowley, who died in 1964. According to historians of occultism, he was a heroin addict and a frenetically promiscuous bi-sexual, too decadent even for the turn-of-the-century English occultists in the Hermetic "Order of the Golden Dawn", who expelled him. He set up a perverse "abbey" of satanic occultism, dissipated his life in systematic practices of vilest "sex magic" and left behind a trail of women degraded and terrified into madness.

Most current followers of "the Craft" insist that it is a benign nature cult, concerned with subjective psychological development (the expansion of "human potential") and preservation of the environment, having nothing to do with satanism, sorcery, drug use or horrifying sexual orgies. Insofar as that is true, neo-paganism might be regarded as the practice of comparative religion. But it inspires little confidence in such protestations of innocence to learn that Gardner's widely used rituals were written in collaboration with Crowley or that the well-known English "white witch" Sybil Leek praised Crowley's "contribution to occultism" on the cover of Francis King's chilling biography of the man.[28] In her noteworthy book *The Changing of the Gods*, Naomi Goldenberg, a feminist who teaches the psychology of religion at the University

[27] Gerald B. Gardner, *Witchcraft Today* (London: Rider, 1954; reprinted New York: Citadel Press, 1955); *The Meaning of Witchcraft* (London: Aquarian Press, 1959).

[28] Francis King, *The Magical World of Aleister Crowley* (New York: Coward, McCann & Geoghegan, 1978).

of Ottawa, mentions "the expression of sexuality in the ritual" without elaboration,[29] adding later that "witchcraft lets sex follow its own laws to a very large degree".[30] With a calm Christian readers are unlikely to share, Margot Adler admits that some Wicca groups do employ sexual acts, including the "Great Rite", but she indicates that such ritual practices are rare and finds them not at all horrifying. "In its highest form", when priestess and priest "through ritual . . . have drawn down into themselves these archetypal forces", to "'incarnate' or *become*" the goddess and god, the Great Rite is "a sublime religious experience", she says.[31]

The Church has always taken occultism seriously, condemning as dangerous all spiritualistic practices, even palm reading, tarot cards and ouija boards. As recently as October 1989, the Vatican warned of the spiritual and psychological risks in seeking mystical experience apart from the divine.[32] Those who believe in the objective reality of the supernatural order admit the possibility that mysterious forces may take possession of those who invite them to do so, but Heaven's angels can never act in opposition to divine revelation. Any spirits encountered in neo-pagan rites are unlikely to be holy, as the fruits of such experiences bear out. One repentant former member of a Wicca group has described her experiences in terms that strip away any illusion of harmlessness:

> When I was a witch, I performed rituals. I evoked spirits. I called entities. I cast spells, burned candles, concocted brews. The only thing I didn't do was fly on a broom, but I probably would have figured it out if given time. But where did it lead

[29] Naomi Goldenberg, *The Changing of the Gods: Feminism and the End of Traditional Religions* (Boston: Beacon Press, 1979), 88.

[30] Goldenberg, *Changing of the Gods*, 114.

[31] Adler, *Drawing Down the Moon*, 110; see also 143, 309.

[32] Joseph Cardinal Ratzinger, prefect, and Archbishop Alberto Bovone, secretary, Congregation for the Doctrine of the Faith, "Letter to the Bishops of the Catholic Church on Some Aspects of Christian Meditation", Vatican City, CDF, Oct. 15, 1989. See also Jacques Servais, S.J., "In Search of the Hidden God", *30 Days*, Jan. 1990, 33.

to? Into darkness, depression and the creation of an aura of gloom around me. I was frequently under demon attack. The house where I lived was alive with poltergeist activity . . . due to residual "guests" from rituals. My friends and family were afraid of me. I knew I had no future; all I had was a dark present. I was locked in by oaths and "destiny". But I had *power*, something I'd always wanted. It wasn't Satan's fault. He didn't exist—or so I thought. I gave it all up, and came to Jesus on my knees. . . . He freed me from the oppression and gave me back my soul—the one I had so foolishly given to evil in exchange for power. . . . Our salvation was bought at a great price and all we have to do is reach out for it. But we cannot serve two masters.[33]

Religion as Psychology

When contemporary goddess worshippers claim to be reviving an ancient belief system from a matriarchal golden age, they know they are drawing on a doubtful record, filling in the gaps with invention. Since what they offer is a personally autonomous religion, it cannot be expected to be coherent or consistent. These deficiencies do not trouble them. They are concerned with creative self-realization and ideological usefulness, not with objective truth. "A remembered fact and an invented fantasy have identical psychological value", writes Naomi Goldenberg. "Thus matriarchies are functioning in modern covens and in modern witches' dreams whether or not societies ruled by females ever existed in past history. . . . Modern witches are using religion and ritual as psychological tools. . . . In a very practical sense they have turned religion into psychology."[34]

Those who call themselves witches today usually follow the old pagan calendar of eight sabbats, or festivals: Samhain (Halloween), the Celtic new year and festival of the dead; Oimelc or Imbolc (February 1), a winter purification festival celebrating the

[33] Carmen Helen Guerra, "The Practice of Witchcraft", letter to the editor, *National Catholic Register*, May 18, 1986.

[34] Goldenberg, *Changing of the Gods*, 3, 25, 89.

Celtic triple goddess Brigid as goddess of fire and heralding the approach of spring; Beltane (May 1, Walpurgisnacht), the major fertility festival, celebrating the mating of the goddess and her son/lover; Lughnasadh or Lammas (August 1, a firstfruits festival), marking the death of the sacred king; the summer and winter solstices and the spring and autumn equinoxes. It is true, as neo-pagans charge, that the early Church, to help new converts resist any temptation toward backsliding, absorbed many of those pagan festivals into such Catholic observances as All Saints' Day, Christmas, Candlemas, Marian feasts and Ember days. Echoes of the pagan past can also be heard in the Wiccans' non-standard definition of the word *virginity*. "The maiden Goddess is a woman who remains a virgin", Goldenberg writes. "Although she may be quite active sexually, the woman is a virgin in the sense of being independent of her lovers."[35]

The moon is an important symbol in witchcraft, always seen as female. According to Goldenberg, "Acceptance of physiological change is also fostered by linking the triple Goddess to the cycles of the moon. The waxing moon is the maiden, the full moon is the mother and the waning moon is the crone."[36] A related belief holds that time, life and the universe are not "linear" but "spiral" or "circular", repeating a cycle of birth-death-rebirth. Many witches believe in reincarnation. Related to moon worship are water rituals, symbolizing both the moon as mistress of the tides and the son/lover as the river god of the old fertility worship.

Contemporary witches tend to use common ritual elements. First is the casting of a "sacred circle" to create a "sacred space" or "portable temple" for the proceedings. Next is "going within" or "centering the energy", in order to inform the "forces of the universe" that they are being called. This is followed by "raising energy", drawing it up from the earth through "guided meditation", dance or shouting. Later, the "energy" is "directed" through a "cone of power" to the object of "magick". Many other activities

[35] Ibid., 97.
[36] Ibid., 99.

may be included in the ceremonies, but they routinely conclude with "grounding the energy", or returning it to the earth. Sacred dance, sometimes nude,[37] is typically part of the ritual, to unite the group and to "raise energy". In feminist witchcraft, where the emphasis is on the goddess as immanent—"the goddess within" or the self as goddess—ritual speaking of the names of participants is regarded as powerful and often includes the phrase "I am goddess, you are goddess".

Crystal reading and "dream work", or visualizing a "dream guide" to seek her advice, are frequent practices, as is the use of tarot cards. Rebirth rituals are used in initiation ceremonies, involving passage through a narrow entrance into a new condition. Masking and mask making are common, as are ceremonies marking the menarche and menopause. Some rituals from archaic witchcraft have been assimilated into general culture; maypoles, authorities agree, were phallic symbols of the Horned God. Old beliefs and symbols lingering in European peasant culture were reflected in the fairy tales collected by folklorists like Jacob Grimm. Such stories are popular, read as myths, among the neo-pagans.

Women-Church

Much of this information comes not as criticism but as boast from the heart of today's witchcraft movement. One might expect it to have limited appeal in a presumably enlightened and scientific age and to be abhorrent on its face to Christian believers. Yet the movement is active and growing in Catholic circles well beyond Mankato. Those involved in it are not the ignorant but the educated, members of what has been called the "new Catholic knowledge class". Feminist theologians, students in Catholic women's colleges, middle-aged nuns and laywomen from Church middle management, especially educators and "peace and justice" networkers, are united in this odd pursuit by religious feminism.

[37] Adler, *Drawing Down the Moon*, 112.

For some twenty-five years, in workshops, conferences and writings directed primarily to each other, they have fed a mounting and obsessive rage against male domination and have concluded, finally, that they will not serve a God identified as "Father". Early Christian gnosticism and medieval Catharism, heresies that rejected Yahweh as a God of evil and the Old Testament prophets as his evil servants, echo through their repudiation of God. The definitive feminist position is not merely that a religion in which some roles are closed to women is essentially evil but that all hierarchy is evil, even the supernatural hierarchy. They will serve no transcendent deity, only "the divine within": that is, only themselves. They style themselves "Women-Church".

Not all neo-pagan witches are feminists, nor are all religious feminists witches. But Adler reports that feminists make up a growing minority of today's Wicca practitioners.[38] College departments of religious studies and women's studies, typically in feminist hands, have been centers of neo-pagan recruitment; feminism and orthodox Christian belief appear to be mutually exclusive. Some religious feminists pursue the New Age; some sample Eastern mysticism; many turn from God the Father, Son and Holy Spirit to an androgynous "Mother/Father God" or to process theology's depersonalized "Ground of Being". The "Mother Goddess" of feminist witchcraft is intended to be a transitional symbol, weaning women from the understanding of God as transcendent Trinity to a concept of the Divine as an essentially immanent and mutable Universal Consciousness, not far removed from pantheism. That ultimate abstraction lacks emotional appeal, however, and it is to the transitional symbol that religious professionals have flocked. As they did in Mankato, they call their activities "women's spirituality" and practice them as a feminist replacement for the worship of the triune God.

An apparent majority prefer a feminine deity, revealed only in human experience; they encounter her in their own impulses and worship her by obeying them. Since this immanent "goddess"

[38] Ibid., 70, 228.

illumines them directly, they have no need of the "male-dominated patriarchal Church", which will, they predict, wither away. In their embrace of this gnostic mystique they resemble the thirteenth-century followers of Joachim of Flora, who predicted a "Third Age" of the Holy Spirit in which law and gospel would be replaced by ecstatic contemplation, the sacraments would be withdrawn and the hierarchy would vanish. Joachim's writings were condemned and burned, by papal order, in 1256 and refuted by St. Thomas Aquinas in his *Summa Theologiae*.[39]

Whatever else witchcraft may be, it is clearly a religion, rival and antithetical to Christianity, and those who take part in Wiccan worship are materially idolators. It is a religion without absolutes, dependent for moral direction on subjective "feelings" about "circumstances". It seems to be seductive and subtly corrupting. Even those who deny belief in a supernatural power insist that psychic and physical effects are produced and that *they* are changed as well as the object of their "magick". It acts as a solvent to doctrinal faith, to traditional morality, most noticeably sexual morality, and apparently tends to obsession. The progressive nature of these effects suggests that, whether or not the practitioners think they are addressing a being "out there", someone other than themselves is responding. Readers of C. S. Lewis may be reminded of the scene in *The Last Battle*, in the Narnian Chronicles, where Rishda Tarkaan called on Tash, a god he didn't believe in—and Tash came.

On Halloween (Thursday, October 31, 1985), in the Senate-House Conference Committee, Senator Helms' Amendment 805 to HR 3036, the object of the spell cast at the Mankato meeting, was quietly and anonymously killed. In September it had passed the Senate by a unanimous vote. Since then, I pray with new meaning when I say, "Deliver us from evil."

[39] St. Thomas Aquinas, *Summa Theologiae*, Ia–IIae, Q. 106, a. 4.

Chapter Two

The Daughters of Lilith

Religious feminism is the logical extension of secular feminism into the realm of the sacred. From the beginning its leaders have worked closely with secular and anti-Christian feminists. In the dedication of *The Changing of the Gods*, for example, Naomi Goldenberg offers special thanks to Rosemary Ruether and to Sister Margaret Farley, R.S.M., a noted Catholic feminist theologian. The literature of religious feminism is remarkably frank, but when more orthodox Catholics ask why strategically placed radical feminists should be permitted to subvert Catholic clients while pursuing their "ministries", these revolutionaries grow evasive. They usually claim they are simply encouraging the creative development of female psychology. The obvious question arises: Why do feminists want to remain in an institution they hate and whose Creed they have rejected? Dr. Ruether explained why, without evasion, in November of 1985. She was speaking in Chicago, where efforts to put her theory into practice were well under way.

Stay in the Church and Use It

"Why bother with the Church at all?" Ruether asked rhetorically. Because "Roman Catholicism goes along the same as ever when dissatisfied people leave it, happily relieved of their critical presence". Fresh from the Mankato conference, she was delivering another keynote address, this time to the annual assembly of

Chicago Call to Action. Her remarks were later published in the Jesuit journal *America*.[1]

Agencies of the "spiritual revolution" must remember, she warned, that "unless we manage to insert what we are doing . . . back into . . . main institutional vehicles of ministry and community . . . it will have no lasting impact". Religious revolutionaries should "stay in the Church and use whatever parts of it they can get their hands on". Thus they "will have far more impact, both on the Church and on the world . . . than they could possibly have if they separated from it". The advantage gained is "like the difference between shouting with the unaided human voice and speaking through a global system of telecommunications", she said. "Use these ordinary structures. . . . If one organizes a liberation or feminist theology lecture series . . . try to hold it in a Catholic college or parish." She did not name the goddess, or call for the formation of covens as she had in Mankato, but her record as a religious revolutionary is public and published, and her audience needed no such detailed instruction.

Chicago Call to Action is a still-smoldering ember of the National Call to Action convention held in Detroit in 1976. The capture of the Detroit event by radical forces was so publicly noted that it is seldom mentioned today, though the Catholic left still pursues its agenda. The Chicago offshoot is not formally affiliated with Church bureaucracy. But in an archdiocese whose head, Joseph Cardinal Bernardin, was president of the national bishops' conference in 1976, and where the man who chaired the Detroit convention, Monsignor John Egan, has long been prominent, Call to Action is considered influential. Its Women's Issues Committee had already begun inserting feminist spirituality into the Church by co-sponsoring, with the Graduate Program of Religious Studies at Mundelein College, a year-long series of programs by a local group called "Limina", to introduce the goddess to Chicago Catholics.

[1] Ruether, "Crises and Challenges", 152.

Mundelein Women

Mundelein College was not an altogether surprising setting for unorthodox activities. The only four-year Catholic women's college in Chicago, it was founded in 1929 by Sisters of Charity of the Blessed Virgin Mary (B.V. M.s). By the 1980s, it was reportedly experiencing financial difficulties. Sister Mary Breslin came to the presidency in July 1986 from the position of treasurer. The college had religious troubles as well. One alumna, the mother of seven, told me sadly that there had been "incredible teachers, excellent women" teaching at the college when she was a student. "But now it's all peace-and-justice and women's studies. I couldn't think of sending my girls there."

One member of Mundelein's Board of Trustees, Sister Anne Carr, B.V. M., had been required to resign from the council of women advisors for the NCCB (National Conference of Catholic Bishops) pastoral on women after going on public record as one of the twenty-four American nuns who denied that there is a binding Catholic teaching on the morality of abortion. The statement appeared in a 1984 *New York Times* advertisement purchased by the notorious abortion lobby Catholics for a Free Choice (CFFC).[2] Mundelein offers two master's degree programs, one in liberal studies and another in religious studies. Mary Griffin, director of the graduate liberal studies program, signed a second *New York Times* advertisement expressing "solidarity" with the signers of the first.[3] Sister Mary DeCock, B.V. M., a member of both the liberal studies advisory committee and the religious studies departmental committee and a teacher in the graduate religious studies program, also signed the second advertisement. Her former colleague in the religious studies department was Father Matthew Fox, O.P., who

[2] Catholics for a Free Choice, "A Diversity of Opinions Regarding Abortion Exists Among Committed Catholics", advertisement, *New York Times*, Oct. 7, 1984.

[3] Catholics for a Free Choice, "We Affirm Our Solidarity with All Catholics Whose Right to Free Speech Is Under Attack", advertisement, *New York Times*, Mar. 2, 1986.

founded his Institute for Culture and Creation Spirituality (ICCS) there in 1977. He moved it to Holy Names College in Oakland in 1983, but he is remembered with respect at Mundelein. Sister Blanche Gallagher, of Mundelein's art faculty, taught in the ICCS summer program in 1985, and many other ICCS faculty members have been drawn from the graduate students who acquired master's degrees in Mundelein's religious studies department under Fox.

It was Sister DeCock who arranged for her department to cosponsor the Limina series with the Call to Action committee. The two sponsoring bodies performed a genuine if inadvertent service to the Church by bringing the goddess movement out of the hothouse of feminist seminars into the sunlight of public scrutiny. Orthodox Chicago Catholics, aghast, denounced the Limina program as "paganism and witchcraft" and demanded that it be barred from Catholic institutions.

Goddess-Centered Events

Limina is a small, non-profit Chicago-area organization formed in 1984 by three women with roots in avant-garde Catholicism to present goddess-centered events for women in Catholic settings. The founders are Tesse Donnelly, M.A. (history), Lillian Lewis, M.A. (theology), S.T.L., and Cathaleen Rich, M.Ph. The organization seems to be an expression of their personalities. Flamboyant "Lil" Lewis provides theological lampoonery; officious, patronizing Tesse Donnelly handles public relations with references to Jungian psychology; soft-spoken, retiring Cathaleen Rich is responsible for artistic components.[4] According to its membership information, Limina offered "an empowering community and a protected space . . . between the ordinary and the holy where women can reclaim the sacredness within". Donnelly said the group received no outside funding but operated on income. The price of the conference admission was forty-five dollars.

[4] Rich also illustrated the 1987 Mary's Pence brochure for Chicago Catholic Women.

First in the series was "The Goddesses and the Wild Woman", presented at Mundelein in March 1985. Program notes promised

> TOGETHER—combining ancient text and modern dreams . . . dance, drama and ritual, we shall draw aside a curtain woven by patriarchal consciousness to reveal within each of us the Goddesses and the Wild Woman. TOGETHER we shall reckon with Her dark side and honor Her bright side. Related to one another, we shall draw Her energy into our souls and celebrate Her return to our lives.

Limina's 1986 schedule, handsomely printed on heavy, glossy paper, lavish with artwork and adorned with testimonials, showed that "The Goddesses and the Wild Woman" was repeated in January 1986 at Sheil Catholic Center at Northwestern University. Listed next were "Five Winter's Eves", held in two locations during January and February, to "search out 'the goddess in charge' and the one we've got locked in the basement . . . time for talk and for a quiet going-within".

Back at Mundelein on March 15, Limina presented "Her Holiness: Maiden, Mother, Crone", a program designed around the "triple goddess" familiar in witchcraft. To Limina, Tesse Donnelly explained, it meant "the three phases of women's lives". The program combined dance, guided meditation, dramatization, discussion, slide presentations and ritual and, according to the conference schedule, had such laudable goals as "discouraging precocious sexual activity . . . and post-partum depression". Celebrating what Donnelly called woman's "time of wisdom", it culminated in an initiation ritual for crones. It was repeated at DePaul University on April 12. Another presentation, announced at the March 15 conference, was to be held "to raise women's consciousness" at St. Mary's College at Notre Dame, Indiana. The season was to have ended with a "summer solstice celebration" at Rosary College in suburban River Forest on June 22, but it was not held. "It was never scheduled", insisted John Easton, Rosary's director of publications. "Apparently they talked to someone here, but it never got put on the calendar." He refused to name the faculty member responsible.

Symbol, Trappings and Ritual

The three leaders heatedly denied that Limina's activities had anything to do with religion, witchcraft or the goddess movement, as local critics had charged. Lewis told Chicago reporters that Limina "explores, validates and consecrates the changes that define women's lives. It's not based on Catholic teachings. It's based on biology."[5] The critics were "rightwing, unsophisticated fundamentalists", she grumbled.

Compared to the Mankato Women and Spirituality conference, "Her Holiness" was an amateur production, loosely organized, less formal and explicit in ritual, lacking either celebrity speakers or dramatic power. It was also small. There were perhaps thirty-five women in attendance, and a trickle of departures continued throughout the day. Parts of the program, and Donnelly's interview comments, might have been less ambiguous if prior public controversy had not put the presenters on the defensive; it was made clear that my presence as an observer was intensely unwelcome. Nevertheless, against the accusation that Limina was engaged in witchcraft there was only bare and inconsistent denial. All the evidence of symbol, trappings and ritual indicated that the charge was true. Contrary to prior disclaimers, it became clear that Limina's program was indeed about religion. It was adversarially concerned with Catholicism. It addressed religious questions in religious terms. Its activities were inherently religious in nature, and the religion they expressed was goddess witchcraft.

Wounded by God

Limina's reason for being, it appeared, is bitter and unremitting resentment of the way life treats women: nothing was fair in the past, and fairness was not predicted for the future. The message was that women must be independent of the masculine, because

[5] Bob Kostanczuk, "Cardinal Studying Women's Group", *Daily Calumet*, Mar. 14, 1986.

only women can be trusted. Toward the Church and salvation history, only antagonism was expressed.

In her energetic opening monologue, Lewis, an unemployed "pastoral worker", asked how many of the audience were practicing Catholics. Amid general groans, three or four women held up their hands. "*Partially* practicing?" she asked. Most raised their hands. The rest identified themselves: one Quaker, one Jew, two Protestants, one "yoga" and one Unitarian.

Limina's estimation of its audience was obviously on target. They guffawed over Lewis' jibes at Catholicism. There were laughter and applause when a woman gloated that she and her companion "teach in a *Roman* Catholic school, and we got our *pastor* to *pay* for us to come to this conference!"

Dressed in full witch costume and mask, Lewis peered out at the crowd in mock ferocity. "Is the lady here who's going to interview me for *Chicago Catholic*?" she asked. "Is the reporter here? Are you afraid to admit who you are? C'mon up!" The audience laughed. Lewis held up a witch doll. "Someone sent me this as a gift", she chuckled. "I don't know what the Blue Army would think about this!" Through the windows, a few men could be seen strolling by along the lakefront. Lewis interrupted her performance to squint out at them, muttering, "That may be the Blue Army in disguise." In the persona of witch, or crone, Lewis declared, "We're doing theology here! It's a *God* question, and I'm glad that Mundelein wants to allow me to ask it. They've got some chutzpah here!" Her "theological question" was, "You'll go straight to hell if you picture God as an old black woman; isn't that true?" In passing, she added, "I don't know if anybody believes in original sin anymore. I'm a theologian, and I haven't bothered with it for a long time."

Tesse Donnelly recited a consciousness-raising tally of the "wounds" God and his servants have inflicted on women, beginning with Genesis. "I will multiply your pains in childbearing", she quoted. Leviticus inequitably required sixty-six days of purification after the birth of a daughter, she complained, but only thirty-three days for a son. No lamb was provided as a sacrificial substitute for

Jephthah's daughter, but a ram was substituted for Isaac.[6] And "the Christian folk of Europe" were responsible for "burning nine million witches".

Sacred Space

It became increasingly clear what kind of religion Limina was promoting as, one by one, the standard elements of witchcraft were introduced. The first ritual activity was casting the circle of "sacred space" with dance. "In the old goddess religions, dance was sacred, a religious act", said Lewis. The women were directed to form a double circle, facing each other, for "Jean Houston's Gynosmythos dance". As they moved, holding hands, they were told to maintain eye contact with their partners and at the end to "touch the person opposite you on her cheek, while looking into her eyes". The dance united the group, they were informed. Donnelly said the music was a Greek folk song.

In historic as well as revived witchcraft, members of the coven dance around their ritual leader or a symbol of their deity. Here, the women first danced around a fabric sculpture of a female figure, some seven feet tall. At the end of the day, they danced again, to the same music, around the "Great Mother" tree. The "sacred space" was the scene of another ritual dance at midday. "Ritual is the compressed and poetic statement of life", Lewis said gravely. "When we begin the dance, we are leaving behind the profane world. If you have time on your watch, you have to let go of that. For the witch world, you have to let go of the old space, so we can be in this liminal world." To the recorded strains of Kay Gardner's "Wise Woman", dancers formed pairs at the "well", then skipped together down the center aisle to the Great Mother tree, where Lewis, now wearing a sort of chasuble, presided. So

[6] The scriptural account of Jephthah's sacrifice of his daughter is not one of approval. In vowing a human sacrifice, he was not obeying God but imitating the evil practice of his pagan neighbors. Jg 11:39–40 reports that the Israelite women afterward mourned her death four days each year.

common were such practices in the Middle Ages that churchmen, prohibiting witchcraft, specifically warned against rituals involving wells or trees.

The song "Wise Woman" is from the album *Moon Circles* by Gardner, a "priestess of the Goddess". Her recordings are available through, and recommended by, *Circle Network News*, a newsletter of "Wicca, Paganism . . . Goddess Worship, Positive Magick & related Pantheistic ways", published by Wicca priestess Selena Fox, Circle Sanctuary, Mount Horeb, Wisconsin.

It was not an esthetic success when the three leaders danced together, too, linked at all six elbows, their backs toward each other, revolving to the sound of "There's a woman in the moon . . . changing, changing, ever changing." In turn, they called out, "I am maiden!" (Rich); "I am mother!" (Donnelly); "I am crone!" (Lewis) and urged the group to join them in this chant about "woman's triform reality".

Cathaleen Rich led the group in a guided meditation, beginning, "Feel the earth through the floor, pulling you; feel rooted in the earth". It was strikingly similar to a meditation in priestess Hallie Iglehart's step-by-step ritual guide.[7] Rich told the women to visualize three "dream guides", a maiden, a mother and a crone, and to ask each one for advice. I stayed in Rich's small group when the audience broke into circles to tell about the advice received. There were sympathetic murmurs and nods of agreement when a mother of four declared that she "didn't much like motherhood, even though men and *our Pope* claim all women do!" One attractive young graduate student witnessed to the seductive power of the occult when she said ruefully that she couldn't get to work on her neglected dissertation because "all I want to do is tarot and dream work!"

During the crone initiation, candidates were required to pass through a "stricture"—a human corridor—to be reborn into their new state. For the ceremony, the women wore masks, made as one

[7] Hallie Iglehart, *WomanSpirit: A Guide to Women's Wisdom* (San Francisco: Harper & Row, 1983).

of the day's projects, and "vestments", which were red scarves. Red, the color of blood and thus of life, was traditionally considered a witch color. The initiates were told, "Up until now in life, your flaw, your vice, was an obstacle. . . . But now you are to wear your flaw with pride!"

There were other interesting neo-pagan elements. Cathaleen Rich compared the female idea of "circular" development with the inadequate "linear" theories of a male psychologist. The star of a dramatized fairy tale was Baba-Yaga, the witch of Russian folklore. One of the books offered for sale, *Crone: Woman of Age, Wisdom and Power*, by Barbara Walker, was listed in the January/February 1985 catalogue of Llewellyn Press, a major national supplier of occult materials. Walker is also the author of *The Skeptical Feminist: Discovering the Virgin, Mother and Crone*, an unrestrained account of her own trek to the goddess and her dreams of a "Woman's Utopia".[8] But the most significant element undercutting Limina's professed intent of "discouraging precocious sexual activity" was the repeated use of the definition of "virginity" described in Goldenberg's *Changing of the Gods* as that prevailing in witchcraft. "In Greek mythology, virginity was renewable", Donnelly said in her slide presentation. "Hera regained hers each spring. Persephone returned each year 'younger than springtime'. Aphrodite was not a maiden; she was the lover of many, mother of many. But she was a virgin because she belonged to no man. 'One-in-herself, belonging to no man' is the *real* meaning of *virgin*", she emphasized. "But without you and me, that will not be the meaning given in our culture. We are being called to reclaim virginity, to save our daughters from seeking their identity in a man! Virginity must be an *active* state, modified by motherhood but reclaimed as crones."

[8] Barbara Walker, *The Skeptical Feminist: Discovering the Virgin, Mother and Crone*, (San Francisco: Harper & Row, 1987).

Observers Unwelcome

Brochures for the Limina conference had been prominently displayed in at least one occult bookstore. Later, when I asked Donnelly why, she brushed my question aside; she didn't know all the places where brochures were distributed, but "most of the people who frequent such stores seem to be harmless folk, perhaps open to new trends". It was even possible, she conceded, that some of those in attendance might call themselves witches. "I could not provide assurances, because we don't screen the people who come. But that is not what we consider ourselves."

Limina may have offered an indiscriminate welcome to those who came to take part in the rituals, but my quiet non-participation was plainly unwelcome. "People have been saying terrible things about us, you know. Saying we're witches!" Lil Lewis said to me when I passed near the registration table. She and the others kept a troubled watch on me and muttered together. During the initiation, Donnelly suddenly loomed above me. "I want to tell you that it's very disturbing to see you here just *observing* these other women and not taking part!" she complained.

Late in the day, an older woman who had been watching from the lobby came up to me. "So you dropped out, did you?" she asked. She was Sister Mary DeCock, Limina's link with the Mundelein religious studies department. She admitted having made the conference arrangements but vigorously denied that the college, or her department, was its sponsor. "We just permitted them to use our facilities. That isn't sponsorship. And there are no students here, none at all. I only see one graduate in the group", she said. "You know, people have been saying it's pagan religion, but it's not religion at all!"

What, then, I asked, was the significance of the "Great Mother"?

"Oh, the Great Mother!" she snorted. "*That's* not religion! That's myth and ritual! But you probably want to ask me what relation it all has to religious studies."

I said I did, indeed.

"Feminism and religion have to help women to understand themselves", she said. "But the department didn't sponsor it. That's just an error."

Wasn't printing it on the season program a rather serious error, I asked?"

"Oh, well. People make mistakes", she shrugged.

After the conference, the Limina telephone was answered by Donnelly, who said the group's events were "attempts to affirm women in life transitions". Any suggestion that they involved witchcraft "bordered on justiciable libel", she warned, claiming that "lawyers are being consulted". She declined to let me speak to the other leaders, declined to say whether they were practicing Catholics and declined to provide information about their academic backgrounds. Program notes stated that Donnelly herself had taught at the Jung Institute, an item of some importance, as Cardinal Bernardin had seemed reassured to learn that "the group uses images which are used in the psychological theories of Karl Jung".[9] Thus it was interesting to learn, eventually, that none of the women had psychology as her academic field; Donnelly's degree was in history. She said her knowledge of psychology was that of "a dedicated amateur" and admitted that her teaching at the Jung Institute consisted of a single course, "Women and Their Symbols", ten years earlier. About her own religious status, Donnelly said she was "a practicing Catholic" in an "alternative parish". I asked her to explain the hostility toward the Church exhibited at the conference. "I think a lot of us feel a loving but contentious relationship with the Church", she answered. The contention was plain to see, but not the love.

In view of the language and rituals used, why did Limina call its presentation psychological in nature? If the program was not religious, I asked, why was it sponsored by Mundelein's religious studies department?

[9] Kostanczuk, "Cardinal Studying".

"They are deeply involved with women's psychological development, which is involved with and is at some points co-terminous with women's spiritual development", Donnelly replied.

"If the program has nothing to do with witchcraft", I asked, "why does it speak, as Starhawk does, of 'the goddess within'?"

"On one level, the goddesses are expressions of archetypal images . . . based on Jungian concepts of women's psychological development", Donnelly replied. "On another level, the goddess is used as a transitional symbol, because, like Rosemary Radford Ruether, we agree that women have suffered from our sense of God as masculine."

What was the significance, I asked, of the fir tree, the "well" (a wooden bucket) and the term *Great Mother* as they were used in the rituals? Donnelly dismissed them as metaphors. "The tree is one of the most ancient of religious symbols, and like the water ritual, universal", she explained. "It's the same with initiation. Initiation rituals are very common. You wouldn't call a fraternity initiation sacramental."

Why, then, had Lewis, as liturgical presider, used the phrase "thank you, Great Mother"?

Donnelly hesitated, then said she didn't remember the incident. "Of course, we don't have a creed as such, so if someone used a phrase, I can't tell you what they [*sic*] meant by it."

I said I had been surprised, when the crone initiates were told, "Hang your masks on the Great Mother", to realize that the term referred to the fir tree.

"I'm not prepared to give you a theological rendering of what was meant by the Great Mother", Donnelly snapped. It was "too complicated" to explain to me, she said.

Donnelly explained that her "negative feelings" toward me had been caused "by your very studied and salient nonparticipation. . . . It would be as if you went to a birthday party and everyone sang 'happy birthday', but someone stepped outside the circle and definitely didn't want to sing." And my questions seemed to suggest that I was trying to link Limina with other groups somehow, she added.

Yes, I was, I said.

"Limina", she said, "is an entirely local, autonomous and spontaneous organization."

"But how is it related to the goddess movement that I see around the country?" I asked.

Donnelly said she knew of no such movement.

Surely she was at least aware of it?

"No, I'm really not", she insisted.

How could she explain the simultaneous emergence of goddess-centered groups in many places if there were no contact between them?

"An idea sometimes springs up simultaneously and independently in many places at once", she said, "out of the collective unconscious."

Surely ideas do not travel independently of a material agent? Donnelly conceded that reading might be involved. "I read things, probably the same things you read, but there's no contact."

And had she read Starhawk? "Well," she admitted, "yes. I read *The Spiral Dance*. But I have never attended one of her workshops."

I said Limina looked to be of the same nature as a much larger Wicca conference I had attended but "still in a bud state".

"If it's just a bud here today," Donnelly replied, "*no one* can say what it will be when it's in full bloom."

The Rest of the Plant

In fact, it is possible to predict quite accurately whether a bud will open as a rose or a brussels sprout by examining the rest of the plant. Similarities—in language, symbol, ritual and definition—to the literature of feminist spirituality and the activities of the Mankato conference were too great to accept as coincidental. Some of those elements are used in folk dance, in psychotherapy, even in children's games, but their presence in such concentration, and in connection with the goddess, spelled cultic meaning. It seemed unlikely competent counsel would advise proceeding with a libel action against those who described it as pagan.

Donnelly's denial that she knew of the existence of the goddess movement became ever less plausible as she began to reveal whose books she had read. Starhawk's and Rosemary Ruether's, admittedly. The Limina brochure also quoted Robin Morgan, who as early as 1970 had recommended witchcraft for women. Gloria Steinem, in her introduction to the conference "textbook" *Goddesses in Every Woman*,[10] wrote about the value of the goddess movement.

Other evidence, even more compelling, suggests that Donnelly knew a great deal about the meaning and goals of goddess feminism. In April 1985, she was one of only four members of the Women's Issues Committee of Chicago Call to Action to be named on a brochure advertising a weekend retreat at St. Joseph's Retreat Center in Des Plaines. It was conducted by Sister Madonna Kolbenschlag, H.M., a former congressional aide who was then a senior fellow at Woodstock Theological Center at Georgetown University. Her name was familiar from "Women, Ritual and Religion", a videotape presented three times at the Mankato goddess conference. Appearing with her on the tape had been feminist theologian Elisabeth Schussler Fiorenza, a member of both Women's Ordination Conference (WOC) and the "Catholic Committee on Pluralism and Abortion" (the putative sponsor of CFFC's 1984 *New York Times* advertisement); Naomi Goldenberg, author of *The Changing of the Gods*; Starhawk's mentor Zsuzsanna Budapest and pioneer goddess "thealogian" Carol Christ.

[10] Jean Shinoda Bolen, *Goddesses in Every Woman: A New Psychology of Women* (San Francisco: Harper & Row, 1984).

The Exorcism of God as Father

The Des Plaines retreat had been called *Kiss Sleeping Beauty Goodbye*, after the Kolbenschlag book registrants were urged to read in advance.[11] In her book, Sister Madonna makes approving mention of witchcraft and discusses the goddess movement at some length as a stage, necessary for some, in an evolutionary process that is moving humanity—and the "God-who-is-coming-to-be"—toward transformation in a "New Faith".

"A conversion to matriarchal imagery is often the first and most necessary step" in the "exorcism" of "God as Father", Kolbenschlag wrote. The step is necessary because

> Woman has adapted herself to a relationship with a transcendent being who is radically Other than herself. The closer she comes to this God, the more she loses her own soul. A woman has no choice but to be an atheist. . . . The moment of atheism is also a moment of the expulsion and destruction of idols. . . . God, who has been imprinted in our minds as a transcendent absolute, must somehow be recovered in an epiphany of immanence, of divine self-revelation.[12]

The archetypal images of patriarchy can be "exorcised", Kolbenschlag said, through participation in the "spontaneous Goddess recovery groups" that have (here quoting Carol Christ) "revived ancient mythologies from goddess-worshipping cultures" and "aligned them with wholesome witchcraft traditions". But Sister Madonna does not see this as the final stage of the new religion. The emergence of the New Faith will eventually demand "more than the detached autonomy, static immanence and narcissistic separatism that matriarchal religion may cultivate", she said. In other words, the goddess cult is "transitional", as Donnelly had told me. She could have heard it from Kolbenschlag herself at the retreat she had helped arrange the previous spring.

[11] Madonna Kolbenschlag, *Kiss Sleeping Beauty Goodbye: Breaking the Spell of Feminine Myths and Models* (Garden City, N.Y.: Doubleday, 1979), see especially 166–202.

[12] Ibid., 184–86.

"The sign of ultimate religious experience will surely be . . . its power to release truly spiritual redemptive energies. The first fruit of the truly catholic faith will be the liberation of God", Kolbenschlag continued. In this "truly catholic" New Faith—a Joachist "Third Age of the Spirit"—the Church will wither away, made unnecessary by the direct illumination of "a creative Spiritual Presence that comes from *within* them as well as from *beyond*". The "New Faith" will abandon the "intoxication" of the sacraments, radically invert the concept of sin to place pride first on the list of virtues, reject the ascetic tradition as masochism and understand prayer as "the deepest contemplation of and contact with the self". Experience will replace revelation as the ground of moral judgment, and the New Faith will express itself as politicization, she predicted. It will be a politics of the left, obliterating patriarchal structure in the secular world as, in the world of the sacred, the New Faith obliterates patriarchal theology and the Church.

When experience is the basis for moral decisions, women's "capacity for ethical choice" will increase, and more will move into Lawrence Kohlberg's stages five and six of moral autonomy, according to Sister Madonna. What she meant by female autonomy was clarified by her description of abortion as "a rational and complex act":

> The possibility of rational choice enhances the very autonomy that women perceive is at stake. Abdication from a decision for or against each pregnancy . . . only increases the risk of self-division that is so harmful to the embryonic child and the guilt that is inevitable in a late abortion. . . . Whichever way we choose, there is some evil. . . . Her self respect and personal autonomy demand that she enter into a process of discernment that exorcises invalid heteronomic imperatives and exposes her own hidden fears and motives to herself. Only then will her decision be truly "free", the act of an ethically mature person.[13]

The Third Age and illuminism having been solemnly condemned centuries ago, Kolbenschlag's vision was not original. Her

[13] Ibid., 171–72.

sophistries about the imperative of selfishness in an "ethical" decision to abort what she admits is a "child" makes Frances Kissling appear tender by comparison. Her deliberate encouragement of idolatry as a step toward the New Faith is stunningly cynical and her proposal to "liberate God" presumptuous unto clinical delusion. Yet it all has an authentic ring. It is not an anomalous digression but a logical progression of the fanaticism that rejects not only masculine but feminine nature as well. Definitively gnostic, it wants to change women into beings of another kind by extirpating their natural inclinations to nurturance, compassion, generosity and responsibility. Now, in this final "spiritual" evolution, it would attempt to change even God.

The Daughters of Lilith

The same mentality is revealed in "The Coming of Lilith", a "myth" invented by Judith Plaskow and her committee at a 1972 conference at Grailville, in Loveland, Ohio. Often reprinted in feminist anthologies, it is included in *Womanspirit Rising*, a collection of essays edited by Plaskow and Christ.[14] In the story, God first simultaneously created a human couple, Adam and Lilith. But when Adam began to order her about, Lilith flew away and refused to come back. So God created Eve from Adam's rib. Adam was happy, but Eve too grew restless about her "undeveloped capacities" and resentful of the "excluding closeness of the relationship between Adam and God". At last, she climbed over the wall and met Lilith, and they developed "a bond of sisterhood". God "became confused. . . . He needed counsel from his children. 'I am who I am,' thought God, 'but I must become who I will become.'" So God and Adam were "expectant and afraid the day Eve and Lilith returned to the garden, bursting with possibilities, ready to rebuild it together".[15]

[14] Carol Christ and Judith Plaskow, eds., *Womanspirit Rising: A Feminist Reader in Religion* (San Francisco: Harper & Row, 1979).

[15] Judith Plaskow et al., "The Coming of Lilith", Christ and Plaskow, *Womanspirit*, 206.

Womanspirit Rising is enormously instructive for those who want to know what has been going on, and why, in the world of religious feminism. In a joint preface, the editors explain how, as fellow students in Yale's graduate theology program, they became feminists because they felt their ideas were being ignored and concluded, on hearing an address by Rosemary Ruether, that existing theology was rooted in "male experience".[16] Eventually they determined that religion could be "recreated to speak to the experiences of women".[17] Their book includes essays by many of the inventors of feminist theology: Ruether, Schussler Fiorenza, Goldenberg, Starhawk, Budapest, Mary Daly and Merlin Stone, among others. The final essay, "Why Women Need the Goddess", is Christ's own. She says frankly:

> Even people who no longer "believe in God" . . . still may not be free of the power of the symbolism of God the Father. . . . *Symbol systems cannot simply be rejected; they must be replaced. Where there is not any replacement, the mind will revert to familiar structures at times of crisis, bafflement or defeat* [emphasis added]. . . . A question immediately arises, "Is the Goddess simply female power writ large, and if so, why bother with the symbol of the Goddess at all? Or does the symbol refer to a Goddess 'out there' who is not reducible to a human potential?"[18]

Christ says she asked Starhawk, who answered, "It all depends on how I feel. When I feel weak, she is someone who can help and protect me. When I feel strong, she is the symbol of my own energy. At other times I feel her as the natural energy in my body and my world." Other goddess feminists have other explanations. Christ summarizes: they see the goddess, first, as a symbol of the spiral energy in nature; second, as a personification of "divine female" who can be invoked; finally, as an affirmation of "the beauty and legitimacy of female power" made possible by the women's movement. "*Theologians need to give more than lip service*

[16] Christ and Plaskow, *Womanspirit*, ix–xi, 21f.

[17] Ibid., xi.

[18] Carol Christ, "Why Women Need the Goddess", in *Womanspirit*, 274, 275, 276, 278.

to a theory of symbol in which the symbol is viewed as the primary fact and the meanings are viewed as secondary,[19] Christ concludes (emphasis added).

By definition, Catholic feminist theologians would seem to be in a different situation. Unlike these ambivalent solipsists, they profess belief in a real Divine Being, transcendent as well as immanent, however explicitly they declare their intention of changing the accepted understanding of that Being by exploiting idolatry. They are depending on a form of the rule *lex orandi, lex credendi*—as one prays, so shall one believe. They seem to overlook the likelihood that, insofar as the rule is true, those who practice goddess worship will come to believe what they pray and fail to "transcend" it on command. Kolbenschlag's own later work attests that it can affect leaders as well as followers.[20]

Like other practitioners of the occult, goddess worshippers say they are changed by their ritual acts, drawn progressively deeper into the cult. Given this progression, feminist fury will continue to mount against the Church, because she cannot change God the Father into God the Mother. As Joseph Cardinal Ratzinger put it:

> Christianity is not a philosophical speculation; it is not a construction of our mind. Christianity is not "our" work; it is a *Revelation* . . . and we have no right to reconstruct it. Consequently, we are not authorized to change the *Our Father* into an *Our Mother*; the symbolism employed by Jesus is irreversible; it is based on the same Man-God relationship that he came to reveal to us.[21]

It is precisely the conviction that religion is an amendable human construct that fires feminist theology, not only the neo-pagan variety but that which calls itself Catholic as well. To judge

[19] Christ and Plaskow, *Womanspirit*, 279.

[20] See Madonna Kolbenschlag, *Lost in the Land of Oz: The Search for Identity and Community in American Life* (San Francisco: Harper & Row, 1988).

[21] Joseph Cardinal Ratzinger with Vittorio Messori, *The Ratzinger Report: An Exclusive Interview on the State of the Church* (San Francisco: Ignatius Press, 1985), 97.

from the rest of the organism, it is thus a fair conclusion that Limina is neither a rosebud nor a brussels sprout but a runner of spiritual crabgrass, intended, like the rest of the movement, to choke out Christian belief and replace it with the New Faith.

Archetype Land

Catholic authorities in Chicago nevertheless seemed more defensive than alarmed about Limina's use of Catholic institutions. Sister Joy Clough, R.S.M., archdiocesan communications director, was taking calls about Limina the Monday following the conference. The cardinal had only two comments on the matter, she said: first, he was aware that the conferences were being held; second, he was not fully informed about what they involved. "The cardinal has not taken a position on the workshop or issued a statement", she said.

I explained that the ritual had invoked a "Great Mother" and that it displayed many similarities to rituals used by those who call themselves witches. Did she think it appropriate that such rituals be conducted in Catholic facilities?

Stressing that she spoke only for herself, Sister Joy said the invocation of the Great Mother did not "seem problematic, since God is not a sexual Being", though what I said about the other rituals "raises some questions".

If the cardinal had made no formal statement, he had answered complaints in the letter quoted in the *Daily Calumet*, in which he said it was his understanding that Limina was drawing from the ideas of Carl Jung. "While there is nothing inappropriate in the use of psychological theories or images to assist people in personal growth," he added, "my review has suggested some areas about which I need further clarification. . . . I have begun the necessary inquiry."[22]

The Jungian influence in feminist spirituality deserves attention. A sometime practitioner of the occult, Jung was deeply interested

[22] Kostanczuk, "Cardinal Studying".

in pagan ritual, alchemy and the Hermetic tradition. Some of his theories were in fact adopted by Nazis as confirmation of their own occult theories. Though Jung himself was no feminist, Jungian theory is quite often associated with goddess religion by those who see the immanent goddess in his notion of the Great Mother archetype or who hope to redesign "archetype land" to conform to feminist tastes.[23] Goldenberg quotes his observation that "religion can only be replaced by religion". Because Catholicism "cannot allow individual people to depart from the myths dispensed by the Catholic hierarchy", Jung saw it as "a dying religion", she says, and to replace it "set out to build a psychology that would function like religion". When feminists have "smashed" the "stereotyped molds of Catholic experience", Goldenberg continues, "Jung's criticism of Catholicism might become the 'daily bread' of millions".[24]

Jung's belief that, in the interests of wholeness, evil inclinations should be accepted and integrated into the personality rather than suppressed is also compatible with feminist neo-gnosticism of all shades. It was from that concept of what to do about one's "dark side" that Limina, for example, drew the directive to the new crones to "wear your flaw with pride". Jungian Edward C. Whitmont, M.D., a founding member of the C. G. Jung Training Center in New York, in his *Return of the Goddess* says, "In the depths of the unconscious psyche, the ancient Goddess is arising", demanding "recognition and homage. If we refuse to acknowledge her, she may unleash forces of destruction. If we grant the Goddess her due, she may compassionately guide us toward transformation."[25]

[23] See Erich Neumann, *The Great Mother: An Analysis of the Archetype* (Princeton: Princeton University Press, Bollingen Series 47, 1963). See also Naomi Goldenberg, "Jung and Feminism", *Signs: Journal of Women in Culture and Society* (Winter 1976): 443–49.

[24] Goldenberg, "Jung and Feminism", 47–50.

[25] Edward C. Whitmont, M.D., *The Return of the Goddess* (New York: Crossroad, 1988), viii.

Sponsorship

At Mundelein that week, the word *Limina* drew instant attention. President Mary Breslin, B.V.M., said she had not known about the conference until she saw the brochure. Yes, she was distressed about it, but the religious studies department had assured her that it was *not* a cosponsor. The college did not sponsor it; the department did not sponsor it; Sister Mary DeCock did not sponsor it. Limina was simply allowed to use college facilities, she said. The program statement was an unfortunate error, but she would make no public statement of correction lest more attention be drawn to the matter. "DePaul is hosting the same conference, you know", she said defensively. "And Rosary. And they held it at Sheil Chapel at Northwestern."

When I called the religious studies department, however, I was told that the department *had* sponsored Limina. Since the director was absent, I talked to Jean Brosnan, her administrative assistant. All calls about Limina were being transferred to the public relations department, she said, but she could answer questions of fact.

Was the program accurate in listing the department as a cosponsor, I asked?

"Yes", she said.

Was the decision to sponsor it made independently by Sister Mary DeCock, or was it a departmental decision?

"Oh, certainly not independent", she said. "No one ever does anything like that independently. It's a decision made by the department."

Why had Matthew Fox left Mundelein three years earlier?

"Well, it's hard to say why he left; for new opportunities, I suppose", she said. "But he certainly had a strong, important, *wonderful* influence on the department, and it is on-going."

Then there was no pressure on him to leave?

"Oh, no, no, not at all! Father Fox is a very great, an *international* scholar!"

Next I spoke to unruffled Jean Lachowisz in the public relations office. "No one at Mundelein sponsored the Limina conference", she said. "They were simply allowed to use college facilities." She herself took "no position" on the matter but had dropped by during the morning and found it "quite innocent".

But Miss Brosnan had just told me that the religious studies department *did* sponsor Limina, I observed.

"Oh, well, all right. So it was sponsored by one department. That does not imply approval." She said that the Limina conference held there a year earlier had aroused no controversy. She thought the conference could be described as "in the realm of the arts", but not of religion.

It looked very much like the religion of the goddess movement, I observed.

"I think it was about celebrating the Western philosophical tradition", she said pleasantly. "Or perhaps it was about nature and the earth."

Gnosticism

To analyze the goddess movement from the sanity of a Catholic perspective, it is useful to review the rudiments of gnosticism, the ancient spiritual error that takes its name from *gnosis*, the Greek word for knowledge. The gnostic is certain that he *knows*, absolutely and without reference to external authority, because he is directly illuminated by "the divinity within" and is thus above any law. He is a *dualist* because he believes the material world and its institutions to be hopelessly corrupt, having developed without benefit of his spiritual gnosis. Theologian Robert Grant defines the self-centered perspective of the historic gnostic religions as "a passionate subjectivity".[26] In *The New Enthusiasts*[27] historian

[26] Robert M. Grant, *Gnosticism and Early Christianity* (New York: Harper Torchbooks, 1966), 9.

[27] James Hitchcock, *The New Enthusiasts and What They Are Doing to the Catholic Church* (Chicago: Thomas More Press, 1982).

James Hitchcock writes about the gnostic qualities in contemporary reform movements, religious and political, in terms that read like a checklist for religious feminism. Besides "feminist tendencies", he notes such gnostic characteristics as an exaggerated sense of its own historic importance; an anti-intellectualism that exalts instinct and imagination over reason; hostility toward the hierarchical Church; a vision of a "new and invisible church" centered in the "sovereign, infinite self"; a belief that "self-knowledge is tantamount to knowledge of God"; a claim to authority arising from "direct inspiration by the Spirit"; rejection of a "narrow", objective notion of God; a utopianism that "absolutizes a single view of social justice" yet somehow coexists with a relativism contrarily denying that moral law can be absolute; and a redefinition of mysticism to serve its particular causes. He cites Matthew Fox as an example.[28] Clearly, the feminists seeking to translate their gnostic vision into a New Faith in a new deity take their color from the same dye lot.

Feminist theologians ceaselessly complain about Christian "dualism", usually in reference to the belief that right and wrong are concepts applicable to sexual behavior. The truth is, a gnostic dualism that sees the flesh as a container for the spirit seems to be at the heart of the belief that the androgynous spirit should overcome the confining tendencies of masculine and feminine gender, and its relevance to the idea of reincarnation is obvious. The "libertinism" common in historic gnosticism, Hitchcock observes, followed from the belief that "values" were a projection of the "sovereign will", which could not be limited by external laws. Similarly, today's gnostics regard individual choice as supreme and condemn as rigidly judgmental those who hold objective standards of moral behavior to be obligatory. Far from indicating belief in the holiness of the body, such permissiveness proceeds from a view of the body as a mere vehicle for the real self, a property to be used in any way the imperial self may choose. Catholic doctrine, restated in recent years by Pope John Paul II as the "theology of

[28] *New Enthusiasts*, 118, 142.

the body", teaches to the contrary that man is an incarnate person, a creature subject to God's law in the unity of flesh and spirit, and not imperial at all.

Feminist Infiltration

Limina is one small pocket of subversion in one city. The 1980s were a decade of feminist infiltration across the American Church. Well before Rosemary Ruether told Chicago Call to Action to "stay in the Church and use it", hundreds of local Catholic feminist groups across the continent were already putting that advice into effect. Thousands, perhaps tens of thousands, have done so since, in colleges, parishes, retreat centers, women's centers, peace and justice committees, catechetical training courses and diocesan agencies and commissions, official and unofficial. While they have been utilized in short-range tactical forays—for example, such groups skillfully organized the feminist troops that dominated the "listening sessions" held in connection with the American bishops' first draft letter on women's concerns[29]—their primary purpose has been the long-range one of preparing women to accept the New Faith.

The scattered examples of grass-roots level subversion described below could doubtless be duplicated in almost any diocese. They reveal common demands: for inclusive language; innovative liturgy; feminist interpretations of spirituality, theology, doctrine and canon law; equal access to all Church offices; permissiveness in regard to sexual and marital irregularities; resistance to hierarchical authority; and leftist politics. They cite standard authorities: "The spirit of Vatican II", Matthew Fox and the corps of feminist theologians headed by Ruether. Their typical agents are religious and laywomen in education, bureaucracy and selectively "representative" committees who work in collaboration with independent activists and like-minded priests. Common indoctrinational techniques and activities are widely reported. A few highlights:

[29] National Conference of Catholic Bishops, *Partners in the Mystery of Redemption* (1988).

Where I was best able to observe, in the heavily German-Catholic diocese of St. Cloud, Minnesota, feminist influence has seemed to emanate primarily from three sources: the College of St. Benedict (C.S.B.) and the Benedictine motherhouse at St. Joseph; Christ Church, a Newman Center parish at St. Cloud State University; and the motherhouse of the Sisters of St. Francis in Little Falls. Their broadly diffuse subversive efforts began in the 1960s.

As the 1980s opened, reluctant but obedient older nuns were spending "recreation" hours deleting "non-inclusive language" from lectionaries. Soon, nun lectors everywhere were making awkward impromptu revisions or deletions as they read. Matthew Fox enjoyed soaring popularity; employees at the Catholic bookstore reported, "Fox is our best seller among nuns." The diocesan liturgy commission, directed by Sister Delores Dufner, O.S.B., pressed for liturgical dance, inclusive language and other feminist innovations, except when expressly forbidden by the bishop. First in the three centers, then in avant-garde parishes, the Sign of the Cross was replaced by the invocation "in the name of the Creator, the Redeemer and the Sanctifier", sometimes even in the rite of Baptism.

At the Newman parish, women staff members preached half the homilies and made frequent mention of Matthew Fox's ideas. "Creation-centered" study groups were offered as a Lenten activity in 1985. Newman's inclusive language committee revised the baptismal rite, replacing references to Jesus Christ with references to "Mother-Father God" and, in place of the renunciation of Satan, inserting a promise, addressed to "the four directions", to "refuse to follow the masters of this age".[30] When the bishop learned of this practice, he ordered it stopped, but the pastor and staff remained in place.

At CSB, a "Committee for Incorporation of Women's Perspectives into Curriculum" (CIWPC) began meeting early in 1982 to study the writings of Mary Daly, Shulamith Firestone, Charlotte

[30] Interview and written statement of Mary King, who resigned from the parish with her husband Peter in 1986 when the pastor, Father Nicholas Dressen, dismissed their concerns about these deviations from the rite.

Bunche, Matthew Fox and Starhawk, among others. Late in 1984, it won a $216,645 grant from the Fund for the Improvement of Post-Secondary Education to design a gender-sensitive curriculum, though in fact gender sensitivity already seemed far advanced. Undaunted by public objections to its hosting of Bella Abzug in the late 1970s, the college further outraged pro-lifers by arranging addresses by Judy Goldsmith, president of National Organization for Women (NOW), and feminist theologian Elisabeth Schussler Fiorenza, in the early 1980s.

By 1985, a variety of revised "creeds" written in "non-sexist" language by parish councils, inclusive language committees, liturgists and individual celebrants were creeping into Masses in the usual churches. The mildest avoided masculine pronouns and references to God as "Father", or to Jesus as "Son". Another, used at a "Farewell Mass" at CSB on May 21, 1985, declared:

I believe in God
who created woman and man in God's own image
who created the world and gave both sexes domination
over the earth.
I believe in Jesus, child of God
chosen of God, born of the woman Mary,
who listened to women and liked them,
who was followed and financed by women disciples.
I believe in Jesus,
who discussed theology with a woman at a well and
confided first in her his messiahship
who motivated her to go and tell
her great news to the city.
I believe in Jesus, who thought of pregnancy and birth
with reverence,
not as punishment—but as a wrenching event,
a metaphor for transformation, born again anguish-into-joy.
I believe in Jesus who appeared first to Mary Magdalene
who sent her with the bursting message, GO AND TELL—
I believe in the wholeness of the Savior, in whom
there is neither Jew nor Greek, slave nor free, male or female.
For we are all one in salvation.

I believe in the Holy Spirit as she moves over the
waters of creation and over the earth.
I believe in the Holy Spirit as she yearns within us
to pray for those things too deep for words.
I believe in the Holy Spirit, the woman spirit of God
who like a hen created us and gave us birth
and covers us with her wings.[31]

Dorothy Rollins, associate director of campus ministry,[32] arranged a presentation of "Womanspirit Rising: A Ritual of Symbol and Movement", as an official 1985 Women's Week activity at St. Benedict's. The same month, *Good News*, the campus ministry bulletin, published a lead essay by a senior student praising the "profoundly liberating" effects of goddess religion and citing Starhawk as a "noted spiritual writer". Sister Mary Anthony Wagner, O.S.B., professor of theology and editor of *Sisters Today*, had found the 1983 "Womanchurch Speaks" conference in Chicago so "thrilling", that she went to the 1986 Women in the Church conference in Washington, D.C., too. There she confided to fellow journalists that "fundamentalist" parents posed the most difficult problem she encountered in teaching. She told me, in defense of feminist theology, that theologians no longer believe that revelation ended with the death of the last Apostle. In 1987, Patty Hackett of campus ministry went to Cincinnati for the Women-Church Convergence; the following year, she organized campus ministry's lesbian support group.

Women's Week continued to provide CSB students with consciousness-raising experiences: in 1987, Sandra Bot-Miller came from the Newman Center women's spirituality group to lead a Wiccan ritual in the meditation chapel; in 1989, Newman's campus minister Jacqui Landry was invited to present a workshop on "the New Age movement, women's spirituality, Monika Hellwig, Madonna Kolbenschlag, Elisabeth Schussler Fiorenza and Rosemary Ruether".

[31] "Liturgy of the Word", program for Farewell Mass, College of St. Benedict, May 21, 1985.

[32] See chap. 1, above.

On a rented farm near Annandale, in 1988, two Little Falls Franciscans who were members of their community's administrative board, Sister Agnes Soenneker and Sister Carol Schmit, opened a "women's spirituality" retreat called Clare's Well, as "a different kind of church". Sister Agnes told a local reporter, "We try to model a church that isn't over the people but is with the people." The center, offering "communal prayer and ritual" (and, for twenty-five dollars an hour, body massage), drew three hundred visitors in its first five months. "We see a real interest in spirituality, and we're not talking about religion", said Sister Carol.[33] Notice of their activities was posted in St. Cloud's only New Age bookstore. "Clare's Well", now formally sponsored by the Little Falls community, signed Call to Action's "Call for Reform" advertisement in the *New York Times* on Ash Wednesday, 1990.

Meanwhile, in St. Louis, Missouri, Joleene Unnerstall left the School Sisters of Notre Dame to become a New Age "trance-formationalist". That means "wholeness education and healing with hypnosis", she told a reporter. "I go into a light trance along with the person I'm working with" to do "whole-person readings" about "past lives, health or anything relevant".[34] When she abandoned the order, Unnerstall did not entirely lose touch with her old community. A conference she organized, titled "Women Alive! A Nurturing Network invites all women to catch the wave of 'Womenspirit Rising'", was presented twice during 1987 at Fontbonne College, a local Catholic institution operated by the sisters of St. Joseph of Carondolet, which is noted for New Age class offerings. It was also presented at Maria Center in the S.S.N.D. provincial motherhouse. Among conference workshops were "Creating a Sacred Circle", workshops on "Past Lives and Present

[33] John DuBois, "Nuns' Farm Breeds Peace: Spirituality Runs Deep in Clare's Well", *Saint Cloud Daily Times*, Nov. 6, 1988.

[34] Regina Popper, "'New Age Thinking' Spreading from West to East, Some Say", *West End World*, Dec. 18, 1986, 23.

Wisdom", "Healing the Inner Child", "Chakras: Spiritual Energy Centers", lessons on group "channeling" and using crystals for meditation. Noeli Lytton Wotawa, campus minister and English teacher at Nerinx Hall, a Catholic girls' high school, led a workshop titled "The Goddess Within". The Maria Center conference ended with a tour through the "hallowed halls" of the motherhouse, "where women have dedicated their lives to spiritual growth for over a hundred years". Another member of the S.S.N.D. community, Sister Aline Faul, regularly taught Silva Mind Control classes, complete with instruction on "astral projection" and "spirit messages", in evening classes at the Carondolet Area Community School through the 1980s.

In addition to "telling their stories" of personal experience and taking part in rituals, feminist spirituality groups like to invent new feminine names and "images" for God. In discussing witchcraft as the *creation* of religion, Goldenberg, who believes God is an image existing only within the individual mind, recommends that the witch—who is thus a creator of God—be envisioned as a woman weaving: "Changing natural materials into something useful".[35] All those elements were present at a gathering called "Rising Spirit: Women Weaving Stories of Spirituality", on Sunday, April 23, 1989, at St. Louis University. Printed on the program, a quote from *Imaging God/Women's Experience*, by Sister Gertrude Wenhoff, O.S.B., said in part, "Women's spirituality will not be discovered in a body of doctrines. It is found in the experience of persons". Co-sponsored by the St. Louis Archdiocesan Council of Women Religious, the Archdiocesan Committee on Women in the Church and St. Louis Women-Church, the retreat day combined rituals and consciousness-raising narrations of "my own life journey" as they related to the image of a "Weaver Woman God". The "Weaver" ritual, led by Sister Joyelle Proot, S.S.N.D., closed with the phrase "this we pray in the name of our God with many names".

[35] Goldenberg, "Jung and Feminism", 97.

In metropolitan Detroit, *Kindred Spirits*, the newsletter of the Women's Sources and Resources network, reports five times each year on "women's spirituality" activities held in the area, usually in Catholic settings. Couched entirely in the vocabulary of religious feminism, it announces an endless round of events like "process gatherings" for experience sharing; "process dance" and drumming groups; courses on "creation-centered spirituality"; solstice celebrations by an "on-going Women's Rituals" group; lectures by Sister Joan Chittister, O.S.B., Phyllis Trible or the ubiquitous Rosemary Ruether; "Dreams and Spiritual Growth" workshops and "Peace Center" exhibits. It also promotes courses and publications from national feminist or neo-pagan groups: Women's Ordination Conference; Women's Alliance for Theology, Ethics and Ritual (WATER); the Berkeley Center for Women and Religion; Boston Women's Theological Center; Catholics Speak Out; Bear Tribe, and so forth.

In Schenectady, New York, on April 24, 1988, Mary Hunt, the compleat feminist theologian, became the focus of a storm of protest when, at St. John the Baptist Catholic Church, she gave a talk titled "Being Church in the Twenty-first Century". Her address, part of the lecture series, "The American Church: An Open Future", was arranged by the parish council's adult education program. Five years earlier, Hunt had founded WATER, an organization on the feminist fringe. After receiving a doctorate in systematic theology from Berkeley's Graduate Theological Union and teaching for two years at an ecumenical seminary in Argentina, she had returned to Washington, D.C. Like-minded advisors at the Catholic "social justice lobby", Network, the Catholic "social justice" Center of Concern (COC), the Catholic leftist Quixote Center and feminist theologians (including Fiorenza, Kolbenschlag, Sister Mary Collins, O.S.B., and best friend and co-director Diann Neu, then at the Center of Concern) urged her to implement her "vision" of an ecumenical center for feminist strategy and ritual by establishing WATER. Needless to say, WATER is a member of Women-Church Convergence. Hunt is also an uncloseted lesbian who serves on the board of directors of New Ways Ministry and is active with the Conference for Catholic Lesbians, a member of a Washington Women-Church group called Sisters Against Sexism, a policy advisor to Women's Ordination Conference and a member of CFFC's board of directors.

Organized as the Coalition of Concerned Catholics (CCC) under F. C. Robert Hollman, laymen and women who opposed Hunt's appearance as part of an official Catholic education program publicly and privately pleaded with Bishop Howard Hubbard, ordinary of the Albany diocese, to bar her from speaking in church. He declined to interfere. Diocesan spokesmen said Hunt would not advert to her controversial stands on abortion and homosexuality, and "even persons to whom one is diametrically opposed on most issues may well contribute to an exchange of ideas on other areas of mutual concern".[36] Father Michael Farano, diocesan chancellor, told reporters that Hunt's appearance had been cleared because no other American bishop had banned her from speaking and because her address was not a homily but part of an adult lecture series.[37] Hunt spoke as scheduled, while some two hundred Catholics prayed and picketed outside the church. With them was Father Walter Baniak of Troy, who noted ironically that Hunt was being permitted to speak in church on Good Shepherd Sunday. "It's like allowing the sheep to be brought to the wolf", he said.[38]

Hunt did not, after all, avoid sensitive subjects in her address. She pointed to the fact that "my lecture was not moved off this property today" as an example of diversity appropriate to the future Church. She predicted that "lesbian and gay people in church will become as common as candles" because "the choice will be welcoming diversity or dying on the vine as the people of God".

[36] Statement in *Evangelist*, Apr. 7, 1988, quoted in Doreen Ercolano, "Bishop's Stand on Speech Disappointing to Protesters", *Record*, Troy, N.Y., Apr. 25, 1988.

[37] Mike McKeon, "Bishop Urged to Ban Talk", *Times Union*, Albany, N.Y., Apr. 21, 1988.

[38] Ercolano, "Bishop's Stand".

Such "diversity" will mean "a shift of power" in decision-making authority from the hierarchy to "the people who are the Church"; a priesthood open to women, homosexuals male and female and the married; "celebration of the goodness" of remarriage after divorce, and homosexual marriage. "The reality will come first; the theology will come next."[39] Like others in Women-Church, she said, her own hope is for an end to the ordained priesthood and the emergence of a Church without hierarchy.[40]

It was another irony that while diocesan officials saw value in the exchange of ideas with those, like Hunt, "to whom one is diametrically opposed on most issues", they apparently saw none in exchanges with the Coalition of Concerned Catholics. Three months after Hunt's address, Chancellor Farano was stirred by CCC's membership campaign to place a notice in the diocesan newspaper, *The Evangelist*, warning that the group was not sanctioned by Bishop Hubbard and that he would not respond to matters it brought to his attention. Farano told an Albany newspaper that CCC had "set itself up as a type of guardian of orthodoxy, which is a function that rests only with the bishop. No group can take that on itself, nor can the bishop give it to anybody." He criticized the group for "asking people to report their pastor, monitor what priests are saying".[41]

"Our goal is to support the bishop", CCC chairman Hollman responded courteously. "We want to do everything to help him. He is without doubt a successor to the Apostles."[42] In a follow-up letter to the editor, Hollman pointed out that Bishop Hubbard had told the *Evangelist* only a few weeks earlier that through their Baptism and Confirmation, "all laypersons are commissioned by the Lord himself to participate in the saving mission of the church.

[39] Doreen Ercolano, "Hunt Speaks on 21st Century Catholic Church", *Record*, Troy, N.Y., Apr. 25, 1988.

[40] Tim O'Brien, "Catholics Protest Theologian's Views", *Times Union*, Albany, N.Y., Apr. 25, 1988.

[41] Catherine Clabby, "Conservative Groups Target Liberalism in Catholic Church", *Times Union*, Albany, N.Y., July 30, 1988.

[42] Ibid.

Such mission", Hollman wrote, "does not require the support of a priest or bishop."[43]

Among problems of concern to the coalition was the growing influence of Matthew Fox's thought in the Albany diocese. Two week-long retreats on "creation-centered spirituality" were scheduled during July at Pyramid Life Center, an Adirondack Mountain camp in Altamont owned by the diocese. The retreats were to be led by Father Brian O'Shaughnessy, a staff member at the diocesan Peace and Justice Commission, and Father Kenneth Tunney. The two men had presented a multitude of lectures, workshops and courses on the subject in Catholic and Protestant church facilities around the diocese since returning early in 1987 from sabbatical semesters at Fox's institute in Oakland, California. CCC objected that diocesan sponsorship gave a misleading impression that Fox's eclectic notions, then under investigation by the Vatican, constituted valid Catholic teaching. Again, Father Farano took exception, accusing CCC of treating Foxian spirituality as "guilty until proven innocent". He said it was unlikely that the retreats would be banned, but, in any case, "responsibility for permitting this or not permitting this does not lie with Mr. Hollman".[44] Father Farano predicted correctly: the retreats were held as planned. Later, O'Shaughnessy's name disappeared from the list of diocesan priests, though it remained, without title, on Pyramid Life Center schedules as a leader of creation-centered "spiritual journeys". His co-leaders on these journeys often included two more peace and justice activists: Jay Murnane, a former priest, and Mary Theresa Streck, a former nun.

"Creation-centered spirituality" and other recognizable forms of the new feminist faith have also cut deeply into the diocese of Pittsburgh, apparently by way of retreat houses. When the Retreat Program at St. Vincent Archabbey in Latrobe held "A Day

[43] F. C. Robert Hollman, "Article Appreciated", letter to the editor, *Times Union*, Aug. 11, 1988.

[44] Betsy Sandberg, "Bishop Hubbard Beseeched to Stop Creation-Theology Camp Sessions", *Schenectady Gazette*, July 4, 1988.

with Matthew Fox: Creation and the Cosmic Christ", on April 16, 1988, advance publicity appropriately included a mention in the parish bulletin of Pittsburgh's St. Gabriel of the Sorrowful Virgin. In Pittsburgh, Allegheny Co-Creators, a local "support group" for Friends of Creation Spirituality, offered a day of seminars extending Fox's message to Pennsylvania's Catholics at the independent "peace and justice" Thomas Merton Center on September 30, 1989. The workshop events (fifteen dollars; bring your own lunch) ranged from "The Cosmic Christ Within" through "Mask Making" to "Song-fest and Body Prayer" (i.e., ritual). Also on the Merton Center calendar that fall were a Pittsburgh Women-Church gathering (September 1); a Dignity/Pittsburgh anniversary celebration (October 1); a potluck supper and discussion of *The Chalice and the Blade*,[45] Riane Eisler's feminist reconstruction of the lost golden age of matriarchy and the hope for its restoration (October 9); Jungian analyst Eugene Monick giving a talk titled "Phallos: The Masculine Alternative to Patriarchy" (October 13); Chautauqua presentations featuring television personality Phil Donahue with Soviet public relations man Vladimir Posner (October 30); Geraldine Ferraro with Marlo Thomas (October 31); and so forth.

Villa Maria Community Center, at the motherhouse of the Sisters of the Humility of Mary, offered on a 1990 schedule seasonal retreats on earth (winter), air (spring), fire (summer) and water (autumn) in the "tradition of Creation-Centered Spirituality". They were among a dizzying month-by-month succession of retreats under such New Faith titles as "The Fabric of Our Life: A Prayer of Weaving"; "Tai Chi Chuan Workshop/Retreat"; "Feminine Spirituality"; "Touch the God Within"; and "Hildegarde of Bingen: A Celebration of Spirituality", led by Sister Madonna Kolbenschlag, H.M. As a pontifical order, the Sisters of the Humility of Mary are not under diocesan jurisdiction but are directly responsible to Rome.

[45] Riane Eisler, *The Chalice and the Blade* (San Francisco: Harper & Row, 1988).

In the city of Pittsburgh, at St. Paul's Retreat House, Bonnie Coluccio presented two "creation spirituality" retreats in May 1989. As part of the one, "Earthiness as Blessing", she led retreatants in a lengthy guided meditation on the elements of earth, air, fire and water. During the same month, Coluccio led four retreat days for those newly received into the Church through "the RCIA process" (Rite of Christian Initiation for Adults).

The spiritual invasion extended into the diocesan Department of Religious Education. Among certification and enrichment courses offered under its auspices during the 1988–89 academic year were two ten-hour series in "creation-centered spirituality", presented by the Sisters of Divine Providence.

In Chicago, religious revolution has long been a growth industry. So many Catholic or putatively Catholic feminist groups are headquartered there that only a fraction can be mentioned. Most share interlocking directorates, with each other and with the national religious-revolutionary network. For example, Chicago's Rosemary Ruether, grande dame of religious feminism, is a leading figure in Catholics for a Free Choice, Women's Ordination Conference, WATER and Women-Church Convergence, among others. Chicago Call to Action (CCA) was founded by Chicago Catholic Women, Dignity/Chicago, the Eighth Day Center for Justice, Friendship House, Leadership Conference of Women Religious, the National Assembly of Religious Women (NARW), the Alliance for Catholic Laity, the Association for the Rights of Catholics in the Church, the Association of Chicago Priests and the Chicago Association of Catholic School Teachers. While the American Catholic Lay Network lasted, CCA was its regional center. Most of those organizations are intensely political; few are primarily concerned with fostering goddess witchcraft. To understand the relationship between feminist spirituality and the politics of the radical coalition, it is helpful to keep in mind Ruether's admission that Women-Church is "rooted" in creation-centered spirituality. Although, as in CCA, feminist spirituality may be handled by a subcommittee, a new understanding of God is essential to the rebellion. As long as the Trinity is adored and revelation accepted as God's inspired word, the gnostic New Faith cannot come to power.

The radical perspective prevailing within the Chicago coalition is reflected in its taste in speakers. CCA boasts of providing "regular forums" for such "Vatican-harassed" speakers as Ruether, Charles Curran, Gregory Baum, Hans Küng and Matthew Fox. Chicago Catholic Women's November 1986 conference titled "Spirituality, Sexuality and Survival in Our Churches" featured abortion partisans Frances Kissling (director of CFFC), Beverly Wildung Harrison (author of *Our Right to Choose: Toward a New Ethic of Abortion*), Mary Hunt (who provided the "Catholic lesbian feminist" viewpoint) and Rosalie Muschal-Reinhardt (a former coordinator of Women's Ordination Conference, employed as a religion teacher at Nazareth High School in Rochester, New York).

Within the national revolutionary network, paid advertisements are favored as a means of influencing public opinion and creating an impression of massive support. CCA component groups (Chicago Catholic Women, Eighth Day Center and the executive committee of NARW) were part of the 1980 committee that sponsored a four-page advertising insert, "Even the Stones Will Cry Out", in *National Catholic Reporter*[46] to decry Vatican disciplinary measures against dissident theologians and revolutionary activists as "a new pattern of intimidation" in the Church. In the eyes of traditional Catholics, the actions had been mild and overdue.

Other advertisements followed over the decade. During 1989, at the suggestion of Matthew Fox, O.P., Chicago Call to Action circulated a self-styled "Pastoral Letter from Concerned Catholics", calling for such things as the ordination of women, an end to mandatory priestly celibacy, restoration to service of resigned

[46] "Even the Stones Will Cry Out", advertising supplement, *National Catholic Reporter*, Feb. 22, 1980.

priests, "open dialogue" about Church teaching on sexual morality, adoption of inclusive language and "new forms of liturgy", "academic freedom" for theologians and lay nomination of bishops. Heterodox theologian Hans Küng called it "splendid, balanced, a very clear résumé of the principles I have been stressing over the years", and read the full text aloud at a "Future of the American Church" conference in Washington, D.C., on September 29, 1989.[47] Seventeen hundred people cheered an unchastened Matthew Fox on February 4, 1990, at a CCA forum in Chicago held to publicize its "pastoral letter" and demonstrate support for Fox, newly returned from his silent sabbatical. He said the time had come to admit that the "institutional Church" and the "progressive" Church constitute two churches.

Under the title "A Call for Reform in the Catholic Church", the "pastoral" was published as an advertisement in the *New York Times* Ash Wednesday edition, February 28, 1990, with 4,505 supporting signatures—a modest number, in view of the postage invested in promotion; I myself received copies from four different sources. Signers included one bishop, Auxiliary Emerson Moore of New York, as well as the president of the Leadership Conference of Women Religious, the administrative assistant of the Conference of Major Superiors of Men and "liberal consensus" theologians Father David Tracy, Father Charles Curran, and Sister Sandra Schneiders, I.H.M. Among the general Catholic population, its message was probably accepted at face value by the same people who believe New York Governor Mario Cuomo to be a thoughtful Catholic sincerely opposed to abortion. Of particular interest was the list of co-sponsoring organizations—Friends of Creation Spirituality, Women's Ordination Conference, CORPUS (Corps of Reserve Priests United for Service),[48] Catholics Speak Out (an off-shoot of the pro-Sandinista Quixote Center) and the Association for the Rights of Catholics in the

[47] Tom Fox, "Inside NCR: Call to Action Letter Circulating U.S.", *National Catholic Reporter*, Nov. 3, 1989.

[48] CORPUS wants unrepentant priests who defected to marry, and who share the Call to Action perspective, to be reinstated in the active priesthood.

Church—which tied together most of the constituencies of the religious revolution.

Cause and Effect

Rosemary Ruether's insight that religious revolution cannot be implemented from outside the Church was substantiated late in thc 1980s in two situations that suggest how the hierarchy could defuse the revolution quietly but effectively. In 1986, when Limina events were being presented in Chicago's Catholic colleges, Cardinal Bernardin promised distressed Catholics that he would reverse his non-interference policy "if there were to be clear evidence" that the group "was in opposition to the teaching of the Church". Whether he was so persuaded, or whether the combination of media attention and alumni protests aroused decision-making boards at the colleges involved, *Chicago Call to Action News* admitted early in 1988 that Limina was "definitely not flourishing on Catholic premises" in Chicago any longer. Even "sponsors of earlier Limina events at several Catholic institutions are reportedly shunning the group because they don't want all the accompanying hassle and potentially inflammatory publicity", the newsletter added.[49] In the exterior darkness, Limina continued active. Lewis crowed in a 1987 interview that the group had presented her play, *The Goddesses and the Wildwoman*, "for 100 nuns up in Rochester, Minnesota, and they stood up and clapped and wanted Wildwoman's autograph."[50] Seven Limina events were scheduled for the first three months of 1990, notable among them a "third annual Ground Hag's Day" observance of "Imbolc" or "Brigid Fest", on February 2. But without the sheep's clothing of Church sponsorship, the organization no longer has easy access to normal Catholics, and pastors are unlikely to pay the expenses of feminist employees who may choose to attend its conferences.

[49] "Church Officials Intimidated; Catholic Right Muzzles Speakers", *Chicago Call to Action News*, Feb. 1988, 2.

[50] Jim Spencer, "Worshipping the Goddesses", *Chicago Tribune*, Sunday, Oct. 25, 1987, sec. 6, 1.

The "St. Louis Network of Creation-Centered Catholic Communities [CCCC]" was formed in 1987 under two Matthew Fox devotees, former Franciscan priest Don Kemner and Sharon Plankenhorn, to foster "a spirituality centered in the primary revelation of the divine, in the Cosmos, in our Earth Mother/Father, the Cosmic Christ". Despite discomfort with the word *lay* ("theologically 'dead'" because "it implies elitism"), CCCC affiliated with the American Catholic Lay Network (ACLN), a project organized by Center of Concern in hope of influencing the 1987 Synod on the Laity. According to CCCC's membership information, creation spirituality "*begins* with mystical union" (i.e., union with "the Cosmos Earth-planet") and, like Madonna Kolbenschlag's New Faith, it

> is non-elitist, non-competitive, non-patriarchal, non-dualistic and, therefore, inherently political. For all is secular and the secular is sacred. In our cultural and religious patriarchal context, it espouses feminist affirmative action in the quest for ultimate sexual balance.[51]

CCCC members were to commit themselves to working within their parishes for "systemic regeneration of church", in the belief that the Church is a system "negotiable and subject to transformation . . . [to] death as passage to newness of life".[52] After ACLN was dissolved in 1989, CCCC failed to thrive. According to Kemner, the archdiocese, "a little bit leery" about laypeople perceived as "out of their control", did not provide the necessary leadership and support. CCCC's core committee held all the standard gnostic attitudes, but by 1990 the organization was inoperative, though Kemner said it still "maintains a structure capable of implementing that vision", and "personally, I live it." The fate of the group indicates how little intrinsic appeal gnosticism has for

[51] Membership brochure, "St. Louis Network of Creation-Centered Catholic Communities", P.O. Box 270, Chesterfield, MO 63006, 1987.

[52] Don H. Kemner, "Three Models of Change within the Roman Catholic Church", Chesterfield, Missouri, St. Louis Network of Creation-Centered Catholic Communities, 1988.

ordinary, believing Catholics. If it were not proposed by Church professionals seen as religious authorities, it would expire naturally.

The goddess movement is best understood as one strategy serving the broader, more politically revolutionary gnosticism represented by the coalition of which groups like Call to Action are the base. But defining the matrix does not answer the next question: What is its appeal? In a world torn and aching with genuine suffering, it is doubtful that many women, well fed, educated, free to choose absorbing vocations from motherhood to astrophysics, would repudiate God out of sheer self-pity because the Catholic priesthood is open only to males. No life is without its limitations. The cause does not account for the effect.

Are those drawn to idolatry—to false goddesses and false prophets—seeking satisfactions largely lost to post-conciliar iconoclasm and the sterile feminist mores of American life? Do they hunger for the sacred, for the richly symbolic drama of color, meaning and mystery that has been leached out of contemporary liturgy, for the interior life so seldom mentioned in the prosaic, culturally adapted Catholicism now prevailing, for a compelling sense of ultimate purpose? The false mysticism of neo-gnostic feminism offers an illusion of these. It also maintains that women are not, after all, exactly like men but are more sensitive, more compassionate, more creative, better. In such forbidden fruit there is some understandable attraction. Secular feminism is dying for lack of it.

The trouble with this fruit is the same as the trouble with the first that ever tempted woman, because it is offered by the same tempter. It is not true. His promises are lies. But it is *real*, in the sense that there is someone at the other end, deadly dangerous, coiling down toward the heart. Those who hope to exploit it to serve ideological ends are like foolish, perverse, vulnerable children, playing with a plastic bomb as though it were Silly Putty. The active presence in the Church of missionaries for this New Faith is a grave and growing problem, and one the bishops will have to deal with sooner or later.

Chapter Three

Eve Reconsidered

The Constituency of Dissent

Local organizations are essential but insufficient to a revolution. To be successful, the revolution needs central leadership able to establish policy, set an agenda, plan strategy and tactics, propagandize, raise funds and effectively direct the energies of followers at the local level by means more tangible than "a cone of power". Religious feminism is no exception. During the 1980s, two groups within the religious revolution moved to assume its national leadership.

In one case, it looked like an attempt to keep Catholic feminism within the tent of the "liberal consensus". That apt label for the post-Christian perspective pandemic in North American theological circles was introduced into common usage by Thomas Sheehan, a professor of philosophy at Chicago's Loyola University, in a 1984 review of Hans Küng's *Eternal Life?*[1] Sheehan, himself a man of the consensus,[2] declared that not only Küng but also the rest of today's "internationally recognized" Catholic theologians ("the ones who hold the chairs, get the grants, publish the books and define the limits of scientific exegesis and theology") deny that Mary was a virgin at Jesus' birth, deny that Jesus was or even claimed to be divine, deny that he founded or meant to

[1] Thomas Sheehan, "Revolution in the Church", *New York Review of Books*, June 14, 1984.

[2] Sheehan disclosed his religious opinions to the world in his own book, *The First Coming: How the Kingdom of God Became Christianity* (New York: Random House, 1986).

found a Church, that he established a priesthood or a hierarchy or rose from the dead. Many of the scholars Sheehan named,[3] and others who share their opinions, were irate that he had stated without subtlety precisely what had long been the substance of conservative accusations. But their objections were to the baldness of his statement; few denied its truth.

Theologians holding such views have institutionalized the liberal consensus in Catholic academia. In the words of renowned Jesuit theologian Richard McCormick, they see themselves as a "second magisterium", which ought to be the intellectual guide for the first.[4] They regard credal Catholicism as "fundamentalist folk religion". Their scholarship, like that of nineteenth-century modernism, and the "demythologizing" Protestant historical scriptural criticism from which it follows, consists mostly of deconstruction. In place of supernatural truth it offers humanitarianism and liberal political prescriptions.

The liberal theological consensus is more than an intellectual current; it is a powerful culture, involving not only academics, religious professionals, clergy and ecclesiastical lobbies like Chicago Call to Action but also journalists, publishers, artists, musicians and businessmen. At many levels, the American Church is under the control of its wide and well-connected following, and the sceptical consensus is vigorously promoted.

Time Consultants, Incorporated, a private, for-profit firm that organizes conferences for religious professionals, is one example of its commercial expression. In 1986, Time Consultants announced a new series of annual conferences on "Women in the Church".

The company maintains a muted public demeanor, suitable to

[3] Sheehan, "Revolution". Sheehan said, "The liberal consensus reflects the presuppositions and procedures that Catholic scholars like Rudolf Schnackenburg, Raymond E. Brown, Roland Murphy, Pierre Benoit, John P. Meier, J. A. Fitzmeyer, David M. Stanley, Rudolf Pesch, Walter Kasper, David Tracy, Edward Schillebeeckx, Hans Küng, and hundreds of others use when they do research." See *Commonweal*, Aug. 10, Sept. 21, and Oct. 5, 1984.

[4] Richard A. McCormick, S.J., "The Relation of Theological Reflection and Analysis to the Magisterium", *National Catholic Reporter*, August 7, 1968.

the producers of the East Coast Conference for Religious Education, the Johannes Hofinger Catechetical Conference[5] and the North American Worship Conference. But like many agencies of the neo-modernist consensus, it involves a high concentration of former clerics. President Timothy Ragan is a former deacon. Vice President Michael Balhoff and staff associate Gary Ault were longtime members of the Dameans, a 1970s recording group of "priest-musicians". As a chaplain at Christ the King Student Center at Louisiana State University in Baton Rouge, Balhoff became part of a public conflict with the late Bishop Joseph Sullivan when, against the bishop's express command, the Claretian-run center invited theologian Charles Curran to speak. Balhoff's priestly faculties were suspended for a year as a result. But under Bishop Sullivan's successor, Bishop Stanley Ott, Balhoff was named adjutant judicial vicar and vice-chancellor, titles still listed beside his picture in the 1984 diocesan directory. By 1986, however, he was married and active in the religious conference business.[6] Ault, who had been director of youth activities for the archdiocese of New Orleans, was on temporary leave from the priesthood when he manned the press room for the 1986 Women in the Church conference. He is no longer listed in the Catholic Directory for that diocese.

Those records are not well known, however, and are commonplace in comparison with some of the personal and theological scandals associated with Women-Church. The chief evidence of Time Consultants' position on the theological spectrum is the relentlessly progressive content of its conferences, which has not at all discouraged some members of the hierarchy from endorsing it. Spokesmen say the company was "fostered by" the diocese of Baltimore, though not formally supported by it. Its promotional materials declare, no doubt truthfully, that it has "worked closely"

[5] Since 1986, that conference has been organized by the New Orleans Archdiocesan Religious Education Office.

[6] Jerry Filteau, "Women in the Church: 2500 at Washington Meeting Urge Equal Role", *Catholic New York*, Oct. 16, 1986.

for many years with "dioceses, the USCC, regional groups and universities".

The liberal consensus is a gnostic agnosticism. The secret knowledge of the initiate is that Christian faith is a psychological state unsupported by objective truth, a position not far removed from Naomi Goldenberg's. It was largely due to that neo-modernist scepticism that faith died among so many women religious, and —because human beings must believe in something—feminist witchcraft sprouted in its place, like thistle in an empty field. The liberal theological establishment can be blamed for blasting the heath where the weird sisters now dance. Nor has it discouraged them; there may even be some patronizing smiles at their conspicuous silliness. However, the neo-modernist scholars do not seem to have been the *source* of the bizarre political "thealogy" of the goddess. Feminism fits comfortably with subjectivist religion and the supremacy of dissent, but dancing around smoking cauldrons is not in the characteristic style of the "second magisterium". As a rule, neo-modernism advances by way of theological ambiguity rather than outright denial, by retaining familiar religious vocabulary but changing the definitions, by emphasis and deemphasis in scholarly writings, in liturgy and catechetics. In its attempt to profit from the development of religious feminism, Time Consultants tried to create an appearance of Catholic normalcy. Advertising the conference exclusively in the modernist journal of record, *National Catholic Reporter*, the firm announced that "Women in the Church" would feature a pair of bishops and prominent theologians of both sexes from respected Catholic colleges as well as some of the feminist theologians whom informed readers would recognize as extremist.

While liberal modernism had long dominated American Catholic academia, the most exorbitant theorists of feminist theology had generally stayed out of the public eye, communicating with each other at feminist conferences and in books and journals not widely read by ordinary Catholics. On occasions when their doings were reported as general news—when Women-Church issued some particularly hair-raising statement, or CFFC ran its Catholics-for-abortion advertisements in the *New York Times*—readers had tended to suppose they represented tiny and eccentric splinter groups. But in the mid-1980s, just as Time Consultants began targeting feminists, the boisterous, ideologically uninhibited Women-Church coalition had begun aiming for higher national visibility, hoping to broaden its base beyond its predominantly Catholic, white, middle-aged, middle-class constituency of religious professionals. Though feminist extremists were involved in both ventures, signs of rivalry developed between Time Consultants, the establishment group striving for an appearance of moderation, and Women-Church, the unabashed radicals affronted that males would dare to compete for a share of the feminist market.

These two groups do not represent the sum of radical feminist evangelization, but their strategic ventures deserve examination because they reveal how broadly, and at what exalted levels, revolutionary opinion reigns in the American Church and how such opinion induces and sustains feminism. In public relations rhetoric, both these national groups stress the need for "diversity" and "dialogue" in the Church, yet neither provides any. Although their speakers are drawn from prestigious institutions, from converted or intimidated males, scholars, priests and even bishops, the views represented at their functions range from appeasement to outright madness but never to dissent from doctrinaire liberal and feminist assumptions. Yet enormous audiences of American and Canadian religious professionals greet those speakers enthusiastically, listen receptively and apparently come away convinced.

Women in the Church

The first Women in the Church conference opened at the Shoreham Hotel in Washington, D.C., on October 10, 1986. It drew a handful of men and nearly 2,500 women, some 85 percent of them nuns, a surprising 10 percent clad in habits and veils. It looked like a gathering of Catholics. In reality, it was a consciousness-raising session for Church revolutionaries with feminism as the unifying theme. A comparatively moderate minority demanded priesthood for women, while a stunning majority thunderously applauded calls to defy the Magisterium, repudiate Judeo-Christian theology and work as "guerrillas" toward a religious coup d'etat that would replace God the Father with the goddess within.

As in any social movement, those in attendance varied in their understanding and commitment; clearly, not all of them recognized the nature of religious feminism. As Sister Joan Chittister put it, if you thought of the women's movement on a scale of one to ten, there was someone standing on every number. Some of those present seemed merely out of date, infected with feminist fever a decade after the secular epidemic. Some may have been attracted to the meeting because they were resentful about an incident of male incompetence, not unknown even among clerics. Some naïvely but fashionably supposed women's ordination to be a matter of simple fairness, unaware even that feminist theologians of both sexes reject the notion of female priesthood ordered along otherwise traditional lines. Many were uncritical thinkers, accepting as valid theological commentary whatever was published in the *National Catholic Reporter*, which seemed to be standard convent reading fare. Perhaps only a few fully understood that the ultimate feminist objective is the obliteration of Christianity. Wherever they initially stood on Chittister's scale, they were all moving in the same direction, and the conference was designed to hasten their progress into fully conscious revolutionary feminism. When at least a thousand of them applauded Sister Madonna Kolbenschlag's description of the Blessed Trinity as "a good ole boy, associating intimately only with two other divine males", who has "legitimated religious bigotry, racism, classism, imperialism, clericalism and all the other isms you can think of", it was hard to imagine what could have shocked them.

Unanimity

Optimists who hoped the radical post-conciliar era was drawing to an end would have found no supporting evidence at the Shoreham. The primary agenda included the usual feminist issues of priestly ordination, sexism, feminist theology, feminist spirituality, liturgical and linguistic revision and "mobilizing one's anger" to effect change. As if in example, rage over recent Vatican disciplinary measures against theologian Charles Curran and Seattle Archbishop Raymond Hunthausen emerged as a passionate secondary agenda.

Seven bishops were present as ornaments, five in the audience[7] and two, as promised, among the speakers: Auxiliary Amedee Proulx, from the diocese of Portland, Maine, chairman of the NCCB's Women Religious Committee and a member of the committee drafting an episcopal letter on women's concerns, and Remi DeRoo, ordinary of the diocese of Victoria, British Columbia and a founding member of the World Conference of Religions for Peace. Bishop Proulx's address was the most moderate of the weekend, sympathetic but finally discouraging to advocates of women's ordination. In his talk he carefully and neutrally described the drafting process; afterward he was patient with a crowd of questioners. But finally he broke away, saying, "It's foolish to expect the bishops of the United States to challenge doctrine in a pastoral letter. It's not going to happen."

The rest of the speakers were uniformly progressive in their credentials and in their views, though, with the notable exception of Bishop DeRoo, male speakers provided almost all of the ambiguity at the conference. They included Father James Provost, a recently tenured professor of canon law at Washington's Catholic

[7] Registrants included Bishop Joseph Imesch of Joliet, Illinois, chairman of the NCCB drafting committee for the pastoral letter on women's concerns; Auxiliary Bishop P. Francis Murphy of Baltimore, who had been a member of the NCCB committee engaged in formal dialogue with representatives of Women's Ordination Conference from 1979 to 1981; Bishop John Fitzpatrick of Brownsville, Texas; Bishop Joseph Breitenbeck of Grand Rapids, Michigan; and Bishop Walter Sullivan of Richmond, Virginia.

University; Father Donald Senior, C.P., professor of New Testament studies at the Catholic Theological Union in Chicago; and Father Richard McBrien, head of the theology department at the University of Notre Dame.

The raw meat of feminism issued from the women speakers, among them such movement stars as Sister Joan Chittister, O.S.B.; Sister Mary Collins, O.S.B.; Sister Sandra Schneiders, I.H.M.; Mary Jo Weaver and Sister Madonna Kolbenschlag. Pia Moriarity is assistant professor of pastoral theology at the Franciscan School of Theology in the Graduate Theological Union (GTU), Berkeley, California, and coordinator of the San Francisco Archdiocesan Women's Task Force. Sister Fran Ferder, F.S.P.A., is co-director of TARA Center, a ministerial counseling service of the Seattle archdiocese, and the author of Quixote Center's *Called to Break Bread? A Psychological Investigation of 100 Women Who Feel Called to Priesthood in the Catholic Church.*[8] Unsurprisingly, in view of its publisher, her book concludes that the female subjects were better adjusted than males who felt similarly called.

Spokesmen for Time Consultants admitted that no attempt had been made to provide "dialogue" by including speakers who opposed women priests. When I asked why, press secretary Gary Ault explained that they hadn't intended that the program be feminist, exactly, but they did want it "to be anti-sexist". Vice President Michael Balhoff told a reporter that they had made no attempt to provide a balance of opinion because "we really wanted to deal constructively with the issues". To have brought in spokesmen for the opposition might have created dissension, he indicated. "I really am not experienced at riding wild horses, and I have a feeling that that would be wilder than the wildest horse I could try to ride."[9] Nevertheless feminists, aggrieved that the conference had been organized by a "male-dominated" cor-

[8] Fran Ferder, F.S.P.A., *Called to Break Bread? A Psychological Investigation of 100 Women Who Feel Called to Priesthood in the Catholic Church* (Hyattsville, Md.: Quixote Center, 1978).

[9] Mary Meehan, "Women's Conference Plan, Striving to Be Constructive", *National Catholic Register*, Oct. 26, 1986.

poration, applauded Kolbenschlag when she said, "The structure and process of this conference give evidence of our failure to give up the patriarchal model." There was grumbling, too, over an advance decision to donate Saturday's offertory collection to Bread for the World rather than to a women's organization. As a compromise, the collection was divided between Bread for the World and a shelter for battered women.

Cultural Current

Setting the pitch for the weekend, keynote speaker Sister Joan Chittister, chairwoman of the International Conference of Benedictine Women and a columnist for the *National Catholic Reporter*, praised the strength, endurance, intelligence, non-violence and feminism of women, and she deplored patriarchy in all its forms. In her opinion, Jesus intended a non-sexist, androgynous Church, but his disciples were unable or unwilling to effect it. To avoid using a pronoun for God, she repeated his name six times in a single sentence: "God made women in God's own image, God talked to them, just as God talked to men, and God trusted them with free will, just as much as God trusted men." But the Church contravenes his will, her diatribe continued:

> We live in a society where they turn away women from their empty seminaries in droves while, in a sacramental Church, people are denied the sacraments. We live in a society where a girl-child . . . may not even carry a cruet to the altar . . . the Church that teaches that "the gates of hell shall not prevail against it" can apparently be brought to its knees by a little eleven year-old girl.

Chittister's argument, that women *must* be ordained because men will not, was echoed often during the conference. No one seemed aware that seminaries were crowded where orthodox teaching prevailed, as among the Legionaries of Christ. It appeared that the avant-garde looked on orthodox Catholicism as an alien and eccentric Church, locked in a "pre-conciliar" mindset and beyond the pale of ecumenism. Three days of Women in the Church provided convincing evidence that the conferees did, in large part, represent a different, and hostile, church.

Although Chittister said in her address that "the women's movement is a growing, swelling, ongoing cultural current of social change", she subsequently admitted to reporters that the women at the conference, most of them nuns over fifty from dwindling religious orders, reflected the makeup of Catholic feminism. That fact poses problems for the future, she conceded. The generation of younger women "don't even know how it was" just fifteen years earlier. Nevertheless, she considered it important that so many had come to the conference. "We need articulation; we need to keep asking the questions—because eventually sin runs out of answers." When one reporter asked if she thought the American Church "as institution" was ready to stand in opposition to Rome, Chittister replied, "Do you want an answer or a prayer? Oh God, I hope so!"

Cultural Lag

Like the liberal consensus of which it is a part, feminism among women religious is a Catholic anachronism. Ten years after secular feminism peaked, splintered and began to fade, it was still widely and deeply prevalent among aging nuns whose denatured orders were dying because there was no longer anything about them to attract young women with religious vocations.

The same kind of rhetoric that used to issue from Bella Abzug, Betty Friedan and Shulamith Firestone was heard at the Women in the Church conference, partially translated into theological jargon. In the 1980s as in the 1960s, "consciousness-raising" depended on "hard case" stories of tragic victims, on building and focusing rage against scapegoats identified as the Enemy and on dissolving the convictions and loyalties that had supported traditional ways of life. Secular feminists used to claim that rape was the normative model for male-female relationships. Many of those persuaded that marriage was a male ploy to enslave and exploit women by keeping them sexually available, economically dependent and burdened by unwanted motherhood (i.e., barefoot and pregnant) eventually became the sad "new poverty class" of lonely women, abortion survivors and single mothers.

Religious feminists use the same tactics, appropriately modified. Most are nuns, Church careerists or academics, but their "hard case" stories rarely concern the specifics of their own "pain and anguish". Instead, battered wives, Third World women and battered Third World women serve religious feminism as raped and pregnant twelve-year-olds have served feminist abortion propagandists. Sister Madonna Kolbenschlag, for example, told of a barrio in Peru where *all* the women were beaten regularly until a feminist organizer taught them to talk to each other and join forces to protect each other when their husbands came home intoxicated and abusive. Chittister claimed:

> In two-thirds of all marriages, women are beaten at least once; one fourth of the women in this country are beaten weekly. . . . A woman in this country is beaten every eighteen seconds and raped every three minutes. . . . This very morning, women are being married for dowry and sold for bride price and denied an inheritance and deprived of money, and work, and land, and housing, and food stamps, and child care services, and health and welfare benefits.

Most of the situations described by the speakers sounded deplorable indeed, if occasionally dubious. Dowry and bride price are cultural customs, not necessarily abusive. The claim that Peruvian women need a North American feminist to teach them how to deal with their husbands smacks of ethnic condescension. In general, the atrocity figures seemed improbably high. But even if they had been accurate, it was difficult to see how they would be improved by the ordination of women priests or conversion to goddess witchcraft. It was easy to see, however, that those who believe the prophets of religious feminism are becoming a new class of dispossessed women.

Catholic Progressives

For all the talk of "peace and justice", the issue of abortion was strikingly absent from every conference tally, of injustices or of reform movements. Speakers mentioned it during the weekend only in passing references to the insensitivity and probably base motives of those who oppose it.

Abortion advocates were prominent among conference exhibitors, however. Like the speakers' list, the exhibition hall was dominated by representatives of the Catholic (and ex-Catholic) radical left. The abortion lobby Catholics for a Free Choice (CFFC) had a crowded display. A highly audible group at the Women-Church booth was distributing "Justice Campaign" petition forms, demanding publicly funded abortions for victims of rape and incest; listed among the fund's Protestant and Jewish "convenors" was Sister Margaret Traxler, S.S.N.D., of the National Coalition of American Nuns (NCAN). Women's Ordination Conference (WOC), another vehicle for the theologians of Women-Church, shared a booth with Center of Concern. Other exhibitors included the National Assembly for Religious Women (NARW), *National Catholic Reporter*/Sheed and Ward and Quixote Center. Friends of Creation Spirituality, an adjunct to Matthew Fox's Institute for Culture and Creation Spirituality, drew surprisingly few browsers to its display of Fox's books. More conventional organizations were also represented, including United States Catholic Conference (USCC), Ave Maria Press and Christian Brothers Wines, whose representative said that when women are ready to celebrate Mass, "We'll be ready with the wine." But most booths were stocked with books by conference speakers and their allies (Weaver's *New Catholic Women*, Kolbenschlag's *Between God and Caesar*, *Angry Catholics* by Andrew Greeley and Mary Durkin, *Midwives of the Future* by Ann Patrick Ware, volumes by Fox, Ruether and Beverly Wildung Harrison, among others) and flyers for groups like the Conference for Catholic Lesbians, Priests for Equality and WATER.

While its coordinator, Pia Moriarity, was telling a workshop audience how to organize their own women's commissions, the Women in Worship Committee of the Women's Task Force had come from the San Francisco archdiocese prepared to proselytize. They sought signatures for a petition in favor of altar girls that, along with a petition calling for support of Archbishop Hunthausen, circulated up and down the rows of seats throughout the weekend. The San Franciscans also offered a set of lesson plans on the evils of patriarchy free to teachers. Though it, and indeed the entire weekend, indicated esteem for episcopal authority in no other case, the last page of the lesson plan was titled "Peace and Justice Action Alert: A Serious Church Matter/An Archbishop Is Demoted". It urged students to write, in defense of Archbishop Hunthausen's untrammeled authority, to the Pope, the apostolic pro-nuncio, the prefect for the Congregation for the Doctrine of the Faith and the president of the National Conference of Catholic Bishops; addresses were provided. The same booth distributed packets of brief articles, ready for insertion in parish bulletins, on such topics as altar girls and women priests. Included was a questionnaire for polling parishioners' attitudes after the bulletin series appeared.

Feminism at Prayer

Two religious ceremonies were celebrated during the conference. The first was an unofficial "eucharist" sponsored by Women-Church Convergence, a coalition whose roster included Catholics for a Free Choice, Catholic Women for Reproductive Rights, Chicago Catholic Women, Grail Women's Task Force, New Ways Ministry, Quixote Center, Conference for Catholic Lesbians, WATER, Women's Ordination Conference, the Wheaton Franciscans and the Racine Dominicans. Among the many celebrants, singers and dancers were Diann Neu of WATER, Rosalie Muschal-Reinhardt and Ruth McDonough Fitzpatrick of WOC, Dolly Pomerleau of Quixote Center and Sister Martha Ann Kirk, an Incarnate Word sister from San Antonio. The service was scheduled on Saturday noon, in a small meeting room where some fifty chairs had been arranged around a central table. As people poured into the room, the chairs were stacked into corners, while the crowd swelled to perhaps 350, pressed noses to shoulders into every inch of space and overflowing down the hall. In the middle of the room, women of uneven talent danced and mimed, singing songs composed by Women-Church members: "Song of the Soul", "We Are Women Claiming Power" and "By My Eyes, Be I Opened". There was a litany of feminist heroines, including the recently deceased Sister Marjorie Tuite, O.P. Breads of various kinds were blessed in five languages—not, mercifully, in the words of the Mass—while almost everyone present stretched out an arm in a gesture of concelebration. Diann Neu announced, "We bless this as the eucharist of Women-Church." Then the bread and wine and grape juice were passed around. Sister Martha Kirk wept. Ruth Fitzpatrick urged all participants to repeat the gesture of concelebration, using the words of Consecration, at the official Eucharist that evening.

Standing beside me and joining in the "concelebration" was Father John Real, of Rock Island, Illinois. I asked him why. He hesitated, shrugged and told me, "Well, we did what we did." He said he entirely supported the drive for women's ordination and the general feminist agenda.

Jesus was not mentioned in the feminist ritual. "God" was named once, "goddess" three or four times. It was theater as liturgy that did not attempt to be an imitation of the Mass. Since the participants rejected the authority of the Church, demanded the right to choose their own ministers from their community, said they were "claiming their power now" rather than waiting until it would be given to them and apparently found their ceremony satisfying and even moving, there seemed to remain no real problem about ordination. As long as it was not done under Catholic auspices, they were entirely free to perform such rituals whenever they chose with no objection from anyone; it could just as well have been a Campfire Girls' ceremony. Why, then, were they still holding meetings of Women's Ordination Conference?

Token Veil

Certain that the women wearing habits and veils must be genuine nuns who had stumbled into this conference by mistake, I kept asking them to comment on the weekend's activities. All of them said they were enjoying it very much and supported it entirely. One middle-aged nun said she was "the token veil for the offertory procession". One of the younger nuns was Sister Mary McCall, a Sister Servant of the Immaculate Heart of Mary, her habit crisply traditional, face and voice gentle. "Six months ago I wouldn't have come to a meeting like this", she said. "But I studied at Notre Dame this summer, a class in liturgy and ministry from Sister Mary Collins, and it really raised my consciousness. Now, I really support equality of women in the Church." Eleven other sisters from her community had come with her, she said, because they shared her views.

The real Eucharist was celebrated that evening by Father David Power, O.M.I., president-elect of the North American Academy of Liturgy, another Catholic University theology professor frequently in evidence at Time Consultants' affairs. He began with an apology for his maleness. "We gather in pain", he said. "It is with sadness that I realize my standing here is the centering and evidence of that pain."

Sister Teresita Weind, S.N.D., a pastoral associate from St. Catherine of Siena/St. Lucy parish in Oak Park, Illinois, preached the sermon. "God will not be damned by anything that the Church does to its women", she proclaimed, while WOC activists released red balloons. During the Consecration, about a third of the congregation extended their arms and recited the words of "concelebration". Afterward, there was general dancing in the aisles.

Theologically Conservative Laity

Most of the male headliners were circumspect in their formal addresses, confining their remarks to matters within their academic disciplines. Father James Provost, whose tenure at Catholic

University had been in doubt until he reportedly amended some unorthodox stands, talked about the rights of Catholics under the new code of canon law. While he said that "regrettably, a few isolated examples of sex-based distinction remain", he did not say women should be priests.

Father Donald Senior, C.P., associate editor of *The Bible Today*, talking about women in Scripture, said:

> The perceptive reader can see, even within the span of the New Testament, the inclusive vision of the gospel crashing upon the rock-strewn shore of other deep-seated social and cultural values. . . . While early Christianity made significant inroads in this system and retained, surely in its normative texts, a vision of equality, it is also clear that the early Church struggled with that social setting.

But his assertion that the New Testament distorted Jesus' message was so quietly made that it did not rouse a woman stretched across three chairs beside me, napping.

Speaking critically if not evenly about both camps, Notre Dame's Father Richard McBrien compared the historic heresies of Nestorianism and Monophysitism with what he sees as current excesses in the debate over female roles in the Church. When he cautioned feminists against setting up a separatist "Church of women", he hastened to add that Rosemary Ruether had said it first, so he ought to be permitted to deliver the warning without having his "feminist credentials revoked by some ersatz Sacred Congregation for the Doctrine of the Faith". He expressed no comparable fear of offending his target when he blasted "opponents of sexual equality . . . in the politically and theologically conservative laity" who "hold fast to a pre-Vatican II notion of the so-called lay apostolate", believing that "the sacred, the spiritual and the ecclesiastical belong to the clergy; the secular, the temporal and the political belong to the laity". They insist on a "hard-and-fast distinction between the two realms", he said, "because many of them do not like the recent activist style of the U.S. Catholic bishops" on

> nuclear deterrence and the U.S. economy. They want the bishops to stay out of areas they presumably do not understand and leave them to the people who do: namely, lay Catholics. These same lay Catholics, however, never explain why the bishops have any particular competence in matters of sexual ethics, especially in matters pertaining to marriage and homosexuality.

They fail to understand on the one hand that economic issues and nuclear deterrence have "a moral dimension", McBrien said, so "the hierarchy can and must address them". And on the other hand, "the laity, including women, have as much interest in the inner life of the Church as do the clergy and religious".

Left Brain

Bishop DeRoo's address carried deference to excess. He said he was humbled by the invitation to appear among this "imposing galaxy of talent", that he was deeply indebted for his growth over the previous twenty-five years to both "futurists" and "feminist scholars", who had shown him the need for new "values and priorities", but especially to the feminists, who had "awakened" him to his "personal need" to "balance the left-brain characteristics commonly associated with male attitudes".

As the feminist theologians who had most profoundly influenced him, the bishop named Elisabeth Schussler Fiorenza, Rosemary Ruether, Joan Chittister, Monika Hellwig and Sister Lucy Vasquez. He indicated his own feminist views on key points, though he phrased his controversial conclusions in question form.

Early Christians had scuttled Jesus' plan for a non-patriarchal Church because of cultural conditioning, he said:

> Unless we are prepared to dismiss out of hand the imposing body of evidence concerning the cultural conditioning of early Christian ministry and its developing forms, do we not have reason for reconsideration of our tradition with respect to women in ministry? . . . Could the current tradition of exclusion eventually prove not to be unchangeable? . . . Why was the paradigm shift Jesus wanted not fully realized? Could it be that

> the cultural limitations of his disciples inhibited their capacity to transmit these attitudes integrally to the early Christian community?

A Mother God might be a cultural advance, he suggested:

> A problem . . . arises when God is imaged primarily or even exclusively as male. . . . The "primordial power of the Mother symbol as the Ground of Being" of which Rosemary Radford Ruether has written, could help redress the balance now weighed down on the side of patriarchy.

Until now, the Church failed to understand the nature of our relationship with the Holy Spirit, he indicated:

> A major shift is occurring in the way we perceive the creative role of the Holy Spirit. . . . Nowhere is the ecclesial paradigm shift more obvious. . . . Our entire understanding of ecclesiology rests on, and should be permeated by, a thoroughgoing pneumatology. . . . Who is the real minister in every one of the Church's ministries? . . . It is both a humbling and a kenotic experience to admit that we are only instruments of the Spirit.

The bishop hinted strongly that ordained priesthood ought to be replaced by a newly understood priesthood of all believers, just as feminist ideologues propose:

> We are thus led to the deeper question of the reappropriation by all of the baptized of their responsibility for the proclamation of God's word, *sacramental celebration*, global ministry and ultimately political activity as well. A rethinking of the very nature of ministry could result from this. . . . Clericalism would be recognized as creating and maintaining lay dependency. It should give way to ministry practiced as mutual empowerment and service to humankind by all the baptized [emphasis added].

Finally, Bishop DeRoo proudly reviewed the encouragement given to feminism by Canadian bishops. In 1984, the Canadian bishops' conference had voted to distribute a "Green Kit" of feminist discussion materials, coincidentally titled "Women in the Church", to parish women's organizations throughout Canada.

In its bibliography were such virulently feminist works as *Womanspirit Rising*, Ruether's *Sexism and God-Talk*, Elisabeth Schussler Fiorenza's *In Memory of Her*[10] and others that would indeed serve to acquaint women with feminist thought though not to arm them against it. The kit project had been "quite a success" and the response "overwhelmingly positive", he said, but approval was not unanimous. Seeking "to re-establish what they perceive as orthodoxy" and believing traditional feminine roles to be "divinely ordained", some women began to circulate a "Statement of Affirmation"[11] and developed "a counter kit, now known as the 'Blue Kit'. Through it all," he said, "we have realized the pain" experienced by women in both camps. "The clash of these different visions of women's place . . . illustrates the problems encountered by people with varying perceptions of reality and different models of Church."

The so-called Blue Kit, which includes papal documents, *The Ratzinger Report*, and the *Code of Canon Law* in its bibliography, was offered to the Canadian bishops by Women for Life, Faith and Family with the request that it be distributed to parishes on the same basis as the Green Kit. Instead, they were "given permission" to distribute it unassisted and at their own expense. But the Blue Kit was not given any formal status as an approved resource.

Among Friends

Of the male speakers, only Bishop DeRoo was more restrained off stage than on. He refused to predict whether women will be

[10] Elisabeth Schussler Fiorenza, *In Memory of Her: A Feminist Theological Reconstruction of Christian Origins* (New York: Crossroads Books, 1983).

[11] The statement of affirmation, drafted in 1984 by Women for Faith and Family, an organization based in St. Louis, Missouri, has been circulated around the world spontaneously by faithful women eager for opportunity to voice their loyalty to the Church. More than 40,000 U.S. women have signed it, and thousands of women from a dozen other countries. Unsolicited new signatures continue to arrive at WFF headquarters. Copies of the affirmation are available at P.O. Box 8326, St. Louis, MO 63132.

ordained, saying, "I don't second-guess the Holy Spirit." He told reporters to bear in mind that the women who oppose feminism "are just as intelligent, just as articulate" as those who promote it, for all that their models of spirituality are pre-conciliar; it was the kindest statement anyone made about the orthodox all weekend. Movements often don't get all they want, the bishop observed. Between competing visions, "sometimes, what you get is a synthesis".

The other men and several of the women let down their hair with the press, perhaps feeling, as Joan Chittister did, that they were "among friends". ("I know how much you've done for us", she told reporters.)

Father Donald Senior, bland and ambiguous in his address, answered sympathetically and at length when a Women-Church reporter asked him why many priests were still so ignorant of "biblical scholarship" as to suppose that Jesus had instituted Holy Orders.

"Well, there are a lot of opportunities for continuing education from diocese to diocese", said Senior, apparently conceding her premise. "But I think it's not enough to be exposed to biblical scholarship, to relate that to something like the question of Orders. . . . It's not simply data that's needed. If you're going to have a conversion of viewpoints, or updating, more is involved."

When a reporter asked Father James Provost why he "compromised" his convictions to gain tenure at Catholic University, he stopped smiling and refused to comment. Like many others at the conference, he wore an "I Love Hunthausen" button on his lapel. "Certain right-wing groups in the Church have set out on a deliberate ploy" to destroy the archbishop's good name, he told the press. It was a "theological scandal" that "certain persons in official positions . . . seem to have cooperated". According to canon law, "investigation of dioceses" is the province of "the Congregation of Bishops", yet, according to reports, the Seattle investigation was done by the Sacred Congregation for the Doctrine of the Faith, under Cardinal Ratzinger's authority. Provost said that by taking sides in a "difference of opinion between Catholics", Rome had intruded in an unsuitable way. He hoped the Holy Father would "redress" the Hunthausen scandal, though he conceded that "technically, the Holy See has not violated his rights".

Dodging repeated questions, Provost refused to predict or support women's ordination. "The current structure and practice of the ordained ministry are still in need of renewal, and we have a major crisis in ordained ministry. I see no point in trying to build a consensus on something that is in itself in a troubled condition." The crisis, he explained, was "the decline in the number of seminarians and the increasing number of laypeople who are being asked to handle pastoral functions".

Enfant Terrible

Father Richard McBrien, whose press conference style called to mind television's Phil Donahue, talked less about the authenticity of Scripture or the institution of the sacraments than about himself. It was clear that he enjoyed being interviewed, and he reminded reporters several times that he gets a lot of practice at it. The *enfant terrible* of American theology displayed his liberalism in his anxiety about his "feminist credentials", his defense of dissent and dissenters and his critical irreverence toward Church authority, couched in sociological rather than religious terms. Asked whether Vatican actions in the Curran and Hunthausen cases would affect theological teaching at Catholic colleges, he snorted, "Do *I* look afraid to speak out?" (He didn't.) McBrien patronized the Pope, talked of how brave he would be if he were in danger, ridiculed parents worried about unorthodox teaching and explained in detail why he is unlikely to be "the next Charlie Curran".

Pope John Paul II "functions" as he does because he had always lived in a "political-social situation" where "the government of his own country was implacably hostile to Catholicism. In a situation like that, the last thing you want or need is a Church which encourages, allows, supports, internal dissent", he said. "If *I* were in Poland, as a theologian, I would be very careful about the kind of aid and comfort I might give, unwittingly, to the enemy. . . . If

I were in Poland, I'd wear my collar proudly, because it would be a *political* statement." Quoting Martin Marty, he said, "It's easy to be a Catholic where it's hard to be a Catholic, in Poland."

At home in the United States, McBrien indicated, he feels differently about the clerical collar. Women, he said, should not only be ordained priests but should also be eligible "for the episcopal and the petrine" offices. "The one thing that bothers me most" is the fear that, like ordained Protestant women, "they begin wearing clerical collars. Here the rest of us have been taking them off, and *they* gotta wear them! I hate to see women getting into ministry and then imitating the worst cultural aspects of the male-only ministry."

The Church will get to the ordination of women "just by hanging on", McBrien continued. "The people who are alive now and trying to keep things within a certain structural confinement are not going to be alive in the next century. . . . A puff of white smoke, and the Church is on a different course." There is "a new consciousness in the world and in the Church. You can't put it back in the bottle. What you see now, the noise and the sound and the fury, is really the tail end of the old way of exercising authority in the Church."

Asked whether he expected to be "the next Charlie Curran", McBrien replied, "I'm quite indifferent to that whole question", but he seemed to have given it a good deal of thought. "I'm in a different position from Father Curran for three reasons. First, I'm a tenured professor at a normal university." Curran, by contrast, was "vulnerable" because he taught at Catholic University, a pontifical institution directly answerable to the Vatican. "I offered him a job every year for six years, when I became chairman at Notre Dame, and he turned me down every time" out of gratitude "to the faculty and students who defended him back in 1967. He's a man of enormous integrity." (When Father Curran's tenure was in doubt in 1967, students and friends picketed the university, and the administration backed down.)

"Second," apparently unlike himself, "Father Curran is not known personally by very many bishops", McBrien said. "Going after Hunthausen" was a more damaging "blunder" for the Vatican than disciplining Curran, "because now they've energized a good solid minority of American bishops".

"The third thing is, I have never been identified, as Father Curran is, with leading a movement specifically directed to taking a dissenting position in the Church. Charlie was the one who in 1968 organized the signatures that protested *Humanae Vitae*." Hence he has "always been marked" as responsible "for making the American Catholic community go off a side track on the issue of contraception". To friendly laughter, he said, "These Catholic laypeople would never have used it if it weren't for Curran. See, Archbishop Foley misses the point when he says to the *New York Times*, 'The teaching is clear'. No one is saying it's not clear; we're saying it's not persuasive."

American theologians will not cease dissenting because of the Curran affair, McBrien predicted, because there has been "a sea change in the Catholic theological community in the last twenty years. Some of our greatest, best theologians are not only not priests, they're women—Margaret Farley, Lisa Cahill, Anne Carr, Elisabeth Fiorenza—there's [sic] so many." (Of those he named, all except Cahill signed CFFC's 1984 *New York Times* ad.) "Even those of us who are priests", he continued, "are teaching at senior tenured positions in universities, not seminaries. It's a big difference." McBrien said his only concern was for the loss to Catholic higher education of "the best and brightest" young scholars, "who will not think seriously of an appointment in a Catholic institution; they will be weaned away by the Columbias and the Yales and the Harvards and the Chicagos". There might be some efforts to stifle free thought at

> lower-level Catholic institutions, where a weak president, a theologically naïve board of trustees, and a particularly "vigilant" bishop who kind of likes to dabble in theology—that combination can be deadly when you sprinkle on that a well-organized group of Catholic traditionalists who pick up a smattering of something this person said in class, a line out of a paragraph out of an article out of a book which they didn't read—

might come together to effect the removal of a "junior-level" faculty member. "I can honestly say it wouldn't happen at Notre Dame; I'm sure it wouldn't happen at Boston College."

Noting the presence of a strong pro-Hunthausen element at the conference, he said he found it significant that "Dutch Hunthausen was not relieved of his duties in the areas where he was most controversial". All the matters taken out of his hands "had to do with sex". McBrien did not explain which areas he thought were "most controversial".

Returning to the subject of "these neo-conservative Catholic laymen who have a problem with the bishops'" stands on nuclear arms and the economy, McBrien asked, "Do you think their whole concern is theologically based? I don't see many of them with a low net worth. They've got something to defend!" The demands of discipleship require a willingness to give up one's possessions, he said. "It's easy to beat up on homosexuals. It's easy to say, 'I'm against abortion', especially if you're male. But everyone is governed by the rule of discipleship, and that's the hardest rule."

The neo-conservatives to whom Father McBrien was doubtless referring, since they had attracted a good deal of media attention, were members of the two lay committees organized by Michael Novak to reply to the NCCB letter on nuclear weapons policy and to write a parallel letter on economic policy.[12] They had not, in fact, questioned the propriety of episcopal statements on relevant moral principles. Rather, they had expressed concern that the pastoral letters under discussion ventured in unprecedented ways beyond moral and ethical matters into areas of prudential judgment on which responsible Catholics may legitimately disagree and in which the bishops have no special competence. Statements about sexual morality, by contrast, clearly fall within the traditional province of religious leaders.

[12] The statement by the first committee, the American Catholic Conference, is "Moral Clarity in the Nuclear Age" (*Catholicism in Crisis*, Mar. 1983). The statement by the second committee, the Lay Commission on Social Teaching and the U.S. Economy, is *Toward the Future: Catholic Social Thought and the U.S. Economy* (Washington, D.C.: Lay Commission, 1984).

Inadequate Model

Auxiliary Bishop P. Francis Murphy of Baltimore was one of the males in attendance. When I talked to him, midway through the conference, he had heard addresses by Joan Chittister, Richard McBrien and theologian Lisa Sowle Cahill from Boston College. Bishop Murphy, a member of the NCCB committee on Women in the Church and in Society, was one of the six bishops who took part in "dialogue" with representatives of Women's Ordination Conference between 1979 and 1981. Did he suppose the views of WOC to be those of Catholic women generally, I asked?

The bishop seemed surprised. "They are *brilliant* women!" he said, not answering my question.

Did he think the conference itself should have been more representative of the range of views among Catholics? Should there have been speakers opposed to women's ordination?

Again, he seemed surprised. From his seat at the back of the conference halls, it had seemed to him that "there was a great sympathy and consensus for the themes of the speakers".

Was the thinking evident here a reflection of what the Vatican meant when it called for "a wider role for women"?

"No, the Vatican was thinking of an 'equal but complementary model' ", Murphy said. "But Joan, and Dick McBrien and feminist literature say that men's and women's characteristics are basically equal, so roles should not be based on gender." In his own view, he said, "the Church has to incorporate a lot of modern insights". We have been "socialized to such an extent that we give a religious justification to real discrimination . . . and unless we deal with that", the question of women's ordination ("a very symbolic question") cannot be dealt with. "However, the model of priesthood many feminists are looking for is not a clerical model, not the one we're operating on now."

What kind of model would it be?

"Lisa was saying that we need to have men and women *together* create new models of interaction that would lead to a different model of priesthood", he said. "I know the one we have is not adequate."

How is it inadequate?

"Well, the priesthood is limited to men who are able to be celibate, and history is showing that in this country there is a continual decline, and we're not going to have adequate priests to do the ministry."

"Let Them Suffer"

The remarks of the male speakers, formal and informal, proved to be a pale prologue to the addresses of the female speakers, whose sizzling rage lighted up peculiar corners of the theological landscape. Sister Mary Collins, O.S.B.—co-director of the Center for Benedictine Studies in Atchison, Kansas; co-director of an advisory committee on feminist theology for *Concilium*, the major theological journal of the liberal consensus; past president of the North American Academy of Liturgy; past chairman of Catholic University's School of Religious Studies and an associate of WATER from its founding—insisted from her podium that Jesus *had* included women among the Apostles. His inclusive intention was undone by Church Fathers under the influence of patriarchal cultures; women came to be excluded from ordination because of sexist social structures in "imperial Rome . . . and the Hellenistic culture of the Mediterranean world in the centuries immediately surrounding the birth of Christ". Later Collins told reporters that "serious biblical scholars" question the "selective readings that served to conceal the presence of women" among the Apostles. The twelve Apostles and the seventy-two disciples, she said, are "constructs" meant to indicate "continuity with the Old Testament and the Twelve and the seventy-two there". Bristling, Collins said she could not be bothered to worry about problems that may ensue for priests who defy their training and Church authority to champion women's ordination. "I don't see any need to organize to support male egos", she snapped. "Let them suffer. Women suffer."

Ultra-radical groups like Women-Church perform "an extremely important service to the Church", she said. "I consider them signs of hope."

Sister Sandra Schneiders, I.H.M., associate professor of New Testament and Christian spirituality at the Jesuit School of Theology in the Graduate Theological Union (GTU) in Berkeley, California, said American women religious must be independent of Vatican control. She stressed that nuns are "laypersons", not clergy, and have the right "to enjoy the same freedom as the rest of the laity to participate freely in the activities of the world". Apparently referring to the notion of an "invisible Church" of those directly illumined by the Holy Spirit, she said there had been, since Vatican II, a "gradual espousal of a pneumatological ecclesiology which is not really compatible with the reigning ecclesiology of the Vatican". It has occasioned "a self-understanding and praxis among religious which is in stark contrast, *even opposition, to official teaching about religious life and Church law regulating it*" (emphasis added). Schneiders praised the "costly but real victory" of the religious superiors "who refused to threaten or expel" the twenty-four signers of the infamous CFFC *New York Times* advertisement on abortion. By their defiance, she said, those superiors "eventually negotiated a satisfactory settlement" with Rome "in almost every case".

Creating New Symbol Systems

If previous speakers had given evidence that they shared the modernist consensus, all circumspection ceased when Mary Jo Weaver and Sister Madonna Kolbenschlag took their turns at the microphones. Candidly and with passionate certitude, they announced the *real* feminist agenda.

Genial Dr. Weaver, an associate professor of religious studies at Indiana University and the author of *New Catholic Women*,[13] is named with reverence among Wicca feminists. She explained

[13] Mary Jo Weaver, *New Catholic Women: A Contemporary Challenge to Traditional Religious Authority* (San Francisco: Harper & Row, 1985).

how the "radical transformation" of Scripture can bring it into line with feminist attitudes. "Male religious writers, biblical authors, the Fathers . . . have described religion in such a way that it legitimizes the omission of women", she charged. But despite their efforts, males "have not been able totally to obliterate" all the heroines from the pages of history. Feminist readers find them, then set about "revising the tradition":

> Once we see that the religious traditions of the West are relentlessly patriarchal, we have to ask what we can do about it. . . . We have to ask if we *want* to do anything about it. Why should we stay within a tradition that gives women no vote and precious little voice, a tradition that is overwhelmingly negative about the female body, mind and spirit?

Different answers to those questions have moved feminist theologians in different directions, Weaver said. Some have rejected Christianity as irreformably patriarchal and are attempting instead to build new religious "symbol systems". Her example was Carol Christ, who

> believes that we are living in a revolutionary time, when new religious symbols are being formed by a process of syncretism and creativity. . . . [W]hile many traditionally based feminists agree with her on the tenor of the times and the need to create new symbols, they question her interpretation of the goddess, and some disagree that the new life presented to women through ritual interaction with a feminine Divine Being necessitates a radical rejection of the biblical Tradition.

In other words, some Christian feminists hold that the Judeo-Christian Tradition can be corrected by incorporation of the Mother Goddess and her rituals *within* the institutions of patriarchal religion, where so many of them hold tenured professorships. "Patriarchy" has, in the past, appropriated such a potentially "liberating symbol" as the Virgin Mary by presenting her as "the handmaid of the Lord" rather than as "a new form of divine self-revelation". According to Weaver, a more useful way to "read Mary" as "a legitimate icon for feminists" would be "to find in her one of the principal tenets of goddess feminism—that is, the discovery of the divine within oneself". (In all the reported discussion about "creating new symbol systems", no one seems to have asked, "But is it *true*? Of what *reality* is it symbolic?")

"One of the best parts of feminist theology" is its "inclusivity, and its openness to ecumenical dialogue of a radical nature", Weaver said. "Christian feminists not only open themselves to the religious experiences of Jews and non-Christians" but also "enter into fruitful dialogue" with "pagan religious expressions and practitioners". In this atmosphere of universal interchange, it seems, only orthodox Christian belief is invisible.

Weaver cast some light on the importance to feminists of relating their experiences ("herstory"). "The operative position of contemporary theologians is that revelation is a dynamic phenomenon that continues in the present time", she explained. "What happens right here, right now, *is* revelation. Women's experience is a legitimate context for the continual self-communication of the divine in the human community." That view makes prophets of feminists and thus opens up "one new way of reading old texts":

> Ruether believes that we are engaged in a new revelational encounter with the divine, in and through women's experience, which is right now empowering us to tell new stories. These new stories do not necessarily repudiate the old stories, but they may well enable us to reconceptualize them.

This means that feminists can rewrite the Scripture "stories", enlarging or inventing female roles. The experience, Weaver said, can

> give us a window on a profoundly enlarged understanding of biblical traditions. . . . [W]e are led by the logic of the process to redefine the parameters of the discipline, to redefine theology . . . and to articulate the divine will in its pluralistic and political . . . modalities.

Weaver's perspective, like Kolbenschlag's, implied that the political leanings of the divine will are revolutionary and anti-Western.

"People who write about spirituality don't usually get their teaching credentials revoked or get forced out of their orders or disinvited from lecturing engagements, although this may be a first", said Sister Madonna Kolbenschlag. She was at that time a senior fellow at Woodstock Theological Seminary at Georgetown University, editor of the *Woodstock Report* and a part-time congressional aide. Her unusual history could indicate either an adventurous spirit or vocational instability. After teaching (literature) at the University of Notre Dame and lecturing at Chicago's Loyola University, she worked as a full-time legislative assistant to Congresswoman Mary Rose Oakar from 1980 to 1984. In 1980 Kolbenschlag was the official congressional observer at the trial of the Salvadoran soldiers convicted of murdering four American Churchwomen. She was among the advisors who persuaded Mary Hunt to found WATER in 1983. From 1983 to 1987, she was at Woodstock; in 1988, she was appointed a visiting fellow at the (Episcopal) Washington Cathedral for one year. Her most recent book, *Lost in the Land of Oz: The Search for Identity and Community in American Life*,[14] noted that she was "pursuing further studies", this time in psychology. To judge from her remarks at the Women in the Church conference, the title of her book could be an example of subjective projection.

In her blistering address, she excoriated the papacy, the Church, Western civilization, the Judeo-Christian Tradition, the Holy Trinity and monotheism. Then she asked the audience, in the name of "our elder brother, Jesus", to "be a scandal to patriarchy". "The myth of the Father God", she said,

> ensured a world of dominance and dependence. . . . Patriarchy, embedded in the creation story of Genesis, *is* the universal religion. What explains the persistence of the myth? What explains its selection? There were other myths available at the time. . . . But the Genesis myth marked the establishment of

[14] Kolbenschlag, *Oz.*

monotheism and the legitimation of patriarchy as the way of nature—as God's will!

"Social historians and cultural anthropologists, building on the work of Scripture scholars, have in recent years offered some new insights" into the messages concealed in the story of the Fall, Sister Madonna said. For example, Gerda Lerner[15] sees the discriminatory significance of "the prohibition not to eat of the tree of the knowledge of good and evil". Adam and Eve's sin, Kolbenschlag said,

> was, first, a sexual transgression: they knew they were naked. In the ancient world, images of the snake were always associated with the goddess of fertility, the goddess of life. Thus the snake is a symbol of pre-eminent female power and also of the threat of chaos: female power out of control. The banishing of the snake is the banishing of the goddess and, symbolically, of Eve's free and autonomous expression of her sexuality.

Kolbenschlag continued that the second transgression—

> "*you shall be as gods*"—is a transgression of power. Because of her autonomous act, her curiosity and her aggressive desire to *know*, she is to be punished by being excluded from knowledge and from the experience that is power. It's not just the triumph of the "One True God" over the fertility goddesses and the cults. It is a clear condemnation by Yahweh of female sexuality exercised freely and autonomously. It is above all a condemnation and prohibition of the exercise of female power and authority.

Nor have things improved much since then, in Kolbenschlag's view. "So now we see what a seamless web this is: the Vatican preoccupation with contraception, abortion, female altar servers, ordination, nun's habits and constitutions. It's all part of one piece! It's not about 'the mind of Christ'." (The audience chuckled.) "And the abortion controversy is not about life. It's about control over women's sexuality and power!"

[15] Gerda Lerner, *The Creation of Patriarchy* (New York: Oxford University Press, 1986), 180–98.

The spirituality of this "false god" has "created the world we live in", Kolbenschlag said. "Spirituality of a different kind will create the world we want to live in." While the "dominant myth" is "hardening into a rigid, fascistic and narrow-minded fundamentalism", feminist spirituality is "dissolving that myth and image" and re-creating "a myth of God through the process of alienation from the old myth and the reconstruction of a God-myth through the lens of another experience of humanness". Faith, she said, "is the process of continually replacing our metaphors for God".

> It is women above all who are in the process of reversing Genesis, turning the myth on its head by validating and freeing their sexuality, by theologizing out of their own experience and taking responsibility for symbol making in the public sector. . . . Why should we be surprised that the Holy One is breaking through the consciousness of humanity as the Goddess or as an uppity woman?

Kolbenschlag said someone once asked her what we can "salvage from the traditional god-myth that is not destructive". She dismissed the question. "I don't think that salvaging is any concern of ours", she said. Instead, women must "reclaim their reality",

> especially through the power of a holistic sexuality and the right to a free and personally responsible expression of it. . . . Women have always experienced the interconnection of sexuality, affectivity, religious zeal and the creative impulse. And so we have to ignore the Great Lie that denies this.

To build the world they want to live in, said Kolbenschlag, women must cultivate new "virtues". First, *passion*: not a passion for life but rage and anger against the evils of patriarchy. They must develop their capacity for *resistance*, becoming "guerrillas" in order to

> build the consciousness and alternatives for the new society without losing your leverage on affecting the system. . . . While the old forms harden and fossilize with an implacable rigidity, we can be about shaping something for the future.

Feminist guerrillas need models for patience, she went on. "None of the guerrillas in the hills of Central America believe that change is going to come in their generation, but they work as if it were."

New Covenant

Male feminists have "stood back on the sidelines, hoping change will come in the conventional masculine way, from the top down", Kolbenschlag told them.

> But your belief in the future of women hasn't cost you anything yet. No relinquishment of power, no rejection slips, no blood. . . . My brothers, it is time for you to join your sisters as outsiders. It is time for you to resign your membership in the male club and join us in the back of the bus. . . . What an incredible notion it is, for the patriarchs of the world, whether it's in the Vatican or in the other Ayatollahs . . . to keep using the argument that it is the *mind of Christ* that only men be ordained to ministry!

The age of the patriarchs is over at last, said Kolbenschlag. "They will be left behind in Egypt" while feminists "journey to the promised land and the New Covenant". There, "visible in the light of the end time", they will find their world:

> Eve, reaching for the Tree of Life, for the fruit of knowledge and power, full of desire for godlikeness. . . . True daughters and sons of Eve will, in increasing numbers, reach for the Tree of Life and the fruits of knowledge and power, seeking godlikeness. The question is, how long will other men and women go on reaching for the fruits of patriarchy?

This address, delivered on Saturday morning, was the conference's penultimate note; only Bishop DeRoo remained to be heard. Kolbenschlag's address was broadcast on giant screens to overflow ballrooms and lobbies and preserved on video- and audiotape for later rebroadcast in towns across the United States and Canada. Like the ranting of the village atheist, who does not believe in God but is devoured by hatred of him, its fulminating invective was out of range of rational argument. And like so much of the rhetoric of contemporary religious rebellion, in accusing the Church of a preoccupation with sex, it exposed the obsession as the speaker's own. But the most interesting thing about it was the central place it gave to original sin and especially to Eve's role in the Fall, which does indeed conspicuously resemble the history of contemporary feminism.

The phenomena of frankly occult theory and rituals, cultivated by Zsuzsanna Budapest, Carol Christ and Starhawk and put into folk-level practice at events like the annual Mankato Women and Spirituality conference and Limina's programs, is an authentic acting out of feminist theology. Kolbenschlag and Weaver, Ruether, Mary Hunt, Mary Daly and others provide the rationalization, and the activity directors at the sabbats translate it into rituals for those seeking a substitute faith. Dances, mask making, chants and invocations, the retelling of old myths with a feminist slant: what they all express is the "theology" Kolbenschlag proclaimed in Washington, the ancient gnostic preference for the serpent over the Creator.[16]

If Time Consultants wanted moderation, why did its planners choose to present so pathological an address?

The obvious answer is that the professed moderation was merely cosmetic and merely preliminary at that. Once the conference was under way, with twenty-five hundred receptive listeners in attendance, its real purpose—indoctrination—could take precedence over image. The conference program said that "seventy-five people, including thirty sisters, nearly twenty bishops, fifteen priests and ten laypeople" had served as advisors for the conference. Apparently they knew they were inciting to religious revolution; press secretary Ault said they did not want their names revealed and declined to identify any except Richard McBrien.[17] According to Timothy Ragan, his firm takes a "less radical approach" to feminism than Women-Church does because it concentrates on

[16] Elaine Pagels, *The Gnostic Gospels* (New York: Vintage Books, 1981), 35–36. See also Hans Jonas, *The Gnostic Religion* (Boston: Beacon Press, 1963), 93–97, 226–31.

[17] There are clues to the identity of the unnamed advisors: at least eight

"lectures" rather than "process".[18] But in fact there is only one revolution. Feminist theology flows from the liberal consensus of unbelief wed to feminist petulance, and the sceptical consensus apparently sees no grounds for divorce. It is the respectability and ubiquity of modernist thought that make it possible for a speaker

---

bishops have been among the speakers who rotate through Time Consultants' conferences. In addition to Bishops Proulx and DeRoo, Kenneth Untener, the ultra-progressive ordinary of Saginaw, Michigan, has made repeated appearances; P. Francis Murphy, auxiliary bishop of Baltimore, spoke at the 1987 Women in the Church event. Raymond Lucker, bishop of New Ulm, Minnesota, a pioneer in progressive catechetics, spoke at a catechetical conference; Thomas Gumbleton of Detroit (and Pax Christi) spoke at the 1989 conference on the Future of the American Church; Joseph Faber MacDonald, bishop of Grand Falls, Newfoundland, spiritual director for the Catholic Women's League of Canada, spoke at the 1987 Women in the Church conference; and Robert Morneau, auxiliary bishop of Green Bay, Wisconsin (and author of *Mantras for Midnight*), spoke at a 1989 religious education conference. Other speakers who have made repeated appearances at Time Consultants' events include Sister Sandra Schneiders, Sister Fran Ferder, Father Richard McBrien, Father James Provost, Father Richard Rohr, O.F.M. (a "peace and justice" specialist and director of a lay ministry center in Albuquerque); theologian Lisa Sowle Cahill of Boston College; Father David Power, O.M.I., professor of systematic theology at Catholic University; Father Gerard Broccolo, a "spirituality of ministry" expert from Chicago; Clarence Thompson, director of Credence Cassettes for *National Catholic Reporter*; Father John Buscemi, liturgical consultant on church design; and theologian Joe Holland, long associated with the Center of Concern. Other noted progressives on Time Consultants' rosters have been Rosemary Ruether; Father Charles Curran; Father Hans Küng; Dr. Anthony Padovano, professor of literature and religious studies at Ramapo College in New Jersey; Ruth McDonough Fitzpatrick of Women's Ordination Conference; Father Richard Woods, O.P., *National Catholic Reporter* columnist (and editor of *Spirituality Today*); Sister Theresa Kane, R.S.M. (who as LCWR president publicly confronted Pope John Paul II during his American visit in 1979, demanding priesthood for women); Frank Bonnike, long-time facilitator for CORPUS, an organization of married ex-priests; and Father Richard Hynes, president of the National Federation of Priests Councils. Dr. Daniel Maguire, of Marquette University (and Catholics for a Free Choice), gave the keynote address at Time Consultants' 1984 East Coast Conference for Religious Education.

[18] Charlotte Hays, "Split within Catholic feminism?" *National Catholic Register*, Nov. 15, 1987.

like Kolbenschlag to continue to claim the identity of "Catholic theologian" and to appear as such at Catholic conferences. Thus, even in 1986, the difference between Time Consultants and Women-Church was merely a matter of style.

Women-Church Convergence

Cincinnati was dark the weekend of October 9, 1987. Chill drizzle trickled from a leaden sky. In the city's cavernous Convention Center, a full three thousand eager female disciples (with some half dozen glum males) gathered for a synod of Women-Church. In distant Rome, the bishops of the Catholic Church were meeting in synod, too, but here Sister Theresa Kane, R.S.M., giggled, "I like to think *that's* the alternative one."

Governor Celeste's wife, Dagmar, a Women-Church member, opened the feminist synod Friday afternoon with an invocation. "We are women of faith, hope and love", she said. "Blessed be our faith, our hope and our love for this planet, which needs love so much. Blessed be our work."

"Claiming our power" was the conference theme. Most participants were middle-aged, plump and seething with unspecified grievances. There were token Protestants, Jews and Church-non-affiliates on the program, and dutiful references were made to ecumenism, but most registrants had Catholic backgrounds. The largest proportion seemed to be nuns and ex-nuns, engaged in teaching, pastoral ministry or social service. Only one wore a habit; many wore white tee shirts reading "Priestly People Come in Both Sexes". The next largest segment seemed to be divorced women, employed in Church offices or in the "helping professions". I met only five women who were living with their husbands, and three of them were pro-life observers. Conferees crowded meeting rooms to hear feminist speakers denounce Roman Catholic Tradition, the doctrinal and moral teachings of the Church, Pope John Paul II, most bishops and American public policy, including abortion policy, which was criticized as too restrictive.

Synod Mothers

"Claiming our power is *not knowing 'our place' anywhere, and driving them all nuts*", roared Eleanor Smeal, sometime president of the National Organization for Women. Women-Church, she said, must press for "the total feminization of power".

Ruth McDonough Fitzpatrick, national coordinator of Women's Ordination Conference, told reporters that "the Women-Church coalition really formed to work on the bishops. We said we were going to represent the powerless." The 1983 Women-Church conference in Chicago, she said, "freaked the bishops out".

Rosemary Ruether urged conferees to give money to her Chicago Catholic Women fund—called "Mary's Pence"[19]—instead of to the Church, because "we subvert—we turn around from below—those foundations on which the patriarchy have set up their great ladders of being upon our backs . . . and leave them to collapse into the void."

Lesbian leftist Charlotte Bunche thundered, "The right wing and the Pope have organized against lesbian and gay rights and against reproductive rights. . . . The limitations placed on your sexuality are central to the limitations that patriarchy wants to place on your own self-definition!"

Marjorie Reilly Maguire, board member of the National Abortion Rights Action League, pointed to the Annunciation as evidence that "ensoulment" does not occur until the mother consents to "the pregnancy that is within her".

"The academy is very resistant", said Scripture scholar Elisabeth Schussler Fiorenza. "At the University of Chicago, a young male scholar accused me of emasculating Scripture scholarship. I told him, '*Of course* I am!'"

"Organized religions have a way of making politics sacred",

[19] Chicago Catholic Women shamelessly promoted "Mary's Pence" with the slogan "in this Marian year—we begin Mary's Pence". They promised that funds would go to support "alternative ministries" and "centers for creative theology, liturgy and healing". Board members included Ruether; Sister Mary Luke Tobin, S.L.; Sister Margaret Ellen Traxler, S.S.N.D.; and other theologically creative feminists.

said secular feminist Gloria Steinem. "I recall the statement that monotheism is but imperialism in religion." She described "right-wing religious groups" as "the kind of people our ancestors came here to escape". Praising the Women-Church liturgies, she advised that "changing rituals is very important" lest, "in times of trial", women revert to old forms of prayer. "Maybe we need circuit-riding feminist preachers" going around to "religious institutions once a month, speaking of the Great Goddess".

The voices heard in Cincinnati represented political, secular and religious feminism, from Smeal's screech to the gentle tones of Carmelite Sister Mary Lavin of Cleveland, president of the Association of Contemplative Sisters, who said she was "actively engaged in spiritual direction".

The conference sponsor was Women-Church Convergence, a coalition of twenty-six feminist groups with intricately interwoven directorships, drawn from a narrow band on the ideological spectrum and described as "rooted in the Catholic tradition". The abortion lobby Catholics for a Free Choice (CFFC) had a leading role. Other members ranged from the Conference for Catholic Lesbians; Grail Women's Task Force; Loretto Women's Network; New Ways Ministry; Women's Alliance for Theology, Ethics and Ritual (WATER) and Quixote Center to Women's Ordination Conference. Six were based in Chicago: BVM Network for Women's Issues, Catholic Women for Reproductive Rights, Chicago Catholic Women, Sisters for Christian Community (SFCC), National Assembly of Religious Women (NARW) and National Coalition of American Nuns (NCAN). Two more, the Wheaton Franciscans and the Racine Dominicans, were religious communities headquartered nearby.

Familiar Faces

Some 150 speakers had to be transported, housed, fed and, presumably, paid. Rent for the convention center is not cheap. But Women-Church and CFFC are intimately entwined, and CFFC, prosperous with grants from the Playboy, Ford, Sunnen, Gund and Scherman foundations, might well have helped fund a conference for the cause. Whatever the capital outlay, overflow crowds made it a profitable venture. CFFC's Frances Kissling, conference finance chair, crowed with pleasure.

The faces were familiar. The same women who held the wildcat "eucharist" at the 1986 Women in the Church conference were prominently involved with Women-Church conference arrangements. Former nun Diann Neu, who moved on from the Center of Concern to help found WATER and design feminist rituals, was general coordinator. Lesbian theologian Mary Hunt, WATER's primary co-founder, was a member of the program committee and a major speaker. Sister Donna Quinn, O.P., director of both NCAN and Chicago Catholic Women, chaired a press conference, and NCAN founder Margaret Ellen Traxler, S.S.N.D., led a workshop. WOC's Ruth Fitzpatrick spoke for Women-Church on National Public Radio. Sister Martha Ann Kirk, C.C.V.I., San Antonio's dancing nun, served on the liturgy committee. Among the speakers were perennial WOC advisory council members Ruether (CFFC board member, natural mother of the Women-Church movement and its leading theoretician), Schussler Fiorenza, then a visiting professor (later regularly appointed) at Harvard Divinity School, and Sister Theresa Kane, R.S.M., who as president of the Leadership Conference of Women Religious had confronted the Pope about women's ordination during his American visit in 1979.

The rest of the cast, too, were feminist regulars: Janet Kalven of Grailville; Kay Haughey of Colorado's "Women in Spirit" group; a CFFC delegation including, beside Kissling, Maguire and Ruether, Mary Jean Collins, Pauline Nunez-Morales and novelist Mary Gordon. From the homosexual front there were Sister Jeannine Gramick, S.S.N.D., co-founder of New Ways Ministry; lesbian "pastoral psychologist" Lorna Hochstein; Charlotte Bunche from Rutgers University and Barbara Zanotti from Maine. Sister Maureen Fiedler, S.L., was there from Quixote Center, which was then engaged in a "Quest for Peace" effort to match government aid to the Nicaraguan Contras with "humanitarian aid" of equal value to the Sandinistas. WOC core commissioners Barbara Ferraro and Patricia Hussey, of the Sisters of Notre Dame de Namour, and theologian Mary Buckley of New York's St. John's University were scheduled to talk about life as unrepentant signers of CFFC's *New York Times* abortion ad. Among the other speakers were Mary's Pence board member Sister Carol Coston, O.P., executive director of the Adrian Dominican Alternative Investment program, and Sister Deborah Barrett, S.F.C.C., executive director of Catholic Women for Reproductive Rights and coordinator of the "Justice Campaign" for publicly funded abortions.

It was interesting to discover Dolores Huerta, vice president of United Farm Workers, and Marga Buhrig, co-president of the World Council of Churches, among the feminist celebrities present. Scheduled but absent (reportedly because of illness) was Sister Fran Ferder, who regularly speaks at Time Consultants' events. Methodist Bishop Leontine Kelly and politicians Geraldine Ferraro and Barbara Mikulski were also no-shows. So was Madonna Kolbenschlag's long-time employer, Congresswoman Mary Rose Oakar.

If God Is So Great

More than fifty display booths overflowed the exhibitors' hall and stretched along the corridors. They ranged from the Crazy Ladies Bookshop and National Organization for Women, through NETWORK, Priests for Equality, Center of Concern, Pax Christi and the Association for the Rights of Catholics in the Church to Bear Tribe Medicine Society. Coalition member organizations were fully represented. Presbyterian Bookstore sounded harmless, but centrally featured in its display were witch Margot Adler's *Drawing Down the Moon*, goddess-thealogian Carol Christ's *Diving Deep and Surfacing* and lesbian evangelist Barbara Zanotti's *A Faith of One's Own*. There were petitions urging Pope John Paul II to ordain women, endorse altar girls and "speak out" against the "Star Wars" defense system; note cards reading, in calligraphic script, "Praise Our Goddess in Her Universe"; buttons declaring

"I'm Poped Out" and "Phyllis Schlafly Is a Female Impersonator", and complete supplies for Enneagram enthusiasts.

Even in such unsavory company, Revolution Books of Cleveland Heights stood out. It offered, among other things, *The Revolutionary Worker*, headlining such stories as "The Politics of John Paul II: Pilgrimage for the Hangmen" and "International Women's Day 1987: WANTED! Unrepentant Women for Dangerous Times!" The young man at the booth told me cheerfully that his was one of a chain of "revolutionary communist" bookstores in cities from Massachusetts to Hawaii. Behind him hung posters illustrated with scurrilous caricatures of the Pope, the Ayatollah and Jerry Falwell bearing the legend "If God Is So Great, How Come He Has Spokesmen Like These?"

Victim Outreach

Victims of sexism and classism are not easily identifiable, but the low turnout of victims of racism and poverty was a disappointment to the coalition. "It's true this is a white group," admitted Ruth Fitzpatrick, "but we really tried." Sheila Briggs, assistant professor of women's studies at the University of Southern California, conceded that Women-Church "lacks working women's voices" and recommended that they be recruited through the labor movement and battered women's shelters. Cuban-born Sylvia Cancio of Cincinnati Women-Church said black women would not come because they saw it as "a middle-class white women's conference".

A vigorous outreach effort had been made to Hispanics. Advance notices and program brochures incorporated both English and Spanish. A special "program for young women", which drew fewer than ten teenage girls, was conducted by two Hispanic "youth ministers", Maria Salgado from the Chicago Archdiocesan Office of Hispanic Apostolate, and Jackie Padron, formerly on the staff of the USCC Regional Office for Hispanic Affairs in Miami. Yet, except among the speakers themselves, few Hispanics were to be seen. Poverty, racism, even sex discrimination were condemned in undefined generalities. The real emphasis remained on the standard, overlapping feminist agenda items: abortion, homosexuality, spirituality and revolutionary politics.

Claiming the Middle

Describing the coalition, Fitzpatrick said, "Women-Church is fluid; it is process; it is whatever that group needs." That pragmatic fluidity enabled speakers to define the movement in contradictory ways. Ruether, Schussler Fiorenza, Hunt and Neu all insisted that Women-Church is not a new sect or denomination. On the contrary, said Neu, members "are claiming the center, *re*claiming what should have been ours all the time". Fiorenza, too, said Women-Church must "claim the middle", that it is a reform movement *within* the Church, that members have not left and will not leave the Church.

Women-Church is no better qualified to claim the strategically valuable middle of the Catholic Church than Starhawk is to be named to the College of Cardinals. But in its fluidity, Women-Church uses words to create whatever effect may be desired at any moment. Nothing whatever at the Cincinnati meeting indicated the survival of a Catholic, or any other kind of Christian, component. God was replaced by a female "Mother-Wisdom", Jesus was forgotten and the name of the Blessed Virgin Mary was outrageously exploited. Except in regard to its own agenda, the movement advocates doctrinal and moral anarchy. "Doctrinal fences are really a sign of patriarchy", Schussler Fiorenza declared.

Even a reporter from Toronto's liberal *Catholic New Times* observed that this was clearly *not* a reform movement but "a new lay church". Ruether conceded that as early as 1982, adherents "were already moving away from the institutional Church". Other speakers reported that Women-Church eventually replaces even perfunctory Catholic practice. "Many women have to choose between Women-Church and no church", said Mary Hunt. Sister Donna Quinn said some women who attend Women-Church rituals also go to church, but "we're finding that more and more women do not". Mary Alcuin Kelly, a former sister of Notre Dame and a founder of Sisters Against Sexism, said, "When I go to Women-Church, I do not go to Mass." (Sisters Against Sexism is a feminist "base community" in Washington, D.C., in which Frances Kissling, Mary Hunt, Diann Neu and Sister Carol Coston, O.P., have all claimed membership.)

Women-Church does indeed display a kind of cohesive identity, but it is not a Christian identity. Though shreds of the old language and symbols are kept at hand for occasional public relations cover, Women-Church has become something altogether different in nature, a religious chimera. Whether or not individual members recognize any deity beyond the self is open to argument; most leaders transparently do not. Its catalogue of cardinal virtues begins with pride, embraces divorce and emphasizes such forms of "sexual expression" as contraception, lesbianism and abortion. Its politics are collectivist. As liturgy, it offers gnostic spiritualism. It could be "imaged" as a feminist coven at prayer before a mirror.

The Knowing Ones

Even more than overt witchcraft, this alien religion, bitterly hostile to Catholicism but little understood by most Catholics, shows dramatic similarities in themes, rhetoric, intensity, morality and objectives to the gnostic cults of early Christian and medieval times, which also attracted a disproportionate percentage of female adherents to the ranks of the "knowing ones".

Though often classed as a Christian heresy, gnosticism had pre-Christian origins in Persian, Babylonian, Greek and Jewish heresies and was also an influence in the Roman mystery cults, according to scholar Hans Jonas.[20] It was one way of explaining the evil in the world, says Robert M. Grant, another authority on gnosticism. Grant believes it was born of despair, in the wake of catastrophic events, when "faith was shaken in God, his covenant,

[20] Jonas, *Gnostic Religion*, 33–42.

his law and his promises".[21] There were a multiplicity of gnostic groups whose beliefs varied in mythological details but held in common the major tenets of "radical dualism": (1) that God is unknowable, utterly separate from (2) a material universe created by fallen powers, in which (3) man's spirit (pneuma) is imprisoned and (4) from which he can escape only by being "awakened" from ignorance to gnosis (secret spiritual knowledge) by (5) an illuminating immanent "spirit", thus becoming one of a pneumatic elite. (6) Salvation, in gnosticism, did not depend on God's grace mediated by a Divine Redeemer but on esoteric knowledge, which replaced rational systems and transformed the believer. The gnosis—that his spirit was a divine spark—meant that he could discover the divine will by consulting his own intuition. Religion became psychology, as it does in the contemporary liberal consensus, in Wicca and in process theology.

Wicca was little mentioned at the Women-Church event except around the ashtrays in the lobby. Instead, chief theoretician Ruether made several references, as she had in her *Women-Church* book, to Wisdom as God the Mother. She spoke of "the inner voice of our Mother Wisdom" and "the source of life and new life which we call Mother Wisdom". Gnosticism, too, venerated Wisdom as Sophia, the feminine principle of androgynous Divinity, or its daughter, trapped in creation by disobedience. She was the fallen creator of earth, air, fire and water and mother of the evil demiurge who was the God of Israel. Jonas describes her as "God's erring Wisdom, the Sophia, falling prey to her folly, wandering in the void and darkness of her own making, endlessly searching, lamenting, suffering, repenting, laboring her passion into matter". Some gnostic allegories of the Christian era offered as "the deeper 'knowledge'" a reversal of "the roles of good and evil" found in the original Tradition; in some, the serpent tempter in Eden was Jesus; in some, Sophia (Mother Wisdom) sent the serpent to tempt Eve and Adam away from obedience to the Evil

[21] Robert M. Grant, *Gnosticism and Early Christianity*, 34.

Creator.[22] Despite those echoes, Ruether's use of the term provides an ambiguous link with the Old Testament Book of Wisdom that could be understood, and doubtless will be defended, as referring to the trinitarian Holy Spirit as a maternal aspect of God. Increasingly common among feminist nuns, that usage is theologically erroneous but certainly less startling to hear than talk of "Holy Virgin Huntress Artemis".

As syncretist religions do, gnosticism kept evolving; Jonas says "intellectual individualism" and "non-conformism" were "almost a principle . . . closely connected with the doctrine of the sovereign 'spirit' as a source of direct knowledge".[23] Since the external world was in darkness, the voice of the self was the only certain voice of God, says feminist scholar Elaine Pagels, a religious historian who, in her enthusiasm for her subject, seems to have been converted to it. The gnostic, Pagels says, believed that "self-knowledge is knowledge of God; the self and the divine are identical":[24]

> Whoever comes to experience his own nature—human nature—as the "source of all things," the primary reality, will receive enlightenment. Realizing the essential Self, the divine within, the gnostic laughed in joy at being released from external constraints to celebrate his identification with the divine being.[25]

In New Testament times, Simon Magus, mentioned in Acts 8:10, was a gnostic. Gnostic sects that appropriated Christian elements and language became a "parasitic growth upon early Christianity",[26] a problem addressed at length by the Fathers of the early Church. Writing about the year 180, St. Irenaeus, bishop of Lyons, observed with distress that "foolish women", more than men, were attracted to the gnostic Marcionite cult that had sprung up in the Rhône Valley.[27] Apocryphal Coptic scriptures, called "gnostic gospels", were rejected by the Church but have lately

[22] Jonas, *Gnostic Religion*, 86, 92–93.

[23] Ibid., 42.

[24] Pagels, *Gnostic Gospels*, xix.

[25] Ibid., 172–73.

[26] Grant, *Gnosticism and Early Christianity*, 89.

[27] Pagels, *Gnostic Gospels*, 70–71.

been revived by feminists and New Agers.[28] Gnostic dualism re-emerged in third-century Manicheanism and again in medieval times, notably among the Cathars of southern France. Jeffrey Burton Russell, American academia's leading legitimate scholar of witchcraft, has written about other medieval antinomian sects of gnostic character, such as the Joachists discussed in the previous chapter, the deviant Franciscan Fraticelli and the Amalricians (who held that since God is all things, they must be God). Even in the non-canonical women's communities of Beguines, which had produced admirable and holy women, many fell into decadence and were caught up in the gnosticism of the times. Convinced that a new spiritual age was beginning, these groups evolved from reformist piety into repudiation of the Church, pantheism, promiscuity, homosexuality, occultism and in some cases frankly Satanic witchcraft.[29] In his fascinating study of medieval revolutionary millenarianism, Norman Cohn sees parallels between those movements and contemporary secular revolutionary movements seeking "emancipation" from "external reality", and "the ideal" of "self-divinization" through psychedelic drugs.[30] Cohn's 1970 edition was too early to take note of the even more striking parallels between today's religious revolutionaries and the fourteenth-century Beghards, many of them "former monks and priests and clerks in minor orders", who degenerated, along with some of the Beguines whose spiritual advisors they were, into the sexually libertine and proscribed Brethren of the Free Spirit.[31] Political philosopher Eric Voegelin has identified gnostic elements in modern messianic po-

[28] See ibid., passim. See also James M. Robinson, ed., *The Nag Hammadi Library* (San Francisco: Harper & Row, 1988). Also, *A Course in Miracles*, a popular New Age work reportedly dictated by a "spirit guide", clearly expresses and exemplifies gnostic beliefs.

[29] Jeffrey Burton Russell, *Witchcraft in the Middle Ages* (Ithaca: Cornell University Press, 1972), 136–42.

[30] Norman Cohn, *The Pursuit of the Millennium* (New York: Oxford University Press, 1970), 286.

[31] Cohn, *Millennium*, 159. The Beghards were the subject of the nursery rhyme, "Hark, hark, the dogs do bark, the beggars are coming to town." Cohn also mentions the influence of Sufis on the degenerating sects.

litical movements and regards the belief that evil can be dissolved by knowledge as a perennial heresy.[32]

The identifying marks itemized by historian James Hitchcock[33] —global pessimism, belief in its own absolute importance as precursor to a new age, anti-intellectualism, feminism, exaltation of a new and invisible church centered in the directly illuminated self, consequent hostility to hierarchical religion, social utopianism, subjectively defined "mysticism", moral relativism and libertinism —have been characteristic of gnosticism in its ancient and modern, religious and political manifestations.[34]

The resemblances to Women-Church are not accidental. In her *Women-Church*, Ruether refers to the Beguines and the Fraticelli as "spirit-filled" predecessors of current religious feminists. Like those groups, she says, Women-Church is a movement of "radical Christianity" that "tends to see the traditional religion as false or fallen" and that "anticipates the New Age, expecting it soon to dawn upon the earth and seeking to pattern itself after what it believes to be the social order of redemption"[35]. Elisabeth Schussler Fiorenza, like many feminist theologians, draws on gnostic apocrypha as if they were legitimate sources of information about the role of women in the primitive Church.[36]

Renewed Priesthood

Male or female, recipients of what they take to be direct divine illumination are apt to feel no need of an ecclesiastical license to practice; they can simply "claim their power". Some of the gnostic cults had women leaders and perhaps women clergy. When Women-Church first organized, ordination of women priests was its primary non-negotiable demand. That is still presumed to be its chief priority by many in the press, the pew and the chancery

[32] Eric Voegelin, *Science, Politics and Gnosticism* (Chicago: Regnery Gateway, 1968).

[33] See chap. 2, above.

[34] Chap. 2, above. See also Hitchcock, *New Enthusiasts*, passim.

[35] Ruether, *Women-Church*, 15–23.

[36] Fiorenza, *In Memory of Her*; see esp. pt. III, 243–351.

office. Individual women may indeed still yearn for priesthood, but Women-Church does not, as leaders have made explicit. Mary Hunt has said it was "a smart strategy to start talking about ordination", but "it would at this point be an experience of assimilation if women were to be ordained".[37] WATER's ritualist Diann Neu, writing in the theological journal *Concilium* in 1982, said, "Women would never want to celebrate Eucharist in the present hierarchical-patriarchal Church guilty of the sin of sexism."[38] Ruether wrote in *Women-Church*, "Most Roman Catholic women neither can nor wish to be ordained within priesthood as presently defined."[39] WOC's Cincinnati press release declared that it seeks access for women to "a renewed priestly ministry", and WOC coordinator Fitzpatrick told reporters that the goal "is not to have women ordained into the clerical state but to renew priestly ministry".

Renew in what fashion? By recognizing anyone who feels "called", male or female, as a "priestly person": that is, by dispensing with ordained priesthood, hierarchy, papal infallibility and the authority of the "first Magisterium". Describing how the Church would be changed if Women-Church achieved its goals, WATER's Mary Hunt explained that "components" would include "a non-hierarchical understanding" made concrete in "small democratic house churches and base communities".

One of the standard arguments today's ecclesiastical revolutionaries use in demanding an altered form of priesthood is that declining vocations will otherwise deprive the faithful of the Eucharist. Yet it was clear that Women-Church had no more interest in the Real Presence than in ordination. Mary Alcuin Kelly, one of the younger women present, talked about how to start a local Women-Church. Such groups, she said, "see it as their mission to

[37] Interview, "Mary E. Hunt", in *The Inside Stories: 13 Valiant Women Challenging the Church*, ed. Annie Lally Milhaven (Mystic, Conn., Twenty-third Publications, 1987), 132.

[38] Diann Neu, "Our Name Is Church: The Experience of Catholic-Christian Feminist Liturgies", *Concilium*, no. 152 (1982): 75–84.

[39] Ruether, *Women-Church*, 66.

experiment with new signs and symbols" but usually "come back to blessing bread and wine and distributing it in a eucharistic manner". At first members were concerned about "the question of Consecration", she said, but "that has become a non-question". Now they are content "to create a sacred space and grow from our own experience".

Marianist Sister Christine Hucik, a Cincinnati pastoral minister in attendance at the conference, seemed to approve. When I asked whether she anticipated the ordination of women, she said wearily, "I don't care. If we are true to the Spirit moving in our times, new forms of ministry and consecrated life will arise. It would be a shame to hang on to the old forms when the Spirit is moving us in another direction. But religious women are really not heard at all. The hierarchy won't help women. So I pay very little attention to what they say or do."

Deposit of Faith

Women-Church rejects as "fundamentalist" the belief that the truth could have been revealed "once for all", to be preserved by the Church as the deposit of faith. Sister Sandra Schneiders, I.H.M. (another Time Consultants speaker), explained how to make Scripture serve feminism. She scoffed at the notion that the Bible "contains revelation", that it is "God telling us things, a collection of otherwise unavailable information". If it were, she said, "God would have said everything God had to say, in first-century terms, and this would be normative in detail for all succeeding generations of Christians!"

"Overwhelmingly patriarchal, androcentric, sexist and oppressive of women" as it is, Scripture is still "our connection with our own religious tradition. Maybe we will finally have to give up", Schneiders said. But first, feminists ought to engage not only scholars but also "preachers and teachers and polemicists and translators and ecclesiastical politicians" in "a concerted approach" to "saving it" with new interpretations. Modeling the process, she said that Scripture is not "literally" the word of God "because

God does not literally speak. Speaking is something you do with your mouth and tongue and esophagus [*sic*], and God does not have those parts." For the same reason, she said, "if we say God is our Father, that is absurd", because "God does not have sexual intercourse with a woman, causing conception of a child". New rules will require feminist interpreters to assume that "Scripture is *not* 'the word of God' . . . is *not* a container of revelation" and to "correct as we read . . . in the way one might say to a friend, 'I know that is what you said, but I know that's not what you meant'". In one such reinterpretation, she said firmly that St. Paul's statement "wives, be subject to your husbands" is something that "came from his culture", while "husbands, love your wives" was "counter-cultural" and thus doubtless genuine, because "first-century husbands were not expected to love their wives".

As the sole New Testament authority present, Schneiders had the entire workshop time to herself, and her address was longer and more substantial than most. Like other Women-Church speakers, she showed no interest in questions of truth or God's will; her subject was how to justify the feminist will. She holds a licentiate in sacred theology from the Institut Catholique in Paris and a doctorate in sacred theology from the Gregorian University in Rome. Her sophistries were unworthy of her education. It is not God's Word and God's Fatherhood that are metaphors but human speech and human fatherhood, which have meaning as shadows of his utterance of his divine Word and of his Fatherhood.

As is typical of feminists, Schneiders seemed to attribute no value to uniquely feminine roles. Complaining of a historic conspiracy against women, she asked, "Where is women's literature? Where is women's art?" Undeniably, most works of art and literature have been produced by men, but while men were making those impermanent things, most women were centrally engaged in more demanding work of surpassing value, bearing and rearing human beings with an eternal destiny.

Further insights into Schneiders' remarkable views came in answers to question from the floor. One woman said she was willing to concede "that Jesus is *an* expression of the divine. But is he the *only one*?"

"The problem of Jesus today is not only, for some women, the problem of his masculinity but also the problem of the *exclusivity* of Jesus", Schneiders agreed. "Is Jesus the sole, unique, *only* absolute revelation of God—a position that invalidates the other great world religions?" For those who wonder, she said, "I recommend to you the book *No Other Name?* by Paul Knitter,[40] who teaches here at Xavier University." As the title indicates, Knitter's book expresses grave doubts of Jesus' uniqueness and reports that other contemporary Catholic theologians share them.

Another questioner asked whether St. Paul's position on homosexuality was "cultural or counter-cultural".

"Use of one particular text to construct an entire morality is a good example of the wrong use of Scripture", was Schneiders' heated reply. "One reference in the New Testament doesn't tell the attitude of the early Church toward homosexuality!" To say that it does would be as bad as "that *awful* thing that came out of the Congregation for the Doctrine of the Faith—and it was *an awful thing*! . . . *anything* but pastoral and anything but caring!"

Lobbying the Church

Advance publicity had suggested that the conference would emphasize internal Church politics. Religious feminists having already demonstrated effectiveness as episcopal lobbyists, it seemed prudent to learn what to expect next. But optimism about clerical politicking appeared low. One after another, speakers complained of persecution by bishops. The feminist notion of proper episcopal sensitivity is unconditional surrender, so they have little appreciation even for bishops who actively support them.[41] Archbishop

[40] Paul Knitter, *No Other Name?* (Maryknoll, N.Y.: Orbis Books, 1986).

[41] In *Women-Church*, Ruether lists the following bishops who endorsed and contributed to the 1983 Women-Church conference: Archbishop Raymond Hunthausen, Seattle; Bishop Maurice Dingman, Des Moines; Archbishop P. Francis Murphy, Baltimore; Auxiliary Bishop Thomas Gumbleton, Detroit;

Hunthausen, for example, was mentioned only as proof that organized lobbying can advance feminist interests. So ferocious were their criticisms that my heart quite warmed toward Bishops Francis Stafford of Denver and John D'Arcy of Fort Wayne/South Bend and even Chicago's Cardinal Bernardin.

Mary Jean Collins, public affairs director for CFFC, past vice-president of NOW and a graduate of Alverno College who "was born and will die an Irish Catholic", starred in a session on "lobbying the Catholic Church" that raised an echo of *Screwtape Letters*. "The average bishop is hearing a lot from the right wing and very little from us, though *we* are the rank and file", she fretted. "CFFC is trying to get people to write to the bishops as the right wing does. . . . The Hunthausen outcome showed that the bishops' organization is just as political as any other political organization." She tried to recruit assistance for CFFC's "Bishop Watch", a tool for creating counter-pressure against the "repressive" parts of the Catholic political agenda. CFFC's "minimum targets" for the project were "the key pro-life dioceses of Chicago", Los Angeles and "Boston, where the cardinal is politically active and has a lot of money". CFFC wanted to "analyze and publicize" what the Church spent "on lobbying reproductive issues". Collins said the value of such information was demonstrated in the Abortion Rights Mobilization suit demanding an end to the Church's tax-exempt status on grounds of the bishops' "electoral political activities". The suit was later dismissed.

Appearing with Collins was five-term Illinois legislator Barbara Flynn Currie of Chicago, who deplored the Church's lobbying and fumed against Cardinal Bernardin for pushing legislation to stop school-based clinics from prescribing contraceptives. Legislators passed "the cardinal's bill" because "politicians are cowards", Currie said. The Church's political power is reprehensible because "it

---

Auxiliary Bishop George Evans, Denver; and Bishop Charles Buswell, Pueblo. Several of those men have since retired, but Auxiliary Bishop Emerson Moore of New York, who signed Chicago Call to Action's "Pastoral" ad in the *New York Times* (Feb. 28, 1990), seems one likely recruit.

does not rest on moral suasion". It doesn't have to, she claimed; the Church "can list the legislator's votes in the parish bulletin. We've seen it happen: 'She's not back this year because they were reading her name out in the pulpit every Sunday because she voted against the cardinal.'" Yet Currie also insisted, inconsistently, that "rank-and-file" Catholics do not support the Church's moral teachings.

When floor discussion opened, audience members were bursting to talk about their own bishops. "The *good* piece of news I heard, about the time the Hunthausen affair was being settled", a woman volunteered,

> was—I'm from Los Angeles, and Archbishop Mahoney was asked by a reporter, "Was the Vatican pressured in any way, and did they respond?" The reporter had heard that the Vatican received five thousand telegrams a week from people, particularly in the Seattle area. And Archbishop Mahoney sort of laughed and said, "Well, *of course* they responded to that! If five thousand people a week telegraphed the Vatican from this country, we would have an entirely different kind of Church!" and that's the archbishop speaking! So they are lobbyable.

"In my experience, there is often more responsiveness at the local level than there is in the hierarchy", Currie replied. "I've had experiences in my local neighborhood Church in which the pastor, who, well, doesn't exactly strike me as a left-wing intellectual out of Harvard Divinity School, is just a much more *flexible* person than anyone in the chancery downtown."

"I'm from a very conservative diocese. The bishop has been there two years, and he threatens to transfer pastors when people from the parish write letters disagreeing with some of his actions", said an irate woman from South Bend, in Bishop D'Arcy's diocese. "Some of us get together and agree to give our money to Mary's Pence. . . . But how do you deal with that kind of situation? The pastors are afraid for their jobs. You know, they've got a good place to work, a good progressive church to be at, and the bishop would pull 'em out."

Another woman broke in, proposing a campaign against the papal nuncio, Archbishop Pio Laghi.

> I come from Denver, where we have just received one of those bishops [Bishop Stafford], and it's like everything has come to a *dead stop*! I think one possibility would be to exert some pressure to get rid of Pio Laghi. He has a big voice in who are nominated as our bishops. I think this man's record when he was in Argentina, during those terrible years, is certainly something that would provide us with some ammunition.

"That's good. That's good," Collins murmured.

Off the Record

South Bend spoke again. "This particular bishop, when he found out from someone in the parish that we were coming here, sent a representative down to investigate us! . . . There are some you can't work with, you have to work around."

"Right. And try to figure out a way to get the other bishops to put pressure on them . . . try to hem the guy in. Like, I think O'Connor . . . has gotten pressure from his brother bishops", Collins said. "There is some pressure to be brought when the guy's really out of line. On the other hand, you have to figure out who can really do that, whose neck isn't on the line."

"We're very fortunate in Kentucky", another woman said. "We have a very progressive archbishop [Thomas C. Kelly, O.P., archbishop of Louisville]. But he can just go so far, because he knows that he will lose all the clout he has if he steps too far out of line. I don't know; what can an archbishop do? . . . He's so terribly effective, and he could really blow that."

"Get support in to him", Collins offered.

> If he's progressive, you can bet he's hearing from the readers of the *Wanderer* in Louisville, and that there's a lot of pressure on him from the right wing. Well, that means writing to the diocesan paper . . . that you don't even want to *look* at, but you might have to write letters to the editor and say, "Blah blah blah, and I support the bishop's stand." . . . On the other

hand, we can't be too concerned about his political future. I mean, these guys have big important jobs that we don't even have access to, and we shouldn't feel too sorry for them.

Before the Pope's last visit, Collins said, she traveled to all the cities where he would appear

> to organize the reproductive rights people. And in every newspaper, the Sunday before the Pope came . . . there were puff pieces. They got very good press, the bishops themselves. Bernardin had one, too. . . . And basically all of them say, sort of tongue in cheek, what you know they *must* say off the record, because it comes through: "Rome is a big pain in the neck. Well, I'm caught between this crazy Pope and these crazy people, and poor me." And they *are* in the middle, because they know—even your guy in South Bend has to know—he *can't* make what Rome wants done, done. He *can't* get it done; he can't do the job they want him to do.

Currie interrupted. "The point is to keep the pressure on and *keep* them in the middle. You don't want them shifting off to the other side."

"When have we been successful with lobbying in getting a bishop to change his point of view?" a woman asked.

"The Hunthausen thing is the best example of that kind of lobbying", Collins replied. "But as for a case where a bishop's point of view was actually changed, I can't think of one."

No one proposed a toast.

Creative Survival

Internal politics was the subject again when Sister Mary Luke Tobin, S.L., told a workshop on "creative survival in religious institutions" that, "as Rosemary Ruether says, we need the Church because it's the global power it is; we need it across the world as a force for change". Tobin, founder of Denver's Thomas Merton Center for Creative Exchange, said she had been an advisor at the Second Vatican Council ("a mistake they haven't repeated") and believes that the Council "made some important steps, beginning with the phrase 'the people are the Church'". It was significant because "once you get a statement through, they think it's *male* to stand by it".

"Threats are dangerous" and strategically unwise, she said. "Win them over if you can. We had to do this in Roman Catholic sisters' groups, and that's why I'm standing here in pastel!"

In the campaign for change after Vatican II, strategic language was of the greatest importance, Tobin said. "'*The Church is changing.*' Wow, did we use *that*! People didn't know how to respond!" In those good old days, people didn't ask why it was changing or who was changing it, she said. "So we ran with the ball while we had it." Today a rising tide of neo-orthodoxy makes progress more difficult, but Tobin said her practical advice stands. "Run with the ball while *you* have it, around the end or straight down the middle."

If Women-Church leaders have more elaborate plans for Church politics, they did not share them in Cincinnati. In the area of secular politics, attention was concentrated on supporting rebellion in El Salvador and South Africa and on opposing it in Nicaragua. "We are creating a spirituality of social struggle", said Ruether. "A simply political base without a spiritual base can not sustain it."

Sexual Empowerment

About sex, Women-Church's message seemed to be that men are up to no good. There were workshops on domestic violence, on rape and incest, on moving beyond the patriarchal family, on teenage sex and contraception, on prostitution and even one—attended by twenty-two conferees but understandably closed to the press—on "sexual affairs between women and priests".

Abortion, as usual, held center stage, but lesbianism was a close second. Ellie Smeal left early for a mammoth "gay rights" march in Washington, and nearly all subsequent speakers said their hearts were with her. At the beginning of a Saturday workshop, "Lesbians Keeping the Faith: Is It Possible?", one woman put her head in the door and bellowed, "Is this where all the dykes are?" Her companion giggled, "Doesn't it feel good to just say it right out loud?" They went in to hear Lorna Hochstein, an openly lesbian "pastoral psychotherapist" from Boston, assure them that although the *official* Church has nothing valuable to teach about sex, many priests and nuns will be sympathetic and supportive.

With Diane Raffle of the Conference for Catholic Lesbians, Sister Jeannine Gramick of New Ways Ministry presented the workshop "Confronting Homophobia". The early Church was not intolerant of homosexuality, Gramick said, but attitudes were later deformed by "a hierarchy of dogma [with] positions on human relations that could be considered homophobic". Homophobia also flourished within "the family structure that is advocated by the Moral Majority", she said, and among people who feel "guilt about their own sexual impulses".

Lesbian Charlotte Bunche, who was the first woman resident fellow at the leftist Institute for Policy Studies, talked about "the most empowering experiences of my life". The day she realized that "womanspirit is redefining our whole concept of what it *means* to be spiritual" was one, she said. "Sexual empowerment is central to the empowerment of women. One of the *other* most empowering moments for me was the day I decided I could come out as a lesbian and *still* speak on any issue in the world." In closing, she urged the conferees to new heights of zeal, predicting that "a Women-Church movement can be one of the most politically powerful movements in this country".

Hearing Barbara Zanotti and Frances Kissling within the same hour vindicated the Fathers of the Church of any misogyny of which they might be accused. The listing of Kissling as speaker was a clue that the workshop called "Sexuality: Healthy, Good and Holy" might not be G rated. But even more bizarre, if possible, was Zanotti, who views her lesbianism, with vast solemnity, as a religion. Goddess religion.

"Sexuality is an historical construct, socially created", said Zanotti, who was once married and didn't like it. "Just as we have come to expose and dismantle the myth of patriarchal religion, we have tried to do the same thing with sexuality." She went on to describe "the sexuality of self-acceptance", a term apparently meaning assertive female auto- and homo-eroticism, about which she provided graphic detail. "So, this act of honoring our bodies and experiencing our bodies as manifestations of the goddess, I think, is a very *subversive* aspect of femininist spirituality". It had been "quite a journey", she said, to where she could say, "I *love* my body; I love every part of me!" Then she named the parts she loved.

The previous summer, she had found it "a wonderful experience . . . on many, many levels" to attend the Annual Women's Music Festival at Hart, Michigan, where seventy-two hundred women wander ninety-two acres of land, "and some choose to wear clothes and some do not. It was the beautiful variations in the female body that were so wonderful to behold!" she said. "It was a very transforming experience for me."

"It all comes back to sexuality, spirituality, autonomy, power, identity", she crooned. "Loving and cherishing our bodies as manifestations of this divine source of life because that is the *truth* of who we are! . . . In closing, let me remind you of Starhawk's words, which she puts in the goddess' mouth: '*All acts of love and pleasure are my rituals.*'"

I was bemused to discover later that Ms. Zanotti had been a member of the Women's Ordination Conference panel during its 1979–80 dialogue with an NCCB committee of bishops.

Frances Kissling brought a change of pace. Chunky and fortyish, she retains the manner of a pubescent misfit trading ribald boasts with the tough boys on the street corner. As "an unreconstructed unmarried heterosexual woman, I personally face the question of reproduction or the possibility of unwanted reproduction on a monthly basis from the time I am thirteen years old . . . until . . . forty-five or even fifty", she said. "Since I have believed since young womanhood that sexuality per se is a positive good, I had to deal both personally with the question of procreation, the possibility of pregnancy, and personally with the question of developing a sexual ethic." What "impedes us from developing a positive sexual ethic is the depth of the burden we all bear in the formation of our values from the *overwhelming disgust*, REVULSION AND HATRED that the Fathers of our Church have shown toward sexuality from time immemorial", she said. "Even the use of sexuality in marriage was to be watched quite carefully. We see this even now in John Paul II, one of the greatest minds of the fifth century." The audience chuckled. "I mean, back to the lust in your heart!"

"So is it any wonder", she asked, "that there aren't a lot of us standing up here and saying, 'I *do* it'? 'Guess what? I *had sex*! *Recently*! And I didn't go to confession! And I used birth control!' " Audience members howled their delight.

The penitential practices of women saints of the past, "the Little Flower, St. Catherine of Siena", she called "a form of anorexia to subjugate their bodies". (One glance established that Kissling, unlike so many contemporary joggers and dieters, had not subjugated hers.) Today, instead, "we have the good wife and mother. Anyone who doesn't fall into those categories is out. We are, as I call it, 'the best and brightest of the bad girls'. And I think that's where we want to stay, most of us."

In the past, Kissling said, such women were called witches: "Women who tried to take control of their bodies, control of their spirituality, control of worship, control of healing. Aren't we glad we aren't allowed to be burned at the stake anymore? The most they can do now, as my friend Mary Hunt says, is to call our mothers and tell them we're bad girls. And since many of us have bad mothers, it's not going to work!"

"We are people who believe in sharing, and sexuality is a form of sharing. Masturbation is fine, massage is fine," she said, "but now we have to stretch ourselves and find ways to share with others as well. . . . So we need to ask ourselves some serious questions. When is it moral to enter into a sexual relationship with another? Is lifetime monogamy a pre-condition? Can we only have one sexual relationship at a time? What about sex for knowledge, for growth, for experimentation? . . . What about sex for priests and nuns? Same-sex sex? Sex for teenagers? I think we are blocked in even attempting to find those answers", she concluded, "because of the burden we bear from the kind of revulsion, *disgust* and *hatred* of women and their bodies that is our patrimony."

Revulsion and disgust never seemed more appropriate.

We Catholics

"Moral Perspectives on Abortion" proved to be a panel about the moral superiority of abortion. It was the only one where orthodox infiltrators revealed their presence. When she was first challenged, lead speaker Marjorie Maguire tried to cut off the objector in mid-sentence.

"We all know that personhood transcends the material, the genetic makeup", Maguire declared. "The theory I have developed is that personhood begins when the woman consents to the pregnancy." Her "symbolic authority" for that criterion rests, she said, "in the story of the Annunciation. We Catholics are always taught that Mary was not obliged to become the Mother of Jesus. . . . If we don't say that . . . we make Mary guilty of sin if she refused. . . . Similarly, I think every pregnancy is an *invitation* by God which a woman is free to accept or reject without sin." No one pointed out that when the Blessed Virgin made her free decision to become the Mother of God she was not yet pregnant.

Maguire denied that an individual human life has a beginning. Conception is merely something that happens to "one of our cells of this huge mass of humanity that's been here since the beginning and didn't begin anew with conception but just continues in a new way." Later she added, "God doesn't automatically do things just because biology happens."

Three other speakers followed. Patricia Camp of Religious Coalition for Abortion Rights said abortion is a purely private option. Former CFFC staffer Pauline Nunez-Morales, now bringing "reproductive technology" to Hispanic women in the southwest, denounced Archbishop Sanchez for opposing school-based clinics in Albuquerque. Deborah Barrett of the non-canonical Sisters for

Christian Community called Cardinal Bernardin's "consistent life ethic" a sham.

After they had finished, Marsha Garland of Lexington stood up. "I am a Roman Catholic. I am the mother of five, and I have lived in poverty in the past", she said. "I would *die* in poverty rather than murder my unborn child . . ."

"Someone else?" Maguire interrupted.

A voice called out, "Let her finish."

"Offering so-called ignorant women free abortion is a further exploitation of women", Garland continued. "And of unborn women." She picked up her papers and walked out. There was a brief pause.

"I'm sorry that woman left. I'm a Roman Catholic nun, and I am *so* pleased that this discussion is happening here", said a woman from the audience. "When I spent a couple of years recently at a male seminary, I was exposed to Beverly Harrison and Maguire. . . . How do we get ourselves out from under patriarchy? We have assumed that since patriarchy has defined the fetus as human life, we then call ourselves murderers when women choose to abort. . . . I'm *sick* of males defining our morality. For God's sake, let us, *as women*, decide." She sat down to applause.

"Religion has a lot to offer us, OK?" Patricia Camp offered. "Our particular belief in our *particular* god enriches our life, OK? But we can't impose *our* morality on others, all right?"

There were other dissenters in the house, however. One woman said she did not agree that we cannot impose our morality. "What about abolition? What about slavery?"

An abortion escort from NOW said she wished "those people who are quote prolife would come to Louisville some Saturday morning and see the cruelty and the pain—the cruelty of those who harass women going into the clinic and the pain on the faces of the harassed women".

Maguire spoke excitedly about the "cruelty of people who try to hand rubber fetuses to sometimes very young women going into clinics. I abhor it!"

"I want to tell you about some other people who are pro-life, who really believe that every woman should have the right to make a well-informed decision about her pregnancy, that she should know what's happening in her womb at the time she's considering an abortion", another woman said quietly. "And she should also know that there are people who would be willing to help her. . . . I work with a group in Omaha. . . . They know we won't walk with them to the abortion clinic, but they know they're welcome to come back afterward if they need help. And many do." There was applause for her, too.

"Some women feel pain because they've had a guilt trip laid on them by the Church", said Maguire.

"You shouldn't have tried to turn to someone else so quickly when that first woman spoke", a woman said. "We need to engage the debate, to put women in the consistent life ethic. It's a whole question of looking at life. When does life begin? Does life *never* begin? Do we have the right to terminate old people's lives somewhere down the line because they're not productive in society? Whose life is important?"

Earler, Maguire had explained that she and her husband, CFFC board member Daniel Maguire, had a son, Danny, elder of two boys, who was born with Hunter's syndrome, a genetic disorder causing progressive retardation and degeneration of the brain and nervous system. Danny Maguire died on October 6, 1983, at ten years of age.

"Sometimes the best respect you can show for a person is the ending of life", Maguire said.

Dry Bones and Death

Some fifteen hundred women crowded a ballroom to hear an odd quartet. Their panel, "Spirituality: Stretching the Circle" was moderated by Sister Nadine Foley, O.P., prioress of the Adrian Dominican Congregation, who became president of the Leadership Conference of Women Religious the following year.

Sylvia Marcos, a CFFC board member identified her as the director of the Center for Psychoethnological Research at Cuernavaca, Mexico, unwittingly proved that gender complementarity is acceptable to feminists if presented as pagan and primitive. Her subject was native folk priestesses "capable of summoning the spirits". She found their cosmology "empowering", first because their magic can "do something to alter God's will" and second because it contains a balance of "masculine and feminine principles", which she called "a duality of complementaries". Her talk was roundly applauded.

Ecology as animist religion was proposed by Wabun (aka Marlise James Wind), a 1960's drop-out from conventional society, who was introduced as "co-founder of the Bear Tribe, an intentional community based upon the visions of Sun Bear, a spiritual teacher of Chippewa descent".

"To bring our energies together and call upon the energies around us . . . the powers of the four directions", Wabun led the huge audience in a chant that, she promised, would "change the way you look at life". Obediently, the women repeated her phrases:

The earth is our mother;
We must take care of her.
Hey yunga, ho yunga,
Hey, yung yung.

"Bring the earth and the other kingdoms into your spirituality", Wabun urged. "When you take a drink, thank the water spirit."

Mary Jo Weaver's address was the *pièce de résistance* of the spirituality forum. Weaver reviewed the "two major streams" of feminist theology and their common plight. The *reformers*, in exile, want to revise religion along feminist lines, while the *revolutionaries*, in exodus, have rejected the Church for goddess religion. "Exile or exodus, we're still in the desert", she observed. "Whether we eventually go home or whether there *is* no home . . . is immaterial. The point for me is, what are we going to do *now*?"

Feminist religion "begins with experience", she said, and borrows from "paganism, Eastern religion, Native American traditions, black women's experiences" and the folk religions of Latin America and Africa. Weaver said they should feel equally free to borrow from Catholic spiritual traditions.

Her ultimatum enunciated the position of feminists who want spiritual experience but reject the limitations of reality. "We have come to say in unison: we cannot, we *will not*, return to patriarchal religion. In this wilderness of loneliness and desire, we can find . . . a divine being infinitely richer than anything imagined by the patriarchy . . . the deity as male and female, as god and goddess or gods and goddesses."

In almost pure form, Weaver expressed the underlying truth about feminist spirituality and other sects on today's scene. They are not attempts to *discover* the truth about a God who really exists but attempts to *invent* a deity with whom, in her words, "we could feel comfortable". Like the arguments for abortion as a good, they betray a conviction that there is no reality outside the self. Feminism becomes, precisely, idolatry, with the self as idol.

Weaver admitted the anomalous position of feminists who continue to claim membership in the Church. "If the pain of our exile, or our exodus, or whatever it is, makes it impossible to find *any* redeeming features in the Christian Tradition", she said, "let us turn to someplace else."

What she seems to want already exists in the tiny Liberal Catholic Church, a sect that originated in a split after Vatican I and survives in an ambiguous eclecticism combining traditional altars, candles and incense with theosophical occultism and what-have-you. Such spiritual adventures may indeed offer contact with the supernatural, though probably not with God. The shimmer on the horizon that Weaver takes for living water is a mirage concealing sand, dry bones and death.

A workshop on "creating contemplative communities" answered the question "What is a cloistered contemplative doing in Women-Church?" Carmelite Sister Mary Lavin, of Cleveland, said in a sweet voice that she had been happy in her cloister for fifteen years, until she began meeting with the "brave women" who eventually formed the Association of Contemplative Sisters (ACS), of which she had since become president. "We discovered . . . we needed each other to grow", she said. "Of course, Rome didn't like that too well." Since then, she had gotten over being "God oriented" and come to live "in the areas of mysticism and feminism". She credited Ruether with stimulating her new understanding that cloisters should be opened, as hers had been, so contemplative nuns can "bond" with laywomen in search of more "creative" prayer. "As we heard in that wonderful talk by Mary Jo Weaver", she said, we have to look into "all the traditions, all the cultures, because there is something in there for each one of us, and no one can legislate your way to pray. Listen to your own inner wisdom and trust that."

Fruit of Our Power

The ritual main event was a "feminist eucharist" consisting of the "consecration" of many breads and chalices as representations of the many women present. The prayers indicated that the consecrated elements became the body and blood of the participants. "This prayer is the consecration prayer of all our life in the woman body that we are", a celebrant intoned. "Take this bread. . . . Blessed are you, O Sacred One, Creator of bread and blood. . . . We have this wine to drink with honor and celebration. It is the fruit of our power. It is the blood of our life."

There were feminist songs. There was a litany that did not, I think, achieve the desired effect. The congregation chanted, in English and Spanish, "I am good. We are good. I am power. We are power. I am womb water. We are womb water." Wabun offered a blessing prayer to "the kin of the earth", the water spirit and the spirits of "the seven directions" (north, south, east, west, up, down and "the energy we breathe together"). It praised "the waters of the cosmos, of the earth we call mother, the water of our bodies and of our mothers' bodies". It failed as theater. There was a collection.

Articulate the Teaching

A frequently heard objection to the Pope's American visit was that the money spent should have been used for the poor. Yet participants in the Women-Church synod had paid from seventy-five to one hundred dollars for admission alone. It seemed hypocritical that community funds should be expended on sending active nuns to the Convergence while basic care for their elderly sisters remained a financial problem. Sister Nancy McMullen, a recently elected superior of the Precious Blood Sisters of Dayton, Ohio, and a high school religion teacher, said her expenses had been paid out of community education funds. She had also attended recent conferences of Network and LCWR but had skipped the Ohio Catholic Education Association conference to come to Women-Church. "It has been a delightful experience," she said, important to her as a teacher, "but especially as a woman." Schneiders' talk had "answered important questions" for her. "I have been enriched with the spirit of the group."

One of the few men present was Father Robert Nugent, co-founder of New Ways Ministry, one of many dubious offshoots from Quixote Center. Nugent said sadly that he has ministered to homosexuals for fifteen years, yet his organization "has been rejected in some dioceses". His most recent rejection had come when Archbishop McCarrick told him he could no longer work in the Newark archdiocese. Earlier, he said, he and co-founder Sister Jeannine Gramick had been dismissed from the archdiocese of Washington, D.C., by Archbishop James Hickey.

Where would he go next? "I don't know", he said. "That's one reason I came here—looking for connections. I feel called to articulate the teaching of the Church in my writing and in my workshops." Nugent said he had never been charged with unorthodoxy and had a supporting letter from Bishop Thomas Costello of Syracuse.

Why doesn't Father John Harvey have similar problems with the hierarchy? Harvey is the founder of Courage, an organization that supports homosexuals in celibate living with the help of the sacraments.

"Father Harvey has the support of Cardinal O'Connor, I suspect basically because he permits no discussion. He's not gay positive. He thinks it's a sickness." Nugent disagrees; he views homosexuality "not as a psychological or emotional sickness but as an orientation. Gays do not see their orientation as abnormal. If the Church had more willingness to dialogue", he said, "I think the Church has a lot to say to gays about freedom. Gay liberation in some instances does not lead to liberation."

No Pious Do-Gooders

Mary Hunt was not apologizing when she proclaimed to the final session, "We have shown this weekend that religious feminists are *not* pious do-gooders, genuflecting in the face of oppression. We are committed agents for social change!"

"The future of Women-Church rests with our children", said Hunt.

> The education of our children is now a serious and important priority for us. . . . When the Pope was here recently, the most frightening part of his otherwise stock-in-trade message was that Catholic schools should be kept pure of the likes of most of us. . . . It signals to me the need to create . . . centers, schools, think tanks, retreat centers, theological centers where feminist approaches will be normative. I believe it is the students of those schools . . . who will be at our conference in 2037.

Hunt's warning of intent to build tomorrow's Women-Church on today's children should be taken seriously. Gloria Steinem was right when she said, "Women-Church *is* the women's movement." Feminism is cooling in secular society. If Women-Church is to survive beyond the present generation, it must have new members. But like Hunt, a childless lesbian, most of these feminists have no children. It is other people's children they seek.

Their operatives are already in place in Catholic institutions everywhere. Most of the women who attended this conference are even now teaching in Catholic schools, working in diocesan offices, chancery offices, parishes, retreat centers and youth programs, where feminism is often the dominant force. Unless Church authorities take action, the subversion can continue without any need for separate establishments. If, however, feminists lose their official positions, they will lose access to the young and thus most of their destructive power.

The time is late for American bishops to stop trying to appease these unappeasable revolutionaries. Nothing short of the extinction of the Church could placate them. Their hatred and contempt for her, and for the bishops, is open. In Cincinnati, no one bothered to make the usual protestations of "love for the Church".

Many speakers expressed a sense that their day in the Church is ending; they foresaw the loss of posts where subversion had been comfortable and easy. Schussler Fiorenza pouted, "*They* can say I'm not a Catholic theologian, but it depends on the women who listen to me." Sister Mary Luke Tobin talked of the "rising tide of neo-orthodoxy" making revolution more difficult. At the Synod in Rome, the world's bishops dismissed proposals by feminist sympathizers to move one step further toward institutionalizing minor liturgical roles for women. Even the *National Catholic Reporter* reflected the judgment that the radical era is ending. "The pope didn't budge. . . . Catholicism American-style is headed for rocky times", Marjorie Hyer wrote there on October 2. "Vatican II Catholics in America may have to confront anew the implications of the question . . . 'Why don't they leave?'" The same edition reported the impending departures from USCC of influential "progressives" Father Bryan Hehir, Monsignor Daniel Hoye and Ronald Kreitmeyer; those departures were lamented at the Convergence. Reform was in the wind. But it will not come from bishops whose right hands indulge the contradictory doings of the left hand.

To understand why, it is unnecessary to look further than Cincinnati, where Archbishop Pilarczyk had warned against Women-Church the previous August, in an unequivocal communication:

> In October, the second national "Women-Church" conference will take place in Cincinnati. . . . It features some speakers who are notoriously opposed to the teaching of the Catholic Church, and includes feminist "liturgy" and feminist "eucharist." Please be aware that this conference is not being held with Church sponsorship and is in no way whatsoever under the auspices of the Archdiocese of Cincinnati.

Word of his position failed to penetrate the archdiocesan apparat, however. In September, Family Life Director Dan Roche wrote in the archdiocesan Family Life and Education *Newsletter*, "We are looking forward to . . . the national convention on women-church convergence to be held also in October." It would, he said, "undoubtedly raise issues about change in families and the church". The same edition offered detailed information about speakers and registration fees.

In its post-Convergence October 16 issue, the official *Catholic Telegraph* ran sixty column inches of adulatory reporting on the meeting, including a five-column story about Ruth Steinert, the local Women-Church founder who was also council president at St. Robert Bellarmine parish. One photograph showed three picketers outside the convention hall, with banners reading "Women-Church is pro-abortion", "Women-Church is devil worship" and "Abortion: the ultimate child abuse". The newspaper failed to identify the protesters. Perhaps they were angels.

As the conference opened, Steinert and Ruth Fitzpatrick had appeared on National Public Radio in a joint interview with Father Dan Conlon, archdiocesan chancellor. What did they talk about? According to Ray George, archdiocesan communications director, "He welcomed them to Cincinnati. And it was a very nice little interview." How did that fit with the archbishop's cautionary statement? "Ah", said George. "The archbishop is aware of it. He had no problem with it."

"Our biggest concern", George confided, "was the possibility of a very serious confrontation between Catholics United for the Faith and some of the delegates. . . . I could just see some very pro-life people getting involved, as well as CUF, and, you know, we didn't want any of *that*." In fact, he said, "we *prayed* that would not happen. Because, you know, we were concerned about any kind of—of confrontation that would blacken the eye of the city. Or of the Church."

Did he think the conference itself had "blackened the eye" of city or Church? "Not at all. Not at all", George said. "Why, they dealt with issues that are very *real*."

Feminist infestation, recalcitrant adjutants and a reluctance to stir controversy have been among the major causes of disorder in the Church these past decades. Pastoral concern for the women involved may be another factor. But pastoral responsibility extends to the rest of the flock as well. A generation of Catholic children —and many of their parents—have been left ignorant of their Faith and confused if not converted by ceaseless exposure to the catechism of secular liberalism and eviscerated theology in Catholic colleges, parochial schools, religious education programs and pastoral ministries of all kinds.

Mary Jo Weaver offered the best advice of the Women-Church weekend when she said, "For heaven's sake, let us turn to someplace else." A few years in the desert might lead some of them to remember and long for home. Or they might remain obdurate. In either case, it would be real love, tough love, love that respects both their autonomy and the souls of the little ones to tell them they cannot continue as they are, enemy agents within the Church. That is what shepherds are for.

The Future of the American Church?

Rendered overconfident by the unexpected turnout at its 1986 feminist event, Time Consultants moved its second annual Women in the Church conference to the larger Washington Hilton Hotel and increased the number of workshop sessions by 40 percent. Again, most of the women present were nuns. This time there were three bishops among the speakers: Kenneth Untener, the ordinary of Saginaw, Michigan (who confessed, "I'm a member of a sexist Church"); Auxiliary P. Francis Murphy of Baltimore (who described his conversion to feminism); and Joseph Faber MacDonald of Grand Falls, Newfoundland, spiritual director for the Catholic Women's League of Canada, an organization that parallels the National Council of Catholic Women in the United States. Militant Canadian Catholic feminism was further represented by Jean Forest, former chancellor of the University of Alberta and a member of the Canadian Bishops' Committee on the Role of Women in the Church, and by Mary Malone, formerly Mother St. Bernard, now a lay professor of religious studies (University of St. Jerome) and of Church history and catechetics (St. Augustine's Seminary and Toronto School of Theology), who was a driving force behind the Canadian bishop's "Green Kit". Sister Carolyn Osiek, R.S.C.J., professor of New Testament Studies at Chicago's Catholic Theological Union, associate editor of *Catholic Biblical Quarterly* and *The Bible Today* and the author of *Beyond Anger: On Being a Feminist in the Church*, said monotheism "becomes bad news" when you have to decide "whether to have a male or a female God".[42] Loretta Jancoski, then a visiting scholar at the University of Notre Dame and an authority on training catechists, predicted that Catholic women who "defend the traditional male values . . . which patriarchy has been fine-tuning for two thousand years" will never be able "to take the Church anywhere. . . . We are *never* going back to pre-Vatican II hierarchy, complacency and comfort."[43] When Sister Sandra Schneiders said the American "spirituality of liberation" is "incompatible with the spirituality of those who presently hold power in the Church", her disapproval was directed at the Vatican.[44] Other speakers included Sister Mariella

[42] Hays, "Split?"

[43] Ibid.

[44] Ibid.

Frye, M.H.S.H., staff assistant to the NCCB women's pastoral committee, and several dissenting former priests, the most prominent of them Bernard Cooke, professor of systematic theology at Holy Cross College, and Thomas Groome, professor of theology and religious education at Boston College.

Nevertheless, Women-Church zealots saw too much compromise. Attendance at the 1987 Women in the Church conference dropped to only 1,250, half as many participants as the previous year. One reason, no doubt, was the timing, just three weeks after Women-Church converged in Cincinnati. The Convergence group was further antagonized because abortion and homosexuality were not openly advocated at Time Consultants' conferences, as they are at Women-Church events. Sister Donna Quinn told a reporter, "The sadness I have is that they aren't doing anything" on those issues. "It would be really helpful if in their plans they'd invite more of us who've done Women-Church to participate."

The dispute apparently ended in agreement that there was turf enough in the revolution for both divisions of the rebel army. By 1988, the "annual" Women in the Church conferences had become annual "Future of the American Church" conferences. As Donna Quinn had advised, a larger contingent of Women-Church members were on the speakers' list: along with Mary Jo Weaver, there were Rosemary Ruether, Ruth Fitzpatrick of WOC and the outspoken Sister Theresa Kane, R.S.M. Among the male speakers were dissident theologian Charles Curran and two ex-priests involved in CORPUS, Frank Bonnike, former president of the National Federation of Priests' Councils, and Anthony Padovano, professor of religious studies at New Jersey's Ramapo College.

At Time Consultants' 1990 conference the keynote speaker was Milwaukee's controversial Archbishop Rembert Weakland, O.S.B. Other "major speakers" included Rosemary Ruether, Sister Mary Luke Tobin and Father Lucien Deiss, C.S.S.P. In supporting roles, speakers were sociologist Dean Hoge (on the priest shortage); Patricia Mische ("Ministering to an Endangered Planet"); Sister Maria Riley, O.P. ("Women in the '90s"); Sister

Mary Daniel Turner, S.N.D. ("Religious Life"); and a host of "theologians and academic leaders".

In the competition for control of Catholic feminism, Women-Church has clearly been the victor, maintaining ideological leadership of the movement. Time Consultants has apparently settled for a market fair concession that permits it to recruit and indoctrinate mutineers of both sexes under a new label. The real losers were American Roman Catholics. Evidently, concern for appearances is no longer necessary. No one seems to fear the taint of radicalism anymore: not the feminist constituency, still undiversified, not the theologians of the liberal consensus, not the cooperating religious bureaucrats and educators, not even the bishops. Or the archbishops.

The only natural comfort to be found in the face of that realization is that the rebels are growing older, and their ranks are not being replenished. There is supernatural comfort in Christ's assurance that the gates of hell will not finally prevail. But for the present, much of the American Catholic Church is occupied by enemy forces.

Chapter Four

The Journey Within

Proverbially, the late decades of a century are marked by strange currents of thought. As the dark twentieth century moves toward its close, the distinguishing characteristic of religious thought is self-absorption. Among America's educated elites, including Catholic elites, religion is now understood as a symbol for personal opinion, faith as a metaphor for imagination, mysticism as altered consciousness however achieved: meditation on the self, sensory deprivation, hallucinatory drugs, vigorous exercise or standing on one's head. The religious impulse is turned away from the transcendent Creator to center on subjective consciousness as the source of spiritual truth, the principle of moral judgment, the object of veneration and service and the explanation for the persistence of traditional belief among the simple peasantry. Every man is his own god, every woman her own goddess. Little interest is shown in questions of ontological truth; many believe there is no truth, and the rest behave as though they agree. Accordingly, individual feelings outweigh intellectual and moral criteria, and it is to emotion rather than objective truth that public debate is directed.

On that landscape, within the province of the modernist theological scholarship that defines religion as a psychological phenomenon, implicitly gnostic religious feminism overlaps an explicitly gnostic New Age movement. That broadly fashionable form of spiritualism displays, in textbook purity, the gnostic characteristics of despair with present society, the search for enlightenment within and the vision of a transformed global order, including a new world religion of naturally altered consciousness. Flourishing at a cultural point where superstition, pop-psychology and scientific speculation intersect, the New Age movement is a manifestation of the same revolutionary rejection of monotheism and Christianity found in goddess feminism. Indeed, its ingredients, including spiritualism, fanatic environmentalism, zeal for abortion, sexual permissiveness and leftist politics, are almost entirely interchangeable with that phenomenon.

Embracing the Asp and the Basilisk

All the strands of the Catholic collapse—the repudiation of doctrine, the flight from gender as incarnational reality, from hierarchy in society, in the Church, in creation and in the supernatural order, to feminism, revolutionary ideology, sexual libertinism and spiritualism in its goddess-Wicca and New Age manifestations—can be examined, entwined, at the Grail, a once-vital Catholic women's apostolate with American headquarters in suburban Cincinnati, Ohio.

It was here, at a 1972 conference, that feminist theologian Judith Plaskow and her committee invented the "myth" called "the Coming of Lilith", described earlier in chapter two. At a 1974 "conscientization" meeting of the International Grail, held in Toronto, the United States Grail Team reported:

> We recognized that, to achieve real socialism, change in the economic spheres would not be enough, but that new social, political, cultural and religious values and institutions would be necessary. . . . We recognize that the use of words like "Marxism" and "Socialism," etc., present a problem in some countries. . . . We recommend that the work group set up acceptable forms of communication with these countries.[1]

In a final report on the meeting, International Grail leaders wrote:

[1] U.S. Grail Team, "A Context for the Conscientization Report", *Conscientization Issue Meeting Report*, Toronto meeting, July 27–Aug. 4, 1974, 35, 38.

> We agree that capitalism is the root of the problem of our world. Therefore we affirm the need for a new socialist society. . . . A. Socialized means of production . . . B. without classes . . . C. for new structures and new type of government . . . D. the creation of new man/woman . . . [and] new forms of the church. . . . To achieve our goal, [we need] a common strategy which recognizes "potential groups for change": 1. . . . marginalized people; 2. women . . . 4. Christian groups with . . . a political option for Socialism; . . . 6. Political groups organized toward socialism.[2]

A major 1982 Grail conference, called "Women's Spirit Bonding", was considered so significant to the development of religious feminism that the proceedings were published in their entirety.[3] Among those participating were movement stars like Judith Plaskow, Mary Hunt, Diann Neu, Carol Christ, Elisabeth Schussler Fiorenza, Sister Carol Coston, O.P.,[4] Ada Maria Isasi-Diaz, Rosemary Ruether and Starhawk. But the most remarkable paper presented—perhaps the most remarkable address in the entire history of the Catholic feminist movement—was "Why Women Need the War God", by religious sociologist Karen McCarthy Brown, who explained her "marriage" in an "ecstatic" ritual of "trance and possession" to the Yoruba voodoo god Oguo. "It can be dangerous to attribute only goodness and light to the realm of the spirit", she said, with unarguable accuracy. Other contributions ranged from the merely heretical to a nightly "series of Wicca rituals", facilitated by Starhawk and described as "an important experience", part of "the recovery of a lost heritage" for many conferees. At a 1984 Grail conference, a young woman who grew up a few doors from my home learned the witchcraft rituals she has since been teaching in and around St. Cloud, Minnesota.

[2] International Grail teams, councils and representatives, *Conscientization Issue Meeting Report*, Toronto, Canada, July 27–Aug. 4, 1974, 31–32.

[3] Janet Kalven and Mary Buckley, eds., *Women's Spirit Bonding* (New York: Pilgrim Press, 1984).

[4] Sister Carol Coston is an Adrian Dominican, the founder and original director of the "social justice" lobby Network.

Under the direction of Grail member Joyce Dietrick, a "certified psychosynthesis guide and trainer", psychosynthesis training workshops have been a staple at Grailville for some years. Psychosynthesis is a variety of New Age psychology, "based on the understanding that individuals and humanity are evolving toward greater wholeness and that we can learn to manage our growth in a conscious, holistic way", through "guided imagery" and "other creative processes", a program brochure explains. It was devised by the late Italian psychologist Roberto Assagioli, sometime associate of theosophist Alice Bailey and her Arcane School, and represents "a link between Theosophy and the human potential movement", says a historian of the theosophical movement.[5] Headquartered at Meditation Mount in Ojai, California, Assagioli's organization is "The Meditation Group for the New Age". In 1987, psychosynthesis programs were on the Grailville schedules for February, March, April, October and December.

"Buddhist scholar" Joanna Rogers Macy, a contributing editor for Matthew Fox's magazine *Creation*, conducted a conference at Grailville in September 1986 to "explore the intersection of personal and spiritual growth with social justice or peace concerns" through "guided meditation, body movement and small-group sharing". "The Gaia-hypothesis and the Council of All Beings ritual" were "a central focus" of the event.

Rosemary Ruether led a conference there on "building Women-Church" in November 1986. Another popular "retreat leader" has been Rev. Carol Parrish-Harra, identified by New Age journalist Ruth Montgomery as a "walk-in", a spiritual entity living—by invitation—in a "host body".[6] In a more mundane view, Parrish-Harra is the formerly Catholic mother of ten who, since the arrival of her "walk-in" personality, has divorced, remarried and founded a New Age church and community in Sparrow Hawk Village, Oklahoma, where she teaches "new spirituality".

[5] Bruce Campbell, *Ancient Wisdom Revived* (Berkeley: University of California Press, 1980), 155.

[6] *Cincinnati Inquirer*, Oct. 3, 1983.

The 1986 conference year at Grailville began and ended with programs on liberation theology. On January 10, "the roots of liberation theology" were outlined by Christine Gudorf, who "studied under Peruvian theologian Gustavo Gutierrez". Gudorf, an associate professor of theology at Cincinnati's Xavier University, also addressed the 1987 Women-Church Convergence. In late December 1986, at a conference titled "Making Global Connections", Elisabeth Schussler Fiorenza provided opportunity for conferees to "strategize together on ways to transform oppressive structures".

Some twenty-eight Grail members signed the *New York Times* advertisement of March 2, 1986, asserting the right of Catholics to support abortion. Among the signatories were the first American members of the Grail, Mary Louise Tully, Janet Kalven and Mary Catherine Leahy, as well as longtime member Frances Kern Crotty, parenting educator at Catholic Social Services Bureau, Covington, Kentucky. Kalven, veteran Grail member Mary Buckley and Dr. Mary Jo Weaver were on the committee that coordinated the advertising project.

Yoruba voodoo priestess Luisah Teish conducted a Grailville conference called "The Ancestral Journey" in mid-March 1987. During the meeting, she urged participants to open themselves to the energies of their ancestors and the earth, through "ritual, dance and visualization". Her program was co-sponsored by the Grail-affiliated Women's Institute on Religion and Society and, appropriately, the Crazy Ladies' Bookstore. Ms. Teish is Starhawk's colleague on the faculty of Matthew Fox's Institute for Culture and Creation Spirituality.

All those activities notwithstanding, the Grail was one of the Catholic women's organizations permitted to testify before the committee of bishops responsible for writing *Partners in the Mystery of Redemption*, the 1988 NCCB letter on women's concerns. When I asked Janet Kalven, the longtime leader, whether the Grail is still officially Catholic, she chuckled and made a Sign of the Cross. "Oh, yes, we're still in the Catholic Directory", she replied. But, she said,

It's a convenience, mainly, for the IRS. Of course it can't go on forever. In today's climate, it's just a matter of time. Especially with all the crazy things coming out of the Vatican, it's only going to get worse. The University of Dayton had Rosemary Ruether to speak last fall, and some of these people from CUF [Catholics United for the Faith] and Jericho—that's the far right—went all the way over from Cincinnati to protest! They said a Catholic institution had no business having her as a speaker because she's pro-choice! And she wasn't even speaking about that, and she isn't even identified—well, a little—on the pro-choice issue! So with *that* kind of mentality around . . .

Last Stage

Late in March of 1987, I went to Grailville for Mary Jo Weaver's weekend conference, titled, like Time Consultants' conference the previous fall, "Women in the Church". Daffodils were out along the farm fences, and violets bloomed in beds beside the buildings, but if spring was in the air, it was not in the atmosphere. The forty-five participants, like the buildings themselves, seemed worn and dispirited.

The conference was not about Wiccan or New Age practices. Neither was it a rerun of Weaver's address at Time Consultants' Conference of the same name. Instead, it was an effort toward the "last stage" in the construction of the New Faith: the presentation of process theology as an intellectually defensible doctrinal base for the new feminist religion. Thus, though it involved no spell casting, the conference served the purposes of Wicca's immanent goddess, gnostic feminist spirituality and New Age monism.

Weaver sounded genuinely wistful, lonely and disoriented, like a runaway child too stubborn to come home; those echoes outweighed even outrageousness in her remarks. She was also more detached about what she asserted, more willing to concede some elements of blamelessness and even beauty to organized religion, less strident and absolute in her condemnation of the Church, than the standard feminist theologian of my experience. She is the only one for whom ideas about God, however mistaken, seemed to be of intrinsic interest rather than merely an occasion for excoriating Catholicism. She is gravely wrong, and her comparative restraint —which was not well-received by her audience—may have been strategically motivated. But she was humanly likeable, and there was pathos in her hunger for the God she will not serve.

"That old God—the 'neurotic father' of Christianity—does not work for me, and I gather it doesn't work for a lot of you either", Weaver said. "We *cannot* return to the security of the past, but we cannot always go forward with confidence, and we are sometimes bitter with the bleak present. Religious alternatives are not clear or are not congenial, and, as Roman Catholics, our own Tradition is killing us."

The new God she offered "isn't God the Father but is this different, more nuanced, process, 'suffering with', God", whom she sees as "related to the biblical personal God" in Isaiah's presentation of God as comforter. "The water images are pure and tender." These symbols were used later, by Christians, as messianic texts about Jesus, she said, "but the Jews saw something else in them. Wandering in the desert, the Jews found exodus harder than slavery, the wilderness harsh, the people contentious", resentful that they had been taken from Egypt, where there was plenty of food and drink. Isaiah, Weaver said, "introduced tenderness, a God who suffers with his people and responds".

Christian feminists are also "in exodus from patriarchy", and in order to believe that "God is leading them to a new place, when the wilderness experience grows too oppressive", they too are using exodus to "make something different". Summing up feminist complaints against Catholicism, Weaver said they find "liturgy oppressive and deeply painful", dominated as it is by an "insensitive and hostile priest". They experience "alienation" because, "before the women's movement, everything was written by celibate males" who offered only two visions for women: "either the Virgin Mary or the temptress Eve". Women still working in parishes "feel invisible and trivialized". They are "oppressed, tired, not nourished, enslaved, in bondage to the whims of their pastors, dependent on the bishop" for "the quality of priests". They are powerless, their "identity decreed for them", forced to endure "sexist language" and the attitude that women are "ritually unclean". And all these torments are "fobbed off on us as 'God's will'", Weaver said. "Why? Because God creates women as inferiors, to be complementary to men?" The question for the future is not whether the middle-aged will stay in the Church but whether "your daughters can accept life in this land of the pharaohs". Yet women rebels in parishes "find little support from other women", she admitted. "Feminists may have moved on, and others may resist." Thus rebels still in the Church are "both fueled by and drained by their anger, lonely and tired".

However, life is not satisfactory for those who have left the Church, either. They still "desire transcendence, ritual and prayer. Many are involved in goddess worship, a rich source of new religious experience", Weaver continued. Others have become part of "Women-Church, in exile from patriarchy" and unwanted in the patriarchal Church, especially since they have taken to celebrating their own eucharists, she said. "They are genuinely open to insights from the goddess movement, but open to the rich traditions of the Church, too. Abandoning patriarchy is not leaving the Church."

Battle for Supremacy

Feminist grievances against the Church are largely baffling, including as they do much that is exaggerated and much that is simply life, in the Church or out of it. Many orthodox Catholics could repeat without alteration Weaver's phrase about liturgy, for example. As the twenty-five otherwise varied interviews in Peter Occhiogrosso's *Once a Catholic*[7] indicate, it has apparently been adapted until it pleases no one. But Weaver's routine list of grievances seems inadequate to explain feminist rage and hatred. Why do such feminists always interpret cautions against sexual sins

[7] Peter Occhiogrosso, *Once a Catholic* (New York: Ballantine Books, 1987).

as a condemnation of women? Why not as concern about male weakness? Or as gender-neutral cautions against lust? A clue to some of the sources of their anger may be their non-negotiable agenda items of "freedom of choice" for abortion and homosexuality.[8] Novelist Mary Gordon, a director of Catholics for a Free Choice and a Women-Church Convergence speaker, told Occhiogrosso, "Most of the people I know who left the Church left it because of sex." Only "inferior people" will "knuckle under sexually", she said.[9] There seems to be a good deal of self-justification at the roots of the religious revolution. Unappeased by civil legality, revolutionaries crave religious endorsement of those activities as positive goods.

Two religious paradigms are "engaged in a battle for supremacy today", Weaver said. "The pre-Vatican II paradigm was monarchical and patriarchal. The old paradigm supported the old God, controlling, immutable, almighty, omniscient, predicated on absolute truth. The role of the theologian was to interpret and translate truth. All their ducks were in a row." The post-Vatican II tradition began in the eighteenth century and is "an ecumenical paradigm" acceptable to feminists. Its "process God" is not absolute, "not a static given", not all-knowing, "but involved, suffering and rejoicing with his people". Feminist theologians, Women-Church, "the reform-minded and those who have abandoned the Church are all looking for new sources of spiritual nourishment. Some are searching for the passionate, creation-centered goddess. All are seeking new relations to the divine, new rules of conduct. Feminist spirituality is a wilderness search", she said. "We sift the history of witchcraft and goddess religion, tarot, the new physics, Eastern and American Indian religion, looking for spirituality, for a divine being who respects our identity. If our system gains support, the walls of the old paradigm collapse."

[8] See Janet Kalven, "Epilogue", in Kalven and Buckley, *Women's Spirit Bonding*, 371.

[9] Occhiogrosso, interview with Mary Gordon, "The Irish Catholic Church", in Occhiogrosso, *Once a Catholic*, 84.

Process theology, as developed by British mathematician Alfred North Whitehead after he came to teach at Harvard in 1924, holds that God and the universe are not separable but exist only in each other, inter-connected, both eternal, both continually changed and modified by experience. God, in that view, is incomprehensible except in relationship with the universe, because, in Weaver's words, "He is the structure that makes the world possible, but he needs creation; that primordial nature needs fulfillment and relationships in order to be real." Process theology "asks us to give up absolutes. Everything is relative, even the deity. . . . We must let go of God, believing that God lets go of everything all the time, that it may all be new all the time." Whitehead held that God is not omnipotent, Weaver explained; he cannot coerce, only persuade. Jesus is "the embodiment of true religion, who sets forth no metaphysical systems". She said she is a "closet Carmelite", moved by the "loving, luring God" she finds in process theology, some parts of Scripture, and in mystics like Teresa of Avila. To a question about where Jesus fits into the process scheme, she answered, "I just haven't done any work on that. I don't do theodicy, christology or ethics. It's outside my competence." She admitted that her sources of information about process theology were limited to "only essays—not whole books—and some conversations with people more expert on the subject."

"Tell us how to get in touch with your primordial being", one conference participant asked her.

"I can't", Weaver replied. "You'll have to do your own. I don't even ask whether it's true or false but just whether it expresses experiences I've had."

Since the universe "is not made up of stuff" but of energy and process ("we are energy, not things"), "perfection resides in movement", and anything that adds to the process is creativity. "More experience contributes more to the process." In process theology, she said, there is "no need to control—self, body or women. It's hard to imagine it growing out of a sexist society. The utopian possibilities of process theology have been finding resonances in the feminist theological vision."

Because it holds that all experience contributes to the enrichment of process reality, this theology could make a virtue of any action anyone might choose to regard as self-actualizing: revolution, certainly, or divorce, abortion, lesbianism, witchcraft, voodoo demon marriages or any of the other desperate acts taking place in the tragic, perilous, self-inflicted feminist wilderness exile. Utopianism, lacking an absolute measure for selfishness and perversity, tends to decay quickly. In process theology, God's Kingdom *is* of this world, and since its residents create themselves, they *become* God.

Absolute Future

Process theology did not spring full blown from Whitehead's brow; it is a form of pantheistic gnosticism. The assumption that God exists *only* within his creation, said C. S. Lewis, is "certainly congenial to the modern mind . . . not because it is the final stage in a slow process of enlightenment, but because it is almost as old as we are. It may be the most primitive of all religions . . . the attitude into which the human mind automatically falls when left to itself."[10]

Contemporary process theology differs from ancient forms of pantheism in being anti-Christian. Its most basic belief is that nothing in the universe has a permanent nature; everything, including its limited, contingent, immanent creative force, is eternally becoming. "A theology founded on evolution rather than on the existence of a transcendent God and salvation by Christ necessarily implies a rejection of the Christian faith", Edwin C. Garvey wrote in *Process Theology and Secularization*.[11] Father Garvey sees process theology as a rejection of the possibility of knowing objective truth. He traces its progress from the first half of the seventeenth century, when René Descartes held that man can know

[10] C. S. Lewis, *Miracles* (New York: MacMillan, 1947), 84f.

[11] Edwin C. Garvey, C.S.B., *Process Theology and Secularization* (Houston, Tex., Lumen Christi Press, 1972), 1.

only his own ideas of reality, not objective reality, through Benedict de Spinoza, the late-seventeenth-century philosopher who taught that "God is not a transcendent being with an intellect or will; rather God is everything". Man is an aspect of that one divine substance, and "man's knowledge is God or Reality or the Ground of Being becoming aware of itself".[12] In the nineteenth century, Georg Hegel kept Spinoza's pantheistic God, but "in a more emphatic way Hegel's God is constantly evolving". There can be no supernatural revelation because there is no transcendent God. This world is all there is, and "revelation" means man's becoming aware of "the never finished manifestation of reality in its ongoing process". Man's consciousness gives meaning to reality, and man creates the future of God. "Theology becomes a theology of temporal hope, of what is sometimes called a theology of the Absolute Future."[13]

The theology of the liberal consensus also implies or at least allows for such a belief, by assuming that unless the object of faith can be empirically proven, it must be assumed to have originated in the purely natural, i.e., in human psychology. Similar notions have been an undermining influence in Catholic catechetics over the past twenty-five years, partly due to the influence of Pierre Teilhard de Chardin, S.J., whose ideas of a materially and spiritually evolving universe, the Cosmic Christ and the Omega Point, gained immense popularity among religious professionals. Of the devastating results, Garvey wrote, "Catechists who follow process theology can teach adaptation to a changing world, and that is all. They may fall back on the claim that they can teach attitudes and fraternal love, but what is love divorced from truth but a sentimental Rousseauian humanitarianism? With love uprooted from truth, there is, in fact, no doctrine to teach."[14] Nothing is absolute; nothing is permanent; nothing is superior to the world. Since in this theology man is the highest achievement of the evolutionary process, Garvey says, "Psychology becomes the highest

[12] Ibid., 7.
[13] Ibid., 8.
[14] Ibid., 22.

science, the new theology."[15] Jesus is not God incarnate, except as all men are manifestations of the cosmic dynamism; he is merely an example of humanity at its evolutionary best.

Philosopher Marcus Berquist, a tutor at Thomas Aquinas College in California, told me "The view that there is no transcendent, no truth beyond this world, that reality *is* evolution, that there is no distinction between the natural and the supernatural, is an essential component of Marxism. It is the theoretical basis for liberation theology, which is why liberation theology gets so entangled in Marxism."

The process view also provides a convenient theoretical base for all the other current gnostic variants, from feminist theology through the muddled thought of Matthew Fox to secular New Age enthusiasms, which see individual intuition as the source of "individual" truth. Though most rank-and-file Women-Church followers probably learn it by osmosis rather than as explicit theory, the appeal to process theology is increasingly common among feminist theologians, who classify their specialty as a variety of liberation theology.

The Grailville conference was the second time within weeks that I had heard process theology proposed as the Truth in a purportedly Catholic setting. The first time, Sister Rosina Schmitt, O.S.B., a tenured professor of theology at St. Benedict's College in Minnesota, was speaking as part of the college's lecture series "Images of God for a New Age". Having become a "Whiteheadian" while taking a course on his work, Sister Rosina was, with perfect logic, on her way out of the Benedictine order, but as plain Rosalyn Schmitt, she continues teaching in the college theology department.

Since then, process theology has been ever more commonly proposed as the theological system appropriate for the feminist New Faith that Sister Madonna Kolbenschlag predicts in *Kiss Sleeping Beauty Goodbye.*[16] The "God-who-is-coming-to-be" of

[15] Ibid., 19.

[16] See references in chap. 2, above.

whom she speaks there is a process God. More recently, in *Lost in the Land of Oz*, Kolbenschlag depicts God as Gaia, "the Great Mother", but even at that reach of fantasy, she describes a process vision of "a self-conscious universe realizing itself to be whole and interconnected, in which knower and known are one".[17]

Less exotically and with a flood of scholarly attributions, Sister Anne Carr, B.V.M., a theologian at the University of Chicago Divinity School, recommends process theology as a way for feminists to understand God and remain in the Church. "To envision God as future, as ahead, rather than above and against the human and natural world, is a reorientation that helps women to see the feminist dilemma in the church as a temporary one", Carr writes in *Transforming Grace*.[18] Whitehead, she says, expresses a "deeply biblical understanding" of God.[19] Approvingly, she quotes process theologian Wolfhart Pannenberg, who sees a denial of human freedom in the old notion of God as "an almighty and omniscient being thought of as existing at the beginning of all temporal processes".[20] Protestant theologian Paul Tillich shows her how religious symbols "are borne out of the collective unconscious" and "die when the situation in which they were created has passed". Feminist theology, Carr says, "exposes the idolatry that occurs when symbols" such as "God and Christ" are "elevated to unconditional significance".[21] Edward Schillebeeckx "holds that the new culture of a 'self-made world' recognizes the primacy of

[17] Kolbenschlag, *Oz*, 186.

[18] Anne E. Carr, *Transforming Grace: Christian Tradition and Women's Experience* (San Francisco: Harper & Row, 1988), 152–56. The grace to which the title refers is not divine grace but "Christian feminism and the spiritual vision it entails". It is interesting to note that, in her acknowledgments, Carr thanks Mary Jo Weaver, as well as Justus George Lawler, another member of the CFFC "Catholic Committee on Pluralism and Abortion" that coordinated the notorious *New York Times* abortion ads. The book is dedicated to Sister Marjorie Tuite, O.P., who, like Carr, signed the offending ad.

[19] Ibid., 152.

[20] Ibid., 154.

[21] Ibid., 101–2.

the future. . . . God is 'the One who is to come' ".[22] Karl Rahner, Carr reports, thinks "of Christianity as the religion of the *absolute* future, that 'absolute future is . . . another name for what is really meant by God' ".[23] Such concepts, according to Carr, "fit the experience of contemporary women who struggle toward a future that still remains promise and hope".[24]

Ambivalence

To judge from the women gathered at Grailville, the exodus from Catholic Faith to radical feminism and process theology has not soothed the prevailing rage or brought happiness to most of the wanderers. Revolutionary theology, occult spirituality and variants of theosophy are growing like jungle vines in the American Church. But in this center where they sprouted early, they have produced a general blight: a withered little company of bitter women in a dying organization.

Dr. Weaver seemed untypically ambivalent in her rejection of the faith. At one point she read aloud, with obvious affection, the passage from Dante's *Divine Comedy* describing the Beatific Vision. Dante, she said, had been very advanced in showing all creation existing within God, though he was of course "too medieval" to show *God* as existing in the universe. The audience listened in chill silence, though they laughed and applauded whenever the Church was criticized.

There were other indications of Weaver's mixed feelings. One woman groaned that Protestant traditions can be as "enslaving" as Catholic; her own included "revivalism".

"But I see a certain beauty in all these things", Weaver responded. "I guess my attitude comes from my family. I have an uncle who follows the statue of the Pilgrim Virgin around, a brother who thinks Vatican II should never have happened, a sister who follows the goddess. And I teach Christianity." She said

[22] Ibid., 155.
[23] Ibid., 155.
[24] Ibid., 155f.

she is no longer formally associated with the Church, but "I'm getting increasing respect for those trying to hold out for the Tridentine, pre-conciliar model. I'd even say I think that shouldn't disappear, but of course, it's exclusive and allows no room for abortion or for lesbianism. It just doesn't fit with my experience. But there never was a golden age when we had it all right."

On the subject of sexual roles, Weaver admitted that "male dominance seems to be universal. Male hatred and fear of women seem to be universal." The attitude, she said, can even be seen in nineteenth-century medicine: graham crackers and corn flakes were intended, like saltpeter, to diminish the sexual impulse. "Don't think the Church is the only nutso thing . . . that the rest of the world was perfectly lusty until Augustine came along."

The single most surprising part of Weaver's presentation was her astringent rejection of some central tenets of feminist theology. She declined "sisterhood" with other women and said she "does not agree" that women are naturally superior to men. Nor does she accept the view that feminists are either prophets ("Prophets do not choose themselves; they are the smelly, dirty little people who keep shouting out unwelcome truths and get killed for it") or that they are an unparalleled transforming force, as "subversives", in the Church. The Church, she said, has encountered worse challengers and survived. "And I don't agree that when we sit around talking at meetings like this we're 'doing theology'. I don't think women's experience is divine revelation. Maybe, maybe not. Perhaps the experience of the suffering in the Third World is revelation, or the Buddhist-Christian dialogue."

What, I asked her, does she believe determines whether something is in fact divine revelation?

"Time and content", she said. "For example, the people who believe in Fatima consider it revelation. What is the content of the message? The conversion of Russia. I don't think that holds up against the gospel message. We just have to wait and see."

Since she differed from the standard feminist position on these matters, I asked, did she also differ on the goal of a socialist society?

"I don't see myself as someone with goals in that way," she answered, "although I am drawn to democratic socialism. Again, it's a matter of 'wait and see'."

Weaver's dispassion was apparently not what her audience came seeking. There were murmurs against her preference for a classroom seating arrangement instead of the usual circle. During breaks, some of the people standing around in little knots complained of boredom. They appeared to prefer less equivocation. Before one session, the people sitting near me were enthusiastically planning a "pro-choice" rally to be held in Cincinnati on May 16 ("nice weather and close to Mother's Day"), and an announcement urging attendance at the big Women-Church Convergence to be held in Cincinnati the following October stirred ripples of excitement.

When Grail member Mary Bohlen first introduced Weaver, she said she had written her dissertation on "the abortive early modernist movement, another attempt to bring imagination to bear on religious questions". The word *imagination* is a significant one in all gnostic religious movements, because they hold it to be the source of the theological "creativity" they value above logical consistency. Those involved in feminist spirituality always talk about "imaging" God, as though their image could create the god or goddess of their choice. Thus process thought denies even the possibility of any body of revealed truth. In claiming that all reality is an "energy event" better described by "the cosmic dance" of modern physics than by traditional theological belief in an intelligent, transcendent, personal God, it more closely resembles science fiction than theology. It could be a plot from "Star Trek". A religion originating in fiction is not unprecedented. L. Ron Hubbard's "Dianetics" was first published in *Astounding Science Fiction*, and, unlikely as it would seem, Garry Wills argued, in *Bare Ruined Choirs*,[25] that Teilhard de Chardin wove his theological concepts out of the novels of Monsignor Robert Hugh Benson. It was interesting but not astonishing to learn that Teilhard had

[25] Garry Wills, *Bare Ruined Choirs* (New York: Doubleday, 1972).

had a powerful influence on the thinking of Grail leaders. But Dr. Weaver, despite her role as advocate for process theology, clearly appeared to be looking for something more than dancing energy: for a transcendent Mind, external, personal and loving, for God as St. Teresa of Avila knew him. She was looking in the wrong places. I hoped someone was praying for her and for all the lost sheep.

Philosophical Tide

Just as religious feminism looks to process theology for intellectual legitimization, the closely related New Age movement looks to the language of contemporary physics. Because its muddle of theosophy, Eastern mysticism, "eco-feminism", occult spiritualism, "cosmic consciousness" and "futurism" is covered with a sauce of scientific rationalism, the New Age movement is admitted where witchcraft, frankly named, may still raise eyebrows. It is with New Age language and techniques that Catholic religious professionals most often insinuate the elements of feminist gnosticism into their own professional organizations.

They do not generally do so under the New Age label. In the vulgar forms associated with Shirley MacLaine and occult paraphernalia shops, the movement is apt to be dismissed as a phenomenon of the lunatic fringe. It was the milieu of such irretrievably discredited figures as Charles Manson, the Reverend Jim Jones and Bhagwan Shree Rajneesh. There one finds ESP, UFO and Edgar Cayce cultists, crystals for "balancing energies" and decorative pyramids in which to retune and display them, "past-life regression", "out-of-body" travel, chakras and tantric sex. New Age "channeling", one of the movement's many profit-making activities, is much like the old seance, except that the spirits contacted are thirty-five-thousand-year-old strangers instead of deceased family members. There, too, are shamanism and the purportedly ancient "earth religions" of recent feminist mythology, worshiping the planet as Gaia, a living Mother Goddess. Theosophical mysticism is enjoying a strong revival in the

New Age movement, complete with reincarnation, "occult wisdom", "spirit guides" and "ascended masters".

Those genuine but peripheral expressions of New Age ideas are not the whole story on this spiritual phenomenon, however. For example, the New Age notions one hears from the speakers' lecterns at National Catholic Education Association conventions are more subtly presented. The late Father Anthony de Mello, S.J. was only one of many Catholic teachers of similar meditation techniques.[26] The New Age movement is not a centrally directed cult like the Unification Church. It is an esoteric socio-religious worldview shared by many loosely affiliated autonomous groups on different intellectual and cultural levels, which at first glance seem to bear little resemblance to each other. The Vatican warned against the movement generically in a 1986 report on sects and cults[27] and more recently issued warnings against the dangers of Eastern mystical techniques divorced from Christian Faith.[28] Carl Raschke of the Institute for Humanities at the University of Denver has called it the spiritual equivalent of AIDS. Its central premise animates an incoming philosophical tide that reaches far beyond the local Psychic Fair.

In her instructive introduction to the New Age movement, *The Aquarian Conspiracy*,[29] "participant observer" Marilyn Ferguson, publisher of *Brain/Mind Bulletin*, described it as an "open conspiracy" of "spiritual subversives" ready to lead mankind from

[26] Anthony de Mello, *Sadhana: A Way to God, Christian Exercises in Eastern Form* (St. Louis: Institute of Jesuit Sources, 1978). Similar exercises, directing would-be mystics to seek and follow the spiritual guidance of imaginary figures, have become very common at Catholic retreats, though they are more likely than Wicca leaders to suggest imagining Jesus or an angel in such meditations.

[27] Joint report from the Secretariat for Promoting Christian Unity, for Non-Christians, for Non-Believers and the Pontifical Council for Culture, "Challenge of New Religious Movements (Sects or Cults)", *Pope Speaks* 31, no. 3 (1986): 270.

[28] Ratzinger and Bovone, "Letter to the Bishops". See also Servais, S.J., "Hidden God", 33.

[29] Marilyn Ferguson, *The Aquarian Conspiracy* (Los Angeles: J. P. Tarcher, 1980).

impending doom into an era of unprecedented fulfillment. As a phenomenon in American society, the movement is new, but its ideas, Ferguson concedes, are rooted in an ancient underground search for mystical illumination: in the Hermetic tradition, gnosticism, alchemy and the Kabbalah. It reemerged down the centuries, she says, in Masonry, Rosicrucianism, the transcendentalist concept of an "Oversoul", the "collective unconscious" of Jungian psychology, Whitehead's process theology and Teilhard de Chardin's vision of spiritual evolution to an Omega Point, summed up by Aldous Huxley as the "perennial philosophy". Today, adherents look expectantly for a "quantum leap" in spiritual evolution when a "critical mass" of the human race comes to recognize "the god within" and realize that "All is One". To hasten the process, they, like their gnostic predecessors, are trying to invent a new religious mythology. They see themselves as prototypes of the higher species that will build a "planetary society" glorious in unspecified ways.

Middle-class Respectability

Adorned with middle-class respectability, that gnostic thesis turns up in unexpected places under such labels as "creation spirituality"; "the human potential movement"; humanistic or "transpersonal" psychology; and whole-brain, confluent, planetary, global or holistic education, medicine, psychology, spirituality, transformation or what-have-you. In 1922, for example, theosophist Alice Bailey founded the Lucifer Publishing Company; she saw the fallen angel as a "bringer of light". Today the company lives on as Lucis Trust, whose World Goodwill division is affiliated with the United Nations as a non-governmental organization and holds frequent forums with representatives of Planetary Citizens, the World Future Society, Greenpeace, Amnesty International and American Friends Service Committee, among others.

New Age ideas have acquired credibility by association with prominent names. Joseph Campbell, the late scholar of mythology, endorsed the movement's basic assumptions in his popular interview series, "The Power of Myth", on the Public Broadcasting System. Nobel laureate physicist Fritjof Capra and social scientist Willis Harman of the Stanford Research Institute, former astronaut Edgar Mitchell and Carl Rogers, the late founding father of the Association for Humanistic Psychology, have contributed to the appearance of scientific validity.

New Age thought has poured into American Catholicism, too, under the sponsorship of such figures as Father Thomas Berry, the Passionist "geologian", and the omnipresent Matthew Fox. Fox's ICCS faculty witch, Starhawk, has been dotingly featured in a front-page interview in *National Catholic Reporter* and her writing respectfully reviewed by the *New York Times.* "Futurist" Hazel Henderson was a "resource person" for the ambitious Catholic Education Futures Project. "Sacred psychologist" Jean Houston is a frequent speaker at education conferences, including those of the National Catholic Education Association (NCEA). Former United Nations Assistant Secretary-General Robert Muller, now chancellor of the UN University for Peace in Costa Rica, whose name appears ubiquitously on New Age letterheads, has also addressed the NCEA. Some of these people identify themselves as New Agers. Others reject such a classification and even disagree about details, but internal evidence in their works conspicuously included in New Age bibliographies and catalogues, betrays their ideological affinity. The linkage between more and less plausible expressions of New Age thinking is apparent in their common vocabulary and symbology and in the common pool of prophets, heroes, teachers, activists and authors whose names keep turning up on their boards of advisors and speakers' platforms.

Cosmic Unity

The central theme of all New Age theorists, like that of the process theologians, is the depiction of God as a limited, changing and impersonal force, co-extensive with the created universe. God is not seen as a transcendent Trinity of Persons, partially known because he has revealed himself and because his glory is reflected in his creation. Instead he is held to be the immanent consciousness of the evolving universe, which we can all know by direct experience because we are part of it. Fritjof Capra terms it the "cosmic dance of energy". Jean Houston calls it the "emerging evolutionary process". Matthew Fox, in *The Coming of the Cosmic Christ*, speaks of "the divine 'I am' in every person and creature" and of "the Cosmic Christ who will usher in an era when the whole notion of private salvation has gone the way of Newtonianism".[30]

The argument that God exists in immanence is deliberately ambiguous. St. Thomas Aquinas taught that God is in all things by his power (i.e., all is subject to him), by his presence (all things are open to his knowledge), his essence (as the cause of their being) and, in a special way, in rational beings who love him, by his grace (S.Th. I, 8, 3). But he is in them by his own essence; he is not of their essence. Those who talk of "God within", as well as those who speak of God as the "absolute future" of a "selfmade world", are denying that the Creator is other—and infinitely more—than his creatures. In their view, God's eye is not *on* the sparrow but *in* the sparrow, because, like everything else, the sparrow is God.

Strange Gods

In New Age exhortations, everything points inward to the self. As one enthusiast, University of California (Irvine) professor of psychiatry Roger Walsh, puts it, "Authority and guidance are not 'out there,' in someone else. . . . Rather the ultimate source of wisdom is within."[31] From seeing oneself as one with the divine essence to seeing oneself as a divine being is a short step. To paraphrase G. K. Chesterton, that Shirley MacLaine shall worship the God within her soon turns out to mean that she worships

[30] Matthew Fox, O.P., *The Coming of the Cosmic Christ: The Healing of Mother Earth and the Birth of a Global Renaissance* (San Francisco: Harper & Row, 1988), 241, 152.

[31] Roger Walsh, "The Perennial Wisdom of A Course in Miracles", *Common Boundary* (Jan.–Feb. 1989): 10–17.

Shirley. Before long, New Agers are exulting, "I *am* God!" which gives fresh meaning to the term *strange gods*.

If man is God, why does evil persist? Because too few have so far been "illuminated". Once man recognizes his "godself", New Agers believe his limitless potential can be "empowered" by mystical techniques. Such aims were identified as gnostic by political philosopher Eric Voegelin in his 1960 essay "Ersatz Religion":

> Knowledge—*gnosis*—of the method of altering being is the central concern of the gnostic. . . . All gnostic movements are involved in the project of abolishing the constitution of being, with its origin in divine, transcendent being, and replacing it with a world-immanent order of being, the perfection of which lies in the realm of human action.[32]

This neo-gnosticism ends in the presumption that the self creates its own reality. The notion that the material is illusion, very old in Eastern philosophy, seems utterly incompatible with Western science. Yet Stanford neuroscientist Karl Pribram suggests that the world may be a holographic illusion projected by the mind, subject to alteration by the right kind of thinking. The study of subatomic particles led Fritjof Capra to conclude that "the electron does not *have* objective properties independent of my mind".[33] "Ultimately, in a radical, ontological sense . . . the world is a creation of the mind", declares Roger Walsh.[34] Marilyn Ferguson believes that "events are affected by what we imagine, what we visualize. An image held in a transcendental state may be made real."[35] Transpersonal psychology—the theology, so to speak, of the "godself"—makes the same claim. These are beliefs on a collision course with disappointment.

[32] Eric Voegelin, "Ersatz Religion", in Voegelin, *Science, Politics and Gnosticism*, 87, 99.

[33] Fritjof Capra, *The Turning Point* (New York: Simon & Schuster, 1982), 87.

[34] Walsh, "Wisdom".

[35] Ferguson, *Conspiracy*, 183.

A New World Religion

In public, New Age spokesmen often profess impartial benevolence toward rival religions, though they hint that all of them will be spontaneously replaced or reinterpreted into monist syncretism in the new order. "In our lifetime we will see the rise of essentially a New World Religion", Jean Houston has predicted. "I believe a new spiritual system will emerge."[36]

Some, like Edgar Mitchell, frankly express the hostility for Christianity that is inherent in New Age logic. Mitchell sneers at "grapevine" religions based on "somebody else's experience of divine reality", which mistakenly teach "that we're guilty, sinful, need to be saved."[37]

"The great religions are actually road maps for the induction of transcendent states of consciousness", Roger Walsh told the 1988 conference of the Association for Humanistic Psychology. He was speaking in praise of the New Age re-education program, "A Course in Miracles", which, he reported, was "channeled" through psychologist Helen Schucman during the 1960s by a spirit voice that told her "Christianity is in need of correction" because it has suppressed the gnostic wisdom that would have made it "consistent with the mystical forms of other major religions". In gnostic writings, Walsh said, "the picture of Jesus is not of someone claiming to be forever unique or in any way ontologically set apart from the rest of mankind" but simply one who "has arrived at a state that is latent within us all".[38]

Revisionist Catholic theologians like Paul Knitter, Monika Hellwig[39] and Raimundo Pannikar provide support for such opinions with their "non-normative Christology". Knitter's book *No*

[36] Quoted in Dave Hunt and T. A. McMahon, *The Seduction of Christianity* (Eugene, Oreg.: Harvest House, 1985), 53, from an interview in *Tarrytown Letter* (June/July 1983), 5.

[37] Quoted in Dean C. Halvorson, *SCP Newsletter* (Jan./Feb. 1984), 4.

[38] Walsh, "Wisdom", 10.

[39] Hellwig was the keynote speaker at Time Consultants' Aug. 1989 North American Conference on worship.

Other Name?[40] reports their doubts about whether God really became man in Jesus Christ, whether Jesus is in fact the *only* "savior figure" or whether, perhaps, that notion is a too-literal understanding of the mythic language early Christians used to convey their sense that Jesus was their "place" of "radical encounter with God". Just as these conjectures are welcomed by feminists unwilling to accept a male Savior, they are useful to the New Age movement, particularly because, of the three theologians, only Pannikar has been much identified with neo-gnosticism.

A Search for Meaning

Secularized Americans lived for several generations on the dwindling spiritual capital of their ancestors. By the 1960s, that capital was much depleted. When disillusioned materialists began to search for a new spirituality to give meaning to their lives, they followed a familiar path into the ancient and persistent error of pantheism.

Spiritual waifs might understandably look for God in the wrong place. But it is stunning, though sadly not inexplicable, that educated Catholics, who knew where to find him, not only failed to light the way for their lost sisters and brothers but also set off down the same false trail. For a believing Catholic to enlist in a movement intended to replace Christianity is patently inconsistent. Yet today many Catholic religious professionals, especially women, are involved in this new religion through "goddess feminism", "Cosmic Christ" mysticism or the human potential movement. Either they do not understand what they are doing, or they have lost their Catholic faith.

Doubtless a substantial proportion are the credulous, who swallowed neo-gnosticism without checking the label; even among the educated, people often parrot fashionable jargon without assimilating it. They may be uncritical listeners, who feel at home wherever they hear familiar words like "spiritual", "peace", "love"

[40] Knitter, *No Other Name?*

and "light". Many may be confused because New Age rhetoric, like the modernist theology so prevalent during the past generation, uses Christian terms invested with new meanings. Its "spirit" is not the indwelling Third Person of the Blessed Trinity, nor is its "Cosmic Christ" Jesus of Nazareth, but some deluded Catholics may assume they are. Tragically, many others have indeed ceased to believe in Christian revelation. Now, as Chesterton predicted, they believe not in nothing, but in anything.

Not all those involved are misled, however; some know exactly what they are doing. Frequently their new faith is not spiritual at all, but political. Cynically, they pull simpler souls behind them into idolatry because it seems expedient to the service of maniacal environmentalists, homosexual politics, Marxism, or feminist revolution.

The Goddess Within

Of the three New Age sub-groups where Catholics are likely to be found, goddess feminism looks the least scientific; it looks nothing so much as deranged. It is in fact largely political theater, aimed at attracting attention to its hatred for patriarchy. But as "eco-feminism", it has become a staple of the movement. Its speakers are frequently presented on National Public Radio and on California's Pacifica station. Like Sister Anne Carr, B.V.M., Sister Madonna Kolbenschlag and Mary Jo Weaver, growing numbers of Catholic and ex-Catholic feminist theologians urge women to interpret goddess feminism from the immanentist perspective of process theology. And the middle-aged women grotesquely engaged in the spiral dance are not simply worshipping Yahweh as a mother. Their chant, "We all come from the goddess, and to her we shall return, like drops of rain flowing to the ocean", refers to "the goddess within", a feminist version of "All is One".

Like other ideologies, feminism sees religion as a human construct, and it is engaged in designing one compatible with its aims. Witch Starhawk says she invents myths and rituals as "seed crystals of new patterns that can eventually reshape culture around them".[41] As Kolbenschlag states the argument: "Our civilization's idolatry of the abstract, omnipotent God has clouded our vision and our capacity for divinization."[42]

Kolbenschlag says she and her peers have, nevertheless, "over the period of a lifetime shed our notions of God like so many worn-out husks or snake skins". She sees "possibilities for personal and social transformation" among the women who "are today forging their own authentic spirituality" as part of "the reconstruction of a God myth through the lens of their own experience". Her own experience, she reports, "opened me to myself, to my reality as a woman, and to the Holy within me. . . . I met the Holy in the revelation of my own being, and She was loving, a verb."[43] The goddess of the new order is the politically correct self.

Matthew Fox and the Cosmic Christ

Father Matthew Fox is the most renowned Catholic apostle of the new mysticism that so much resembles the old pantheism. For a dozen years, he has played Pied Piper to religious professionals, clerics, liberation theologians, eco-feminists and other ecological immoderates. If one cannot hear his tune, apparently pitched outside the range of ordinary human ears, it is impossible to explain what attracts them. In light of Genesis 1:3 it would not seem to be news that creation is good, yet Fox has persuaded countless followers that his "creation spirituality" represents a theological breakthrough of prophetic proportions. He seems to be leading them toward a New Age mirage, far, far away from the Catholic world. He calls them to transfer to the cosmos, as he interprets it, the religious passion they once directed toward Jesus Christ. Their obedient proselytizing has intensified the already grave situation of Catholic catechesis throughout the nation.

[41] Carol Zaleski, "What Is Your Most Politically Incorrect Fantasy?" *New York Times Book Review*, Apr. 10, 1988.

[42] Kolbenschlag, *Oz*, 138.

[43] Ibid., 128, 132, 137.

Fox has built his noteworthy career as director and star of the eclectic Institute for Culture and Creation Spirituality (ICCS), which he founded at Chicago's Mundelein College in 1977, then moved in 1983 to Holy Names College in Oakland, California. His permissive "spirituality" has attracted not only disaffected Catholics, Protestants and non-believers but also well-meaning listeners with short attention spans. Some who hear him praise the created universe and demand that we protect as our brothers and sisters even the "tree people" and the "rock people" apparently stop listening before they discover that his concern does not extend to unborn human people. Fox sees abortion as a necessity that must be provided in safe facilities. He lauds committed homosexual relationships—including genital acts—as celebrations of creation. He finds the Mass less "boring" when it incorporates witchcraft chants and dances. And he calls for more irrationality, which is understandable, given what he has to say.

The friar's unorthodoxy has hardly been covert. An essay he wrote in 1978, "Meister Eckhart and Karl Marx: The Mystic as Political Theologian", raises the suspicion that his apparent madness may be method concealing a political agenda. Less rambling and incoherent than his books, it praises Eckhart as "a mystic of the left" and philosophical predecessor of Karl Marx who made a seminal "historical contribution to socialism". Fox summarizes the clues:

> Eckhart's position on capitalism (merchant mentalities kill God in us);[44] on class (there is none: we are all nobles); on democracy (all people give birth to God); on realized eschatology (heaven is now and is not to be projected into another life); on self-criticism as including criticism of one's own institutions, including religious ones; on human history as divine history.[45]

[44] Even the "merchant mentality" that does "pious works" in hope of Heaven.

[45] In Richard Woods, O.P., ed., *Understanding Mysticism* (Garden City, N.Y.: Image Books, 1980), 541, reprinted ("slightly revised") from *Listening* (an earlier Fox-founded publication) (Fall, 1978). Father Woods, another central province Dominican, is a featured columnist in *National Catholic Reporter*

Among the heirs to Eckhart's thought Fox identified the Beghards and Beguines, Martin Luther, Georg Hegel, Ludwig Feuerbach and Karl Marx.

In *Original Blessing*, his 1983 book, Fox declared that "no one believed in original sin until Augustine".[46] He denounced belief in God's transcendence as "the ultimate dualism" and blamed it for separating God from humanity "and reducing religion to a childish state of pleasing or pleading with a God 'out there' ".[47]

On November 15, 1987, Fox was the chief celebrant at a bizarre "Cosmic Mass of Thanksgiving for the Body" sponsored by ICCS at Holy Names College. The public was invited, so Oakland resident Jerald Cooper attended as an observer. In the dimly lit college gymnasium, smoky with "cleansing" cedar-chip smudge, throbbing with drumbeats, some 150 people gathered before a large movie screen for a litany in praise of body parts. As photographs flashed on the screen, they successively intoned, "*te laudamus Domine*", for lungs, heart, mitral valve, stomach, colon, testes, ovaries, gallbladder, sweat glands, earwax and so on, bowing from the waist before each slide. Then the congregation separated into small circles of ten. After dancing widdershins and repeating a Wiccan chant ("the earth, the water, the fire, the air, return, return, return, return . . ."), Fox and the small-group leaders, some of them women, jointly recited the words of Consecration over bread and wine. It was, Cooper said, "beyond parody".

In San Francisco on April 7, 1988, Fox was a panelist at a "Gaia Consciousness Conference and Celebration of the Re-emergent Earth Goddess" held by the California Institute of Integral Studies at the Franklin Street Unitarian Center.

---

and the author of *Another Kind of Love* (Fort Wayne, Ind.: Knoll, 1988) on "the positive dimensions of same-sex love".

[46] Matthew Fox, O.P., *Original Blessing: A Primer in Creation Spirituality* (Santa Fe, N.M.: Bear, 1986), 48.

[47] Ibid., 89.

Intellectual Magpie

Fox's 1989 sabbatical was welcome news to those concerned about the common good. Clearly, he ought to be prevented from spreading poison as a priest-theologian in apparently good standing. But the accompanying media flurry brought him attention far beyond his intellectual merits. Fox lacks stature as a theologian; in academic circles, he is not considered a serious figure. By comparison, men like Fathers Charles Curran, Richard McCormick, Hans Küng, David Tracy and perhaps even Richard McBrien look like flawed but credible scholars. They are dissenting theologians, and some of them are shallow. Fox, though he holds a doctorate in theology, is less a theologian than an intellectual magpie, collecting snips and snatches of other writers' ideas, often distorted in translation or out of context, as though to dignify his absurd message by attributing his opinions to others. He even dares appropriate that giant of Dominicans, Saint Thomas Aquinas, as an earlier exponent of "creation-centered" mysticism.[48] "Aquinas would be on my faculty if he were alive today", says Fox.[49] When Father John Boyle, president of the Catholic Theological Society of America, and McBrien, head of Notre Dame's theology department, spoke out to protest Fox's silencing, both made it a point to say they were unfamiliar with his work. Apparently the lack of peer recognition hurts; he told *National Catholic Reporter* that his order had published a magazine "devoted to United States Dominican theologies", but "I wasn't in it". His plaintive question: "If I'm not a United States Dominican theologian, what am I?"[50]

ICCS draws less than one hundred students each year (more than half of them nuns and priests) for a four-month sabbatical program, a nine-month certificate program or a nine-month master of arts degree program, in "Culture and Spirituality", "Cre-

[48] Fox, *Cosmic Christ*, 114–16.

[49] Barry Eberling, "Jesus Never Heard of Original Sin: Original Blessing Shapes Theology of Matthew Fox", *National Catholic Reporter*, Sept. 13, 1985, 4.

[50] Ibid.

ation Spirituality and Geo-Justice" or "Creation Spirituality and Transpersonal Psychology". Nonetheless, Fox's influence is pervasive, especially among women religious. ICCS graduates have gone on to careers in campus ministry, youth ministry, retreat centers, feminist organizations, Catholic schools and colleges and other parish and diocesan positions, including pastorates. And while Curran, McCormick and Tracy inflict their direct damage primarily on those in the academic world, Fox has long functioned as a side-show barker for an esoteric New Age religion, taking his mystical stew directly to the naïve, the rebellious and the trendy. He reaches thousands with traveling workshops held throughout the United States and Canada and in Australia, New Zealand and Ireland, often under Catholic auspices. In addition, he is executive editor of the glossy bi-monthly magazine *Creation*. Friends of Creation Spirituality, a non-profit, tax-exempt corporation, of which Fox was founding president, claims "25,000 adherents".[51]

He is also the author of a dozen books, including such titles as *On Becoming a Musical, Mystical Bear*; *Whee, We, Wee All the Way Home*; *A Spirituality Named Compassion*; *Breakthrough: Meister Eckhart's Creation Spirituality in New Translation*; *Original Blessing: A Primer in Creation Spirituality* and *The Coming of the Cosmic Christ*. At the Catholic bookshop in my hometown, employees tell me Fox is their top seller to nuns. His books are also available in at least one local Christian bookstore, at New Age shops and on the New Age shelves at B. Dalton.

Variations on a Theme

In November 1988, I heard the tireless Dominican speak six times during three days in San Diego: twice at the (Catholic) University of San Diego and once each at St. Paul's (Episcopalian) Cathedral, First Unitarian Church, San Diego State University and First United Methodist Church, where he conducted an especially

[51] Matthew Fox, O.P., "My Final Statement before Being Silenced by the Vatican", advertisement, *New York Times*, Dec. 14, 1988, 11.

noisome all-day workshop.[52] Each time he drew overflow crowds, disproportionately female. More troubling than their attraction to his ambiguous "panentheism" was their tolerance for his ranting against patriarchy, "Christolatry" and the "institutional" Church, which could appeal only to audiences seething with the same fury. Under various titles, Fox gave, each time, essentially the same speech, drawn directly from his latest book, *Cosmic Christ*, with minor adaptations to suit particular audiences. By the end of his stay, though it had ceased to shock, its inconsistencies had become so conspicuous that I marveled that Fox himself could ignore them.

His central themes were (1) original sin versus "original blessing", (2) ecological abuse versus primitive reverence for Mother Earth, (3) "pseudo-mysticisms" versus the "new mystical story", (4) "boring" liturgy versus "playful" rituals and (5) "homophobia" versus "sexual mysticism". They deserve a detailed look, not only for the insights they offer on Fox's own turbulent psyche but also as disturbing clues to the emotional and spiritual condition of Catholic feminists. It is in this odious theology, Rosemary Ruether says, that Women-Church is "rooted".

1. According to Fox, the Church should focus on the "original blessing" of creation rather than on the "anthropocentric", "individualistic", "sexist", "anti-mystical" "Fall-Redemption" theology invented by St. Augustine. Fall-Redemption theologies "have a strong tendency to become Christolatrous and to zero in almost completely on Christ as Redeemer", he said. "The 'Jesus' dimension to religion paralleled the individualism of the Enlightenment and the industrial age." He claimed at intervals, however, "I don't deny original sin". It is "dualism, the separation of body and spirit", that is "the sin behind the sin".

However one interprets Fox's stand on original sin, he made it clear that he recognizes "social sin". He calls "homophobia" a "grave, grave sin". And, he said, the Church commits "a very

[52] San Diego's Friends of Creation Spirituality had also arranged for Fox to speak at USD-affiliated University High School, but Bishop Leo T. Maher canceled that appearance.

serious sin of omission" in "hiding its head in the sand" about "population control". Personal sin, on the other hand, he sees as a source of growth.

Fox is at his most appealing when he talks about the wonders of the natural world. It is of course true that creation is good. The Church has always taught so, just as she has taught that man is a being composed of soul and body, Fox to the contrary notwithstanding. But as soon as man comes on the scene—long before St. Augustine—original sin disturbs the harmonious universe God has created. The universal discordance between his good creation and flawed human nature is empirical evidence of original sin. In the darkness of the twentieth century, it is a marvel that anyone would doubt it.

Fox's denigration of Jesus implicitly denies his divine nature—you cannot commit idolatry by adoring the real God—and is consistent with his rejection of the Fall. He seems to say that Jesus' mission was not to redeem mankind but to warn against littering and "homophobia".

2. Before they were invaded by genocidal European imperialists (despite "an occasional ritual of human sacrifice"),[53] "native peoples had more advanced civilizations than European Christians". Their "cosmological, non-dualistic, matrifocal cultures reverenced Mother Earth" and saw all creatures—"rock people, tree people" and so on—as brothers and sisters. Convinced that native peoples had no need for Christianity, Fox opposed the canonization of Father Junipero Serra.

Western civilization has lacked a cosmology[54] since the Enlightenment, or the Middle Ages, or St. Augustine, depending on the point Fox is making when he says it. Now, ecologically speaking, the sky is falling, he declares. "First World" man, no longer "at home in the universe", centers his attention on "the two-legged ones" without care for the fact that "the earth is dy-

[53] He repeated this in print, in *Cosmic Christ*, 24.

[54] *Cosmology* is "the theory or philosophy of the nature and principles of the universe", according to *Webster's Unabridged Dictionary*, 2d ed. (New York: Simon & Schuster, 1983).

ing" of overuse. "What we are doing to the soil and the water, the rain forest and the air, and therefore to our children's children's children" comes out of the "loss of cosmology". The Vatican, he charges, "is deaf to the suffering of Mother Earth. If you don't believe that divinity is in the soil, then you tolerate the destruction of six billion tons of topsoil every year."

Fox's doomsday statistics are undocumented in his speeches and referenced in his books to such dubious sources as Sierra Club publications, ICCS cosmologist Brian Swimme or Paul Ehrlich. "Within thirty years, Iowa will be a desert", he claims. Within twenty-five years, the United States will be importing food ("but from whom?"). Within fifteen years, "one-third of all the world's forests will be gone". In fifty years, "in the United States, not one tree will be standing". Within one hundred years, "there will be no living species left on the planet, including humankind".

The truth is that man has not been at home in the universe since the Fall. Lower animals, like everything else, are indeed sometimes victims of human sin. Nevertheless it is man, flawed as he is, who bears the image of God, whom Christ has redeemed and who is destined for eternal life with him.

Economist Jacqueline Kasun offers a saner and better documented view of earth's natural resources than does Fox:

> No more than one to three percent of the earth's ice-free land area is occupied by human beings, less than one-ninth is used for agricultural purposes. Eight times, and perhaps as much as twenty-two times, the world's population (5 billion) could support itself at the present standard of living, using present technology; and this leaves half the earth's surface open to wildlife and conservation areas.[55]

3. The loss of cosmology "destroyed mysticism" and encouraged "pseudo-mysticisms" like fascism, nationalism and consumerism. "Christofascism" is another "pseudo-mysticism" Fox sees in Protestant fundamentalism and in "the papal fundamentalism we are now

[55] Jacqueline Kasun, *The War against Population* (San Francisco: Ignatius Press, 1988), 206f.

getting in considerable doses". Opus Dei, he said, is an example of a fascist organization.

The Church contributed to the suppression of mysticism by "*sleeping*! on top of her mystical treasures" like the Bible's Wisdom literature. "Of course, most Wisdom literature comes from North Africa", where they worship "a black Mother Goddess named Isis", Fox went on. "This kind of freaks out the *Heilsgeschichte* German agenda of salvation history we've been getting from patriarchal German religious education for three hundred years." Yet, without understanding what she was doing, the pre-conciliar Church "rolled out all these wonderful texts from Proverbs" and applied them to "Mary, the Mother Goddess of the Christian Church".

Goddesses aside, Fox thus contradicted his charge that the Church abandoned her treasure of Wisdom literature; if he was not deprived of that cosmological vision, neither were other Catholics. It is true, however, that the Church has always approached mysticism with caution, both because imagination can be mistaken for mystical experience and because not all spiritual experiences are from God. The common doctrine of the Church is always the final authority for obedient Catholics. Even such a giant as St. Teresa of Avila was docile in submitting to her spiritual directors.

Fox also cautioned that "today we have to beware of false mystics". How would he know a *true* mystic? When asked to define mysticism, he said it is impossible, because it is "a right-brain experience", and definition is "a left-brain activity". But he offered, as images of mysticism, "standing rapt in awe", "hanging upside down in a tree" and "all our unitive experiences".

A new cosmological vision, a new "mystical story", is now being created by the union of science and religion, Fox said. In its light, mankind "is being asked to change its way of seeing the world" from the old theism ("dualistic, bad, deadly") to "panentheism", or the Cosmic Christ. With this "paradigm shift", man finds himself "at home" in "the kingdom/queendom of God". Those who resist it are fundamentalists, "freaked out" by "this psychic earthquake" and desperate for security.

The old revelation is superseded. Scholars must be liberated from "the quest for the historical Jesus" so they can devote their attentions to the "deep ecumenism" that assimilates primitive wisdom. "It has become increasingly evident to me how the concept of the Cosmic Christ is pre-Christian", Fox said. "The divine 'I am' in every person and every creature is no particular tradition's private legacy." Native cultures knew the Cosmic Christ before the arrival of European Christians, who didn't.

In announcing the "paradigm shift", Fox advanced the basic claim of the New Age movement. While a "cosmically lonely" agnostic might indeed find such a vision appealing, it is difficult to see why the faith of a believing Catholic would be affected, since he would have known all along that "the heavens declare the glory of God". Science can offer fascinating detail, but never a new revelation. Many in Fox's audiences, however, seem poised for the leap into New Age faith. After his talks, middle-aged women twitter around him like teen-agers around a rock star.

4. Father Fox declared that Catholic worship has cut off from its mystical roots to become a ("boring!") matter of "reading and being read *at*". As he sees it, liturgy without "play" is the literally deadly reason "the young are dying". "One American adolescent in ten attempts suicide. On Indian reservations, one in ten succeed in killing themselves", he said. "In California, one of every three young men between nineteen and twenty-nine is in jail." Why? According to Fox, "adultism" is to blame. "Cannibalistic" adults control everything—religion, politics, education—while the cries of young people "in despair"—from fear of nuclear war, unemployment, violence, alcoholic parents—go unheard. "Adultism" arises from "the repression of the child in the adult . . . the mystic, the divine child in us wanting to play in the universe". At its worst, "adultism" becomes fundamentalism, spawning "religious and spiritual abuse" with "hellfire and brimstone" sermons. Knowing "how vulnerable our species is to the wounded child inside", he fears that the young, in turn, will become "killer adults" unless they are helped.

But how to help? Our educational systems "don't have room for the right brain; our religious traditions have forgotten their mystical traditions". The Church has "zeroed in so much on sexuality as morality, we're not teaching young people about sexuality as mysticism". The Foxian prescription is "playful" worship: "Step out of the rational to cure the rational—get out of the box of rationality" with "sweat lodges, wilderness education, drumming, mask work" and stories that give them a vision "of their own divinity".

"Adults have to learn to play again", Fox said. Worship should be "an oasis where the child can emerge from adults". It should be about "getting our hearts together—getting our bodies together, because, believe it or not, our hearts are in our bodies!" To "redeem worship", we must "get people to dance to drums and take off their clothes in a sweat lodge".

Questions arise. Why not just bring back Latin, incense and Gregorian chant instead? In *Cosmic Christ*, Fox explains that "liturgy in its present context is not redeemable" because "neither the old Latin Mass nor the current vernacular one offered a living cosmology".[56] We need to worship "in circles", preferably "on Mother Earth". Starhawk, he says, has shown us how to do it with "basic chants and spiral dances from ancient women's religions".[57]

If sweat lodges and drumming are the answer to the despair of the young, why is the youth suicide rate highest on Indian reservations, where those customs survive? The despair of the young seemed to have been merely an introductory hook, quickly forgotten in Fox's excitement about bringing out "the child in the adult". Yet there is indeed despair behind the frantic and sometimes suicidal sensation-seeking of many American adolescents. There would be none if drumbeats and nakedness and sexual freedom were the answer, for those they already have to excess. What they do not have are answers to the perennial human questions "Who made me?" and "Why did God make me?"

[56] Fox, *Cosmic Christ*, 216f., 220.
[57] Ibid., 217, 218.

5. It was not the subject of faith, however, but of "sexual mysticism" that moved Fox to greatest intensity. His exaltation of homosexual lovemaking as a religious pursuit could bring a blush to the cheek of an ACT-UP zealot. "The Cosmic Christ celebrates sexual diversity", he told his audiences, in a kind of litany.

> The Cosmic Christ is not obsessed with sexual identity. The Cosmic Christ is both female and male, heterosexual and homosexual. . . . The Cosmic Christ is ecstatic and excited when lovers make love. . . . The Cosmic Christ is saddened when the mystery and mysticism of sexuality are reduced to moralizing about sexual acts. . . . Sexual behavior and its expression as the art of lovemaking need to find their expression in committed love relationships between two persons.
>
> Creation-centered tradition does not traffic in "mortification of the senses", because it recognizes passion, body, senses and sensuality as part of that divine gift, that original blessing,

"In fact," he said, "I think it's the first gift of the Cosmic Christ." In some ways, homosexuality is superior to heterosexuality. "There's no better birth control", said Fox. And there is cosmological merit in the fact that it is not "productive; there's a lot of merit in rediscovering sexuality as play".

Aborting Imagination

"You spoke so eloquently in defense of the rain forests; what is your position on abortion?" I asked Fox.

"I'm against abortion in principle", he answered. "I'm not against people who have abortions, and I'm not against abortion clinics for the poor, because abortion at this time in history is a sociological fact, and the very reason I'm against abortion is the reason I want clinics for people who are going to have abortions—so that *their* lives won't be threatened at the same time the fetus' is." He put the stereotypical hard case. "We don't have the sense of extended family! So you have like a single woman in America today, *poor*, maybe already with a couple kids, and she feels *in conscience* she cannot give another twenty years to another kid. So what is she gonna do in a culture that isolates her so much?"

"I think the real issue is the abortion of imagination", Fox went on. "Why is it that we have so many abortions today on the one hand, and so many impotent and sterile parents on the other, who want kids and can't adopt them anyplace? Why can't we create some computer banks, putting together the people who are going to have children they can't raise and those who want children and can't get them?"

"Isn't that what adoption agencies are for?" I asked. But he is not an easy man to interrupt.

"I never met a woman who found abortion an easy moral decision. And I think to add guilt and burden and grief to their burden is—is—not correct," Fox said. "You know, one thing that bothers me about right to life is this quasi fanaticism. For example, in the Catholic Church there's a lot of trumpeting against abortion, and yet the Catholic Church itself is involved today in aborting spiritual movements in Latin America and in North America. Abortion is an analogous term. It's not just mothers who have abortions; it's hierarchy who abort things. We have to raise our whole level of awareness about reverence for everything, including ideas, and thinkers, and movements and artists!"

Doonesbury Theology

Fox's flower-child message, which has evolved in little but vocabulary since 1972, is part vulgarized Teilhard de Chardin, part vulgarized Thomas Berry/Sierra Club, part Harvey Cox's *Feast of Fools*, part "gay liberation", part Starhawk, part Women-Church, part New Age, part Rousseauean "noble savage". That may seem like too many parts, but even *National Catholic Reporter* described Fox's work as "a combination Doonesbury cartoon theology and Shirley MacLaine spirituality".[58]

Fox's diatribes against "dualisms" oppose not only distinctions

[58] "Silencing Fox a Fruitless Exercise", editorial, *National Catholic Reporter*, Oct. 21, 1988, 10.

between mind and body but also those between creature and Creator. And between man and beast; he likes to say that because his dog, Tristan, "enters into ecstasy without guilt", he chose him as his spiritual director. Despite his fevered talk about lovemaking and his enthusiastic emphasis on "the child within" the adult (usually the "wounded child"), Fox scarcely mentions marriage or babies except to fret about overpopulation. And when he does, he quotes Stanford University's Paul Ehrlich, author of *Population Bomb*.[59] In Fox's ideal universe, trees would be safer than unborn babies; if you tried to chop one down, he would try to stop you.

Though Fox claims that "creation spirituality" was lost with Augustine, his "Family Tree of Creation-Centered Spirituality" includes St. Benedict, St. Dominic, St. Thomas Aquinas, St. Catherine of Siena, St. Teresa of Avila, St. Thomas More and St. John of the Cross, not to mention most of the major artists, poets, social reformers and scientists of Western history.[60] In fact, except for his consistent praise of homosexuality and his consistent if inaccurate environmentalism, most of what he says is contradicted somewhere else by something else he says. The result is not only adulterated Catholicism but also an ambiguous muddle of Pelagianism, pantheism, primitivism, syncretism, irrationalism and theosophy. What he means by "the Cosmic Christ" seems to be a life force closer to the monist "oversoul" of Eastern religions, New Agers and Starhawk's "immanent goddess" than to Jesus Christ.

Preparation for Sweat Lodge

From time to time in his magazine *Creation*, Fox has attempted to distance "creation spirituality" from the New Age movement. Similarly, in *The Coming of the Cosmic Christ*, he lists "New

[59] Paul Ehrlich, *The Population Bomb* (New York: Ballantine Books, 1968).
[60] Fox, *Original Blessing*, 307–15.

Ageism" (between "fundamentalism" and "asceticism") with current "pseudo-mysticisms", because, he says, its interpretation of "past life experiences" is "excessively literal".[61] It is a relief to suppose that First Communion classes will not be trying "past life regression" at his suggestion. But a reading of the book reveals multiple parallels between Fox's thought and New Age ideas. *Creation*, and ICCS catalogues, list classes, faculty members, guest speakers, authors and subjects certifiably associated with the movement. Charlene Spretnak, co-author with Fritjof Capra of *Green Politics*,[62] author of *The Spiritual Dimension of Green Politics*,[63] and editor of *The Politics of Women's Spirituality*,[64] served for years on *Creation*'s editorial board with such noted New Agers as Joanna Macy and Brian Swimme. In the pages of the magazine, readers find Passionist Father Thomas Berry, the "geologian" who wants to "reinvent the human" in a universe freed of "hypermagical ultra-omnipotence",[65] Hazel Henderson, Marija Gimbutas and Daniel Ellsberg, originally of Pentagon Papers fame, now deep in New Age affairs. Fox's "On the Road" calendar lists speaking engagements at such New Age centers as Unity and Religious Science churches. Bear & Company, a New Age publishing house Fox founded with friends in 1982, lists among its authors both José Arguelles, the art historian who arranged the 1987 "Harmonic Convergence", and Chris Griscom, the Light Institute guru who introduced Shirley MacLaine to her higher self.

Starhawk is not the only ICCS faculty member whose specialty might be considered unusual in the academic world. Sister Jose Hobday, O.S.F., teaches "Native American ritual". Jeremy

[61] Fox, *Cosmic Christ*, 45f.

[62] Charlene Spretnak and Fritjof Capra, *Green Politics: The Global Premise* (Santa Fe, N.M.: Bear, 1987).

[63] Charlene Spretnak, *The Spiritual Dimension of Green Politics* (Santa Fe, N.M.: Bear, 1986).

[64] Charlene Spretnak, ed., *The Politics of Women's Spirituality: Essays on the Rise of Spiritual Power within the Feminist Movement* (Garden City, N.Y.: Anchor Books, 1982).

[65] William Birmingham, "Thomas Berry", *Cross Currents* (Summer/Fall 1987): 178.

Taylor "teaches and facilitates dream work" both at ICCS and at Berkeley's Graduate Theological Union. Physicist Brian Swimme, author of *The Universe Is a Green Dragon*, regularly teaches "cosmology". "Transformation instructor" Shanja Kirstann, a Sufi instructor who used to work with Jean Houston, teaches "a rite of passage for soul making" that has to do with "free movement, chalk doodles, journal writing and sacred drama". "Gestalt therapist" Jean Lanier teaches "personhood as a work of art". Sufi teacher Robert Frager, founder of the California Institute of Transpersonal Psychology, presents "Aikado as a spiritual discipline". Sister Marlene DeNardo, S.N.D., teaches "geo-justice" and "feminist studies"; before coming to ICCS, she was with Basic Christian Communities, Maranhão, Brazil, for seven years. (Fox says ICCS teaches "liberation theology for *First* World peoples".)[66] Yoruba voodoo priestess Luisah Teish has taught West African and Caribbean "ritual dances". Faculties have included masseuse Paula Koepke, "ritual guide" Jim Roberts (teaching "male liberation: storytelling, drumming, movement, heyoka power . . . unleashing our animal roots and our ancient brotherhood") and Lakota Sioux Buck Ghost Horse, teaching "preparation for sweat lodge" ("no previous knowledge or physical conditioning necessary"). Visiting professors have included Father Berry, Patricia and Gerry Mische of Global Education Associates, feminist theologian Pia Moriarity and Ron Miller, a scholar of comparative religion whose specialty is approaching Scripture with the right brain through dream analysis. When ICCS was at Mundelein, Rosemary Ruether taught feminist theology there, and she remains an ally. While Sister Alexandra Kovats, C.S.J.P., was ICCS' "spiritual director", she drew on "creation-centered spiritual tradition" to "elicit the power within". Jungian analyst John Giannini has offered dream interpretation. After some years on the ICCS faculty in Oakland, Brother Joseph Kilikevice, O.P., went back to Illinois and now travels throughout the country conducting

[66] Friends of Creation Spirituality advertisement, *New York Times*, Dec. 14, 1988, 11.

retreats. Each week, students participate in ritual, body prayer (dance of sorts) and group process ("response to conceptual ideas" of creation spirituality and "sharing of autobiographies").

These are not the only fascinating connections between ICCS and other strains of "cosmic unity" religion. The "Cosmic Masses" with which Fox and his associates scandalize orthodox Catholics in Oakland are adaptations of a liturgical form introduced in 1975 at New York's Episcopal Cathedral of St. John the Divine by Pir Vilayat Inayat Khan, world leader of Nizami Chistiyya Sufism. As the Pir's "Mass" ended, he intoned, "I am the One I love; there is but One. One in All. All in One."

Sufism is a heterodox Islamic mystical sect that teaches, as his chant indicates, that God is everything, and thus everything is God. It was brought to the United States early in this century by Pir Vilayat's father. His mother was Ora Ray Baker, sister of Mary Baker Eddy, the founder of Christian Science, whose religious thought may have been influenced by that of her brother-in-law. Pir Vilayat now runs a center called "The Abode of the Message" in New Lebanon, New York, and speaks to New Age conferences about such matters as "personal bioluminescence" and "healing with crystals". The journal of the Sufi "Center for the Dances of Universal Peace" carried Matthew Fox's 1988 diatribe against the Vatican, issued on the eve of the disciplinary year of silence imposed by his religious superiors. Editorial notes added that "the Dances are at the 'core' of Fox's ICCS graduate program" and urged readers to write "positive" letters to Cardinal Ratzinger.[67]

Frivolous as it may sound, the ICCS program is not aimless. It is designed to transform consciousness—to replace the content of faith without changing its name. A student molded by ICCS might still claim to be a "Catholic", but the meaning of doctrines and sacraments would be utterly changed. Fox, for example, intermittently says that he does not deny the doctrine of original sin. What he does is effectively disembowel it with ridicule until the listener reaches the obviously implied conclusion that he

[67] *Dance Network News*, Oct./Nov. 1988.

has denied it. Then he redefines it as "dualism", or the failure to see that all is one, and declares his acceptance of its "very minor role in theology".[68] Ambiguity is his method: he describes faith as subsisting in "imagination"[69] and repudiates "mortification of the senses" as denial of the goodness of sense experience.[70] In the "erotic" sacrament of the Eucharist, as he describes it, bread and wine do not *become* the Body and Blood of Jesus Christ but already *are* the "cosmic body and blood of the Divine One present in every atom" of the universe, and its effect is the "awakening of consciousness to the sufferings of Mother Earth".[71] Traditional prayer is something one moves away from as, centered in creation spirituality, one becomes aware that there is no need to plead with a God "out there" because the Cosmic Christ is within each of us, so celebrating oneself is celebrating him. The dualist "theistic" notion of a God "out there" must be replaced, he says, with the vision of "all things in God and God in all things", which he calls "panentheism".[72] That obscure term was also used by nineteenth-century modernists Friedrich von Hügel and George Tyrrell in their effort to describe a middle ground between outright pantheism and the transcendence they considered unacceptable.[73] Fox attempts to distinguish his own "panentheism" from pantheism, but what he describes seems identical to it. Since he fails to advert to God's transcendence, Fox's followers conclude that God exists *only* in his creation, that is, in themselves.

The "Cosmic Christ" of which Fox speaks is not "the historical Jesus", who was a "nondualistic" mystic and prophet who, "like all of us, wrestled with his true self" and whose refusal to "abandon his vision" brought him to an "untimely death".[74] Fox uses "*the*

[68] Fox, *Original Blessing*, 47, 49 and passim.

[69] Ibid., 319.

[70] Fox, *Cosmic Christ*, 38.

[71] Ibid., 214.

[72] Ibid., 57.

[73] Gabriel Daly, O.S.A., *Transcendence and Immanence: A Study in Catholic Modernism and Integralism* (Oxford, Clarendon Press, 1980), 135, 154.

[74] Fox, *Cosmic Christ*, 67–73, 161, 140.

Christ" as a generic title, as theosophists do. Like Paul Knitter and Monika Hellwig, he asks if "the fact that the Christ became incarnate in Jesus" must "exclude the Christ's becoming incarnate in others—Lao-tze or Buddha or Moses or Sarah or Sojourner Truth or Gandhi or me or you?"[75] In common with Thomas Berry,[76] Fox holds that the world is being called to a new "post-denominational", even post-Christian, belief system that sees the earth as a living being—mythologically, as Gaia, Mother Earth—with mankind as her consciousness.[77] Such worship of the universe is properly called cosmolatry.

It is superfluous evidence of the disarray in the American Church that Vatican intervention was required to gain Catholics a brief respite from Fox's ubiquitous theologizing. Various bishops, his Dominican superiors and several noted theologians shrugged him off as harmless. It took an improbable four years and, at last, a direct order for Cardinal Ratzinger to achieve token compliance from the Dominicans with his request that the garrulous eccentric be disciplined.

In 1984, Cardinal Ratzinger first asked Dominican Master General Damian Byrne to investigate Fox's writings and activities. Three Dominican theologians, Fathers Benedict Ashley, Thomas McGonigle and the late Christopher Kiesling, reviewed Fox's work and reported, in 1985, that while certain doctrines could be better integrated into his books, they were not heretical or "completely beyond the pale of Catholic theology".[78] The cardinal replied that those conclusions were "questionable" and expressed doubt "whether Father Fox should be permitted to publish at all".[79] In 1986 and 1987, the Congregation again prodded the

[75] Ibid., 235. For Knitter and Hellwig, see above, chap. 3, n. 40.

[76] Thomas Berry, "Thomas Berry: A Special Section", *Cross Currents* (Summer/Fall 1987): 179–217.

[77] Fox, *Cosmic Christ*, 235–44.

[78] Sidebar notes to "Father Matthew Fox to Begin Period of Silence", *Origins*, Washington, D.C., USCC, Nov. 3, 336. Hereafter, "Fox", *Origins*.

[79] "A Statement Concerning Matthew Fox and the Institute in Culture

Dominicans to stop Fox's dissemination of his heterodox opinions. Father Donald Goergen, O.P.,[80] provincial of Fox's own St. Albert the Great Province, responded each time with a detailed defense of Fox's writings. At last, in April 1988, Cardinal Ratzinger's office insisted that the order remove Fox from his position and prevent him from teaching, writing or speaking his errors. The Master General then directed Father Goergen to ask Fox to take a one-year "sabbatical". Fox himself made the matter public the following October.

Even as Fox's sabbatical year was announced, Father Goergen said, "Theologians, including myself, have examined his writings from a doctrinal point of view and do not think there is sufficient reason to prohibit him from speaking and writing."[81] Goergen told Master General Byrne, "There is no scandal that needs to be remedied." Objections to Fox's activities, he said, have come only from "extreme reactionary groups".[82] Apparently, other religious authorities either concurred or lacked the courage of their offices. Fox continued his tireless trek from podium to podium without visible episcopal interference up to December 15, 1988, the effective date of his one-year "sabbatical". As he departed, he fired a vituperative blast at Rome, published, like so many radical Catholic statements, as a full-page advertisement in the *New York Times*.[83]

---

and Creation-Centered Spirituality", Chicago, Ill., Dominican Province of St. Albert the Great, Oct. 11, 1988, 6.

[80] Father Goergen is best known to the general public as the author of *The Sexual Celibate* (Garden City, N.Y.: Doubleday, 1977), The book, which advocates bi-sexuality (psychological) as the androgynous ideal, was dismissed by Professor Ruth Tiffany Barnhouse as an example either of "appalling ignorance" or of "an unadorned and unsupported statement of the writer's own value system" in her own book, *Homosexuality: A Symbolic Confusion* (New York: Seabury Press, 1979), 108, 186, n. 8.

[81] "Fox", *Origins*, Nov. 3, 1988, 337.

[82] Bill Kenkelen, "Dominican Order, under Vatican Pressure, Silences Matthew Fox", *National Catholic Reporter*, Oct. 21, 1988, 15.

[83] Fox, "Final Statement", 11.

Savonarola

Fox, this apostle of self-affirmation, celebration, sensual delight, permissiveness and play, appears oddly joyless. A slight man, gray of skin and hair, narrow faced, pinch lipped, with lantern jaw cocked above sloping shoulders, arm motions constrained, he speaks with burning vehemence, more Savonarola than Friar Tuck. His malicious witticisms, most of them used in his books and repeated in each address, soon cease to amuse. Listeners may hear a promise of liberation in Fox's message, but his dissonant intensity seems finally tragic. Though he shamelessly exaggerates the degree to which creation is endangered, some of his enthusiasm for the splendor of it rings true. Though the solutions he proposes range from ludicrous to evil, some of the problems he names are recognizable. It is certainly true that worshipers experience a diminished sense of the sacred at Mass since Latin, Gregorian chant, candles and incense have been expunged. Through the fog, glimmers can be seen of the fruitful uses to which Fox might have put his talents if he had made nobler choices instead of escaping into the disintegrating liberty of false spirituality.

Sabbatical Year

In Father Fox's parting advertisement, he identified himself with such other "victims of the Roman Inquisition" as Charles Curran, Leonardo Boff and Archbishop Raymond Hunthausen, denounced the Vatican's "mindless fundamentalism", urged supporters to write in his defense to apostolic delegate Pio Laghi and asked for tax-deductible donations to Friends of Creation Spirituality. Then he subsided into a surprising public silence.[84]

In January 1989, shortly after Fox's visit to San Diego, some twenty former Catholics, Protestants and Unitarians formed a new church, called the "New Creation Fellowship and Renewal

[84] Whether or not Fox made public appearances during his travels is not on record. He did write a new book on the relationship between liberation theology and creation spirituality to be published by Harper & Row, and an editorial and a book review in the Sept./Oct. 1989 issue of *Creation*.

Center", to "rediscover, celebrate and incarnate the transforming power of the Cosmic Christ in our personal and community lives". Their leader, Lawrence Kraus, a former Lutheran minister and a member of the local Friends of Jung organization, said, "We don't know yet what form the church will take for the age of interdependence."[85] While it seems unlikely that Foxian churches will be springing up everywhere, this one at least seems to exemplify the "post-denominational" belief system to which Fox says the world is being called.

Early in February, Master General Damian Byrne, world head of the Dominican Order, issued a statement dissociating himself and the order from the widely published open letter in which Fox had called the Church, and Cardinal Ratzinger, a "dysfunctional family". Byrne's public repudiation may have influenced Fox's unexpected decision to remain out of sight for the entire year as directed. National Catholic News Service was informed in late May that Father Fox had decided to observe the full period of silence after "dialogue with trusted advisors" in the Dominican Midwest Province.[86]

Fox had said he would go to Latin America during his sabbatical to visit fellow "victim" Leonardo Boff. He went at least as far as Nicaragua. The first post-sabbatical issue of *Creation* was a paean to the "revolutionary Christians" of that utopia.[87] It included an overview by ex-seminarian David Gentry-Akin, the magazine's young managing editor, who traveled with Fox, met the Sandinista leaders and saw no evidence of "totalitarianism" except the United States embassy. Fox's own breathless reminiscences of his visit followed, accompanied by an admiring interview with Sandinista "Minister of Culture" Ernesto Cardenal, a former Trappist. There was also a poem by Cardenal with a footnoted editorial apology for its "exclusively male references to God". (After Nicaraguan voters

[85] Rita Gillmon, "Group Formed to Study 'Cosmic Christ'", *San Diego Union*, Feb. 4, 1989.

[86] "Father Fox 'Acquiesces' to a Full-Year Sabbatical", *Saint Cloud Visitor*, June 1, 1989.

[87] *Creation* (Jan./Feb. 1990).

turned the Sandinistas out in the February 25 election, *Creation* suggested that they had not voted "against the Sandinistas" but "*against* the U.S. war".[88]

During the month of January 1990, Fox conducted five-day programs in New Zealand and Australia, but he was back in the United States in early February for Chicago Call to Action's midwest conference, held to publicize the "Call for Reform in the Catholic Church" it co-sponsored with Friends of Creation Spirituality and four other radical groups.[89] Fox told the Chicago audience that the time had come to admit that there are two Catholic Churches.

Fox's year of silence was apparently without educational effect on some Catholic organizations. Most of his speaking dates for the first six months of 1990 took him to Religious Science, Divine Science, Unity, Methodist and Episcopal gatherings.[90] But on May 31, 1990, in Phoenix, he also addressed the fourteenth annual conference of the (Catholic) National Association of Lay Ministry, where Bishop Thomas J. O'Brien joined him in dance. The five hundred members of the association formed a circle, shook hands and chanted "Earth I am. Fire I am. Water, air and spirit I am."[91]

The Troublesome Friar

One of the names listed on Fox's "Family Tree of Creation Spirituality" is that of Giordano Bruno, a troublesome sixteenth-century Dominican whose reputation has lately been revived among New Agers. Bruno was obsessed with a theory of materialistic pantheism; he believed that God and the world are one; that matter and spirit, soul and body, are simply two phases of the same substance;

[88] "A Vote against the U.S. War", earth notes, *Creation* (May/June 1990): 8f. In another post-election development, Father William Boteler, superior general of the Maryknoll order, petitioned the Vatican in June to reinstate the priestly faculties of Miguel D'Escoto, erstwhile Sandinista foreign minister, according to a Catholic News Service report (*St. Cloud Visitor*, June 21, 1990).

[89] See chap. 2 above, 114.

[90] "On the Road—with Matt Fox", *Creation* (May/June 1990): 5.

[91] "From the Mail", *Wanderer*, Sept. 6, 1990, 3.

that the universe is infinite, and every part, mineral, vegetable and animal, is animated. He ran away from the Dominicans, dabbled in "natural magic" and prowled from country to country, restless and troubled. In those more decisive times, he was successively excommunicated by the Calvinists in Geneva and the Lutherans in Germany and finally burned at the stake for heresy in Rome. One can indeed detect a family resemblance between Fox and Bruno.

It is unlikely that Fox will end at the stake, but he does give the impression of a man planting a bomb on his own flight. No one can predict the action of grace in the human heart, but it will be no surprise if his hubris bears him out of the priesthood and out of the Church. That will be sad, but of his own doing. It would be sadder still if his superiors were to indulge his tantrums, condone his egregious errors and let him continue to prey on the flock. Religious authority is a spiritual responsibility that obligates those who command as well as those who obey.

Spiritual Subversives at NCEA

Those infected with the spiritual viruses of goddess feminism or creation spirituality had to make some kind of conscious choice to expose themselves. It has been sadly evident for some years that others, entirely innocent, risk exposure to neo-gnosticism at National Catholic Education Association conventions.

No one, for example, evangelizes for the New Age "transformation of consciousness" with more clarity or drama than Jean Houston, one-time Catholic, director of the Foundation for Mind Research, past president (1978–79) of the Association for Humanistic Psychology and leading voice of the "human potential movement". In addition to her frequent appearances at New Age conferences, she speaks regularly to educators. The persistence of evil demonstrates a terminal breakdown in the old Western worldview, she says, but simultaneously, improved communication technologies, the "global" women's movement and new discoveries in physics and "psychotechnologies" present unprecedented opportunities for a "revolution in consciousness". If the unenlightened masses can be persuaded to accept illumination from those already transformed, they too can be "godded" and so launched on the development of their previously submerged potential. Houston, an early LSD experimenter, is also considered an expert on non-pharmacological techniques for altering consciousness.

In her standard presentation, Houston tells educators that the chief responsibility for "global transformation" is in their hands. "You people right now are among the most important people alive", she told the 1989 national conference of the Association for Supervision and Curriculum Development (ASCD) on March 14. "You are the weavers of the future . . . midwives of souls. All cultures thought that their culture was *it*. They were wrong. *This* is it, right now; *this* time in history! Everything is in place to make the leap—but the *juice* is not on." Stimulating the "juice" that will bring in the new global age is a duty educators must accept, she said. "You are the ones who are creating the whole system transition."[92]

For unexplained reasons, Houston was invited to address NCEA conventions in 1982, 1984 and 1989. Protesters may deserve credit for her last-minute decision to speak atypically, in 1989, about St. Francis of Assisi as a model of transformation. The saint has been appropriated by New Agers as he was by 1960s hippies; one well-known pop singer is rumored to believe himself a reincarnation of Francis. But Houston's talk was ambiguous enough so that it probably did not shake the faith of listening believers, New Age or Catholic.

In 1985, when Houston did not appear, the NCEA had Robert Muller as a major speaker. Muller identifies himself as a Catholic but says he only began to "discover spirituality" from Buddhist Secretary-General U Thant at the United Nations. When he did, his conversion to a cosmic-unity faith seems to have been com-

[92] Jean Houston, "Whole System Transition: The Birth of Planetary Society", address to the Association for Supervision and Curriculum Development, Mar. 14, 1989, Orlando, Fla.

plete. Muller credits Houston with having launched his speaking career, and they often address the same conferences. He too spoke at the 1989 ASCD meeting, where his recitation of "planetary" platitudes was chiefly distinguished by his Charles Boyer accent. Some of his other activities are of more galvanizing interest, however. For example, the "Robert Muller School of Ageless Wisdom", in Arlington, Texas, is an accredited private institution "certified" as a "UN-Associated School". It uses a relentlessly New Age "World Core Curriculum" designed by Muller and promoted internationally by Gordon Cawelti, executive director of ASCD, and intended to instruct students from birth ("Balanced Beginnings") through high school. The school's 1988 resource catalogue offers twenty-eight items—curriculum materials, lesson plans, books and computer diskettes—with such titles as "The Forces of Light", "Education in the New Age", "Toward a World Religion for the New Age", "Teaching the Gaia Hypothesis", "Visions of Peace" and "Whole Brain" teaching. Four are books by Alice Bailey; four are from Helena Roerich and the Agni Yoga Society; one is a tape of Muller's address at Lucis Trust's 1982 World Goodwill seminar.

In conjunction with the United Nations' University for Peace, the Robert Muller School co-sponsored an April 1988 conference featuring, among its "Leading Lights", Muller himself; Ted Turner, the "transformed" president of Cable News Network; Barbara Meister-Vitale, author of *Unicorns are Real*; Willis Harman, president of the Institute for Noetic Sciences at Stanford University (a New Age think tank); and Harmonic Converger José Arguelles.

NCEA Futures

Convention speakers are not the only New Age channel to the American Catholic bureaucracy. Further evidence of its influence showed up in reports on a "Catholic Education Futures Project" in which the NCEA participated between 1985 and 1988 along with twenty other Catholic education agencies associated with the

NCEA or the United States Catholic Conference. It was summarized in the NCEA's glossy journal *Momentum* in September 1988 and discussed at two workshops at the 1989 convention. The *Momentum* overview, "The Dangerous Journey Through Opportunity to Transformation", was written by Sister Suzanne Hall, S.N.D.deN., "chairperson of the planning, study/reflection and symposium phases".

Two accompanying articles by project "resource persons" are worth special notice. Sister Sarah Fahy, S.N.D.deN., wrote about the importance of creation-centered spirituality in educating for "global citizenship". Hazel Henderson, described in the report as an "independent self-employed futurist", wrote briefly about "our responsibility for co-creating positive futures" in an ecumenical spirit. Her name is a staple of New Age advisory boards, and she has the dubious distinction of being the only woman Madonna Kolbenschlag praised by name in *Oz* as representative of the way "women's spirituality . . . is building a kind of chrysalis of the future" out of which the "new world order" will emerge. The sixteen books in the "Planning Phase" bibliography include one by Henderson, two by Thomas Berry, one by Fritjof Capra, one by Raimundo Pannikar and one by Patricia Mische. Simple prudence would recommend that educators plan for future needs; there is nothing alarming in that. But as demonstrated in the relevant NCEA workshops, "futuring" is a lengthy, repetitious, groupthink process, having less to do with designing for the future than with redesigning the participants to think along the New Age lines suggested by the reading list. Such a project holds no promise for a restoration of authentic Catholic education.

Necessary Dissent

As societies where it prevails give witness, the belief that consciousness is the only reality may lead to neglect of practical needs and objectively real evils. Perhaps that explains the striking absence from the 1989 NCEA convention program of several issues of enormous importance to the future of Catholic students. Although the meeting was held in Chicago while Cardinal Bernardin was chairman of the NCCB Respect Life Committee, there was not a single presentation about abortion. Nor was there any on euthanasia, though the Catholic Health Association gave disturbing evidence of the need for it by distributing "model living will" forms at its exhibit booth.

Space was found for the liberal consensus, however, as represented by theologian Ann O'Hara Graff, for example. A professor at the archdiocesan Mundelein Seminary, Graff confronted the cardinal with religious professionals' standard complaint that the Church declines to accept the guidance of the second magisterium. "Religious educators are sometimes in the difficult position of offering a rationale for Church teaching that they feel does not reflect Jesus Christ, is unjust and untruthful", she said during a symposium on religious education. "In conscience, we are bound to examine again both what the Church teaches and what nags at us that we cannot accept." Over the past century, Scripture scholars have peeled away mistaken beliefs about the origins of the Church, she declared. "Today we recognize that the Church appeared as a response to Jesus' person and message. We can no longer read our hierarchical Church order back into the gospel as if there were no history. Jesus proclaimed God's love. . . . He did not appoint a Pope or ordain anyone, male or female." Because Church leaders, slow to accept these conclusions, continue to deny laypeople participation in doctrinal decision making, "serious dissent in the Church is sometimes necessary for the sake of the gospel", Graff said.

Cardinal Bernardin replied that the Church cannot "come to grips" with the questions Graff raised until she has settled the changes "in mission, function and nature of the Church" that have grown out of the Second Vatican Council.[93]

[93] Daniel J. Lehmann, "Bernardin Urged to Boost Laity's Role", *Chicago Sun-Times*, Mar. 29, 1989, 5.

Intellectually Embarrassing

Whether or not the NCEA intends to steer Catholic education into the New Age, it is clearly paying serious attention to the subjectivist theories of humanistic and transpersonal psychology. Yet those ideas are not taken seriously by recognized academic and professional psychologists. A leading graduate-level text by Salvatore Maddi, *Personality Theories: A Comparative Analysis*,[94] includes no references to Jean Houston or to transpersonal psychology.

"Among academic psychologists, transpersonal psychology is almost unheard of", said Paul Vitz, professor of psychology at New York University.

> Even humanistic psychology, which moved into many of those ideas, is considered to be outside the academic world. In the universities, transpersonal psychology is essentially associated with Shirley MacLaine. No transpersonal psychology is taught in our department. But at Sierra Junior College, if there is such a place, who knows what's going on? Somebody there may be teaching a course in transpersonal psychology.

Why does a professional organization like the NCEA focus so strongly on ideas viewed with disdain by legitimate psychologists? "The world of education is an intellectual vacuum filled with everything from Carl Rogers to values clarification—which is the vaporization of any moral position—to Jean Houston", Vitz said. "It's a sign of the pathological condition of most of our educators that they would buy this stuff. It's Shirley MacLaine in textbook form. It's embarrassing."

Marshall Fightlin, a clinical psychologist who practices in Duluth, Minnesota, said he did not know of Jean Houston but was painfully aware that "humanistic psychology has been the source of many of those strange ideas: that you can just follow your instincts and I can follow my instincts and somehow it will work

[94] Salvatore R. Maddi, *Personality Theories: A Comparative Analysis* (Chicago: Dorsey Press, 1989).

out that we're both right! It's saying that you don't have to grow up; you can just continue to function like an infant and be the center of the universe. But an adult has a lot more power to do harm than an infant has." Fightlin said he worries about the social consequences of following "the God within". "There is no doubt that those attitudes contribute to the breaking up of the family. It's a menace, a cancer in terms of family and social stability."

The Journey Within

The continuing disintegration of their communities proves that the "passionate subjectivity" of gnosticism is equally menacing to the stability of professed religious. With the evaporation of Catholic belief, many members have had difficulty finding a new organizing principle, yet some such principle is essential to any community. Searching in obscure corners of comparative religion and the occult, they found among other oddities the Enneagram, a system of personality classification that reputedly originated among monist Sufi mystics in ancient Afghanistan. Wedded to pop psychology (e.g., the Myers-Briggs Type Indicator), it has become overwhelmingly popular in the strata of American Catholics looking for truth within themselves.

According to Enneagram enthusiasts, the Sufis guarded the system as a secret oral tradition for many centuries. It came to the West after the Russian Revolution, when guru Georgei Ivanovich Gurdjieff fled to France and established an esoteric center at Fontainebleau. Publicized by journalist Peter Ouspensky, Gurdjieff acquired an international following. Ouspensky wrote about the Enneagram in his 1949 book *In Search of the Miraculous*. Nothing more about it appeared in print until the early 1970s, when Chilean psychiatrist Oscar Ichazo reintroduced it to the United States by way of the Esalen Institute and *Psychology Today* magazine. Claudio Naranjo of Esalen established a nationwide network of small Enneagram groups. Among his early students was Father Robert Ochs, S.J., who promptly began teaching it in his religious experience classes at Chicago's Loyola University.

Once launched, the fad spread quickly among Jesuits and then to other orders, becoming an important element in the seduction of Catholics into the New Age movement. Today, fascination with the Enneagram has replaced concern about sanctifying grace at retreat houses, in adult education classes, spiritual formation sessions and everywhere else that avant-garde nuns, priests and laypeople gather. Like habitués of singles' bars comparing zodiacal signs, they ask new acquaintances, "What's your Enneagram number?"

The Enneagram symbol is a circle surrounding a nine-pointed star, which represents the nine personality types into which, believers hold, all human beings can be sorted. Oddly, they are all considered to be *false* personalities—defense mechanisms concealing compulsive neuroses. It is no doubt symptomatic of their identity anxiety that Catholic religious professionals are so powerfully drawn to the negative theory that human personality is wholly composed of pathological elements. Under those layers of delusion and illness, what do they think constitutes *authentic* personality?

Authors of a leading Catholic Enneagram text say the basic personality is and will always remain a "sin type". But learning what type it is offers the "new freedom" of awakened "self-criticism", of having "always something to repent, something to confess as sin, something to make resolutions about for the future". *The Enneagram: A Journey of Self-Discovery*[95] consists mostly of descriptions of the nine types, which, like newspaper horoscopes, include qualities recognizable in everyone. It also offers advice about how to overcome each compulsion and even each type's appropriate colors and animal "totems". It attempts to put the Enneagramic system in a Christian perspective by referring to personality fixations as "sin" and representing the "Enneagramic Jesus" as a model of wholeness who possessed all nine personality types yet lived them without the "sin" of compulsion.

[95] Maria Beesing, O.P.; Robert J. Nogorek, C.S.C.; and Patrick H. O'Leary, S.J.: *The Enneagram: A Journey of Self-Discovery* (Denville, N.J.: Dimension Books, 1984).

The chief obstacles to making sense of the book are its failure to define personality and its apparent confusion of person and nature in regard both to ordinary men and to Jesus Christ, who put on human nature while remaining the Second Person of the Blessed Trinity. Do the authors intend to present universally defective personality as a psychological version of original sin? In fallen man, original sin is a flaw in *nature*, not a personal sin to be confessed. In context, what the authors seem to mean would more accurately be termed *temperament*—a characteristic weakness inclining one to a particular kind of sin. If personality is defined as compulsive neurosis, sin cannot be seen as a free act for which the sinner is culpable, and personality cannot be attributed to Jesus, who has no weaknesses. These logical problems arise because the authors are attempting merely cosmetic repairs to a typically New Age "journey within", which is really aimed at the "transformation of consciousness" and focused not on God but on the self. Secular New Agers use a different vocabulary; they see their "Enneagram work" as an aid to becoming spiritually "evolved beings".

Turning to the East

Much else in today's neo-gnostic spirituality is similarly taken, or translated, from romanticized Eastern mysticism, and its pernicious fruits are widely visible on the Catholic scene. Witness the dismal example of the Franciscan Sisters of Oldenburg, Indiana, and Wheaton, Illinois.

Beginning in 1983, Sister Claire Whalen, director of personnel services for the Oldenburg Franciscans, and Sister Sarah Page, curriculum director for the Catholic schools of St. Louis, Missouri, sent successive delegations from their community to "brain/mind revolution" courses directed by the late Beverly Galyean. Dr. Galyean's fame rests on her "confluent education" program, which taught public school students in southern California that "we are all God" in the essential "oneness that is consciousness". Sister Sarah, a teacher in the Franciscan courses, received her New Age indoctrination under Jean Houston. The re-educated Oldenburg nuns subsequently transmitted these ideas to their elementary and secondary students in Catholic schools in Indiana, Missouri and Ohio, with such "mind-expansion" exercises as "meditating on their peaceful center", rhythmic breathing, visualization, "mental journeys" with guided imagery and "painting with love".[96]

The altered consciousness of the Wheaton Franciscans led *National Catholic Reporter* to say that they "have gone to meet the 21st century".[97] In fact, what they have gone to meet is the New Age. The understandably shrinking community has run pleas for new members in the back of Matthew Fox's *Creation* magazine under "Opportunities". Wheaton Sister Gabriele Uhlein, who studied with Fox, is the author of *Meditations with Hildegarde of Bingen*,[98] one in the series of ICCS *Meditations with* books distributed by Bear & Company. At Our Lady of the Angels Convent in Wheaton, Sister Gabriele has presented "enlightenment" classes to "explore" Jewish, Buddhist, Islamic, Indian and Wiccan "traditions" and rituals and to introduce the I Ching, a Chinese fortune-telling system. Sister Gabriele explained her quintessentially New Age motives:

> We no longer have the luxury of a leisurely religious search. We are in the process of unfolding a new human identity, and in the balance hangs our ability to successfully navigate our initiation as planetary people. The convergence is upon us as surely as the evolution of the species.[99]

Another Wheaton Franciscan, Sister Virginia Barta, went in April 1988, at community expense, on a spiritual pilgrimage to India, where she wandered alone from ashram to ashram. Her letters

[96] Unsigned, "Tapping the Mind's Potential", and Sister Sarah Page, "Educator Trains for New 'Wave'", in *Franciscans Celebrate* (Summer 1983). See also Rae Ann Barger, "Not Your Ordinary Field Trip, This One!" *Middletown* (Ohio) *Journal*, Nov. 7, 1983.

[97] Robert J. McClory, "These Nuns Have Gone to Meet the 21st Century", *National Catholic Reporter*, Jan. 13, 1989.

[98] Gabriele Uhlein, *Meditations with Hildegarde of Bingen* (Santa Fe, N.M.: Bear, 1983).

[99] Advertising flyer for her six-session "Enlightenment?" course at the Advent Center for Spiritual Development, Wheaton, Ill.

back to Wheaton told how she greeted one guru by kneeling before him and touching her forehead to the floor "to give him reverence as a God-Realized being". She sat at the feet of Hindu mystics, meditating on "the core of the self" in order to "experience God —the True Self". She spent time at Shantivanam, the Hindu-Christian ashram where English Benedictine Dom Bede Griffiths serves as guru. According to Griffiths, the task of Christians is *not* to bring Christ to India but "to discover Christ already present and active in the Hindu soul".[100] From another ashram, Sister Virginia reported that "cleaning the temple, dressing and feeding the gods was a daily ritual". When she came home two months later, she and several companions founded the "Christine Center for Meditation", an ashram "dedicated to a Unitive Planetary Spirituality", in Willard, Wisconsin. It offers hermitages or lodge rooms to guests who come for "Retreats, Spiritual Development Seminars and Body Energetics Work", yoga, psychocalisthenics, reflexology, acupressure, tarot, astrology, "Transpersonal Psychology" and other illuminative activities consistent with the belief that All is One. The Mass is not among the "spiritual services" offered at the center; anyone who cares is advised to repair to the nearest parish church. The center brochure does not reveal whether retreatants are expected to greet Sister Virginia as a "God-Realized" guru.

Back at the Wheaton motherhouse, community life is rounded out by membership, through the social justice team, in Women-Church Convergence.

The Zeitgeist

Neither a residual sense of the ridiculous nor a fear of consequences has yet slowed the extraordinary contemporary surge of neo-gnosticism. In its numerous disguises it is thriving among post-Christians. It is not uncommon among academics and corporate executives, booming among Unitarians, attenuated mainline

[100] Bede Griffiths, *Christ in India* (New York: Charles Scribner's Sons, 1966), 217.

Protestant churches and public school educators, epidemic among feminists, ecological absolutists, pacifists, "yuppies" and vegetarians. Anxious about personal or social problems, intrigued by the mysteries of nature and the mind, hungry for spiritual meaning, many of them might have turned for answers to Holy Mother Church if her professional elite in America had confidently witnessed to her truth. But sadly, many in Catholic academia, bureaucracy and religious orders failed to offer her answers because, when they encountered the well-known "spirit of Vatican II", they assumed they were supposed to embrace the zeitgeist. And the zeitgeist is the spirit of the New Age movement, promising spiritual superiority, a comprehensive understanding of reality and knowledge of the means to manipulate it, unrestricted by objective moral law: promises as old as Eden. The Franciscan communities of Oldenburg and Wheaton are tragically typical of the majority of religious houses. Those who have lost a vital Catholic faith are proving more susceptible to mystical pantheism than to atheism. Heartbroken nuns who are still believers concede that their orders are dying. The neo-gnostics think they are constructing "America's emerging culture". They may be right.

Or, on the other hand, a religious movement led by exploiters and followed by the deluded could prove to be as ephemeral as a soap bubble. Those who stumbled into it in the course of a genuine spiritual search may be open to Christ when the counterfeit fails, if Catholicism is preached with conviction. Catholic dissidents present more difficult pastoral problems, but appeasement will not move them to repentance. Depriving groups like the Grail of the use of the Catholic label and arranging the early retirement of subversive religious professionals might help. At least it would protect children from contagion.

There is little practical reason for optimism, but the knowledge that Christ is with us sustains Christian hope. Unlikely as it appears on a natural level, he has the power to restore his disintegrating American Church to undeserved health. Mercifully, history is full of surprises.

Chapter Five

The Domino Effect

During the first half of the twentieth century, nuns were almost universally esteemed as living signs of Christian contradiction to the world. Though most women's religious communities now seem to be in terminal decline, reverential awe toward nuns still lingers among lay Catholics, so indelible is their old image and so recent their transformation into religious revolutionaries. How did they get from there to here?

The feminism that is devouring them is an opportunistic disease, insinuated into congregations reeling in pain and confusion from encounters with "new theology". And while their disintegration reached crisis proportions only after the Second Vatican Council, the original infection was contracted in the late 1940s and early 1950s, when the Sister Formation movement began urging that American nuns earn the same academic qualifications as their secular peers. That plausible idea floundered in practice because American higher education, Catholic and non-Catholic, was increasingly contaminated with error, especially in the disciplines nuns usually pursued: education, psychology, catechetics and theology. John Dewey's secularist theories, generic scepticism and a succession of popular psychological notions held sway in state teachers' colleges, while neo-modernism was seeping into Catholic universities from Europe. First exposed to neo-modernist theology in college classes, nuns proved highly susceptible.

The Revolution Begins

Nineteenth-century modernism, contracted from rationalist German Protestant biblical scholarship, struck European Catholic theology late in the nineteenth century. Growing, like process thought in general, out of the Enlightenment philosophy of Descartes, Hegel, Spinoza and Kant, it rejected the historical truth of Sacred Scripture. God does not intervene in human history, it held, and objectively true knowledge about him is inaccessible to the human mind. What is called "revelation" is an expression of human religious psychology, the dynamic voice of "God within". Jesus Christ was not the Son of God made man, not a Divine Redeemer, but a merely human moral teacher of surpassing insight. So the Scriptures had to be expressions of community consciousness, written to provide a religious interpretation of past events. Christianity had been constructed by followers of Jesus to give his moral teachings the binding force of divine commands. According to that reasoning, the Church is a purely human invention, without divine origin or authority. The function of modern biblical scholarship, these men believed, is to use these hypotheses as if they were scientifically established fact to uncover the literary and historical purposes of Scripture in Hebrew and early Christian communities.

Why did they labor over a religious system they considered to be based on lies? Rudolf Bultmann, the most prominent twentieth-century liberal Protestant advocate for "demythologizing" Scripture, seems to see its goal as liberation from doctrine and moral precepts to a blind and unreasoning optimism. In *Kerygma and Myth*, he says that while the idea of Jesus as Divine Redeemer has "ceased to be tenable for us today",[1] his story can nevertheless "evoke religious experience" and thus inspire a subjective sense of "divine activity" within oneself, which he calls "existential" faith.[2]

Such a "faith" must be not only entirely personal and formless

[1] Rudolf Bultmann et al., *Kerygma and Myth* (New York: Harper Torchbooks, 1961), 35.

[2] Ibid., 196–203.

but also contrary to reason. "The man who wishes to believe in God . . . must realize that he has nothing in his hand on which to base his faith. He is suspended in mid-air" yet "ready, as Luther put it, to plunge into the inner darkness".[3] Faith, says Bultmann, *needs* to be "emancipated" from "the sphere of objective reality",[4] because when "God withdraws himself from the objective view", it "makes the world profane and restores to it its proper autonomy as the field of man's labors".[5]

A group of European Catholic theologians, including Fathers Alfred Loisy, S.J., and George Tyrrell, S.J., and layman Friedrich von Hügel, adopted the notions of liberal Protestantism and so popularized them as to create a growing crisis of belief. Pope Pius X condemned modernism in 1907, calling it "the synthesis of all heresies". In 1910, he identified its erroneous propositions in detail and instituted an anti-modernist oath to be sworn by all priests and seminary professors.[6]

However, the ideas continued to smolder underground in theological circles, especially in Scripture scholarship, where they undercut the most basic claims of the Church.

In its starkest formulation, the theological "new paradigm" flowing from those premises maintains that the Church has no special access to the truth about God. God is present or can be known only within the world. His will is revealed by a directly inspiring "spirit" (which may or may not be the Holy Spirit) as one reflects on one's experience. Man can have no "soul" distinguishable from his body; hence "salvation" must mean a utopian "Kingdom of God" built on earth. In such a view, Jesus Christ is God incarnate only as all men are, or can become,

[3] Ibid., 211.

[4] Ibid., 210.

[5] Ibid., 211.

[6] Pope Pius X's encyclical on modernism, *Pascendi Gregis* (London: Burns & Oates, 1907), is available in a 1982 facsimile edition from Neumann Press (Long Prairie, Minn., 1982). The Pope's condemnation of sixty-five specific errors of modernism, *Lamentabile Sane*, and the "Oath Against Modernism" appear as appendices in Michael Davies, *Partisans of Error: St. Pius X against the Modernists* (Long Prairie, Minn.: Neumann Press, 1983).

"incarnations" of God, if they follow the "spirit" within them as he did.

Usually summed up today as "the spirit of Vatican II", this body of neo-modernist opinion has penetrated deeply into the Church. It represents the substance of the new theological "liberal consensus", which is shared even by some prelates. Liberation theology and process theology are among its expressions. But nowhere has its impact been greater than among Catholic women religious, where its poisonous spiritual fruits include rabid feminism, goddess-Wicca and New Age thought. When women religious understood themselves as brides of Christ, their consecration expressed not what they *did* but what they *were*. When they lost their faith, they were convulsed by a crisis of identity so profound that it threatens to destroy the very possibility of consecrated life. Their rapid disintegration has no precedent in the entire history of the Church.

The Modernization of Religious Life

When the sisters went back to school, qualities that had been among their virtues contributed to their undoing. They proved to be the same submissive, uncritical and assiduous students at State U.—and, alas, at Catholic U., and at catechetical centers like Lumen Vitae in Belgium—that they had been in the days of orthodoxy back at dear old Mount St. Swithin's. But what they were taught was notably different, and few had the sophistication to strain out the camels. Along with educational theory and remedial teaching methods, many swallowed the neo-modernist reinterpretation of Scripture and catechetics, the new morality and new psychology, already prevailing among avant-garde professors. The result was a rapid group conversion in worldview, quickly translated back home into a new vocabulary, new policies and the new excuses that eventually became clichés of deconstruction. Even before the death of Pope Pius XII, many Catholic grammar schools had ceased to require student attendance at daily Mass, explaining that routine is deadly; if the children attended less often, the Mass would "mean more to them". During the late 1950s, nuns in classes I attended were already beginning to refer to Scripture as "mythology", explaining to questioners that "calling it 'myth' doesn't mean it isn't true, because a myth is a story that communicates some kind of a truth". The Second Vatican Council was not the cause, but the precipitating occasion, for a revolution already under way.

During the Council, Leon Joseph Cardinal Suenens of Belgium, author of *The Nun in the World*,[7] was the most outspoken advocate for the "modernization of religious life". It was he who suggested inviting a few women to attend the third session as auditors. The only American among them, Sister Mary Luke Tobin, S.L., president of the Congregation of Major Superiors of Women (CMSW), was irreversibly radicalized by her Roman experiences.

In debate on *Perfectae Caritatis* (the "Decree on the Appropriate Renewal of the Religious Life"), Cardinal Suenens said the naïveté of women religious endangered their apostolates. Nuns must become acquainted with the modern world, alter their "distinctive but ridiculous garb" and be given the freedom necessary to pursue apostolic action and to travel alone. Infantile obedience was out of date; representative government should replace congregational rule by a single powerful mother superior.[8]

As finally adopted, the decree orders an "up-to-date renewal" of religious life "in harmony with the present-day physical and psychological condition of the members". "Obsolete prescriptions" are to be pruned from constitutions and customs. General chapters are authorized to set their own norms for renewal, seeking approval from the Holy See and local bishops only "when the law requires this". Superiors are to "consult their subjects" and "listen to them". Even contemplative communities are directed to pursue "renewal", though without sacrificing their "withdrawal from the world" or their prayer life. Sisters preparing for active ministry are to

[7] Leon Joseph Cardinal Suenens, *The Nun in the World* (Westminster, Md.: Newman Press, 1963).

[8] Rev. Ralph M. Wiltgen, S.V.D., *The Rhine Flows into the Tiber* (Rockford, Ill.: Tan Books, 1985), 217f.

be "instructed" about modern society, and young nuns are to acquire their degrees before assignment. Religious habits are to be "simple and modest . . . poor and becoming" yet "suited to the times". However, *Perfectae Caritatis* also reminds women religious that as followers of Christ, they must "seek God above all else", remembering that they have renounced not only sin but also the world and that "religious obedience" requires them to "be humbly submissive to their superiors".[9] In tribute to the merits of the decree, its title was incorporated into the name of the Consortium Perfectae Caritatis, the American minority organization of orthodox women religious formed in 1970.

But the majority congregations represented by the already liberalized CMSW had been engaged in wildcat renewal throughout Vatican II, introducing neo-modernist theology to a far wider population of nuns than had been affected through Sister Formation. Accustomed to obedience and as credulous as Cardinal Suenens had warned, many nuns accepted it as an accurate reflection of the Council. Because they trusted the authorities who taught them, many came to believe that doctrines are *symbols* of the yearning human spirit rather than objective *truths* about God's dealings with mankind and, with astonishing speed, found that their faith had dissolved. Along with the inerrancy of Scripture and the immutability of dogma, the vision of the Mystical Body was dismissed. In its place came an interpretation of the Church as a pyramid, specifically designed to keep all power at the top, in the hands of the Pope and the bishops, and to oppress the voiceless faithful at the base. Those perceptions made women religious feel they had sacrificed their lives for a confidence game. Many were desolated by the loss of religious certitude. Many were enraged.

Sent to earn a doctorate in theology at St. Mary's College at Notre Dame in 1957, Sister Pascaline Coff, O.S.B., learned a "new theology of the Eucharist" from Passionist Carroll Stuhlmueller,

[9] "Decree of the Up-to-Date Renewal of Religious Life", in *Vatican Council II: The Conciliar and Post Conciliar Documents*, ed. Austin Flannery, O.P. (Collegeville: Liturgical Press, 1984), 611–23.

later reinforced by Benedictine Godfrey Diekmann: Christ was no longer a "static" presence in the Eucharist but a "dynamic" presence in the community. As a result, her congregation's priories replaced the "five-foot monstrance" used for perpetual adoration with "a small one-foot chalice monstrance". Some sisters, she admits, felt "that Christ was being dethroned and displaced" and warned that the change was "the beginning of a spiritual landslide". Adoration gradually dwindled from "perpetual" to "two nights a week" in each community. Coff herself turned eastward, to India, and eventually established an ashram in Sand Springs, Oklahoma, where Benedictine nuns, and Trappist and Tibetan monks now jointly practice inter-religious meditation.[10]

According to her diary, Sister Emmanuel Lucas, of the Franciscan Handmaids of Mary, was so happily traditional at the beginning of 1964 that she voted against even minor changes in the habit. But by mid-summer, after her introduction to new scriptural interpretation, she joined in a celebration of "the death of God . . . the untouchable one in the heavens, that Recorder of all our misdeeds", who "had to die so that the 'Ground of my being', as Tillich [one of the major Protestant theologians of this century] calls him, could truly live in me".[11] Eventually, Patricia Lucas left consecrated life.

Sister Rea McDonnell, S.S.N.D., says she suffered a "devastating" loss of faith in 1968, when her teacher in a graduate theology class announced, "God is not a person." With her "whole theological system" shattered, she began the "never-ending task" of reconstructing "a theology from below".[12] Others in her order encountered devastations of their own; between 1960 and 1985, the School Sisters of Notre Dame shrank from eleven thousand to eight thousand.

[10] Pascaline Coff, "Go East New Nun", in *Midwives of the Future*, ed. Ann Patrick Ware (Kansas City: Leaven Press, 1985), 82–94.

[11] Patricia Lucas, "Diary of Change", in Ware, *Midwives*, 175.

[12] Rea McDonnell, S.S.N.D., "Dying and Rising", in Ware, *Midwives*, 200.

To assess the effects of liberalizing programs conducted in many communities during the Council with their approval, the leaders of CMSW in 1967 circulated a so-called *Sisters' Survey*, a massive psycho-social questionnaire about theological beliefs, political views, reading habits and attitudes toward religious life. It was regarded with intense seriousness; 150,000 nuns completed it, for a phenomenal response rate of 88 percent. Like many such instruments, it was designed to shape as well as test opinions. Woven into the multiple-choice answers were the ideas of a process God, of human experience as revelation, of a Eucharist without priests and a Church without a hierarchy. Sister Marie Augusta Neal, who directed the survey, suggested in her 1969 interpretation of the results that traditional answers indicated a "proneness to Fascism" and a reprehensible concern "with saving their own souls" *instead of* "helping in the renewal of the world",[13] surely an odd either-or perspective on salvation.

Community Reform

Psychological "discoveries" have been the justification for many recent innovations in Catholic life, yet, if what they intended was not destruction, those responsible for inaugurating abrupt and sweeping post-conciliar change displayed not even an elementary understanding of human psychology. The Council Fathers had intended only to initiate wholesome reforms, but by the time the Council ended, leaders of most women's communities had lost interest in Vatican approval. The call for experimentation and new constitutions was implemented in most orders as wholesale disestablishment that intrinsically altered the structure of religious life. Inevitably, the upheaval in community life profoundly disoriented even those who promoted it and set off a chain reaction of disintegration. The directive to re-examine their current works in the light of their founders' intentions seemed like a message

[13] Msgr. George A. Kelly, *The Battle for the American Church* (Garden City, N.Y.: Image Books, 1981), 259. See also Weaver, *New Catholic Women*, 84.

that their past sacrifices had not been appreciated. Most nuns experienced it, at a deep psychic level, as a repudiation of the transcendent purpose to which they had vowed their lives.[14] The ensuing collapse is still sending shock waves through the Church. In comparison to the lost generation of the young, their numbers are small—and growing ever smaller—but the consequences of their tragedy reach far beyond their convents.

Radicals in the ranks, shrewder in their generation than the children of light, maneuvered their way into control. Sister Maureen Fiedler tells how "those of us who wanted fundamental change in community structures held late-night meetings in basements, developed phone networks to keep allies informed and learned the importance of setting agendas, preparing proposals in advance and determining who would speak most effectively".[15] To manipulate their communities, they used techniques that have since become maddeningly familiar to lay Catholics as well: "small-group" discussions, where a "facilitator" notes members' remarks in highly selective summary, then reports them to the discussion leader. The resulting "consensus" tends to consist of conclusions desired by those in control, whether or not anyone in a small group actually stated them. Thus many nuns who doubted the wisdom of drastic change were pressured to accept it as "democratically" chosen. Many who recited the rote explanation—that their new freedom from obedience and custom was a superior state because it made service voluntary—felt in their hearts like discarded wives, disvalued, dispossessed and bereaved. As one Sacred Heart sister put it, "It just feels like somebody died."[16]

[14] Dr. James Hitchcock discussed the phenomenon at greater length in a two-part article, "The Rebellious Heart: The Unravelling of the Church Since Vatican II", *Catholicism in Crisis* (Oct. and Nov., 1985).

[15] Maureen Fiedler, "Riding the City Bus from Pittsburgh", in Ware, *Midwives*, 43.

[16] V. V. Harrison, *Changing Habits: A Memoir of the Society of the Sacred Heart* (New York: Doubleday, 1988), 190.

Collapsing orders have tended to follow a standard sequence. First, exposure to neo-modernist theology produced a counter-conversion, away from religious conviction ("the belief that God is absolute truth, that the Roman Catholic Church has a direct line to the Deity")[17] to acceptance of secular values ("autonomy and self-definition, freedom, commitment to key issues, affirmation of themselves as change agents").[18] Laxity in community prayer, especially eucharistic prayer, soon followed. Next came permissive new rules and refusal to obey ecclesiastical authorities. Finally, feminism flowed in to fill the void where faith had lived. "I will not serve" has become their common message. Examples can be cited in a wide range of communities.

The Grail

Though feminism directly contradicted its professed principles, the Grail was in the vanguard of the movement. Because the Grail was an autonomous, non-canonical movement, its evolution away from orthodoxy cannot be blamed on hierarchical misdirection. Early and deliberately, it became an interdenominational cross-road for feminists lay and religious, academic and non-academic. Why? The North American group was inevitably affected by the mounting turbulence of the Church in Holland, its international headquarters. But like canonical women's communities, the Grail was propelled from orthodox certitude into feminist derangement chiefly by the ideas of male theologians.

Founded in Holland in 1921 by Father Jacques van Ginneken, S.J., the Grail was a lay community with an elite core committed by promises to lives of celibacy, poverty and obedience. Unless the Church offered modern women Christ, Father van Ginneken warned, spiritual hunger would draw them to the secular women's movement, "Bolshevism", "occultism, spiritism and theosophy".[19] The Grail was to be a spiritual training center, fos-

[17] Weaver, *New Catholic Women*, 87.

[18] Ibid., 89.

[19] Alden Vincent Brown, *The Grail Movement in the United States, 1940–*

tering the "womanly virtues" of spiritual receptivity, self-sacrifice and compassion, to form liturgically centered, vibrantly apostolic Catholic laywomen who would work in their families, parishes and communities, or as lay missionaries, for the conversion of the world.

Dr. Lydwine Van Kersbergen brought the Grail to the United States in 1941. Early recruits were attracted by her conferences on "The Christian Conspiracy", presented at cooperating parishes. Janet Kalven, a convert from Judaism, left a job with Mortimer Adler at the University of Chicago to join the Grail in 1942. National headquarters were established in 1944 on a farm at Loveland, Ohio. According to Kalven, Father van Ginneken had told them, "Always deal directly with the bishop, because he'll be too busy to interfere." So the movement did, further avoiding masculine control by refusing to have its own chaplain.

Some fourteen thousand young women eventually participated in Grail programs, which included summer courses and a "year's school of the apostolate", a program of rural living and Christian culture: farm work, canning, bread baking, music (especially Gregorian chant), meditation, weaving, sculpture, dance, writing and study of the literature of the Catholic Revival.[20] Courses were accredited by Catholic University, and Dorothy Day, Joseph Jungmann, H. A. Reinhold, Christopher Dawson, Jean Danielou, Evelyn Waugh and other prominent figures came to present them. For twenty years, Dr. Van Kersbergen's powerful personality shaped the American Grail. Her book *Woman* seems prophetic today in its grasp of feminism's anti-feminine heart. Van Kersbergen sees the sexes as complementary, divinely designed to form "a functional whole rather like our right and left hands, which can grasp

---

1972: The Evolution of an American Catholic Laywoman's Community (Ann Arbor, Mich.: University Microfilms International, 1983), chap. I, 5, 19.

20 Ibid., 223. Among the better-known Grail affiliates was Delores Leckey, staff director for the NCCB Committee on the Laity from its foundation in 1977.

so firmly precisely because they are opposites."[21] The contrasting feminist thesis, proposed by those like Simone de Beauvoir, "identifies the human with the masculine", she says, in urging woman to strive for

> a situation identical with the man, not only externally, but psychologically, having the right to homosexuality, taking the initiative in heterosexual love, as well as every other avenue of life. . . . Two notable waves of resentment rise beneath the surface of this argument: a deep-seated, misogynist aversion for everything connected with the specific womanly role in love and motherhood . . . and an equally deep conviction that the achievements which our society designates as masculine are the only really valuable achievements.[22]

Dr. Van Kersbergen believed the world was wearying of that destructive ideology, "now that its earlier goals of equality before the law, identical education and free entry into business and professions have been achieved".[23] "A reaction against the masculinized ideal of the feminists is growing," she says, "and from many quarters a new slogan resounds: 'Be yourself; be true to woman's nature.'"[24]

In fact, feminism was just about to burst the seams of society. And while the "new slogan" is at last being heard from some quarters, Grailville is not one of them. In a painful irony, the Grail adopted precisely the positions Van Kersbergen had delineated as pernicious, to become precisely what Father van Ginneken designed the movement to oppose—a seedbed of feminism, occultism, theosophy, liberation theology and Marxism—as though it had itself become a New Age "walk-in".[25] Janet Kalven, in her seventies, agreed that there has been "a *drastic* change. One hundred and eighty degrees!" Of her once popular pamphlet *The Task*

[21] Lydwine Van Kersbergen, *Woman: Some Aspects of Her Role in the Modern World* (Loveland, Ohio: Grailville, 1956), 120.

[22] Ibid., 11–12.

[23] Ibid., 10.

[24] Ibid., 12.

[25] See chap. 4 above, 196.

of Woman in the Modern World, she laughed, "In 1948, I wrote that. Now I do not believe *one thing* that's in it!"[26]

When American Grail members began serving as lay catechists in Latin American and African missions in the early 1950s, their training program was influenced by progressive European theological, scriptural and liturgical scholarship. Father Johannes Hofinger, S.J., came to Grailville from Germany in the summer of 1955 to present a survey class in contemporary theology. After that, members were sent for training to Lumen Vitae in Belgium or to other catechetical institutes. By 1958, Grailville had formed its own catechetical department. German theologian-psychologist Josef Goldbrunner came to speak on "Depth Psychology and the Spiritual Life" in 1958, returning in 1959 to teach modern catechetics. By 1960, in the Grail's catechetical journal, editor Eva Fleischner expressed the progressive view that religious education at its best is not "primarily concerned with a series of abstract tenets that must be memorized and believed, but with *life*, the life of God communicated to man".[27]

Like other hypotheses of the time, the statement implied a false dichotomy. Dogma is essential to religious education *because* it communicates the truth about God to man. The Church gives those truths concrete life in liturgy, sacraments, moral teaching and the holiness of the saints who live them in the world. There is no either-or choice; both dogma and its concrete expression are necessary to the life of the faithful. Without doctrinal truth, a Catholic culture quickly becomes a sepulchre.

By 1960, confusion about the Grail's identity was beginning to trouble its members. Oddly enough, many felt that their formation had focused too much on immersion in "life"—especially manual labor—and too little on intellectual development. Some wanted the curriculum to encourage the development of the "self" and the

[26] Interview with Janet Kalven, Mar. 28, 1987.
[27] Brown, *Grail Movement*, 183–87.

"variety in tradition" found in the secular world.[28] Doubts were growing about the value of the lay missionary program, and half a dozen members of the "nucleus" had been released from their lifetime promises.[29]

Van Kersbergen was replaced as North American president in January of 1962 and returned to Europe. New leaders took over, Janet Kalven among them, and the demolition of the Grail began in earnest. Seven hundred members and alumnae, single and married, were invited to a Grail National Conference the following October 12, just one day after the opening of Vatican II, to consider "new perceptions of person, community and world that were emerging".[30] Certitude was traded for a new "openness" to contemporary society and to "the religious experience of women outside the Catholic tradition".[31] Drastic reorganization and a rash of resignations followed.

According to Kalven, Grail feminism was inflamed by the example of European religious feminists from St. Joan's Alliance, who were already suggesting that women be ordained.[32] Speakers at Grailville tended ever more toward the progressive: Fathers Bernard Cooke, S.J.; Daniel Berrigan; Godfrey Diekmann, O.S.B.; Carroll Stuhlmueller, C.P.; Gerard Sloyan; Gregory Baum; Charles Davis. (Davis, Baum and Cooke all defected from the priesthood later, Davis with longtime Grail "nucleus" member Florence Henderson as his prospective bride.)

Only 165 Grail associates continued as full members for the group's 1964 "Aggiornamento Year",[33] when a Catholic-Protestant weekend conference was presented by Frances Maeda of the World Council of Churches. The year-long School of Formation was discontinued in 1965. "We had discovered at the Grail by the mid-

[28] Ibid., 224–28.

[29] Ibid., 229–33.

[30] Ibid., 235.

[31] Ibid., 321.

[32] Janet Kalven, "Women's Voices Began to Challenge—after Negative Vatican Council Events", *National Catholic Reporter*, Apr. 13, 1984, 15.

[33] Brown, *Grail Movement*, 229–41.

1960s that something was wrong with complementarity", Kalven says.[34] In 1966, at her request, Kalven's celebrated pamphlet *The Task of Woman in the Modern World* was withdrawn from circulation. Grail historian Alden Brown observes that members in the 1960s exhausted themselves in "discussions of change, openness and relevance", that is, in looking within.[35] By 1967, the shrinking nucleus agreed that "conversion of the world" was a triumphalist term, bearing "connotations of condescension" and "totally without meaning to most people with whom we are involved in this world".[36] Seeing the natural world as the only possible source of knowledge about God confirmed a view of their "spiritual journey" as a search for truth (which would never finally be found) through action. At the end of the decade, outgoing President Dorothy Rasenberger reminded her Grail sister that their task was "still to reflect and act, act and reflect". In such action, she said, "belief, itself open ended . . . is refined and transformed".[37]

From 1968 through 1975, in place of the Year's School, a non-sectarian "semester at Grailville" offered courses on black history, group process, sexism, death and dying, socialism and Virginia Woolf. Still accredited by Catholic University, the program moved the Grail further toward "a non-credal position".[38] In 1969, after an international Grail conference on "the feminist critique of the churches", Kalven joined a "consciousness-raising" and planning group in Church Women United (CWU), an interdenominational liberal coalition.[39]

During the 1970s, the Grail extended its influence on American religious feminism. Seventy-five women, Rosemary Ruether and Elisabeth Schussler Fiorenza among them, came to a week-long 1972 conference, "Women Exploring Theology", sponsored by

[34] Kalven, "Voices", 15.
[35] Brown, *Grail Movement*, 303.
[36] Ibid., 300.
[37] Ibid., 303.
[38] Ibid., 260–65.
[39] Kalven, "Voices", 15.

CWU.[40] It was there that Judith Plaskow and her committee wrote "The Coming of Lilith" for a "liturgy". Repeated in 1973, the Grail-CWU conference focused on "more inclusive theology and liturgical language".[41] To institutionalize the project, a "Seminary Quarter at Grailville" was established in 1974, offering a "unit of theological education" in which "women's concerns are central rather than peripheral".[42] It drew students from twenty-eight seminaries and eight colleges before expiring in 1977. By the end of the 1970s, the Grail itself was expiring; in the United States, only forty nucleus members remained.[43] Grailville had become more a conference center than a community, filling its calendar with a parade of Wicca, voodoo, New Age, process- and liberation-theology conferences, arranged by one or another of its last three task forces: on woman, the search for God, and liberation.[44] *Women's Spirit Bonding* is the hair-raising report of one conference.[45]

Though the precipitous drop in membership suggests otherwise, Kalven assured me there was never a policy division among Grail leaders. Its transformation was "in many ways a natural development", she said, easily accomplished because of its independence from clerical control.[46] She seemed to consider it an achievement.

[40] The rest included ordained Protestants, seminary students and professional Church workers. See Weaver, *New Catholic Women*, 127; also Brown, *Grail Movement*, 305.

[41] Weaver, *New Catholic Women*, 127.

[42] Brown, *Grail Movement*, 306.

[43] Ibid., 302.

[44] Ibid., 305.

[45] See chap. 4 above, n. 8, esp. "Why Women Need the War God".

[46] Interview with Janet Kalven, Mar. 28, 1987. In the same interview, she volunteered the interesting information that many religious orders today, seeing the benefits of such independence, "have formed two legal corporations—one of the things you can do under the law—and the one that owns the property is not the one that's subject to Rome". They do so, she said, because "they may want to take a stand—for example, a pro-choice stand. A lot of the orders are pro-choice. Or a stand for the ordination of women. So, if it came to a choice, they wouldn't lose the property."

Glenmary Sisters

Back from their re-education at Lumen Vitae, the Glenmary Home Mission Sisters of Cincinnati so far relaxed their rules that Archbishop Karl Alter stepped in to restore discipline. Rather than submit, fifty sisters withdrew in 1965 to form a new lay association, leaving only fifteen members in the order.[47] By 1988, only three remained.

School Sisters of St. Francis

"Renewal" turned into insurrection among Milwaukee's School Sisters of St. Francis between 1966 and 1976. The membership of three thousand declined by more than one-third, and new admissions virtually ceased, but Sister Francis Borgia Rothluebber, the mother general, said too many women had entered religious life in the old days anyway.[48] There has been no subsequent recovery. By 1990, according to the order's public relations office, membership in the United States was down to 1,450.

Immaculate Heart of Mary

Astonished Catholics followed in the press as the once thriving Los Angeles Sisters of the Immaculate Heart of Mary fell apart in 1968 after several years of feuding with Rome and Cardinal McIntyre. Under dispute was their version of "renewal", which included encounter group therapy with "human potential" psychologist Carl Rogers,[49] abandonment of the religious habit, individual autonomy in regard to prayer and community life and anarchic

[47] Weaver, *New Catholic Women*, 92–93. According to Janet Kalven of nearby Grailville, Grail members had learned the same new attitudes at Lumen Vitae as the Glenmary Sisters had, but because the Grail did not have canonical status, it caused them no problems with the bishop.

[48] Kelly, *Battle*, 280.

[49] W. R. Coulson, "Tearing Down the Temple: Confessions of a Catholic School Dismantler", *Fidelity* (Dec. 1983): 18–22. Dismayed by its consequences, Dr. Coulson, who was Rogers' associate in the I.H.M. project, says he now "specializes in treating drop-outs from the human potential movement".

refusal to recognize ecclesiastical authority. In 1964, there had been 637 nuns in the IHM community. More than two hundred had left by 1969, when 354 of the remaining members relinquished canonical status but kept the community's property, including a college, a high school, two hospitals and a retreat house.[50] The impoverished minority group of fifty-four faithful sisters eventually moved to Kansas, where they continue to provide orthodox Catholic teachers for the diocese of Wichita.

As Immaculate Heart Community (IHC), the non-canonical majority ran the college at a deficit until 1980, then sold the campus to the American Film Institute for just under five million dollars. At last report, IHC's educational enterprises had dwindled to an "Immaculate Heart College Center" offering "multi-cultural seminars" and master of arts degrees in feminist spirituality and global education from offices over a bank in West Los Angeles. Its resident and visiting faculty have included such familiar feminist names as Rosemary Ruether, Elisabeth Schussler Fiorenza, Dorothee Sölle (of Union Theological Seminary), Toinette Eugene (a consultant to the bishops' committee for the pastoral on women's concerns, from Colgate Rochester Divinity School), Sister Rosemary Rader, O.S.B. (of St. Paul Priory in Minnesota), Diann Neu (co-director of WATER), Anita Caspary (who led the IHM disintegration as Sister Humiliata) and Patricia Reif, another IHM old-timer.[51] Perhaps reluctant to make their present status clear, IHC members continue to use the initials "IHM" after their names.

Sisters of Loretto

Sister Mary Luke Tobin, the American woman auditor at Vatican II, had been president of both the Congregation of Major Superiors of Women (CMSW) and of her own community, the

[50] See Kelly, *Battle*, 261–71.

[51] Kathleen Hendrix, "A Recreation of the IHC Experience", *Immaculate Heart College Alumni Newsletter* (Spring 1985): 7; also a registration bulletin, "Immaculate Heart College Center: Spring '85 Offerings" and *IHC Center: Annual Report 1988–89*.

Sisters of Loretto at the Foot of the Cross, in the early 1960s. Under her leadership, the Loretto sisters were already on the road to sweeping change before the Council began. Nuns who "had gone to study at good theology schools in Europe and in this country" came home with new ideas, Tobin recalls, and "we paid attention to those new theological voices and psychological insights".[52] Tobin had greeted Cardinal Suenens' *The Nun in the World* as a "breakthrough book" and met with him frequently during the Council. Thanks to liberal *peritus* Bernard Häring, Tobin was able to attend the commission meetings where the "Constitution on the Church in the Modern World" (*Gaudium et Spes*) and the "Decree on the Apostolate of Laypeople" (*Apostolicam Actuositatem*) were drafted. Her activities drew the interest of the world press.

When the Council ended, Tobin led the Sisters of Loretto speedily on to community secularization, ecumenism, anti-war agitation and political and feminist activism. But after years near the center of high international affairs, she apparently lost all taste for the quiet of the cloister. In 1970 she went to Vietnam on a "fact-finding" team for the Fellowship of Reconciliation. In 1973, she took a staff post as citizen action director of Church Women United and went to Europe with five liberal clergymen, including the fashionably adaptable theologian Harvey Cox, as the only Catholic in a "peace pilgrimage". She was active in Women's Ordination Conference from its inception and deeply involved in Network.

At the 1987 Women-Church Convergence, Tobin reminisced about the high-handed tactics she and her allies had used to quell the resistance of less-revolutionary sisters.[53] Affronted and unsettled, many left the Lorettos. The remainder were thoroughly modernized. Sister Maureen McCormack, later the Loretto president, came to see *herself* as "a sign of the times", standing for "the

[52] Mary Luke Tobin, S.L., interview with Cecily Jones, "Doors to the World", in Ware, *Midwives*, 183.

[53] See chap. 3 above, 173f.

building of an earthly city where there will be no more crying or weeping, where death shall be no more".[54]

The order became a haven for radical nuns. Sister Dorothy Vidulich of the Sisters of St. Joseph of Peace, a devotee of liberation theology and a veteran of fifteen years of activism for the Equal Rights Amendment, Women's Ordination Conference, disarmament and Nicaragua's Sandinistas, became a Loretto "co-member" in 1979 as a gesture of "solidarity".[55] Today Vidulich is a reporter for the *National Catholic Reporter.* Sister Maureen Fiedler, co-director of Quixote Center, departed the Sisters of Mercy of Erie and joined Loretto at a 1984 "liturgy" she said was "in the Catholic feminist tradition".[56]

On March 30, 1989, the Loretto Women's Network was a party to the *amicus curiae* brief submitted to the United States Supreme Court by Catholics for a Free Choice in opposition to the Webster decision.[57] Later that year, to commemorate her 1979 public challenge to Pope John Paul II, the Loretto Women's Network began circulating a videotape of Sister Theresa Kane's "tenth-anniversary" address, in which she proclaims a "decade for women" to "re-image" God. For its rounds of Catholic feminist centers, the film, *One Woman's Voice*, is packaged with detailed instructions for presenting it within a "sacred circle" ritual that addresses "God our mother" and incorporates song, bongo drums and the standard symbols for earth, air, fire and water.[58]

[54] Maureen McCormack, "Uprooting and Rerooting", in Ware, *Midwives*, 99.

[55] Formerly the Sisters of St. Joseph of Newark, the St. Joseph of Peace Sisters were firmly in sympathy with the Loretto objectives. Her move was a gesture of "solidarity", not an escape. See Dorothy Vidulich, "Finding a Founder", in Ware, *Midwives*, 170.

[56] Fiedler, "City Bus", in Ware, *Midwives*, 37.

[57] The Eighth Circuit Court of Appeals had upheld the right of the Missouri legislature to limit abortions in publicly supported medical facilities. That decision, challenged by Reproductive Health Services et al., was upheld by the U.S. Supreme Court in July 1989.

[58] The model ritual "Faithful to the Vision" notes that it is adapted from a LCWR prayer service, "Bonded with Suffering Women", by Mary Fran Lottes, S.L.

How was it possible for the very women who had been models of self-sacrificial devotion to lose their faith, apparently overnight, and turn to rend the Church they had loved? Psychiatrist Leo Alexander, who worked with the chief of counsel during the Nuremburg war crimes trials after World War II, found that the most significant motive of German Christians for converting to Nazism was fear of "ostracism by the group".[59] Society has been mistaken, he concluded, in believing that conscience, once formed, is permanently fixed. "It may be that the lesson learned in youth has to be continually re-learned in adult life to be durable, and that the ideals acquired in youth must be continually striven for again, in order to remain valid and desirable", he said. "Maturity is a level hard to maintain."[60] His observations may shed some light on the astonishing change of course by Catholic religious since 1965. Subjective conscience is a frail guide to moral judgment because fallen human beings are easily misled by personal considerations and group pressure. Conscience needs an infallible teacher and, once formed, a sustaining community, which is why men need the Church, and why they ought to pray for the grace of perseverance.

Self-Realization

After the Council, most American Catholic congregations of women ceased to be sustaining communities. In the peak year of 1966, there were 181,421 women religious in the United States. By 1976, some fifty thousand had abandoned their convents and sought new careers; by 1990, only 103,421 remained. A substantial proportion of those who left became lay religious professionals. Community life disintegrated almost everywhere. Many nuns moved out to share apartments with a few companions or went back to graduate school to train for "ministries" of their

[59] Leo Alexander, "Medical Science Under Dictatorship", *Ethics and Medicine* 3, no. 2 (1987): 31.

[60] Leo Alexander, "The Molding of Personality under Dictatorship", *Journal of Criminal Law and Criminology*, Northwestern University School of Law, 40, no. 1 (1949): 9, 27.

own choosing. The remnant faithful to their original beliefs and vocational vision have often suffered freezing discrimination and callous persecution.

Re-educated, the nuns became theologians, directors of religious education, parish administrators, hospital and prison chaplains, social workers, masseuses and hair dressers. A startling number headed centers for victims of domestic violence, divorce, career displacement and even sexual maladjustment. Some of the most revolutionary became lobbyists, "peace" activists and free-lance fomenters of political and ecclesial upheaval of other kinds. All but a handful abandoned the parochial schools, and those who stayed on, usually as administrators, announced that they would require the same salaries as lay teachers. In my diocese, in 1960, 314 Benedictine sisters were teaching in fifty-one schools; in the 1990–91 school year, only eighteen are still teaching.[61] Faced with staff shortages and costs beyond their means, the Catholic school system that had been an ornament to the Church and a marvel to the world began to shrink. In 1965, there were 13,400 Catholic elementary and secondary schools in the United States; by 1989, only nine thousand remained. Compounding the tragedy, those still operating are more apt to teach neo-modernism and the liberal causes of the movement than authentic Catholicism. Their scholastic performance, however superior to that of state schools, in most cases does not flow from the sources of the Faith.

Thousands of sisters took administrative jobs in diocesan and national Church bureaucracies. As part of the "new Catholic knowledge class" of professionally educated social activists, they helped launch the "American phase of *aggiornamento*", an organized movement to create and implement a liberal "Catholic social policy". Sister Marie Augusta Neal, S.N.D.deN., was a member of the NCCB Advisory Council when she suggested the national consultation eventually held as the 1976 Call to Action assembly in Detroit. Another nun, Sister Margaret Cafferty, as national

[61] James Engel, "Sisters in the Classroom Are a Vanishing, but Dedicated Breed", *St. Cloud Visitor*, Aug. 23, 1990, 10.

staff coordinator for the "justice sub-theme" on "personhood", was among the most visible participants in that extravagantly progressive venture.[62]

No longer remote from the profane world but increasingly alienated from the "folk Catholics" in the pews, liberated nuns have refused to make a formal break from the Church, for two reasons. First, they might not be able to continue their new "ministries" without the support of bishops and the faithful. Second, while they have ceased to believe the articles of the Creed, they have not lost their apostolic spirit. They see themselves as "change agents",[63] engaged in a "long march through the institutions" that will transform the Church to conform to their new vision.

A misogynist might read this bleak history as an argument against higher education for women. The problem is not education as such but erroneous education. Nuns seem to have had no more immunity to the toxins of neo-modernism than Massachusetts Bay Indians had to Pilgrim measles. The chief reason why education has corrupted so many is that they learned what they were taught. If education had no effect, who would build schools? But these women cannot be seen only as victims. Sin is also a factor; as Catholic feminists never tire of repeating, they are not merely subjects acted upon but also decision makers, and some of their decisions have been terrible. To survive perverted education requires conscious and constant resistance, prayer and grace. It is dangerous for anyone, male or female, but the naïve, the shallow and those who navigate by feeling instead of principle are first to succumb.

Liberation Theology

The feminism that drives "updated" nuns is a symptom; their disease is loss of faith. Like spiritual bag ladies, they scrambled

[62] For a detailed examination of that movement, see Joseph A. Varacalli, *Toward the Establishment of Liberal Catholicism in America* (Lanham, Md.: University Press of America, 1983).

[63] Weaver, *New Catholic Women*, 89 and passim.

in the late 1960s into a frantic search for a new belief system as compelling as the one they had lost. Many involved themselves in such fashionable leftist causes as anti-war protest, nuclear disarmament, global awareness, homosexual rights and environmentalism but not, with honorable exceptions, in the pro-life movement.[64] Crank theories from the occult fringe began to sprout in their midst—iridology, reflexology, graphoanalysis, Enneagrams. Alcoholism and lesbianism became publicly noted problems. Their rootlessness made them extraordinarily vulnerable to the secular feminism sweeping through American society. Sure that the Church had exploited them, they were easily moved to self-pity, rage, lust for retribution—even to the arrant lunacy of witchcraft—when feminists brought liberation theology's "consciousness-raising" techniques into their communities.[65] One sister, prudently anonymous, said the systematic use of such methods damaged the faith of nuns who had never attended subversive theology classes by dredging up forgotten grievances and depicting "self-realization" as obligatory. "They've been gazing at their navels ever since", she said.

Improbable as it seems that a theory of social revolution designed for destitute Latin American peasants should be used to

[64] Among the brave and talented exceptions: Sister Paula Vandegar, S.S.S., of Los Angeles, has been actively involved in pro-life education, counseling and publishing, from the beginning; Sister Jean Therese Condon, C.S.J., of St. Paul, Minnesota, founded and still directs TLC (LifeCare) Centers, a state-wide chain of neighborhood centers offering pro-life counseling and referral as well as general medical screening; three Handmaids of Mary Immaculate from the Blue Army Shrine in Washington, New Jersey, Sisters Mary Joseph Breck, Mary Frances Nagle and Mary Michael Eliason, were sentenced to ten days in prison, on June 7, 1989, for participating in an Operation Rescue in Dobbs Ferry, New York.

[65] See Paulo Freire, *Pedagogy of the Oppressed* (New York: Continuum, 1970). In Brazil in the 1960s, Freire systematized "consciousness-raising" as a subversive technique. In his literacy programs, group dynamics were used to lead students to see previously unrecognized oppression in their lives and to practice resistance. His method has been used in Third World Marxist literacy programs, in North American feminism and in liberation theology's "base communities" in Latin America.

lure middle-class North American nuns into witchcraft, it is indeed true, as Rosemary Ruether repeatedly states, that religious feminism is a form of liberation theology. Both are expressions of the immanentist perspective adherents call the "new paradigm" of reality, though the rhetoric of Third World liberation theology evokes greater sympathy.

Liberation theology has its roots in German theology, but its fullest bloom has been in Latin America. Many American religious who went there after Vatican II were galvanized by pity to support it. Even the NCCB and its bureaucratic arm, the USCC, resonated to its arguments and seemed embarrassed that Rome should find flaws in a theological "option for the poor". It was because they considered it a field trial of liberation theology that so many North American religious professionals displayed uncritical ardor toward the Sandinista regime.

The Vatican has commended the genuine compassion underlying Third World liberation theology but has warned against its tendency to politicize the gospel.[66] As generally understood, it is a synthesis of idealistic Marxism and neo-modernist Christianity, marked by typically gnostic characteristics: (1) despair with the world (in Latin America, with wealthy classes and nations; in feminist liberation theory, with "patriarchal power"); (2) an emphasis on "structural" sin co-existing with antinomian disregard for traditional rules of personal morality; (3) a sense of its own absolute importance; (4) a claim to direct inspiration by the spirit of God, speaking through "the poor" or "women's experience". Rejecting any distinction between the supernatural and the material as "dualism", it sees all reality as political and in conflict. To justify revolution and encourage the creation of a "popular Church", in opposition to the Catholic Church,[67] it redefines Christian terms:

[66] See Cardinal Joseph Ratzinger, "Instruction on Certain Aspects of the 'Theology of Liberation'", in *Theology and the Church: A Response to Cardinal Ratzinger and a Warning to the Whole Church*, ed. Juan Luis Segundo (San Francisco: Harper & Row, 1987), appendix, 173–92.

[67] At Puebla, Pope John Paul II warned that liberation theology tends to develop "an attitude of distrust toward the 'institutional' and 'official' Church,

revelation means interpretation of one's experience of oppression; *incarnation* means God as immanent within the world; *salvation* means a new, utopian social order. Pope John Paul II cautioned the Latin American Bishops' Conference against "re-readings" of the gospel in which "the divinity of Christ is passed over in silence" or he "is presented simply as a 'prophet'" or "as the subversive from Nazareth" rather than as "the center and object of the gospel message".[68]

Rosemary Ruether praises liberation theology for exactly that perspective. "Redemption is not confined to the individual soul, to interpersonal relations, or to the ecclesial sphere", she says. "It is fundamentally the redemption of humanity, the redemption of creation, the overcoming of systemic injustice. . . . It sees the church not as a separate sacred place that points away from society toward heaven, but as a harbinger of these hopes for a redeemed humanity in history."[69] She calls it "a historical falsehood that Jesus founded . . . an institutional church and established the structures of priesthood and sacraments and hierarchical government".[70] The *real* Church, she says, exists "where the Word of God is preached as the denunciation of social evil and the annunciation of an alternative possibility of justice, and where people are motivated and empowered to enter this struggle".[71] Ruether accuses Rome of opposing this "real Church" only because it wants to maintain "control", not out of concern for truth.[72]

"Marxist-Christian" liberation theology thus becomes a new re-

---

which is described as an alienating force and contrasted with another, 'popular' Church or Church 'born of the people' and concretized in the poor". Pope John Paul II, "Truth, Unity and Human Dignity", address to the third General Conference of the Latin American Episcopate, Jan. 28, 1979, reprinted in James V. Schall, *Liberation Theology in Latin America* (San Francisco: Ignatius Press, 1982), 341.

[68] Ibid., 335f.

[69] Ruether, *Women-Church*, 25.

[70] Ibid., 33.

[71] Ibid., 25.

[72] Ibid., 26, 28.

ligion; even what is not Marxist in it is not authentically Christian. It is process thought, expressed in a Christian vocabulary but with little else to distinguish it from atheistic humanism. One enthusiastic interpreter, Father Dermot Lane, fits it into the now-familiar "post-modern paradigm" from which the broader religious revolution is flowing:

> The emerging paradigm employs categories like holistic, organic, indivisible, and integrative in its understanding of reality. It is inspired by a process philosophy (A. N. Whitehead and C. Hartshorne), the new physics (F. Capra), a feminist perception of human existence, and an ecological view of life today (J. Cobb). . . . Precisely because the world is in process, the goals of social praxis are now realistically available to us.[73]

If God is not a transcendent and incomparably superior Person but, as neo-modernism maintains, simply the depersonalized "spirit" of mankind yearning for meaning, there can be no divine moral law, because there is no One "out there" whose nature it expresses. Man is adrift in an existential sea—with no hope of finding the right way home, because there is no right, and no home. Process thought sees his yearning as evidence of his collective divinity, creating the future. Man "perfects" God by cooperating in the prescribed revolution and establishing the utopian Kingdom.[74]

Cardinal Ratzinger specifically notes the modernist influence of Rudolf Bultmann on such liberation theology and criticizes its "immanentist perspective". Because it holds that "every dualism

[73] Dermot A. Lane, *Foundations for a Social Theology: Praxis, Process and Salvation* (New York: Paulist Press, 1984), 95, 109.

[74] See Teilhard de Chardin, *The Heart of the Matter* (New York: Harcourt, Brace & Jovanovich, 1979), 54, 92. See also Marie-Dominique Chenu, "A New Birth: Theologians of the Third World", in *Concilium: Tensions Between the Churches of the First World and the Third World*, eds. Virgil Elizondo and Norbert Greinacher (New York: Seabury Press, 1981), 18–23. See also Gustavo Gutierrez, *A Theology of Liberation: History, Politics and Salvation* (Maryknoll, N.Y.: Orbis Books, 1973), 232–39. See also Weaver, *New Catholic Women*, 151–52, and Carr, *Transforming Grace*, 150–52.

must be overcome" ("the dualism of body and soul, of natural and supernatural, of this world and the world beyond, of then and now") so the "kingdom" can be realized in "politico-economic reality", the liberation movement has "ceased to work for the benefit of people in this present time", the Cardinal says, and begun to "destroy the present in the interests of a supposed future: thus the real dualism had broken loose".[75]

Marxists, who see history as the inevitable clash of social forces, are not alarmed by that prospect; they consider destruction a necessary stage in the dialectical "class struggle". But Christians cannot be excused for such unwisdom. The twentieth century has become a vast mausoleum of uprooted cultures, shattered churches, martyred priests and murdered innocents, sacrificed to just such utopian schemes. Feminist liberation has added empty convents, broken families, and millions of aborted infants to the list of victims.

Feminist "Conscientization"

Catholic feminists borrowed the technique of radicalization through dialogue from Brazilian educator Paulo Freire. Because men resist change unless prevailing circumstances are intolerable, Freire saw that consciousness-raising was required—to create resentment of previously unrecognized domination—before established political, social and religious structures could be overthrown. He coined the word *conscientization* to describe his method for "awakening" revolutionary political consciousness in his students with carefully planned group dynamics.[76] His literacy classes, structured on "dialogue", presented reality "as process, as transformation—rather than as a static entity". All reality, he taught, is in the process of "*becoming*".[77]

Liberation theologians embraced Freire's methods. He has long

[75] Ratzinger with Messori, *The Ratzinger Report*, 173–86.

[76] In Freire, *Oppressed*.

[77] Ibid., 81, 72.

been an advisor to the liberal international theological journal *Concilium* and was awarded UNESCO's Prize for Peace Education in 1986. The "father" of Latin American liberation thought, Father Gustavo Gutierrez, praises Freire's system as "one of the most creative and fruitful efforts" to establish the "context" for a "true cultural revolution".[78] When the religious left waxes sentimental about Sandinista literacy classes in rural Nicaragua, they are referring to programs like Freire's, whose chief purpose was political indoctrination and radicalization.

Because Freire's methods can be used to radicalize naïve groups while preserving an appearance of democratic procedure, they have become a staple of feminist "social analysis". Feminist theologian Doris Donnelly, a perennial speaker at religious education conferences, recommends them as the means to replace the "pyramidal model" of the Church with a "circular model" in the minds of the laity.[79] Sally Cunneen, co-founder, with her husband Joseph, of the liberal Catholic journal *Cross Currents*, uses Freire's techniques in her freshman English classes at New York's Rockland Community College, to help students—especially Catholics—overcome any notion that "the Church asks obedience, good behavior and right thinking of them" and to learn to depend instead on imagination, critical thinking and the "right to make mistakes".[80] Pia Moriarity, coordinator of the Women's Task Force for the San Francisco archdiocese and an assistant professor of pastoral theology at Berkeley's Graduate Theological Union (specializing in "the application of Paulo Freire's philosophy in North American situations")[81] spoke at Time Consultants' 1986 Women in the Church conference about "organizing women's commissions".

Feminist liberation theory paints women as victims of a patri-

[78] Gutierrez, *Liberation*, 91.

[79] Dody Donnelly, C.S.J., *Team: Theory and Practice of Team Ministry* (New York: Paulist Press, 1977), 93:158, n. 37. Donnelly is also a visiting professor at Fox's ICCS.

[80] Sally Cunneen, "Growing Pains", *Critic* (Winter 1989): 22.

[81] Time Consultants, "Women in the Church", conference program, Oct. 10–12, 1986.

archal conspiracy of oppression and sees deliberate affronts even in the inexorable reality of creation. Like ancient gnosticism, it makes God himself the ultimate villain, because he created them as women in a world where patriarchy has been undeniably universal. The hierarchical and patriarchal Church, as the representative of his authority on earth, is the accessible target for their rage. But feminism sees itself as a Promethean force. "A new God is being born in our hearts", Rosemary Ruether declares, "to teach us to level the heavens and exalt the earth and create a new world."[82]

The late Sister Marjorie Tuite, O.P., head of National Assembly of Religious Women (NARW) and an employee of Church Women United, packaged a feminist "political skills" kit, bearing the labels of both NARW and CWU, which goes far beyond politics to the invention of that new God.[83] The kit contains step-by-step directions—straight out of Paulo Freire—for "conscientizing" small groups. Session one introduces a new feminist "worldview" of reality as "conflictual". Session two teaches the interpretation of reality according to personal experience, as opposed to the "false consciousness" of received beliefs. In session three, participants "do social analysis" of "our present hierarchical system", where those who hold power employ "tactics of misinformation and disinformation".

Session four directs members to "do" collective and "dynamic" feminist "theologizing". Each one is to tell *herstory*, "consciously

[82] Rosemary Radford Ruether, *Sexism and God-Talk* (Boston: Beacon Press, 1983), 11.

[83] Marjorie Tuite, Jo'Ann De Quattro, Rhonda Meister and Judy Vaughan, "'How to' Skills with a Feminist Perspective", leadership training packet, Chicago, National Assembly of Religious Women, 1984. The other items enclosed are also interesting: an NARW membership brochure, an order form for NARW tapes and publications (predominantly of Women-Church speakers, including Barbara Zanotti, Wabun, Maureen Reiff—here identified as a "Women-Church activist"—Sister Maureen Fiedler of Quixote Center and Tuite herself); a feminist bibliography; and a reprint of a speech by Sister Carol Coston, O.P., founding director of Network (Carol Coston, O.P., "Feminism: Values and Vision", Network, Nov.–Dec. 1980). The kit was distributed from NARW's booth at Time Consultants' 1986 Women in the Church conference.

and politically", to "define ourselves and to name our reality". Here the process turns openly against the Church; members are to search their "religious heritage" for "cultural sexism and patriarchalism" and to reject any "aspects of theology" that "legitimate . . . the oppression and domination of women". As feminists define the terms, members have no trouble finding them. Then the construction of the new faith begins. "Rejecting a tradition imposed", they "claim" a "spiritual tradition as women", which "is often discovered outside the official context" of "what has been defined by 'the authorities' as theology", says the guide. Where will they find it? In "new translations, new interpretations, new language and new namings of the holy . . . expressed in a vast array of religious forms". (A passage from Alice Walker's *The Color Purple* is offered to help " 'conjure up' new images of God".) Finally, members are told, "celebrate, in a way appropriate to your group, a new image or name for God".

The last session has to do with "creating alternatives" by "politicizing ourselves and others", assuming "a militant stance" against the "oppressors", "confronting, acting against, separating from or using the system".

"Reflection" questions are provided for dialogue in each session. In striking resemblance to the questions prescribed for the "listening sessions" preceding the bishops' pastoral on women, they are designed to elicit anger by suggesting grievances. All nuns but the most fortunate, and most Catholics active in parishes, will recognize elements of the process as something they have personally endured.

The second draft of the American bishops' pastoral letter on women, while disavowing goddess worship, witchcraft, sexual immorality and support for abortion, speaks with approval of "Christian feminism".[84] Mary Jo Weaver, who knows the feminist

[84] National Conference of Catholic Bishops, Ad Hoc Committee for a Pastoral Responding to Women's Concerns, "One in Christ Jesus: A Pastoral Response to the Concerns of Women for Church and Society", *Origins* 19, no. 44 (Apr. 5, 1990): 731f., nn. 130–32.

movement more intimately than the bishops do, calls the term *Roman Catholic feminist* an oxymoron and says it will be necessary "to force a choice between the two" because "a conjunction of the two is impossible".[85] Fear of a mass exodus of women from the Church may well terrify the bishops into "standing with the oppressed", she says.[86] But while renewal "made feminists of many sisters",[87] it has not had the same effect on most laywomen, Weaver admits. If confrontation with the hierarchy is to end in feminist triumph, she believes, women religious must "lead the women's movement in the Catholic church".[88] Laywomen may not be disposed to follow. It is certainly not for lack of opportunity that most are not feminists, and some in fact were, when feminism was fashionable and unexamined. Now, those of an age with the feminist nuns are more likely to be praying that their doctrinally illiterate children—and grandchildren—will return to the Church. A more germane question about Weaver's scenario is whether there will continue to be radical nuns to do the leading. A 1989 publication from the Leadership Conference of Women Religious suggests that there may not be, and illustrates why not.

LCWR Reflects on Its Experience

In 1970, the Congregation of Major Superiors of Women (CMSW) dissolved into the Leadership Conference of Women Religious (LCWR). Stressing autonomy and self-realization instead of corporate identity and self-sacrifice, LCWR encouraged the exodus from traditional apostolates, and initiated or supported many of the organizations and coalitions formed to hasten the radical "renewal" of its members. It collaborated with Network and the Center of Concern, two liberal "social justice" lobbies founded in Washington in 1971. It coordinated the formation of "Sisters Uniting", a forum of extremist groups like the National Coalition of Ameri-

[85] Weaver, *New Catholic Women*, 49.
[86] Ibid., 38.
[87] Ibid., 108.
[88] Ibid., 70.

can Nuns (NCAN), the National Assembly of Religious Women (NARW), Las Hermanas and the non-canonical Sisters for Christian Community. LCWR endorsed the Equal Rights Amendment and sent representatives to the 1975 International Women's Year gathering in Mexico.[89] In 1983, the virulently pro-abortion Daniel Maguire was a featured speaker at LCWR's annual meeting. Three of its most renowned leaders spoke at the 1987 Women-Church Convergence: Sister Mary Luke Tobin, Sister Theresa Kane and Sister Nadine Foley, O.P., who assumed the presidency the following year. Another past president, Sister Helen Flaherty, S.C., and incumbent president Sister Helen Marie Burns, R.S.M., signed Chicago Call to Action's Ash Wednesday 1990 "Call for Reform" ad in the *New York Times*.

Nevertheless, LCWR is still officially recognized as the liaison between women religious, the bishops' conference and the Vatican Congregation for Religious. Its membership includes the lion's share of American nuns.[90] After James Cardinal Hickey of Washington, D.C., raised the question of their separate recognition at the 1989 "summit meeting" in Rome, he was appointed as liaison to congregations not affiliated with LCWR, many of them small, vigorous, consciously orthodox communities formed since the Council. But recognition was not withdrawn from LCWR. Instead, the divergent organizations were instructed to settle their differences through dialogue.

In the tradition of the 1967 Sister's Survey, LCWR conducted

[89] Ibid., 85, 234.

[90] In an interview (May 31, 1990), Father James Downey, O.S.B., director of the Institute on Religious Life, said that, although LCWR claims to represent more than 90 percent of American nuns, figures from the 1988 *Catholic Directory* show only 456 communities affiliated with LCWR, 135 affiliated with the traditional Institute on Religious Life (IRL) and 287 other communities unaffiliated. However, according to Father Downey, LCWR has "more numbers" than those figures suggest; 70 to 75 percent of all nuns belong to LCWR-affiliated communities, 13 to 14 percent are members of IRL affiliates and 9 to 10 percent belong to the independent orders. Sisters in the Consortium Perfectae Caritatis join as individuals rather than as communities. Its constituency overlaps but is not identical to that of IRL.

a "consultation" with selected communities among its membership in 1985. At a "Think Tank Writers Seminar" in 1986, the responses were translated into papers in a characteristically collective feminist process: each "team" writer was assisted by as many as five members of the LCWR task force that developed the survey questions. The lamentable final product, *Claiming Our Truth*,[91] is thus more significant than a volume of personal essays; it is an official joint statement of LCWR positions. They are not the positions of Catholics. St. Irenaeus would have recognized them as gnostic.

Although "Christian feminism" is the book's declared theoretical base, the essays disclose a desperately uncertain religious vision, only tenuously related to the "symbol" of Jesus Christ, which looks to a feminist version of "liberation" for the world's earthly salvation. The notes and reading lists constitute a comprehensive bibliography in feminist theology. They list Father Raymond Brown, S.S., Father Joseph Fitzmyer, S.J., Rosemary Ruether, Elisabeth Schussler Fiorenza, Sister Sandra Schneiders, Patricia Wilson-Kastner, Phyllis Trible, Sister Agnes Cunningham, Sister Joan Chittister, Sister Marie Augusta Neal, Sister Elizabeth Johnson, C.S.J., Mary Jo Weaver, Thomas Groome, Paulo Freire (*The Pedagogy of the Oppressed*), Carl Jung, Marina Warner (*Alone of All Her Sex*), Carol Gilligan, Jean Shinoda Bolen (*Goddesses in Every Woman*), Alice Walker (*The Color Purple*), Mary Daly, Carol Christ and Judith Plaskow (*Womanspirit Rising*), Gerda Lerner, Sister Madonna Kolbenschlag, Charlene Spretnak, Barbara Walker and Starhawk.

In the first paper, "Woman's Center: Incarnational Spirituality",[92] Sister Catherine Osimo, C.S.C. (aided by editor Foley and Sisters

[91] Nadine Foley, O.P., ed., *Claiming Our Truth: Reflections on Identity by United States Women Religious* (Washington, D.C.: Leadership Conference of Women Religious, 1988). Sister Foley was president of LCWR when the book was published.

[92] Sister Catherine Osimo, C.S.C., "Women's Center: Incarnational Spirituality", in Foley, *Claiming Our Truth*, 9–32.

Anne Clifford, C.S.J., Mary Elsbernd, O.S.F., Valerie Lesniak, C.S.J., and Mary Daniel Turner, S.N.D.), outlines the theological view underlying the enterprise. She names the sources of the nuns' "theological shift" as the "evolutionary consciousness" of the general culture,[93] the "impact of biblical criticism"[94] and Father Karl Rahner's "ascending christology".[95] Osimo says the Council implied, "without saying so directly", that "theology itself will move away" from the belief that "reality (truth) is essentially static, unchanging and unaffected by history".[96] Citing Father Raymond Brown, she explains that historical criticism "alerts us" to the cultural and theological limitations "of those who developed" Church dogmas.[97] The faulty old "descending christology" saw revelation as a "divine deposit of faith", requiring "only passive intellectual assent" to "clearly defined doctrines", with no parallel demand for "ongoing conversion".[98] It was possible "even to imagine Jesus raising himself up in order to prove his divinity one more time".[99] Having rejected all that, Osimo says, women religious now believe that revelation is "mediated to them as women" through what they "perceive, think, act, feel and experience".[100] They view God not as "perfect, remote in heaven" but as "immanent in creation", "involved in human affairs", affected by suffering.[101] They "image" him as "mother and father" or as a woman giving birth. They "do not focus on" original sin;[102] they see Jesus as a sign of "God's own self-emptying of divinity, *rather than* a figure who comes 'from above' to 'assume' a humanity defined as male".[103]

Their new Christology, says Osimo, holds that "Jesus had no

[93] Ibid., 13.
[94] Ibid.
[95] Ibid., 16.
[96] Ibid., 14.
[97] Ibid., 15.
[98] Ibid., 22.
[99] Ibid., 21.
[100] Ibid., 23.
[101] Ibid., 28.
[102] Ibid., 24.
[103] Emphasis added. Ibid., 25.

divine foreknowledge"; that his death "is not a ransom to satisfy the punishment due to sin"; that "the resurrection does not reveal Jesus' omnipotence" but "the salvific meaning of his entire life".[104] It is difficult to know what she means here by "salvific", having dispensed with man's Fall, Christ's Divinity and the redemptive meaning of his death, but it is one of many such ambiguities scattered through the book, perhaps for cosmetic purposes. In any case, what she calls "ascending christology" is the uncertain impression someone might have had who was standing on the edge of the Palm Sunday crowd—or in front of Pilate's court—of Jesus as a compassionate man, perhaps even as a great moral teacher. As C. S. Lewis noted, such a view is untenable because if Jesus of the New Testament is not God, as he claimed, then he is either "a lunatic or a fiend".[105]

Lacking the "security of certitude and stability",[106] Osimo continues, nuns expend their energies in working toward the liberation of "peoples, cultures, male-female, the poor" rather than in "worry about their personal immortality".[107] They welcome "the possibility of sharing with other religious traditions" because "a triumphalist ecclesiology is not possible".[108]

Other essays in the volume develop the same themes. *Incarnation* is used to mean immanence. God, they indicate, can be known only in immanence, i.e., in one's intuition. The LCWR respondents reportedly do not see themselves as consecrated brides of Christ but as committed social reformers, directed, by the god within, to stand in "solidarity with the oppressed".[109] "Incarnational spirituality has replaced an other-worldly emphasis on saving one's soul", announces Sister Anne Clifford, C.S.J. And, sensitized by partic-

[104] Ibid., 25f.

[105] C. S. Lewis, *The Case for Christianity* (New York: Macmillan, 1974), 45.

[106] Ibid., 29.

[107] Ibid., 27.

[108] Ibid., 29.

[109] Patricia Wittberg, S.C., "Outward Orientation in Declining Organizations: Reflections on the LCWR Documents", in Foley, *Claiming Our Truth*, 93.

ipation in the women's movement, she says, "we are attentive to the dualisms" in "magisterial teachings about human sexuality".[110]

"We know that we cannot look for a God 'out there' to save us and take us to heaven 'up there.' We cannot seek God as an object separate from our world, outside our lived experience", says Sister Elaine Prevallet, S.L.

> Naming and imaging an immanent God is a difficult and even paradoxical process. . . . The paradox comes with the sense that God disappears into life. . . . For some, God is a clear presence and Jesus, a very available image through whom to relate to God. For many others, among whom I count myself, that is not the case. . . . God is experienced not so much as a separate Being, but God is sensed as the deepest dimension of our own being. What we find is not God but *ourselves*. . . . The process of self-knowledge is the process of knowing God.[111]

Sister Sheila Carney, R.S.M., proposes that nuns "reappropriate" the Blessed Virgin Mary—"not for purposes of traditional devotion" but to establish a relationship of equality—using Fiorenza's "hermeneutic of suspicion" to reinterpret Scripture and Marian Tradition. "Moving away from a strictly physiological definition" of Mary's virginity, Carney suggests Mary can be seen as the model of "an entirely new order" if "the term 'virgin'" is understood to mean "one whose personal power center wells up, who is autonomous, 'one-in-herself,' who is free from male domination or control".[112] She seems to understand Mary as a paradigm of feminist liberation, a kind of icon for NOW.

Rahner's interpretation of a pluralistic "world church" is the theme of another essay, by Sisters Margaret Gannon, I.H.M.,

[110] Sister Anne Clifford, C.S.J., "Women Missioned in a Technological Culture", in Foley, *Claiming Our Truth*, 44–45.

[111] Sister Elaine M. Prevallet, S.L., "From the Inside Out", in Foley, *Claiming Our Truth*, 69–71.

[112] Sheila Carney, R.S.M., "Women of Presence, Women of Praise", in Foley, *Claiming Our Truth*, 107–18.

and Mary Elsbernd, O.S.F.[113] Elsbernd also collaborated with Sister Marilyn Thie, S.C.[114] (and five assistants), in an essay on the "subversive and hence political" act of "imaging" God in non-masculine ways.[115] Many women religious, the authors say, use such impersonal images as "life force", "wholeness and growth", "vision of future life" and "cosmic energy". And while others still like to think of him as "a someone", no responses to the LCWR survey spoke of God as "'Supreme Being,' self-existing" or "infinitely perfect Spirit", they report. Only one respondent used the term *trinitarian*, and there were two references each to God as "indwelling Spirit" and "incarnate in Jesus".[116] "Naming God from our experience" is one way women religious can help transform the "patriarchal Church", the authors conclude.[117]

Saddest of all the sad essays in *Claiming Our Truth* is "Outward Orientation in Declining Organizations: Reflections on the LCWR Documents", by Sister Patricia Wittberg, S.C., a professor of sociology at Fordham University.[118] It is her fairly astringent observation that women's religious communities will cease to exist within a generation unless they change course. In thirty years, the number of American nuns has shrunk by seventy-eight thousand. Their median age is in the middle sixties, 40 percent are older than seventy and attrition by death has become precipitous. According

[113] Margaret Gannon, I.H.M., and Mary Elsbernd, O.S.F., "A World Church and Christian Feminism", in Foley, *Claiming Our Truth*, 121–38.

[114] The presence of Sister Thie on LCWR's consultation task force is evidence of its uncompromising radicalism. She is associated with WATER; see her article on feminist spirituality in *New Directions for Women* (Nov./Dec. 1984): 1. She signed CFFC's first (1984) *New York Times* ad. Her participation in the consultation in an official capacity would be unthinkable if LCWR were concerned about maintaining an appearance of Catholic orthodoxy.

[115] Sisters Mary Elsbernd, O.S.F., and Marilyn Thie, S.C., "What's at Stake: Women Religious Naming Ourselves Women", in Foley, *Claiming Our Truth*, 143–62.

[116] Ibid., 144–46.

[117] Ibid., 158.

[118] "Outward Orientation", in Foley, *Claiming Our Truth*, 89–102.

to Wittberg, religious organizations do not survive their original leadership unless they emphasize their distinct group identities, institutionalize community commitment and actively recruit new members. An association in which members "retain virtually full personal autonomy" becomes merely a "cooperative venture in support of its members' individual self-interests" and can rarely "produce a second generation". In the past, religious congregations typically "enforced homogeneity of members, communal sharing and renunciation of private property, communal work", and allowed little contact with "the corrupting values of the larger society". Such "self-abnegation" sustained their commitment from erosion by secular values, but it led, Wittberg says, "to immaturity at best and to outright pathology at worst". One might argue that "outright pathology" has become far more evident since self-abnegation was abandoned, but LCWR members indicate, the author says, that they have chosen "decline and extinction" rather than a return to the "psychologically destructive group survival mechanisms of the past". Reluctant to face the "cognitive dissonance" it evokes, they avert thoughts of the future by focusing on "outside" issues. Now they must choose between active recruitment and "redemptive letting-go".[119]

The obvious question is why young women are no longer entering. Wittberg's suggestion that "marketing research" might show how to correct "inaccurate" images of religious life and thus attract potential members seems disingenuous. "Little is known of the reasons" for the lack of vocations, she says. Yet she does know. Summing up the causes of their numerical decline, Wittberg identifies an attitude ironic indeed in women who profess unshakable "solidarity with the oppressed". Religious congregations, she says, may have "adopted the values of mainstream U.S. society, in which the only persons who actively promulgate their religious views are members of lower-class sects with whom middle-class Americans do not want to be identified".[120] It seems they have

[119] Ibid., 96–100.
[120] Ibid., 99.

assimilated elitist disdain as well as demythologized Christianity from dying mainline Protestantism.

Rudolf Bultmann asked rhetorically, at the beginning of *Kerygma and Myth*, "If we once start subtracting from the kerygma, where are we to draw the line?"[121] American women religious in the past twenty-five years have answered, "Nowhere!" They have been subjects in an experiment in neo-modernism, and its sorry fruits can be counted in their congregations: loss of faith, institutional ruin, moral disintegration, scandal and death.

Their decline and fall have been tragic, and not only for themselves. As the agents of subversion closest to the young, their activities had grave consequences for the rest of the Church. Even if authoritative action is not taken soon, the corrupt communities will disappear by natural attrition, perhaps within twenty years. Only then will it become possible for health, order and concern for truth to be restored in whatever remains of the Church.

121 Bultmann, *Kerygma*, 9.

Chapter Six

Marching through the Institutions

There are few seminal Catholic feminists. Anyone who follows their revolutionary doings in the news soon notices the same names appearing over and over, like characters in a play. Possibly excepting witchcraft, their religious opinions largely echo those of the reigning theologians from whom they learned them. How have so few made so deep an impact on American Catholic life? By ferocious drive, compounded by the unaccountable passivity and sometimes the collusion of authorities in the Catholic hierarchy, bureaucracy and institutions.

Catholic feminists seized control of women's religious orders with relative ease because nuns were a closed, naïve, dislocated and aggrieved population. It has not enjoyed similar success among most laywomen, the overwhelming majority of whom do not see the Church as a means to power, do not want to be priests, do not want to be witches. From Catholicism, laywomen like laymen require truth, sacramental nurture and moral guidance. Their faith withers if they do not find them. They may even abandon the Church for fundamentalism, the New Age movement or secular materialism, but trying to recruit them into independent "feminist base communities" is an unpromising enterprise. The feminist conquest of the American Church does not depend on winning their allegiance, however.

As the serpent knew when he spoke to Eve, the first step in any revolution is to discredit established authority.[1] That was accomplished by the theological establishment with the help of Catholic feminists. The second step was the capture of Church career women; feminist leaders now count on them as "change agents". For the third step, the consolidation of power, it is only necessary that Catholic institutions remain under feminists' control. Feminists believe that bishops will not drive them out, that adult women have nowhere else to go, that the captive young can be indoctrinated *within* the institutions. Consequently, while they continue to hurl denunciations at the hierarchy, their chief revolutionary strategy is a shrewd, relentless "long march" through Church agencies concerned with liturgy, theology, spiritual direction, moral instruction, catechetics and sex education by a corps of self-identified "subversives", many of them shaped in Women-Church groups. Like members of liberation theology's "popular churches", they remain "outside institutional control" while maintaining "footholds" within the Church and using her own resources to destroy her, "without being stifled or controlled" themselves.[2] Rosemary Ruether calls this "the positive working of the dialectic".[3]

It is a strategy Catholic feminists have long pursued, with more dramatic effect and less official opposition than liberation theologians ever achieved in Latin America. And they have done so in a society where the rhetoric of exploitation was by comparison ludicrous. A review of their devastating march through Catholic institutions has the fascination of a history of the Black Death.

[1] For an enlightening discussion of the ideology and tactics of revolution, see Peter Collier and David Horowitz, *Destructive Generation: Second Thoughts about the '60s* (New York: Summit Books, 1989), esp. 11–17.

[2] Ruether, *Women-Church*, 28–31.

[3] Ibid., 2–7, 25–40.

Feminists in Theology

Mary Daly

Mary Daly is usually named as the first of the radical American Catholic feminists. Her landmark book, *The Church and the Second Sex*, first appeared in 1968.[4] Though its ideas were not original,[5] it contains in rudimentary form most of the concepts still current in religious feminism. It declares that the Church ("misogynist" since New Testament times) should discard the "perverted notion" that God is immutable, because it establishes a "worldview" closed to "theological development and social change".[6] Catholics must abandon an "institutionalist view" of the Church ("a root of many evils") and see her instead as a prophetic "movement in the world". While Daly says that "exclusion of women from ministerial functions is unreasonable", she also suggests that the "clerical caste" itself is "irrelevant and doomed". Anticipating Matthew Fox, she says that the "sin-obsession and antisexuality" expressed in the story of Fall and in the Church's "understanding of the Incarnation" should give way before the "evolutionary awareness of modern man".[7] Birth control should be "readily available to all women",[8] and, in hard cases at least, the "moral ambiguity and complexity" of abortion should be recognized.[9]

The Second Sex would not have been written, Daly says, if her "most secret thoughts" about the Church had not been reinforced by the dissidents she encountered when, as a graduate student in

[4] Mary Daly, *The Church and the Second Sex* (Boston: Beacon Press, 1985).

[5] As authorities on her side of the arguments, Daly cites a familiar list, including Simone de Beauvoir, Rosemary Ruether, Betty Friedan, then-unmarried Elisabeth Schussler, Sidney Callahan, Arlene Swidler, Rosemary Lauer, Krister Stendahl, Father Bernard Häring, Father Teilhard de Chardin, Paul Tillich, Father Hans Küng, Gregory Baum, Harvey Cox, Leslie Dewart, then-Brother Gabriel Moran, Father John McKenzie and then-Father Eugene Kennedy.

[6] Daly, *Second Sex*, 183.

[7] Ibid., 182–85.

[8] Ibid., 218.

[9] Ibid., 135.

theology at Fribourg, Switzerland, she visited the Second Vatican Council in 1965. There, she says, only the "strangely foreseeing 'conservatives' . . . in some perverse way knew" that "what was really going on" was not the overthrow of the Church. Everyone else, she says, thought it was "the greatest breakthrough of nearly two thousand years", admitting "an endless variety of human possibilities".[10] She came home breathing fire. Reportedly presuming that her new doctorate in sacred theology automatically conferred membership in the Catholic Theological Society of America (CTSA), Daly attended its 1966 assembly. Founded in 1946, CTSA had been opened to qualified lay members and nuns in 1964.[11] Daly was permitted to remain for the addresses but, as a non-member, was barred from the banquet. When she forced her way in, authorities threatened to call the police. In response, Daly threatened to call the press. Her will prevailed.[12]

After her book appeared, Daly was told that she would not be retained on the faculty of Boston College. Her outrage attracted what she calls "national, international, supernatural publicity". Electing her "a symbol in their crusade for 'academic freedom'", fifteen hundred students demonstrated, and twenty-five hundred signed a petition, in her behalf. During a seven-hour "teach-in", some "local self-declared witches came and hexed Boston College". Boston media reported the uproar; the *New York Times* picked up the story; newspapers across the country published it. As the 1968–69 academic year ended, Daly looked out from her apartment building to the towers of Boston College and understood that "there was some primary warfare going on . . . an archetypal

[10] Ibid., "Autobiographical Preface to the 1975 Edition", 9.

[11] Before Vatican II, no Catholic theological institution in the United States accepted lay students, male or female, at the doctoral level. CTSA membership was open to priests, clergy and religious brothers but not to nuns or laity. During the Council, CTSA's constitution was changed to admit qualified laity, and the first two women members joined in 1965. By the late 1970s, CTSA had its first woman president, Sister Agnes Cunningham, S.S.C.M.

[12] George Kilcourse, ed., *Proceedings of the Forty-Second Annual Convention of the Catholic Theological Society of America*, 135, Weigel, *Catholicism*, 40.

battle between principalities and powers . . . and I willed to go all the way in this death battle".[13] Where she has in fact gone could serve as a cautionary lesson for other feminists.

Either the hex worked or the hostile media attention pitched on "academic freedom" seemed intolerably embarrassing. Boston College granted Daly promotion and tenure, thus inflicting on itself a source of perennial embarrassment and of potentially eternal harm to students. Daly was not appeased but angrier than ever. Correctly seeing her triumph as evidence of patriarchal cowardice, she decided that "liberation" begins "when women refuse to be 'good' and/or 'healthy'". Deliberately, she chose "the role of witch and madwoman".[14]

In the Academy

Academic associations like CTSA and the Canon Law Society began to draw increasing numbers of feminist members through the 1970s. A growing trend toward interdenominational theological unions open to women students enabled feminists to influence Catholic seminary education. In Boston, where the Jesuit seminary joined eight non-Catholic seminaries to form Boston Theological Institute (BTI), a 1970 conference was held to design a "feminist theological curriculum". Conference "resource people" included four prominent Catholic feminists: Mary Daly, Sister Marie Augusta Neal, Arlene Swidler and Elizabeth Farians.[15] Subsequently, a Women's Theological Coalition was established within BTI. A Center for Women was also formed at the Graduate Theological

[13] Daly, *Second Sex*, 12.

[14] Daly, *Beyond God the Father: Toward a Philosophy of Women's Liberation* (Boston: Beacon Press, 1973), 65.

[15] Farians, a director of Catholics for a Free Choice in its pre-Frances Kissling days, aired her exegetical views in March 1972 in the *Andover-Newton Quarterly*, a theological journal, where she said, "Then we can say with a clear conviction and without fear or guilt that if Jesus was not a feminist, he was not of God." Quoted in Ralph Martin, *A Crisis of Truth: The Attack on Faith, Morality and Mission in the Catholic Church* (Ann Arbor, Mich.: Servant Books, 1982), 22.

Union in Berkeley, California, a consortium of three Catholic and six Protestant seminaries. "Probably the largest pools of women studying and teaching theology are in those two places," Janet Kalven said in 1984, "but women theologians/biblical scholars are scattered across all the leading seminaries and schools of theology."[16] Among the products of Berkeley's GTU is Mary Hunt, the foundress of Women's Alliance for Theology, Ethics and Ritual (WATER).

Daly and Ruether helped form a women's caucus within the American Academy of Religion in 1970. Also involved were Carol Christ and Judith Plaskow, who had previously been inspired by Ruether to invent goddess witchcraft.[17] While Ruether was by then bent on assaulting patriarchy from within the Church, Daly chose to follow the Wiccan path.

Daly had been "transformed" by her duels with CTSA and Boston College into the vengeful fury who wrote *Beyond God the Father* in 1973, *Gyn/Ecology* in 1978 and *Pure Lust* in 1984.[18] In a new preface to a 1975 edition of *Second Sex*, she looked back on the original edition as incomprehensibly restrained. Abandoning not only Catholicism but also the Holy Trinity, she evolved into an openly lesbian witch and anti-Church militant who calls herself "unhinged".[19] Her writing evolved into incoherence. She refuses to sully her classes with male students, should any register for them. Her books, still read, cited and recommended by movement revolutionaries, helped to shape the feminist genre. But private activities seem to occupy most of her attention now.[20] She is no

[16] Kalven, "Voices", 20.

[17] Christ and Plaskow, *Womanspirit*, x–xi.

[18] Mary Daly, *Beyond God the Father*; *Gyn/Ecology: The Metaethics of Radical Feminism* (Boston: Beacon Press, 1978); *Pure Lust: Elemental Feminist Philosophy* (Boston: Beacon Press, 1984).

[19] Daly, "New Archaic Afterwords", in Daly, *Second Sex*, xxviii.

[20] She attracted some attention with a flurry of protests (including the burning of an effigy of "patriarchy") when Boston College denied her promotion to full professor in 1989. Harvard Divinity School Professor Harvey Cox, one

longer much in evidence on the Catholic feminist lecture circuit[21] or in the major feminist organizations. Other feminist witches who withdraw entirely from the Church will doubtless follow her to obscurity.

Rosemary Ruether

By contrast, Rosemary Ruether has become the best-known feminist figure in the American Catholic revolution. She speaks so often and so widely as to appear homeless. She was a formidable voice for Women's Ordination Conference during its 1979–81 "dialogue" with the NCCB. In 1983, *U.S. Catholic* gave her its award for "furthering the cause of women in the church".[22]

Ruether first attracted public notice in 1964, when she wrote that the Catholic teaching on contraception makes one "an unwitting slave of biological fecundity". To risk having more children, she said, would "demand that I scuttle my interests, my training, and in the last analysis, my soul".[23] Having years earlier ceased to believe in the immortality of the soul, Ruether had far broader differences with the Church, however. In 1968, she proposed that Catholic revolutionaries found an "autonomous reformed church" of small communities with elected leaders, linked by a national council, to "express the most advanced insights of contemporary

---

of three hundred scholars who signed a petition from the American Academy of Religion pleading that Daly be promoted, said, "It is hard to imagine where the whole field of religious and theological studies would be today were it not for the contributions she has made." See Leila Prelec, "BC Campus Scene of Small Daly Protests", *National Catholic Register*, Apr. 30, 1989, 1.

[21] An exception was Daly's April 1990 address "Be-Witching: Recalling the Courage to Sin" at St. Rose's College in Albany, New York. She reportedly ridiculed the Second Coming of Christ and urged her audience to sing "O come, let us ignore him". See "From the Mail", *Wanderer*, June 14, 1990.

[22] "People", *Catholic Bulletin*, St. Paul, Minnesota, Mar. 24, 1983.

[23] Rosemary Ruether, "A Question of Dignity, a Question of Freedom" in *What Modern Catholics Think About Birth Control*, ed. William Birmingham (New York: New American Library, 1964), 233–40.

Catholicism".[24] Sadly for American Catholics, she changed her mind. By 1973 she was advising like-minded dissenters that remaining nominally within the Church offered more revolutionary opportunities than leaving. They need never "see the inside of a parish church" or bother about moral rules, she said, because the Council had brought "protestantisation" to Catholicism. "Pluralism of the most rampant sort has come", she said, and the bishops are "powerless to expel it".[25]

Ruether, like Elisabeth Schussler Fiorenza, cites ancient gnostic writings as in many ways more reliable than the "patriarchal" canon of Sacred Scripture.[26] She portrays the sacraments as mere symbols and urges the declericalization of the Church, insisting that priestly power arises not from ordination but "from the community's collective experience".[27]

"Eucharist is not an objectified piece of bread or cup of wine that is magically transformed into the body and blood of Christ", she says. "It is the people, the ecclesia, who are being transformed into the body of the new humanity, infused with the blood of new life."[28] Anyone can be designated to celebrate the Eucharist; no "sacramental power" is needed "that the community does not have". The ritual meal at the 1987 Women-Church Convergence expressed just that interpretation of Eucharist.

As a "feminist Christology", Ruether proposes that "the mythology about Jesus as Messiah or divine *Logos*, with its traditional masculine imagery", be discarded.[29] Women "must emancipate themselves from Jesus as redeemer and seek a new redemptive disclosure of God and of human possibility in female form", she says.[30] "Feminism represents a fundamental shift in the valuation

[24] Ruether, "On the New Reformation: Creating a New Kind of Religious Community", *National Catholic Reporter*, Oct. 30, 1968.

[25] Ruether, "Continuing Reform after Vatican II", *Month* (Mar. 1973): 93–97.

[26] Ruether, *God-Talk*, 34–37 and passim.

[27] Ibid., 208f.

[28] Ibid.

[29] Ibid., 137.

[30] Ibid., 135.

of good and evil", because "past descriptions of evil", rooted in patriarchy, were "themselves ratifications of evil".[31] Destruction of "blasphemous" patriarchy—"the idol with flashing eyes and smoking nostrils who is about to consume the earth"—is, she announces, the primary goal of feminism.[32]

According to Ruether, the image of God as "Father" is an idolatrous projection of "transcendent male ego" that "sacralizes" patriarchal culture and "inferiorizes" woman as symbolic of nature.[33] Its "underside" is the conquest of nature "imaged as the conquest and transcendence of the Mother".[34] Insofar as her perspective is representative, it explains the tie between religious feminism and ecological fanaticism. "We cannot criticize the hierarchy of male over female", she says, "without ultimately criticizing and overcoming the hierarchy of humans over nature."[35]

According to Ruether, the male enslaves the female because he images her as "a threatening lower 'power'" seeking to "drag him down" to the "realm of body and nature".[36] That anthropology is not entirely consistent with her view of matrimony, which, polemical though it is, suggests considerable masculine enthusiasm for the "realm of body and nature".[37] What she seeks, in any case, is not a greater appreciation of women as women. Androgyny is her model for a human species liberated from "dualistic" gender into "psychic wholeness", though she indicates that achieving it is easier for females, since males typically "identify their ego with left-brain characteristics".[38] The very name of God, Ruether proposes, should be replaced with gnosticism's androgynous term "God/ess".[39]

[31] Ibid., 160.
[32] Ruether, *Women-Church*, 73.
[33] Ruether, *God-Talk*, 66, 72ff.
[34] Ibid., 47.
[35] Ibid., 73.
[36] Ibid., 74f.
[37] Ibid., 260–61.
[38] Ibid., 112 and passim.
[39] Ibid.; see esp. 34, 46, 67–71.

It is in the practical rather than the theological order that Ruether has made her greatest contributions to the religious revolution. She had a formative hand in several of the Catholic feminist groups that sprang up between the late 1960s and the mid-1980s. She spoke at the first meeting of Women's Ordination Conference (WOC), was a founder of Women-Church (née "Womanchurch") and, in 1983, helped unite many of the feminist groups into Women-Church Convergence, a coalition of questionable importance in view of their already interlocking memberships. Her zeal for abortion has never wavered. She was a founding board member of Catholic Alternatives, a short-lived front established in New York in 1976 to provide a "Catholic" public relations presence for abortion advocates. Among her Catholic Alternatives fellows was Mary Calderone, president of the Sex Information and Education Council of the United States (SIECUS) and past medical director of Planned Parenthood Federation of America.[40] By 1977, Ruether was chairing a committee at Catholics for a Free Choice (CFFC). Since 1985 she has been a member of its board of directors. She was part of the organizing committee for CFFC's two pro-abortion *New York Times* ads.

Elisabeth Schussler Fiorenza

Another major Catholic feminist theologian, German-born Elisabeth Schussler Fiorenza, says not only that feminist theologians *need not* be objective scholars but also that they *must not* be. Fiorenza studied New Testament theology at Wurzburg, then came to teach at the University of Notre Dame in 1970. When Carol Christ established a women's caucus in the Society of Biblical Literature (SBL) in 1971, Fiorenza became co-chair.[41] She found Grailville's 1972 "Women Exploring Theology" session "a

[40] Also on that board were feminist canon lawyer Clara Marie Henning and Gloria Fitzgerald, a former Ursuline nun working with Bread for the World. See Patricia McCormack, "Sex Data Offered Catholics", *St. Paul Sunday Pioneer Press*, Oct. 31, 1976, 9.

[41] SBL is a group within the American Academy of Religion.

very decisive conference for the development of feminist theology".[42] Unlikely as it seems, she claims her speech to the 1975 Women's Ordination Conference drew objections from Notre Dame's theology department, that she was not permitted to use her own book, *In Memory of Her*, in her classes there and that those restrictions led to her resignation.[43] At the 1987 Women-Church Convergence—though she boasted of an invitation to speak to the American Catholic bishops about patriarchy—she grumbled about her standing among male Catholic theologians. To claim that feminism represents "the middle" in the Church, as she does, requires an appearance of scholarly respectability. Any such problem was solved when, in 1988, she accepted a prestigious appointment as Krister Stendahl Professor at Harvard Divinity School, where her husband was already a faculty member.[44]

Fiorenza considers biblical interpretation a political act,[45] and, as she practices it, it is. Taking liberation theology as her framework, she says feminists must be "engaged", as distinguished from "neutral", scholars. None is really neutral, anyway, she declares; those who believe they are neutral really are "androcentric".[46] The "basic insight of all liberation theologies, including feminist theology", she says, is that "intellectual neutrality is not possible in a world of exploitation and oppression".[47]

[42] Annie Lally Milhaven, "Elisabeth Schussler Fiorenza" in *The Inside Stories: Thirteen Valiant Women Challenging the Church* (Mystic, Conn.: Twenty-Third Publications, 1987), 45.

[43] Ibid., 55, 60.

[44] As president of the Catholic Theological Society of America, in April 1986, her husband, Francis Schussler Fiorenza, sent Cardinal Ratzinger a statement of support for Charles Curran signed by 727 North American theologians (Anne Roche Muggeridge, *The Desolate City: Revolution in the Catholic Church* [San Francisco: Harper & Row, 1990], 204). Ironically, the chair Francis Schussler Fiorenza holds at Harvard is that of Roman Catholic studies, endowed by the entirely orthodox Chauncey Stillman in 1958 for the orthodox, internationally renowned Christopher Dawson, who was the first Catholic ever to hold a chair there.

[45] Fiorenza, *In Memory of Her*, 7.

[46] Ibid., xx.

[47] Ibid., 6.

In an "engaged" feminist hermeneutics, no texts may be considered "revelation" unless they "critically break through patriarchal culture", Fiorenza says. Since many biblical texts are undeniably patriarchal, biblical theologians may regard Scripture neither as "the Word of God" nor as a collection of early "theological responses to pastoral-practical situations".[48] The New Testament should no longer be seen as an *archetype* ("an ideal form" establishing a "timeless pattern") but should instead be regarded as a *prototype* ("critically open" to "its own transformation").[49]

How is Scripture to be transformed? By reading it with the feminist "hermeneutic of suspicion", then improving it with "feminist reconstruction": that is, by invention. The feminist scholar must weave women into scriptural texts where she thinks they should have been. Fiorenza recommends drawing on gnostic and apocryphal sources, written by history's "losers", because they escaped "patriarchal" revision.[50] *In Memory of Her* includes a heavy-handed model of the reconstructionist genre by one of her Notre Dame students. An "epistle" by a Gentile "Apostle Phoebe", it describes her worry that St. Paul may be reverting to sexist attitudes from his pre-Christian past. It also reports Phoebe's outrage with the "infuriating" St. Peter, who gives "scandal to all the saints" by refusing to listen to "Apostle" Mary Magdalen.[51]

This is not "reconstruction" but new construction built on rejection of historical reality. What can be its purpose? Not to transform Scripture but to transform the writer, her fellow students and, eventually, her own students so they will read not only Scripture but all reality through a feminist lens.

Concern for respectability has not inhibited Fiorenza's political activism. Having ascertained in 1975 that WOC was not interested in "ordination at any price" but instead sought a self-defined,

[48] Ibid., 48, 3–5.
[49] Ibid., 33.
[50] Ibid., xiii–xxiv.
[51] Ibid., 61–64.

non-hierarchical priesthood,[52] she became a founding member, board member and vocal participant in the group, serving on its team in the NCCB dialogue. She says she "coined the notion of 'Women-Church'",[53] that is, the claim that feminists continue to *be* "church" even as they leave the hierarchy behind. With Judith Plaskow, she founded the *Feminist Journal in Religion*.[54] Mary Hunt credits Fiorenza as one of the "bunch of friends" who urged her to found WATER in 1982.[55] When Daniel Maguire wanted to recruit signers for CFFC's pro-abortion 1984 *New York Times* advertisements, she served on the recruiting committee and permitted her name to be published as a member.

Such activism seems to have done her career little harm. Fiorenza professes a desire not to destroy but merely to "reform" the Church; her theological writings are less polemical and more scholarly in style than Ruether's; her position at Harvard Divinity School reduces many churchmen and -women to stammering awe. Perhaps for those reasons, she is welcomed even in circles where Ruether might be considered too controversial. During 1989, for example, Fiorenza presented keynote addresses not only at WATER's annual conference but also at the first national convention of the Catholic Campus Ministry Association, where she talked about "women's ministry and the discipleship of equals". In addition, she presented "distinguished lectures" not only at Pacific School of Religion, Oberlin College and Occidental College but also at (Catholic) Seton Hall and St. Louis Universities.[56] She is on *Concilium*'s editorial board. In 1987 she was presented with *U.S. Catholic*'s annual award and was elected president of the Society of Biblical Literature.

It is true that Fiorenza seems more interested than Ruether in retaining not only the machinery but also some of the religious

[52] Milhaven, "Fiorenza", 55.

[53] Ibid., 57.

[54] Ibid., 63.

[55] "Mary Hunt and WATER", *National Catholic Reporter*, reprint no. 10, n.d., distributed at Women in the Church conference, Oct. 10, 1986.

[56] "Faculty News", *Harvard Divinity Bulletin* (Winter 1990): 17.

references of Christianity. On closer examination, however, her relative traditionalism looks entirely strategic. She opposes the notion of Women-Church as an "exodus" community, but does so because separatism "concedes that women have no authentic history within biblical religion"[57] and because the Church can only be changed by feminists "claiming the center" as the new model of Christianity.[58] Mildly, she criticizes feminist spirituality as "occupied with meditation and incantations, spells and incense, womb chants and candle gazing, feminine symbols for the divine and trance induction", not because she sees anything intrinsically wrong with these activities, only because they are not useful to the reconstruction of "the Jesus movement".[59] She even criticizes Rosemary Ruether—for the "neo-orthodox implications" of her "hermeneutics", which I confess I had not noticed[60]—because Ruether discusses the "classical prophetic tradition" of Scripture without condemning its "patriarchal polemics" or its "repression of the cult of the Goddess".[61]

Because she is more realistic than the goddess-separatists of "feminist spirituality", the kind of Church Fiorenza advocates probably would not put witchcraft rituals on the altar. But she explicitly rejects any possibility that it would be "*Roman* Catholic".[62] Instead it would be a hybrid, political religion, transformed by feminist reinterpretation of Scripture and Tradition and gnostic additions to Scripture and theology. It would teach a revolutionary process God and an alien moral doctrine. It would not be Christ's Mystical Body but a collective. "The gospel is not a matter of the individual soul", she declares, but "the communal proclamation" of an "alternative community and world".[63]

This is another false dichotomy, designed to confuse. Yes,

[57] Fiorenza, *In Memory of Her*, xviii.
[58] Ibid., 348.
[59] Ibid., 344.
[60] Ibid., 16–19.
[61] Ibid., 17.
[62] Milhaven, "Fiorenza", 60f.
[63] Fiorenza, *In Memory of Her*, 344.

Christ's gospel is a call to community—the community of his Mystical Body—but it is first a call to each individual soul. Jesus offers himself as "the Way, and the Truth, and the Life"[64] for each one of his children through his Church. When he said, "Seek and you shall find",[65] he was not addressing civic search committees or designers of utopias. Catholicism teaches that while Jesus died for all men, he would have died for only one.

"Feminist theology" is corrupted by ideological bias on every level; it lacks not only faith but also scholarly integrity. Ironically, it renders to revolutionary feminism the submission of mind and heart it refuses to the Church, fully aware that in feminism it is not truth that is served but political strategy. Fiorenza both practices and endorses that expedient morality, softening her criticism of "feminist spirituality" because Carol Christ understands that "at the heart of the spiritual feminist quest is the quest for women's power".[66] In a moral universe where political control is the ultimate object of worship, feminists exploit everything sacred as a means, not an end: God himself, the Eucharist, Scripture, theology, charity, compassion. As Mary Daly understood in some perverse way in 1968, Christ's Church is besieged by principalities and powers, by the spirit of wickedness in high places.

The Feminist Network

The so-called quest for "women's power" is a quest for feminist power. Inspired by the "new theological paradigm" and aided in the practical order by secular feminists from NOW,[67] Catholic feminists began spinning an intricately entangled web of organizations shortly after Vatican II. The most important groups in their network, in order of their founding, are National Assembly of Religious Women (1968), National Coalition of American Nuns

[64] Jn 14:6.

[65] Lk 11:9; Mt 7:7.

[66] Fiorenza, *In Memory of Her*, 18f.

[67] Charlotte Hays, "NOW Attacks Church's Stance on Abortion", *National Catholic Register*, June 23, 1985, 1.

(1969), Catholics for a Free Choice (1970), Network (1971), Center of Concern (1971), Chicago Catholic Women (1974), Institute of Women Today (1974), Quixote Center (1976), Women's Ordination Conference (1977), New Ways Ministry (1977), WATER (1983) and Women-Church Convergence (1984). All are relatively small and drawn from the same membership pool; many are merely paper organizations, dormant between conferences. Church Women United is another link in the web and, though Protestant, it seems to be drawing the mainline National Council of Catholic Women into the feminist orbit.

With some differences in emphasis, their characteristic marks are hostility to law (especially the teachings of the Church); defense of sexual libertinism, including contraception, abortion, homosexuality and unrestricted "sexual expression" (as manifestations of antinomian freedom); and leftist political activism (as the path to utopia). If large numbers of Catholics openly disobey the law, they claim, Church authorities will be forced to legitimize altar girls, "inclusive" language, married priests, women priests, self-ordained priests, contraception, homosexual practice and abortion, as they did Communion in the hand. Sister Fran Ferder, stating their common wisdom, says, "One of the basic principles of change is that practice precedes law."[68]

Such groups could be dismissed as eccentric if their members were expelled from their "footholds" in the Church or at least disdained by Church officials. But no such clear line has been drawn. Instead, many of them have been permitted—even invited—to function as speakers, advisors and consultants to official Catholic bodies.

Sister Marjorie Tuite, O.P.

A key figure in the organization of the feminist network was the late Sister Marjorie Tuite, O.P., whose personal evolution recapitulated that of the Catholic feminist movement. In the 1950s, as Sister Veritas, Tuite taught in New York parochial

[68] Reported in *Seattle Progress*, May 14, 1990.

schools. Under the influence of "new theology", she moved to Chicago in the late 1960s to direct adult religious education and work with the National Urban Training Center. With civil rights organizer Sam Easley, she presented sensitivity sessions ("Marge and Sam workshops") to men and women religious throughout the country. She played a central role in the formation of the radical National Assembly of Women Religious in 1968. In 1973, she joined the faculty of the Jesuit School of Theology in Chicago as a "specialist in social justice ministry".[69] When Women's Ordination Conference formed in 1975, she was on its core commission. In 1981, she took a staff post at Church Women United (CWU) as national director of Ecumenical Action, a committee serving the stock agenda of the political and feminist left.[70] Sister Marjorie's name appeared, with the identifying tag "Church Women United", in the CFFC *New York Times* ad of October 7, 1984, calling for abortion "pluralism" in the Catholic Church.

Enamored of the Sandinista regime, Tuite went to Nicaragua more than a dozen times, once for a protest fast with foreign minister and sometime Maryknoller Miguel D'Escoto. During treatment for hepatitis after a 1986 visit there, Tuite was found to

[69] For biographical information on Tuite, see Charlotte Hays, "A New Nun's Story", *Catholic Twin Circle*, Nov. 1, 1987, 5. See also "Sister Marjorie Tuite: Activist for Peace, Justice Issues", *Catholic New York*, July 3, 1986, 39; and Mary Bader Papa, "Women Set Siege on Male Bastions", *National Catholic Reporter*, Nov. 10, 1978, 1.

[70] In 1986, for example, Tuite's committee opposed (1) aid to the Nicaraguan contras, (2) Star Wars, (3) the death penalty, (4) South African investment, (5) table grapes, (6) human rights abuses in South Korea (no mention of North Korea), (7) "the TV miniseries 'Amerika'" (for its "negative portrayal of the United Nations" and "false fears of the Soviet Union". At the same time, the committee warmly supported (1) the United Nations in general and, in particular, the U.N. Convention to Eliminate All Forms of Discrimination against Women, (2) "Forward-Looking Strategies" adopted by the 1985 Nairobi conference on the UN Decade for Women, (3) the Witness for Peace demonstration in Washington, D.C., (4) the World International Year for Peace Congress and (5) the Women's Coalition Against U.S. Intervention in Central America and the Caribbean.

have a pancreatic tumor. She died at a New York hospital on June 29, following surgery.[71] At her funeral Mass, in her girlhood parish of St. Vincent Ferrer, the pastor properly asked that non-Catholics not come up for Communion. WOC's executive director, Ruth McDonough Fitzpatrick, tells what followed:

> William Sloane Coffin, people from National Council of Churches, Church Women United—her funeral was packed with people of all faiths. . . . In a loud voice . . . I called . . . "You know that's not true. You're all welcome." At the consecration the priest on the altar was surrounded with women. He was trying to elbow them back to give him his sacred space. But all of us extended our hands and said the words of consecration. . . . Before communion, [Sister] Maureen Fiedler . . . went up and down the first seven rows saying, "Everybody, please come to communion" . . . . At that point we saw William Sloane Coffin walking back from communion, and people who had meetings scheduled—Protestants—all stayed so that they would receive communion. . . . Women-Church came into its own at Margie's funeral in the way that Margie wanted.[72]

Tuite's body was cremated and some of her ashes shipped to Managua for veneration and eventual burial. Her CWU duties were temporarily assumed by Sister Ann Patrick Ware, S.L., a part-time CWU employee (also executive coordinator of the National Coalition of American Nuns, executive coordinator of the Institute of Women Today, a member of Women-Church Convergence and former chairman of the theology department at Webster College in St. Louis).[73] Early in 1987, Ada Maria Isasi-Diaz, a Cuban-born ex-nun (also national contact for Las

[71] "Sister Marjorie Tuite," *Catholic New York*, 39.

[72] Milhaven, "Ruth McDonough Fitzpatrick", in Milhaven, *Inside Stories*, 41–42.

[73] Webster College made early news in the secularization of Catholic colleges in 1967, when its president, Sister Jacqueline Grennan, announced to students, faculty, and the world that it would no longer be a Catholic college, because "it is my personal conviction that the very nature of higher education is opposed to juridical control by the Church". Grennan herself then left religious life (*America*, Jan. 28, 1967).

Hermanas, past director of WOC and a NARW board member), assumed Tuite's post on a permanent basis.[74] Like Tuite, Isasi-Diaz had been one of the WOC team in its 1979–81 dialogue with NCCB. Also like Tuite, both Ware and Isasi-Diaz had signed CFFC's *New York Times* ads.

In a foreword to *The Inside Stories*, a collection of interviews with Catholic feminists,[75] Rosemary Ruether lauds Tuite as "a personal mentor to at least half of the women represented" and as a martyr to patriarchy. After Tuite signed CFFC's ad, she "found her very existence in the Catholic Church threatened", Ruether declares melodramatically. The conflict "with its ruthless demands for submission from the hierarchy killed her, or at the very least, hastened her death. This death makes Marge Tuite close to a new Christ figure for Catholic feminists."[76]

National Assembly of Religious Women

The National Assembly of Religious Women was the first group in the feminist chain and in many ways the paradigm. Founded in 1968 as the National Assembly of Women Religious by nuns who reportedly considered Leadership Conference of Women Religious (LCWR) stodgy and elitist,[77] it claimed a member-

[74] On Isasi-Diaz' background, see Papa, "Male Bastions", 1. On personnel changes at CWU, see "Annual Report, 1986–1987: Ecumenical Action", Church Women United.

[75] Milhaven, *Inside Stories.* Interviewees include Sister Theresa Kane, R.S.M.; Marjorie Reilly Maguire; then–Sisters of Notre Dame de Namour Barbara Ferraro and Patricia Hussey; Elisabeth Schussler Fiorenza; CFFC Director Frances Kissling: WATER coordinator Mary Hunt; ex-Sister of Mercy and director of Michigan's Department of Social Services Agnes Mary Mansour; WOC Director Ruth McDonough Fitzpatrick; novelist Mary Gordon; ex-Sister of Mercy and representative to the Rhode Island state legislature Elizabeth Morancy; former director of Planned Parenthood of Rhode Island Mary Ann Sorrentino; assistant professor Bernadette Brooten of Harvard Divinity School.

[76] Rosemary Ruether, "Foreword", in Milhaven, *Inside Stories*, x.

[77] Weaver, *New Catholic Women*, 128.

ship of two thousand when it was opened to laywomen and renamed after Tuite became its national coordinator in 1981.[78] Tuite significantly influenced its passionate hostility to Rome. NARW promotes feminist spirituality, sexual permissiveness, abortion and leftist political causes through its newspaper, *Probe*, in writings, addresses, political education, demonstrations and conferences. Its characteristic temper was exemplified at the 1983 convention in Chicago, where members boosted their spirits by singing, "I have a fury deep inside my very soul. I will not live forever on my knees. Waves of hate wash over me and wash me clean of fear."[79]

The theme of the 1985 NARW convention, held in Los Angeles, was titled "The Politics of Struggle: Building a Community of Hope". Workshop subjects ranged from "setting the context of the struggle" through "strategizing our dissent from hierarchical, patriarchal Church structures" to "building lesbian communities of resistance and hope". The text of CFFC's second ad was circulated for signatures. In her address, Tuite said, "Patriarchy in the family unit is disabling. And to me the vertical, patriarchal power of the Church hierarchy is violent."[80]

A February 1986 NARW conference in Chicago was moderated by Sister Kaye Ashe, O.P., of Rosary College, the newly elected president of the Sinsinawa Dominicans. She sounded an encouraging note of gloom when she said, "I think we are experiencing a dark period ever since the *New York Times* ad." Rosemary Ruether talked, as usual, about Women-Church as "the feminist expression of the basic Christian community of liberation theology". Rosalie Muschal-Reinhardt was asked about the validity of Women-Church sacraments. In answer, she reported happily that her daughter hadn't wanted her baby baptized because

[78] "Sister Marjorie Tuite", *Catholic New York*, 39.

[79] *National Catholic Register*, Nov. 27, 1983. Quoted in Muggeridge, *Desolate City*, 140.

[80] Terri Vorndran, "NARW Explores Strategies for a Dissenting Community", *National Catholic Register*, Aug. 25, 1985, 1.

she felt "'my baby has already been baptized in the waters in my womb'". So the family held a welcoming ceremony instead. "And if that wasn't Baptism!" Muschal-Reinhardt said. "If that wasn't Eucharist!" Choked with emotion, her voice broke off.

Mary Jo Weaver, in her address on "why we're angry", said she no longer went to Mass and felt "less and less comfortable speaking of 'we' in the Church". Quoting Marjorie Tuite, Weaver said feminists are angry because "they don't want us; they've never wanted us; they never will want us!" Tuite had been "overwhelmed by the evil of patriarchy", Weaver said.[81]

In March 1989, NARW joined St. Louis Catholics for Choice, thirty Jewish and Christian organizations and eight bishops of the Episcopal Church in an amicus curiae brief to the United States Supreme Court opposing Missouri's Webster law.[82]

Church Women Divided: The National Council of Catholic Women

Tuite is less reverently remembered by orthodox members of the National Council of Catholic Women (NCCW), who see her as partly responsible for compromising trends in their organization. Founded in 1921 under the direction of the American bishops, NCCW has a nominal membership of more than ten million women from parish Altar and Rosary societies across the nation, and has been loyally Catholic at its grass roots level. Its opposition to abortion is steadfast; it opposed the Equal Rights Amendment (ERA); it holds that the sexes have naturally complementary roles and that woman's role is as valuable as man's. Mary Jo Weaver criticizes NCCW's "pre-conciliar mentality",[83] which in fact tends

[81] Audiotape, "Women-Church: Its Struggle and Its Vision", NARW conference, Illinois province, Feb. 16, 1986.

[82] Liz Schevtchuk, "Two Groups of Nuns File Pro-Choice Briefs", *Florida Catholic*, Apr. 14, 1989, 4.

[83] Weaver, *New Catholic Women*, 121.

to be in harmony with the Vatican's. Most members are wives and mothers from small towns or suburbs, devout, generous, modest about their own qualifications and charitable in their judgments, sometimes to excess.

With the mass conversion of Church career women to feminism and the leftward shift of the episcopal bureaucracy, NCCW's traditional posture has tended toward erosion from the top. Some who rise to national office feel inadequately informed and ineffectual in comparison to the professional staff in Washington, D.C., and even the strongest willed NCCW president can do little to change matters from her distant home during her two-year term. Margaret Mealey, NCCW executive director from 1950 to 1977, was a member of the national planning committee for International Women's Year and, on a "Meet the Press" broadcast from Houston during the 1977 IWY conference, endorsed the ERA despite the NCCW's official stand against it.[84] In 1981, an NCCW convention adopted a resolution favoring disarmament. A troupe from Chicago Call to Action presented a musical skit, "Between the Times", at NCCW's 1987 national convention in Minneapolis. Pro-life speakers who had been refused permission to distribute printed materials were appalled when Call to Action was permitted to hand out membership brochures and promotional materials.[85] NCCW's successive executive directors and others from its national office have

[84] Interviews with Betty Hillemeier, July 1990, who was then president of NCCW, and Phyllis Schlafly, who as a guest on the same "Meet the Press" show was left as the only woman among five panelists to oppose the ERA. As Mealey had retired from her position as NCCW director only days earlier (at the NCCW national convention), she could claim to be expressing merely her personal opinion. Nevertheless, her stand left the NCCW's formal position unstated and thoroughly compromised.

[85] Permission was denied on the estimably cautious policy grounds that distribution of any materials not screened and approved in advance was prohibited. Nevertheless it is an argument against the effectiveness of the policy that Call to Action's promotional literature should have survived review while a simple pro-life bookmark was rejected because it had not been screened.

attended board meetings of Church Women United (CWU) for years,[86] and there have been sporadic attempts to appoint women from NCCW's province-level leadership to CWU's state boards.

CWU is structured like a feminist version of the National Council of Churches. Affiliated local churches, organizations and individuals continue to support their own activities, many of them entirely blameless. CWU uses their contributions, collected at such annual events as World Day of Prayer and World Community Day, and also uses their names to add weight to the activities of its national staff and elected board of managers. It issues position papers, holds political action briefings, offers testimony at congressional hearings, provides conference speakers, makes grants to approved groups and otherwise "builds coalitions" within a network of like-minded organizations. Formal NCCW membership would lend credibility to CWU's claim to represent church women from all denominations.

Such an affiliation would violate NCCW's integrity, however, because CWU's stands on specific issues conflict with Catholic positions not open to compromise. For example, in 1970, CWU's national board of managers (made up of state presidents and representatives from all member groups) adopted a policy statement calling "termination of an unwanted pregnancy" a "basic human right".[87] Subsequent protests led the board's executive committee to state, in 1973, that "there are Catholic and Protestant women

[86] The present executive director is Annette Kane. Her predecessors, since Mealey's retirement late in 1977, have included Mary Helen Madden (1977–80) and Winifred Coleman (1980–85).

[87] "Resolution on Abortion (1970)", Church Women United National Board of Managers. For access to NCCW and CWU documents, I am indebted to Delores Boyle, Darlene Gerber and Elaine Zitzman, members of the St. Paul/Minneapolis Archdiocesan Council of Catholic Women Committee for a Statement on Church Women United, 1986–87, and board members, Minneapolis Deanery CCW. Mrs. Boyle served as legislative information vice-chair from 1982 to 1986. Mrs. Zitzman's research on CWU very thoroughly covered the years from 1973 to 1987.

on both sides of this controversial issue", and "Christian respect" ought to keep them from condemning each other.[88] Today CWU insists that the 1970 resolution "was an action of that particular Board only, and is not binding on any other", which while unsatisfactory seems to be a move in the right direction. A third statement, written by CWU's ecumenical action committee and adopted by its executive council in 1982, says "Church Women United has no collective position on the abortion issue".[89] But along with National Abortion Rights Action League, CWU vigorously supports the "U.S. National Women's Agenda", a declaration left over from International Women's Year 1975.[90] The "agenda" demands a vast array of "rights", including "the legal right of women to control their own reproductive systems"; "protection of the right to privacy" between "consenting adults" and legislation to end "discrimination based on affectional or sexual preference".[91] In 1987, CWU's newsletter, *lead time*, rallied members to the pro-abortion campaign against Robert Bork's appointment to the Supreme Court.[92]

NCCW's traditional members are also distressed about CWU's policy statement on "children's rights", drafted by Tuite's ecumenical action committee and adopted by CWU's Common

[88] Veronica Rohr, chairman, "NCCW-CWU Relationship Task Force Report" (circa 1978), n.d.

[89] "A Statement of Concern about Abortion (1982)", written by the Ecumenical Action Committee and approved by the executive council, Church Women United, June 1982.

[90] International observance of the U.N. Decade for Women opened with an International Women's Year in 1975. Then-Congresswoman Bella Abzug persuaded the U.S. Congress to fund a U.S. International Women's Year in 1977. The agenda was a product of the first "year" (1975) but fully reflects the positions of the second. Among many other supporting groups listed are Lesbian Feminist Liberation, National Organization for Women, National Education Association, National Coalition of American Nuns, Institute of Women Today and Leadership Conference of Women Religious.

[91] "U.S. National Women's Agenda", information sheet, St. Paul, Minnesota, Democratic National Committee Women's Caucus, n.d.

[92] Anne Martin, *lead time* (Sept./Oct. 1987): 11. Martin is identified as CWU's "controller".

Council in June 1985. Endorsing school programs for "prevention of adolescent pregnancy", the policy declares support for Children's Defense Fund, "both financially and programatically".[93] Children's Defense Fund has led the nationwide lobbying effort for "school-based clinics", where children are given contraceptives and abortion referrals without their parents' knowledge.[94]

Most NCCW members trust the judgment of their leaders, know little about CWU and are unaware of the relationship between the two organizations. Some, better informed, strongly oppose any ties, while a minority want to make NCCW a more progressive organization. In 1987, NCCW's "Task Force on Church Women United" recommended acceptance of CWU's invitation to full membership in its common council.[95] President Toni Bischoff urged that NCCW continue sending representatives to CWU meetings "without bringing the matter before the national Convention".[96] No formal policy change was adopted; there is no official tie between the two groups. Yet according to Patricia Janik, NCCW's national program director, personnel from NCCW and CWU enjoy an "open relationship" of "dialogue and cooperation", exchange publications, attend each other's meetings as non-voting "observers" and lobby Congress jointly.[97] These activities are summed up in NCCW promo-

[93] Policy statement on "rights of children and youth", approved by Church Women United Common Council, June 1985. In 1987, *lead time* urged members to order the Children's Defense Fund's booklet "Preventing Children Having Children" and commended an Oklahoma CWU affiliate for its role in establishing a school-based clinic. See Church Women United, "How We Can Help Combat the Problem of Teen Pregnancy", *lead time* (Mar.–Apr. 1987): 11.

[94] See Donna Steichen, *Population Control Goes to School* (Gaithersburg, Md.: Human Life International, 1988).

[95] Betty Miller, chairman, "Task Force on Church Women United", July 1, 1987.

[96] Letter from Toni M. Bischoff, president, to NCCW board of directors, July 7, 1987.

[97] Interview with Patricia Janik, July 17, 1990.

tional brochures as "working ecumenically with women of other faiths".[98]

"So they're up there lobbying for things that we're down here fighting", said one Minnesota NCCW member. Another Minnesotan, Province Director Isabel Meyer, was startled to find her name listed without authorization on CWU's 1988 state-level directory as one of its "local unit presidents and denominational representatives".[99] Tension continues, and disillusioned Catholic women continue to drop out.

Pressure for the alliance comes in part from elected NCCW leaders who have learned to conform to the feminist worldview. To a greater degree, it arises from a bureaucratic caste system in which a professional peer (like the late Sister Tuite) may command greater loyalty than members with traditional Catholic principles. Those "folk Catholics", far away in the grass roots, can come to seem like irksome obstacles to progress, just as congressional constituents can. But inevitably, someone's principles prevail. Ten million committed Catholic women could change the face of society if their impact were focused. Instead, the principles of the revolutionaries prevail so often as to recall William Butler Yeats' chilling lines:

> The best lack all conviction, while the worst
> are full of passionate intensity.[100]

Catholics for a Free Choice

Catholics for a Free Choice (CFFC) is neither Catholic nor a membership organization but a lobbying and disinformation arm of the abortion movement, annually funded by more than

[98] "Together We Can Make a Difference", promotional brochure, Washington, D.C., National Council of Catholic Women, 1990.

[99] "Church Women United in Minnesota: Denominational Presidents or Representatives, 1987–1988", *CWU/MN Update* (Jan./Feb. 1988).

[100] William Butler Yeats, "The Second Coming", *Master Poems of the English Language*, ed. Oscar Williams (New York: Washington Square Press, 1968), 887f.

$275,000 in grants from foundations that either advocate population limitation, represent birth control manufacturing interests or, like the Playboy Foundation, otherwise profit from the sex trade.[101] Headed by Frances Kissling, a former administrator of legal and illegal abortion facilities[102] (and co-founder and past executive director of National Abortion Federation, an abortion trade association), CFFC exists to provide a putatively Catholic presence in the pro-abortion alliance.[103] *Conscience*, its bi-monthly news journal, provides insight into the activities and logic of Catholic abortion advocates for readers with strong stomachs.

In 1984 and 1986, CFFC initiated a crisis by persuading hundreds of Catholic feminists to sign two full-page *New York Times* advertisements declaring that there is no single "legitimate Catholic position" on abortion, that Catholics may dissent from the Church's teaching and remain in good standing. Both ads were drafted by CFFC board member Daniel Maguire, a former priest, with his wife Marjorie; both were purchased by CFFC for more than thirty thousand dollars each. The first, published to aid Geraldine Ferraro's vice-presidential campaign, appeared on October 7, 1984, with only ninety-six signatures, twenty-four those of nuns. The second, a declaration of support for signers of the first, ran on March 2, 1986. It bore more than one thousand names, representing a large percentage of the Catholic feminist constituency.

CFFC was founded in New York in 1970 (as Catholics for the Elimination of All Restrictive Abortion and Contraceptive Laws)

[101] Long-time foundation supporters include Ford, Brush, Sunnen (Emko contraceptive profits), Veatch (Unitarian-Universalist), Scherman, George Gund, Educational Foundation of America, Mary Reynolds Babcock, Ms and Playboy. CFFC's 1983 income was about a quarter million dollars, 97 percent of it from such grants. See Richard Doerflinger, "Who Are Catholics for a Free Choice?" supplement to *Catholic League Newsletter* 13, no. 2 (n.d.): 1–4. See also Joan Turner Beifuss, "Pro-Choice Catholics Reap Widespread Publicity", *National Catholic Reporter*, Jan. 11, 1985, 4.

[102] *Washington Post*, Aug. 24, 1986.

[103] Adelle-Marie Stan, "Call to Dissent", *Ms* (Dec. 1985), 92. See also "NOW Nuns and the 'Pro-Choice' Sisterhood", *Mindzenty Report* (Feb. 1985): 1.

with the crowning of the local NOW director as "Pope Patricia" on the steps of St. Patrick's Cathedral. Intended to counteract Church opposition to New York's permissive abortion law, it first operated out of a donated office in Planned Parenthood's building. Through the 1970s, most of its twenty-thousand-dollar annual budget came from a Unitarian Universalist church in New York.[104] When the Supreme Court legalized abortion in 1973, CFFC was a useful public relations addition to the Religious Coalition for Abortion Rights. Its role remained minor through the 1970s, under founding director Father Joseph O'Rourke, S.J., who was expelled from the Jesuits and the priesthood in 1974 but continued to use the initials "S.J."[105]

CFFC's offices were moved to Washington, and Kissling became director in 1980. Her audacity and fund-raising talents have greatly expanded its public profile. Since her coming, CFFC has enjoyed such media attention that reporters actually quote her entirely predictable opinions on Catholic matters. This absurd situation exists chiefly because the media is dominated by abortion advocates, but the collusion of the Catholic feminist network has also been indispensable. Notre Dame Sisters Barbara Ferraro and Patricia Hussey,[106] who shared a season of publicity for their refusal to retract endorsement of the first *New York Times* ad, issued all their press statements through CFFC, including the

[104] Doerflinger, "Free Choice?" 1–2.

[105] A pre-Kissling brochure from CFFC's early days in Washington, D.C., listed Janice Gleason, president; Denyse Barbet, vice president and treasurer; Meta Mulcahy, vice president; Carol Maxwell, secretary; directors Virginia Andary, Carol Bonosaro, Glenn Ellefson-Brooks, Dr. Elizabeth Farians, Anne Fremantle, Dr. Jane Furlong-Cahill, Dr. Joseph T. Skehan, Joan G. Stanley and Father Joseph O'Rourke, S.J.; honorary advisors Dr. Hillary Appleton, Gabrielle Burton, Mary Kelly, Esq., Lt. Gov. Mary Ann Krupsack, Father Edward McGowan, S.J. and Dr. Janice Raymond. For a chilling account of O'Rourke's later life, see Joe O'Rourke, "Ruminations of a Father to Be", *Conscience* (Sept./Oct. 1988): 1, a report of his wife's 1988 pregnancy and their decision to abort their only child.

[106] Ms. Hussey has even referred to Kissling as a "theologian". See her WOC award acceptance speech in *New Women/New Church* (May/June 1987): 6.

announcement that they had at last resigned from their order.[107] Women-Church Convergence, which lists CFFC as a coalition member, held its 1989 meeting in Washington on April 8. The following day, flocks of Women-Church members marched under CFFC's banner in the highly publicized pro-abortion March on Washington. Chicago Catholic Women (CCW), NCAN, Loretto Women's Network and many other Convergence groups and individual members joined in CFFC's pro-abortion amicus curiae brief, filed on March 30, 1989, while the Supreme Court was deciding the Webster case.[108]

Unintentionally, the feminists' association with CFFC has served the interests of real Catholics by exposing some of the most virulent subversives within the Church. Many who endorsed the ads came to rue their impetuosity when they discovered that in the Church, both as hierarchy and as "people of God", there is indeed a single Catholic position on abortion. By denying it, feminists intend both to support the "right" to abortion and to deny that the Church has magisterial authority established by Jesus Christ to guard and transmit his saving truth.

If the involvement of Catholic feminists in CFFC activities seems to be represented here as a litmus test, it is because abortion is indeed a watershed issue in the yawning division between Catholics orthodox and revolutionary. No "dialogue" can make traditional Catholics doubt the immorality of abortion; they may not understand the theological nuances of every question facing

[107] See Donna Steichen, "Showdown in St. Louis: Catholic Laity 1, Proabortion Nuns 0", *Fidelity* (Apr. 1988).

[108] Margaret Conway, "The March on Washington: Catholics United for Choice", *Conscience* (May/June 1989): 17–18. See also David Shaneyfelt, "Who's Prolife and Who's Not?" *Catholic Twin Circle*, May 14, 1989, 7. Among individuals listed by the court as parties to the brief are Rosemary Ruether, Mary Buckley, Geraldine Ferraro, ex-nuns Barbara Ferraro and Patricia Hussey, Ruth M. Fitzpatrick, Christine Gudorf, Sister Donna Quinn, Dolly Pomerleau, Janet Kalven, Daniel and Marjorie Maguire, Mary Jo Meadow (religious studies department, Mankato State University, Minnesota), Annie Lally Milhaven, Joseph O'Rourke, Jane Via (San Diego) and Mary Jo Weaver.

society and the Church today, but they know that killing babies is evil. Thus Catholics who offer public support for abortion clarify their status in the eyes of pro-life Catholics. Beyond ambiguity, beyond sincere differences, beyond academic qualifications, beyond the labels of liberal or conservative, they stand revealed as utterly wrong. It is rarely necessary to persuade run-of-the-pew Catholics that abortion is intolerable, though often hard to persuade them that Sister could actually approve it. At the heterodox end of the spectrum, too, abortion is a key issue, a matter on which all the Catholic feminist groups cited here[109] and most Catholic revolutionaries share a common perspective.

National Coalition of American Nuns

Minnesota-born Sister Margaret Ellen Traxler, S.S.N.D., who entered Mankato's School Sisters of Notre Dame in 1941, left the classroom in 1965 to work with the National Catholic Conference of Interracial Justice. Golda Meir gave her a medal for her work with the National Interreligious Task Force on Soviet Jewry. She speaks with moving passion about racial and social injustice and has devoted much energy since 1974 to the needs of women prisoners. She writes of her family with love. But she seems to have lacked the temperament for her original vocation; of the Church she speaks with a bellowing rage reminiscent of Bull Connor at Selma.

Traxler scorns the Church as a collaborator in the universal oppression of women, calls the orderly years between Vatican

[109] An obvious exception is Feminists for Life, which attempts to find a balance on the difficult line between support for liberalism and opposition to abortion. Since its foundation in the mid-1970s, it has professed both to support the Equal Rights Amendment and to demand protection for the unborn as consistent feminist positions. FFL copes more successfully in this ambiguous territory than does the "seamless garment" organization JustLife because, in my estimation, FFL is a pro-life organization first and a womens' rights group second, while for JustLife the abortion issue seems to have no higher priority than any prudential item on the "consistent ethic of life" list. In addition, FFL's "feminist" stands are usually valid, or at least defensible, calls for proper male responsibility for the real needs of women and children, and thus are not feminist but simply civilized.

Councils I and II "an aberrant time for American sisters"[110] and remembers convent life with loathing.[111] Since Vatican II, she says, religious poverty has "moved up" from "giving up things—material goods, money and ownership rights—to giving up attitudes—class distinctions, sexism, racism, elitist privileges, habit and veil, buildings and acceptance by the Church bureaucracy."[112] She says Women-Church rituals are "living liturgies" showing "the direction for future prayer".[113] She describes "the mean bishops" as "pitiful little adolescent boys".[114]

In 1969, Traxler formed the small but vocal National Coalition of American Nuns (NCAN).[115] Mary Daly addressed its first meeting. NCAN won nationwide attention in 1982 when Traxler, Sister Ann Patrick Ware, Sister Donna Quinn, O.P., and Sister Deborah Barrett, S.F.C.C., appeared on the Phil Donahue television show to declare their opposition to the "states' rights" Hatch amendment against abortion.[116] Traxler and Quinn regularly hold public "celebrations" of January 22 as the anniversary of the Supreme Court decision legalizing abortion.

Traxler left Quinn in charge of NCAN's Chicago office, Ware in charge in New York, when she founded the Institute of Women Today (IWT) in 1974. Sponsored by Church Women United, NCAN, NARW and Methodist, Presbyterian and Jewish women's groups, IWT proposed "to search for the religious and historical roots of women's liberation". Traxler says it also has developed programs to train women prisoners for jobs in building trades and established a halfway house for women parolees

[110] Margaret Ellen Traxler, "Great Tide of Returning", in Ware, *Midwives*, 129.

[111] Ibid., 137.

[112] Suzanne Allyn, "Confessions of a Feminist Nun", *Fidelity* (Nov. 1984).

[113] Traxler, "Great Tide", in Ware, *Midwives*, 138.

[114] Stan, "Call to Dissent", 65.

[115] According to Mary Jo Weaver, NCAN has never claimed to represent more than 2 percent of American nuns. See Weaver, *New Catholic Women*, 244, n. 70.

[116] Ware's article about the event, "When Rebel Nuns Go Public", ran in both *Ms* and *Conscience* in Sept. 1983.

on Chicago's west side.[117] Ware, doubling as IWT's New York coordinator in 1985, reported spending "two days a week with women in jail or in court",[118] a remarkable feat considering her other duties as NCAN's New York director and part-time staffer at Church Women United.

Chicago Catholic Women

Chicago Catholic Women (CCW) was also founded in 1974. In 1977, it organized the "Women of the Church Coalition" that grew into Women-Church Convergence.[119] In 1987, CCW claimed a membership of eight hundred and identified busy Sister Donna Quinn as executive director.[120] At the 1987 Women-Church Convergence, Rosemary Ruether crowed that CCW's "Mary's Pence" campaign could dry up "the ecclesiastical bank which is funding oppression around the world" and "pool our resources to fund women's ministries".[121] The Mary's Pence fund drive, created as a feminist alternative to the annual Peter's Pence drive (for the Pope), was inaugurated in April 1987 with Ruether, Traxler, Coston, Sister Mary Luke Tobin, Sister Kaye Ashe, Rosalie Muschal-Reinhardt,[122] Sister Janemarie Luecke, O.S.B.,[123] Sister Teresita Weind, Sister Yolanda Tarango, C.C.V.I. and

[117] Traxler, "Great Tide", in Ware, *Midwives*, 135–36.

[118] Ware, *Midwives*, cover notes.

[119] The coalition, meant to replace "Sisters Uniting", included CCW, NARW, NCAN, WOC, IWT, Quixote Center, Las Hermanas and, as soon as it was founded, WATER. See Weaver, *New Catholic Women*, 132–33, and Ruether, *Women-Church*, 66–67.

[120] "Chicago Catholic Women Begin Mary's Pence Fund", *St. Cloud Visitor*, May 28, 1987, 4. See also conference program, "Women-Church: Claiming Our Power", 5.

[121] Quoted in Charlotte Hays, "3,000 Christian Feminists Hear 'Patriarchy' Rapped", *National Catholic Register*, Oct. 25, 1987, 1.

[122] Muschal-Reinhardt was reportedly the first woman graduate of the School of Theology in Chicago. A married grandmother and past director of Women's Ordination Conference, she has reported it as her dream "that when I die I will be buried a bishop of the U.S. Catholic Church". See Papa, "Male Bastions", 1.

[123] Luecke was then president of NCAN.

Edwina Gately,[124] as board members.[125] Two years later, Ruether revealed that "the major supporters of this project are the Catholic women's religious orders".[126] How is it, one wonders, that those orders can make grants to Mary's Pence but cannot support their own aged sisters?

In 1987, six of the groups represented in CFFC's *New York Times* ads—NARW, NCAN, CCW, IWT, Catholic Women for Reproductive Rights (Sister Deborah Barrett, director) and the Justice Campaign (director: Barrett)[127]—were all using the same Chicago address.[128]

Network

Network, a less-notorious "national Catholic social justice lobby", also has been important to the Catholic feminist movement. It was formed in December 1971,[129] when Marjorie Tuite "gathered

[124] Gately is described as founder of Genesis House, a Chicago ministry to prostitutes. But at the 1977 IWY meeting in Houston, a Franciscan priest, Father DePaul Genska, identified himself as the founder of a Chicago agency of the same name and description.

[125] "Mary's Pence: A Catholic Women's Foundation to Raise Funds for Alternative Ministries", fund-raising brochure (n.d.), distributed at the 1987 Women-Church Convergence in Cincinnati. Subsequent additions to the board include Dagmar Celeste (Ohio's first lady); Sister Yvonne Cherena, O.P. (Washington, D.C.); psychologist Patrick Durbeck (Harrisburg, Pennsylvania); Sister Amata Miller, I.H.M. (of Network); and Margaret Susan Thompson (Syracuse University). Luecke and Weind were no longer listed in 1989. See *Cross Currents* (Spring 1990): 128.

[126] Rosemary Radford Ruether, "Mary's Pence: Promoting Women's Ministries", *Cross Currents* (Spring 1989): 98.

[127] The Justice Campaign was described as "a national campaign to secure public funding for abortion for victims of rape and incest" on its promotional literature distributed at Women-Church Convergence. Listed on its letterhead among "convenors" was Daniel Maguire.

[128] The address: 1307 South Wabash, Chicago. Conference program, "Women-Church: Claiming Our Power", Women-Church Convergence, Oct. 9–11, 1987, 3–7.

[129] Milhaven, "Interview with Elizabeth Morancy", in Milhaven, *Inside Stories*, 90.

forty-seven of us in Washington", ex-Sister of Mercy Elizabeth Morancy recalls.[130] In her words, it has been "an effective tool of lobby for change".[131]

Sister Carol Coston, O.P., was Network's executive director during its first eleven years and later remained on its board of directors. Sister Mary Luke Tobin was also an active board member for many years.[132] Network's "peace and justice" positions, like those of Church Women United, have consistently been fashionable with the media.[133] By refusing to take a public position on abortion, it avoided controversy; Coston did not sign CFFC's ads. By the time she left, Network had an annual budget of three hundred thousand dollars and seven thousand members of both sexes, some of whom doubtless supposed its views represented Catholic thought.[134]

Coston herself was a full voting member of the Women-Church coalition, however. She was a delegate to the 1977 International Women's Year conference in Houston.[135] Along with Starhawk, Karen McCarthy Brown and other noted religious feminists,[136] she was a panelist at the 1982 Women's Spirit Bonding conference at Grailville. When CCW hatched its "Mary's Pence" scheme in 1987, she joined the board. In October the same year she spoke at the Women-Church Convergence in Cincinnati.

In a 1984 autobiographical essay, Coston said her "feminist perspective", developed during the 1960s and 1970s, enabled her

[130] In 1984, Morancy left the Sisters of Mercy after twenty-five years rather than give up her race for re-election to the Rhode Island legislature, a post where, she says, she always voted pro-abortion. See ibid., 94.

[131] Ibid., 89f.

[132] Tobin, "Doors to the World", in Ware, *Midwives*, 197.

[133] For example, Network lobbied *against* the Vietnam War, aid to "oppressive regimes" of the right and military spending; *for* increased social spending, Legal Services Corporation and the Equal Rights Amendment.

[134] Carol Coston, "Open Windows, Open Doors", in Ware, *Midwives*, 155.

[135] Kalven and Buckley, *Women's Spirit Bonding*, xii.

[136] Notable among the other panelists were Carol Christ, Judith Plaskow, Elisabeth Schussler Fiorenza, Rosemary Ruether, Mary Hunt, Diann Neu, Ada Maria Isasi-Diaz, Janet Kalven and Mary Buckley.

to see "domination" on all sides and gave her freedom to "try to transform" it, as well as to choose her own work, companions and "life-style", and to discover "feminist spirituality".[137] She discussed her spirituality in a 1980 speech published by Network and included in Tuite's NARW-CWU "conscientization" kit. It draws heavily on the thought of Sister Madonna Kolbenschlag and recommends the "positive images" to be found in the goddess "traditions" of Ishtar and Isis.[138] Network's staff, says Coston, developed its own "rituals" for office events, legislative seminars and "eucharistic celebrations". She also celebrates "feminist ritual" and "eucharist" with the Washington "women's base community" that Elisabeth Fiorenza dubbed "Sisters Against Sexism".[139] Among the "sisters" are CFFC's Frances Kissling[140] and WATER's Mary Hunt.[141] As if to prove that Coston's attitudes are not alien to Network, Sister Nancy Sylvester, I.H.M., who succeeded her as national director, also spoke at the 1987 Women-Church Convergence.[142]

Network often loses on its lobbying issues, Coston says, but has succeeded anyway by "educating thousands of people, especially women religious, in the whole political process".[143] And so it has, alas. Network's relative respectability makes it useful to those who deny infallible moral authority to the Magisterium but impute it to liberal ideologues.

[137] Coston, "Open Windows", in Ware, *Midwives*, 147–48.

[138] Coston, "Feminism". Distributed by NARW at Time Consultants' 1986 Women in the Church conference. The address was presented to "the School Sisters of Notre Dame and the Sisters of St. Joseph of Carondolet".

[139] Coston, "Open Windows", in Ware, *Midwives*, 158.

[140] Frances Kissling, "I Think of Myself, in Some Ways, as a Very Traditional Catholic", *Chicago Tribune*, Sept. 28, 1986.

[141] "Mary Hunt and WATER", *National Catholic Reporter* off-print (n.d.).

[142] See conference program, "Women-Church: Claiming Our Power", Oct. 9–11, 1987, 43.

[143] Coston, "Open Windows", in Ware, *Midwives*, 159.

Center of Concern

Another Washington "social justice" think tank in the feminist loop is Center of Concern (COC), established in 1971 by three Jesuits, Father Peter Henriot, Father William Ryan and Father William Callahan with the blessings of Jesuit Superior General Pedro Arrupe, the American bishops and U Thant of the United Nations.[144] Ryan was its original director; Henriot held the position from 1977 to 1988, when Father James Hug, S.J., succeeded him. An autonomous body focused on the application of liberation theology to "international development, peace initiatives, economic alternatives, women in society and Church", COC endorses "creation-centered spirituality"; publishes papers, books and a newsletter; holds conferences and consults—with the NCCB, among others.[145]

Though gender neutral in staff and membership, COC is profoundly feminist in policy, and its women's project has been influential. As a staff member from 1974 to 1978, Sister Elizabeth Carroll, R.S.M., past president of LCWR (1971–72), worked on feminist issues. Her perspective can be judged from her description of Consortium Perfectae Caritatis as "a group whose vision limited renewal to the literal application of *Perfectae Caritatis*".[146] Carroll was the keynote speaker at the first Women's Ordination Conference meeting in Detroit in 1975.[147]

[144] The launching of Center of Concern was announced from United Nations headquarters, and the Center is still affiliated there as a non-governmental organization.

[145] Information from *Center of Concern: Annual Report, 1984–85*; Joe Holland, "The Post-Modern Paradigm Implicit in the Church's Shift to the Left" (paper; Feb. 1984); Holland, "Family, Work, and Culture: Strategic Themes for Catholic Spirituality in the Crisis of Modernity" (paper; n.d.); Holland, "American Catholic Lay Network: An Update", *Center Focus* (Jan. 1986); Center of Concern publications catalogue, 1986; *Center Focus* (Sept. 1988, Nov. 1988, July 1989, Nov. 1989); Center of Concern 1990 Catalogue of Educational Resources; other papers, all from Washingon, D.C., Center of Concern.

[146] Elizabeth Carroll, "Reaping the Fruits of Redemption", in Ware, *Midwives*, 65.

[147] Ibid., 66–67.

Sister Maria Riley, O.P., succeeded Carroll as coordinator of COC's "women's project" in 1979.[148] In that capacity, she arranged the May 1981 "Women Moving Church" conference. With Diann Neu, then on COC's staff, she later edited the proceedings in tabloid form.[149] COC has published many of Riley's writings on women's spirituality, one of her chief interests.[150] In 1987, she participated in the Women-Church Convergence in Cincinnati.[151]

International Grail member Anne Hope joined the Center in 1987, after a decade spent training Catholic leaders in Kenya and Zimbabwe in Paulo Freire's "conscientization" techniques. During a 1983–84 sabbatical in the United States, Hope directed seminars for returned missionaries at the Catholic Mission Association in Washington and wrote a three-volume text, *Training for Transformation*, about her methods. She has presented "training for transformation" workshops at various institutes for COC.

COC is treated as credible by some who might shrink from public association with its allies and offspring. Its consultants worked closely with Archbishop John Roach, Archbishop Rembert Weakland and their drafting committees for the NCCB pastoral letters on peace and on the economy.[152] When the first draft of the American bishops' letter on women's concerns was published in 1988, a COC committee headed by Riley prepared a responding

[148] "Center of Concern: Publications", catalogue (n.d. circa 1986).

[149] Diann Neu and Maria Riley, eds., *Women Moving Church* (Washington, D.C.: Center of Concern, 1982).

[150] Maria Riley, *Wisdom Seeks Her Way: Liberating the Power of Women's Spirituality* (Washington, D.C.: Center of Concern, 1987). Other works by Riley on women's spirituality, listed in Center Publications Catalogue, 1986, include *In God's Image*; *Eve and Mary the Mother Are Our Stem: All Our Centuries Go Back to Them*; *Women, Church and Patriarchy*; *Women: Carriers of a New Vision*; and, with Fathers Henriot and Hug, *Energies for Social Transformation*, all published by Center of Concern. Several are also listed as available on videotape.

[151] Participants' list, "Women-Church: Claiming Our Power", Silver Spring, Md., WATER, Dec. 1987, 3.

[152] *Center of Concern: Annual Report, 1984–85*, 1f.

paper.[153] It was the basis for her address to the national assembly of the LCWR in late August 1988 and was later echoed by Catholic feminists across the nation. It was also submitted to the bishops' committee, without causing a ripple of disturbance.

The format of *Partners in the Mystery of Redemption* is an odd one for an episcopal teaching document. Instead of opening with statements of Church teaching, which are then applied to particular cases, each section in *Partners* opens with women's testimony as either "voices of affirmation" or "voices of alienation". Thus it appears that women are teaching bishops, rather than bishops teaching women. Orthodox Catholics were dismayed that quotations from "voices of alienation" outnumber "voices of affirmation" by five to one.[154] On such sensitive matters as the ordination of women and "inclusive" language, not a single word of positive testimony is included. Nor are the grave errors expressed by "voices of alienation" on abortion, contraception and remarriage after divorce ever directly addressed by the bishops. Yet Sister Riley's paper protested the use of the word *alienation* to identify what it called voices of "anger and loyal dissent". These women, it said, "may be extremely critical of some of the stances taken by the institutional church and its response to the reality of women's lives, but most of them feel deeply identified with the church as the community of believers. They are not aliens."[155]

How could she know? No internal evidence suggests that the alienated witnesses were practicing Catholics. None of the "voices" is identified except by diocese, and their own words establish that they either were unacquainted with the teachings of the Faith or

[153] Maria Riley, O.P.; Peter Henriot, S.J.; Anne Hope; Phil Land, S.J.; and George Ann Potter, *Comments on the First Draft NCCB Pastoral Letter Partners in the Mystery of Redemption* (Washington, D.C.: Center of Concern, June 13, 1988).

[154] Dr. Susan Benofy, "A Statistical Analysis on Testimony Quoted in the Pastoral on Women", *Fidelity* (June 1988).

[155] Riley et al., *Comments*, 5.

had rejected them. What the COC paper reveals is that Sister Maria and her team in fact share the perspective of alienation. Though it praises the draft pastoral—for raising the "controversial questions" of women's ordination and preaching, birth control, lesbianism and abortion—most of its content details feminist complaints. It not only accuses the Church of "structural" sins of "sexism", especially in her insistence on a male priesthood, but also expresses sullen resentment with the truth, revealed by Jesus Christ, that God is our Father rather than our Mother.[156] As a corrective, it recommends not only that "male-oriented" language be deleted but also that God be "imaged" as female and that "interpretation of Scripture" be somehow changed. The importance of language, it says, "cannot be minimalized [*sic*]".[157] The paper classes patriarchy with "sexism" as a "structure of sin" and a "moral and social evil".[158] It clearly indicates belief that the Church's magisterial authority is not given by God but is an arbitrary device depriving women of a fair share of "jurisdiction". Quoting Paulo Freire, it urges bishops to broaden their "male" theological views by entering into "dialogue" with women "who have begun to articulate their own experience".[159] The Church must learn from "the experience of the laity and the *sensus fidelium*", it says, that the "sense of the sacred is often experienced beyond the legalistic interpretations of current church teaching" about marriage, in "other forms of sexual expression within relationships of love and involving informed, adult consent". The passage concludes:

> We urge that the committee incorporate into the body of the draft some of the materials on human sexuality that is [*sic*] available from sources beyond the predominately [*sic*] male-authored texts that the document presently quotes.[160]

[156] Ibid., 11–12.
[157] Ibid., 12, 17.
[158] Ibid., 8–10.
[159] Ibid., 6.
[160] Ibid., 14.

Partners lacks "intellectual rigor", COC's paper complains. While "specialists" were consulted to "interpret the difficult questions" for bishops who drafted previous pastorals, "women's studies specialists" were not invited to help with this letter. Thus, the "work of some of the most creative and prophetic women scholars are not apparent" in it. It names Sister Elizabeth Johnson, C.S.J., Sister Anne Carr, Elisabeth Schussler Fiorenza, Sister Margaret Farley, Sister Mary Collins, Sister Sandra Schneiders and Mary Buckley as "only a few" of the women scholars who should be consulted.[161] All except Johnson, Collins and Schneiders signed CFFC's 1984 *New York Times* ad. All without exception are on public record as feminist theologians of the most revolutionary stripe.

The way Riley's paper was utilized serves as an interesting example of feminist tactics. At hearings in my diocese, a statement was presented by two mild-mannered Franciscans fresh from the LCWR gathering, Sisters Rita Barthel and Clara Stang. What they said so closely resembled her paper that some of the phrasing was identical, though there was no mention of consenting adults. Their call for "women scholars" didn't specify which ones, so I asked. Cheerfully they rattled them off: Elisabeth Schussler Fiorenza and Sisters Elizabeth Johnson, Anne Carr, Margaret Farley, Mary Collins and Sandra Schneiders—plus Rosemary Ruether and Mary Hunt.

Shortly afterward, Bishop Imesch held a teleconference about the pastoral on NCCB's television network. Echoes from Riley's paper filled the call-in period. Almost every caller recited from her recommendations for the second draft: that it should have the same "academic excellence" that marked other recent pastorals; that the "work of women scholars" should be incorporated; that it should focus more acutely on the evils of "patriarchy"; that language about God should be "inclusive".

When I asked Bishop Imesch later whether he had recognized the substance of the COC critique in his teleconference calls, he

[161] Ibid., 6, 11.

said he had not. "That's not new", he said of the COC paper. "That came in about four months ago. I don't remember what it said. I haven't heard anything from the LCWR."

It was disheartening to find, when the second draft of the pastoral (now titled *One in Christ Jesus*)[162] appeared in April 1990, that many feminist theologians are indeed incorporated into its endnotes. Never mind the three citations of LCWR; as the bishops' official liaison with American nuns, its presence was predictable, however much of its positions veer from orthodoxy. But what can explain the citation of Sister Anne Carr, who was forced to withdraw from the committee's own panel of consultants because she publicly endorsed abortion? What of Rosemary Ruether? Eleanor McLaughlin? Mary Jo Weaver? Sallie McFague? Monika Hellwig? Elizabeth Johnson? Most of the citations bear little relationship to the text, as though they were merely placating gestures, which is probably the case. Need their inclusion trouble the rest of us, then? Yes, because like everything else, it will be put to political use. When Weaver withdrew from a scheduled appearance as John Courtney Murray lecturer at the University of Toledo on May 6, 1990, because hundreds of pro-life Catholics objected, she expressed astonishment that anyone should question her standing as a Catholic scholar. After all, she told the Toledo *Catholic Chronicle*, her book, *New Catholic Women*, is cited "in a positive way" in the new pastoral.[163]

[162] NCCB Writing Committee for the Pastoral on Women in Society and in the Church, second draft, "One in Christ Jesus: A Pastoral Response to the Concerns of Women for Church and Society", *Origins* (Apr. 5, 1990): 717–40.

[163] Karen Katafiasz, "Dr. Weaver Explains Why She Cancelled Talk at UT", Toledo, Ohio, *Catholic Chronicle*, May 11, 1990. The citation is a note to the sentence "the story of women remarkable for their courage and resourcefulness must form an indispensable part of any account of the establishment and development of the church in the United States", *One in Christ Jesus*, 728, n. 100. While the women glorified in her book, *New Catholic Women*, may indeed be courageous and resourceful, most of them have not used those qualities for the benefit of the Church but against it.

Anyway, Weaver added, she only signed CFFC's *New York Times* ad be-

The Quixote Complex

Father William Callahan moved from COC to found Priests for Equality (PFE) in July 1975, setting off a dizzying proliferation of organizational progeny.[164] PFE is composed of sympathetic priests[165] and others who "strategize" for the ordination of women. The most prominent name on its board of directors is that of Father James Coriden, academic dean of Washington Theological Union, who took a stand for women's ordination in *Sexism and Church Law* in 1977.[166]

On January 1, 1976, Father Callahan and associate Delores "Dolly" Pomerleau branched out to form the hotly activist Quixote Center,[167] which soon became their major vehicle and a point of departure for many radical Catholic causes. Sister Maureen Fiedler joined in September 1976, eventually sharing with them a three-

---

cause she thought abortion "should be discussed". She said she had not been on CFFC's coordinating committee and hadn't made a public statement about her "personal position on abortion" (Katafiasz, "Weaver"). But she had. While she is not listed on the committee for the first ad, her name is included among "coordinators" in the second (*New York Times*, Mar. 2, 1986). And in "Lay Signers Reflect on Statement", an article published both in NARW's newsletter, *Probe*, and in CFFC's journal *Conscience* (Mar./Apr. 1985, 1), Weaver said she and the other lay signers endorsed the ad to "build coalitions to extend the legitimacy of dissent over abortion" and to "reveal Rome's stupidity even while we noted that they were doing a fairly good job of it themselves" (*Conscience*, 6).

[164] Its fascinating history is recounted in *Quixote Center Chronicles: 1975–1985* (Hyattsville, Md.: Quixote Center, 1985), 1–8. Hereafter, *Chronicles 1985*.

[165] Seven hundred priests reportedly endorsed PFE's "Charter of Equality" in the first year. Ibid., 1.

[166] James Coriden, ed., *Sexism and Church Law: Equal Rights and Affirmative Action* (New York: Paulist Press, 1977), ix, 191. Father Coriden was chairman of the theology department at Catholic University of America in 1973 (see Kelly, *Battle*, 120f.) and is currently academic dean of Washington Theological Union.

[167] *Chronicles 1985*, 1.

way directorship.[168] Other staff members have come and gone as needed.

A few projects spun off to separate incorporation: New Ways Ministry in 1977, Christic Institute in 1979,[169] PFE in 1984. Except when some cause needed a list of supporting organizations, others remained under the Quixote umbrella during their life spans: "Catholics Act for ERA" (1978);[170] "Catholic Advocates for Equality" (1979);[171] "Religious Task Force on Latin America"

[168] Ibid., 2.

[169] Sara Nelson, a NOW fund-raiser; Father William Davis, S.J., past director of the Jesuit Office of Social Ministry; and ex-seminarian Dan Sheehan, a Harvard-educated attorney who had previously worked for the American Civil Liberties Union and the Jesuit Social Ministry Office, joined the Quixote staff in 1977 to pursue the Karen Silkwood suit against Kerr-McGee Corporation. See Cliff Kincaid, "The Christic Institute's Legal Terrorism", *Human Events*, Nov. 28, 1987, 13. Silkwood, an employee at a Kerr-McGee plutonium plant in Oklahoma, was killed in an automobile accident. Sheehan claimed she was murdered to prevent her from exposing the company. He accused Kerr-McGee of hiding a black-market conspiracy to smuggle nuclear materials out of the country, but the surrounding publicity and the jury's final $10.5-million judgment against the corporation in 1979 were based on liability for Silkwood's plutonium poisoning on the grounds of inadequate plant safety standards. See *Chronicles 1985*, 2–3. See also Richard Raschke, "Catholic Center Probes Union Organizers' Death" (a Quixote Center reprint of a 1977 *National Catholic Reporter* article, n.d.). See also Kincaid, "Terrorism", 13.

After their 1979 victory in the Silkwood case, the three spun off from Quixote as Christic Institute and made further news during the Contra controversy. Christic filed a bizarre 1986 suit charging that Contra supporters had conspired in drug running and political assassination. The case was dismissed.

[170] *Chronicles 1985*, 3.

[171] When Callahan's priestly faculties were suspended and his Jesuit superiors ordered him to stop promoting the ordination of women, to cease criticizing "clear decisions of the Holy See" and finally to leave the center, Quixote formed the committee to purchase the *National Catholic Reporter* advertising supplement, "Even the Stones Will Cry Out". The ad, linking Callahan's situation to the "repression" of Küng, Schillebeeckx and homosexual "rights" advocate Father John McNeill, ran with supporting endorsements from twenty-six hundred individuals and one hundred organizations. See *National Catholic Reporter*, Feb. 22, 1980.

(1980); "Central American Religious Study Group" and "Central American Telephone Tree" (1982); "Medical Aid for Nicaragua" and "Catholics for the Common Good" (1984);[172] "Quest for Peace" (1985); "Veterans Fast for Peace" (1986); "Let Live" (1986);[173] and "Communities of Peace and Friendship" (1989).

Quixote opened its own center in Nicaragua and organized effective pro-Sandinista public relations and lobbying campaigns in the United States in the 1980s. In 1985, Quest for Peace collected ten million dollars' worth of humanitarian aid—money, clothing and medical supplies—for Sandinista-approved Nicaraguan poor. Quest's total aid, collected with five hundred co-sponsors (mostly religious groups), was valued at an amazing hundred million dollars by 1987.[174] That otherwise sympathetic effort was tarnished when Quixote lobbied vigorously *against* humanitarian aid for the Contras, arguing that its "sole purpose is the overthrow of the elected Nicaraguan government".[175] The 1990 elections there were a bitter pill for Quixote.[176]

Meanwhile, Quixote's feminist activism never flagged. Sister Fran Ferder came in 1976 to write *Called to Break Bread.*[177] As "full participants" in the 1976 Call to Action conference in Detroit, staff members lobbied successfully for "the ERA, women's ordination, an end to discrimination against gay men and lesbians".[178] In 1977, to protest the Vatican "Declaration" against women priests, Quixote distributed "Almighty Dollars"—play money bearing an image of St. Thérèse of Lisieux, of all people, as "patroness of

[172] Formed to campaign for the "Ferraro-Mondale" ticket. See *Chronicles 1985*, 5–6.

[173] An anti-capital-punishment group. *Musings from Rocinante* (newsletter) (Oct. 1986).

[174] Colman McCarthy, "Against Ollie North: Quiet Commitment", *Washington Post*, July 18, 1987. See also "Conservative Forum", *Human Events*, Jan. 9, 1988.

[175] *Chronicles 1985*, 6.

[176] See *Quixote Center Chronicles: 1989* (West Hyattsville, Md.: Quixote Center, 1990), 5.

[177] Ferder, *Called to Break Bread.*

[178] *Chronicles 1985*, 2.

equality for women in ministry".[179] In 1978, Dolly Pomerleau coordinated the second WOC conference, which drew two thousand participants to Baltimore. PFE, then claiming seventeen hundred members, held a conference "in tandem with" that "main event".[180]

In 1979, as "Listen to the Voices of the People", Quixote organized demonstrations against the Holy Father during his American visit, printing posters, issuing press releases and recruiting women to "stand with blue arm bands" while "Sister Theresa Kane spoke out" to the Pope at the National Shrine of the Immaculate Conception.[181] Ruth Fitzpatrick, then on staff, says Quixote urged people not to receive Communion at the Pope's Masses because the rules prohibited lay eucharistic ministers. PFE called on priests to "pull back from giving communion . . . so that lay people would have to do it." Callahan, who "knew how to use the press", put on his Roman collar and chatted with reporters. "The press loved him", Fitzpatrick recalls.[182]

During the 1980 Synod on the Family, Quixote held a conference in Rome titled "Women and Men in Today's Family, Society and Church".[183] As "Catholics Act for ERA", Fiedler, Pomerleau and ten allies chained themselves to the Republican National Committee building in Washington that year. In 1981, Fiedler organized a "Prayer Vigil for the ERA" outside President Reagan's church and toured the country lobbying for ratification; in 1982, she and seven others fasted for thirty-seven press-conscious days for ERA ratification in Illinois. Barbara Cullom, Ph.D. (biblical

[179] See *New Women/New Church*, news publication of Women's Ordination Conference (Nov./Dec. 1987), 20. The explanation, on the face of the "funny money", is that St. Thérèse "felt called to be a priest in a Church that would not test her call. She prayed for death at 24, the age of ordination, so she could celebrate in heaven at the age men could celebrate the Eucharist on earth." Only on items designed for public distribution does Quixote capitalize the words "Church" and "Eucharist".

[180] *Chronicles 1985*, 3.

[181] Ibid.

[182] Milhaven, "Fitzpatrick", in Milhaven, *Inside Stories*, 34f.

[183] The co-sponsor was a European group, *Femmes et Hommes dans l'Eglise*. Some eighty persons reportedly attended. *Chronicles 1985*, 3.

studies, University of Notre Dame), joined with Fiedler to organize the 1983 "Woman-Church Speaks" conference in Chicago.[184] Fiedler's keynote address, "Political Spirituality", was later published in Quixote's newsletter.[185]

Fiedler, Pomerleau, Cullom and Jeannine Gramick all signed CFFC's first *New York Times* ad. Cullom signed the second ad, too, along with Father Callahan and New Ways staff member Brother Rick Garcia, B.F.C.C.[186] On March 4, 1985, to protest the NCCB's closed hearings on women's concerns, Pomerleau and Fiedler, as the "Committee of Concerned Catholics", held parallel "open hearings" where Mary Buckley, Mary Hunt, Ruth Fitzpatrick, Sister Marjorie Tuite, Sister Carol Coston and others complained about "repression in the Church".[187] Pomerleau served on the planning committee for WOC's November 1985 conference, "Ordination Reconsidered"; Quixote and PFE were among its few sponsors.

PFE first published *Miriam's Song*, a tabloid edition of addresses presented at Time Consultants' Women in the Church conference, in 1986. Since then, issues have appeared at irregular intervals. Writers have included Sister Joan Chittister, Sister Elizabeth Johnson, Sister Sandra Schneiders, Sister Fran Ferder, Sister Mary Collins, Rosemary Ruether, Mary Jo Weaver, Sister Anne Patrick, S.N.J.M., Sister Camille D'Arienzo, R.S.M., and Sister Dianne Bergant, C.S.A.

As "Catholics Speak Out", "New Ways Ministry", "Priests for

[184] *Chronicles 1985*, 4–5.

[185] Maureen Fiedler, "Political Spirituality", *Musings from Rocinante*, Quixote Center newsletter (Jan. 1984): 1.

[186] Father Enrique Rueda identifies BFCC (Brothers for Christian Community) as a non-canonical homosexual "religious order". He reports that Garcia had previously been president of a St. Louis Dignity chapter as well as a former "volunteer" for National Organization for Women. See Enrique Rueda, *The Homosexual Network: Private Lives and Public Policy* (Old Greenwich, Conn.: Devin Adair, 1982), 420.

[187] Joan Turner Beifuss and Mary Fay Bourgoin, "Catholic Women Voice Divergent Views, Concerns at DC Hearings", *National Catholic Reporter*, Mar. 15, 1985, 35. See also *New Women/New Church* (May/June 1987): 20.

Equality" and "Quixote Center", the Quixote complex joined Chicago Call to Action and the Association for the Rights of Catholics in the Church to produce another four-page advertising supplement to *National Catholic Reporter* in the fall of 1988 during the annual NCCB meeting. Titled "By Their Fruits You Will Know Them", it demanded (1) that every Church office, including the episcopacy, and all "decision-making positions" be open to women and their advancement speeded by "affirmative action"; (2) that "gender-balanced" language "for humanity and for God" be used in liturgy and Scripture; (3) that "dialogue" be conducted on "issues of sexuality, sexual orientation and reproduction". It bore thirty-seven hundred signatures.[188]

New Ways Ministry and Others

Homosexuality is an abiding interest at Quixote. Dignity "chaplain" Sister Jeannine Gramick, S.S.N.D. (of NARW and NCAN),[189] met Dignity chaplain Father Robert Nugent, S.D.S., on Quixote's staff in 1976, and together they developed workshops "to help people overcome homophobia". In 1977, Gramick and Nugent spun off as New Ways Ministry.[190] Subsequently, New Ways formed such organizations as "Sisters in Gay Ministry Associated" (SIGMA) and "Catholic Coalition for Gay Civil Rights".[191] In 1979, Georgia Fuller joined Quixote to organize an "ecumenical Conference on Homophobia" in the churches.[192] Sister Theresa Kane, R.S.M., was a scheduled speaker at New Ways' "First National Symposium on Homosexuality and the Catholic Church" held November 20, 1981, in Washington, to coincide with the

[188] "By Their Fruits You Will Know Them: A Call to Eliminate Sexism from the Church by the Year 2000", advertising supplement, *National Catholic Reporter*, Nov. 18, 1988.

[189] Jeannine Gramick, "From Good Sisters to Prophetic Women", in Ware, *Midwives*, 234–35.

[190] *Chronicles 1985*, 2.

[191] Rueda, *Homosexual Network*, 337.

[192] *Chronicles 1985*, 3.

closing of the annual NCCB meeting.[193] Sister Jeannine's order, the School Sisters of Notre Dame, reportedly supplied more members to "Catholic Coalition for Gay Civil Rights" than any other women's religious community.[194] Xavieran Brother Joseph Izzo of New Ways Ministry,[195] a Catholic University counselor who temporarily replaced Callahan at PFE, organized Quixote's second "Conference of Gay/Lesbian Christians" in 1982 to form an "ecumenical" coalition against "the onslaught of the New Right".[196]

Because New Ways' message was permissive about homosexuality, the Washington archdiocese never supported or approved its activities. By 1987, New Ways had been expelled from both the Washington archdiocese and the Newark diocese. As early as 1979, the Washington archdiocese had also warned bishops and religious communities against Quixote's activities. Jesuit authorities suspended Callahan's priestly faculties for a year in 1980, and in 1987 Jesuit Superior General Peter-Hans Kolvenbach ordered Callahan to dissociate himself from PFE and "Catholics Speak Out" and stop calling himself "co-director" of Quixote Center or face dismissal. Father James Coriden wrote a letter, co-signed by the other five members of the PFE board,[197] expressing shock that the group should be judged "reprehensible".[198] PFE's 1989 winter newsletter reprinted Callahan's letters to and from his superiors in

[193] Despite Archbishop Hickey's warning to all the nation's bishops and all Washington-area religious personnel, the 150 symposium participants included eighteen major superiors of religious orders and twenty formation directors; 78 percent were priests or religious. See Rueda, *Homosexual Network*, 359, 419, 466 n. 89.

[194] Ibid., 353.

[195] Ibid., 420.

[196] *Chronicles 1985*, 5. By 1988, Izzo's signature in the "by their fruits" ad was listed among non-Catholics.

[197] Fathers Joseph Dearborn and Michael McGarry, C.S.P.; Jeff Bissonnette and Sisters Gretchen Elliot, R.S.M.; Ellen Lynch, C.S.C.; Judith Zielinski, O.F.M.

[198] "Group Hits 'Scarlet Letter'", *Catholic Messenger*, Davenport, Iowa, June 15, 1989.

a twenty-page insert.[199] Quixote's considerable lobbying contacts were alerted to write to Vatican and Jesuit authorities in Callahan's defense.[200] As of midsummer 1990, he was still in place, and PFE said the Jesuit Order had announced no decision in his case.[201]

WATER

Women's Alliance for Theology, Ethics and Ritual (WATER), founded in 1983, is rarely called by its full name. Foundress Mary Hunt became a feminist at Harvard Divinity School, under Ruether and liberation theologian Juan Luis Segundo, S.J.,[202] before going on to Berkeley's GTU for her double doctorate. There she met WATER's co-foundress, co-director and chief ritualist, Diann Neu, then a nun. Neu holds a GTU master's degree in sacred theology and an exaggerated view of her own qualifications. In October 1988, at a CFFC "reproductive options" conference in Albuquerque, Neu said she came to her "approach" to "reproductive rights" with "all the training and *experience* to be a bishop in my church".[203]

Hunt is active in Conference for Catholic Lesbians (CCL), a homosexual "support group" born of Women-Church in 1983.[204] Her involvement, she says, "certainly emerges out of my own life, loving women, and living in a committed relationship with a woman".[205] She airs her odd religious views in *WATERwheel*, WATER's quarterly newsletter. In one edition, she says that a theological image of "divine child abuse"—God the Father "carrying out" the death of his own son—explains the prevalence

[199] *Priests for Equality NEWS & NOTES* (Fall/Winter 1989).

[200] *Quixote Center Chronicles: 1989*, 6.

[201] Telephone interview, July 30, 1990.

[202] "Mary E. Hunt", in Milhaven, *Inside Stories*, 120.

[203] Emphasis mine. Her address was published in CFFC's journal, *Conscience* (Jan./Feb. 1989): 9–12.

[204] Weaver, *New Catholic Women*, 131. See also *National Catholic Register*, Nov. 27, 1983.

[205] "Hunt", in Milhaven, *Inside Stories*, 144.

of abuse in society.[206] Oppression springs from "thc notion of an all-powerful God", which provides "a role model" for the powerful while crushing the "disempowered". Violence is further encouraged, she says, by "the glorification of martyrs" and of the crucified Christ.[207] Her own first theological principle: "Life, pleasure and justice are to be valued equally."[208]

The WATER center in the Washington, D.C. area functions much as do the other groups in Women-Church Convergence, as a vehicle for classes, conferences, speaking engagements and public statements.[209] But it attracts smaller audiences than most; only seventy-five people came to hear Elisabeth Fiorenza at its 1989 annual conference.[210]

Association of Contemplative Sisters and Las Hermanas

Two more groups deserving brief notice are the Association of Contemplative Sisters (ACS) and Las Hermanas. By comparison with other feminists, ACS leaders speak softly, but the difference is in style rather than substance. ACS is in fact one of the oldest Catholic feminist organizations in the country, founded by rebellious superiors in 1969 at Woodstock, Maryland, to repudiate new Vatican directives for contemplative life.[211] The organization

[206] This recent nuance of feminist theology has also been proposed by Joanne Carlson Brown, Rebecca Parker, Beverly Wildung Harrison and Carter Heyward. Heyward was the keynote speaker for the 1990 Women's Spirituality Conference at Mankato State University in Minnesota.

[207] Mary E. Hunt, "Where Charity and Love Are Not", *WATERwheel* (Spring 1990): 1.

[208] Ibid., 6.

[209] Among WATER's speakers, in addition to Hunt and Neu, have been Ruether, Schussler Fiorenza, Quixote's Barbara Cullom and Beverly Wildung Harrison.

[210] William Bole, "Gospel Biased by 'Androcentrism,' Says Feminist Theologian", *Washington Post*, Mar. 18, 1989, C16.

[211] Sacred Congregation for Religious and Secular Institutes (SCRIS), *Venite*

has never been recognized by authorities in Rome.[212] Its incumbent president, Sister Mary Lavin, O.C., of Cleveland, spoke at the 1987 Women-Church Convergence.[213]

Las Hermanas is of interest chiefly as a textbook example of the Potemkin villages common along the Catholic feminist front. A member of Women-Church Convergence, it was organized in 1971, purportedly to advocate the interests of poor Hispanic women. Its telephone number, as listed in Women-Church Convergence's 1987 program directory ("contact: Ada Maria Isasi-Diaz"), was answered in 1990 as "Church Women United". The answering voice was that of Sister Ann Patrick Ware, who said she is now Isasi-Diaz' secretary. Isasi-Diaz herself no longer heads Las Hermanas, though she remains on its national board. She is now national associate general director of Church Women United (CWU) and chairman of its program division, Ware said. The New York office is CWU's national headquarters, she explained, though it also maintains its offices in Washington, D.C., and at the United Nations. Ware told me that Las Hermanas had just been "differently restructured", with no president, but she assured me that it was "still going strong" and referred me to its national office in San Antonio.

The San Antonio number was answered by a recorded message; Las Hermanas, I learned, has no full-time office staff. The recording supplied a third number, which proved to be that of Sister Yolanda Tarango (a member of the Mary's Pence board and a participant in the 1987 Women-Church Convergence) at the Incarnate Word Generalate in San Antonio. Sister Tarango identified herself as Las Hermanas' national president and as the sole current member of its "three-person national coordinating team". She explained, as Ware had, that the organization had

---

Seorsum (*Instruction on the Contemplative Life and Enclosure of Nuns*), Aug. 15, 1969, in *Sisters Today* (Nov. 1969).

[212] Weaver, *New Catholic Women*, 102–5.

[213] Conference program, *Women-Church*, 1987, 19, 39.

"just been restructured". On its new seven-member national board are four nuns, she said: Sister Eliza Rodriguez, S.L. (San Antonio); Sister Rose-Marta Zarati (California); Sister Maria Inez Martinez, I.H.M. (California) and Sister Delorita Martinez, O.P. (Nebraska).

While Catholic feminists do indeed yearn to recruit Hispanic women, they have been spectacularly unsuccessful in doing so. Tarango said Las Hermanas has some two hundred members, publishes a bi-monthly newsletter and holds bi-annual meetings that draw "two hundred to three hundred women", most of whom "have never attended *any* conference before". She insisted that former CFFC employee Pauline Nunez-Morales is simply a four-year member of Las Hermanas who works with the organization on some projects and happens to work for a "reproductive options center" in Albuquerque. Las Hermanas itself takes "no position" on abortion but "supports the Catholic teaching", she said.

"What does it mean to say that you 'support Catholic teaching on abortion' if you 'take no position'?" I asked.

Tarango paused. "Well, we take no position on abortion. We do not advocate abortion. Even Catholics for a Free Choice does not support the right of every woman to have an abortion. . . ." she volunteered.

"Catholics for a Free Choice does indeed support the 'right' of every woman to have an abortion", I interrupted.

"I mean, yes, they support that *right*, but they don't say that every woman should *have* an abortion. They support women's freedom to *decide*", Tarango said.

Originally, Las Hermanas had a more "general thrust", she continued, but now it concentrates on "women's needs and the Church's lack of response".

Women's Ordination Conference

Both Women's Ordination Conference (WOC) and Women-Church Convergence are vehicles for the organizational constituencies listed above. WOC lost membership and importance as the contradiction between its professed reason for being and its real aims became increasingly obvious: though it has had members who wanted to be priests, the organizers' thrust from the beginning has not been toward women's ordination but toward reinterpreting both priesthood and sacraments as expressions of community power. WOC spokeswomen in fact make the strongest possible case against women's ordination, both in what they say and in what they are.

WOC was devised in 1974, to tie the issue of women's ordination to International Women's Year.[214] At its first major meeting, held in Detroit in November 1975, twelve hundred people listened to addresses, celebrated "liturgies" and established organizational machinery; 90 percent were women religious. As keynote speaker, Sister Elizabeth Carroll called on the bishops to enter into "serious, continuing dialogue with women about women".[215] Sister Margaret Farley said women should assert a "moral imperative" for ordination.[216] But it was Rosemary Ruether who set the theme for the new organization when she asked members to consider seriously whether they really wanted ordination in the present "demonic" Church. First of all, she said, they "must demystify in their minds the false idea that priests possess sacramental 'power' which the community does not have".[217] Thus from the outset, WOC's goal was to proclaim and act on a theology of declericalized priesthood and symbolic sacraments.

In its early years, WOC seemed to be riding a wave of wide support. The NCCB-sponsored 1976 Call to Action meeting in Detroit recommended ordination of women to the diaconate and the priesthood.[218] Ada Maria Isasi-Diaz was director of WOC's first office.[219] Rosalie Muschal-Reinhardt later became her co-

[214] Weaver, *New Catholic Women*, 112.

[215] Ibid., 113.

[216] Ibid. Farley later signed CFFC's first *New York Times* ad.

[217] Ibid.

[218] Papa, "Male Bastions", 18.

[219] Joan Turner Beifuss, "A Women's Religious Revolution", *National Catholic Reporter*, Mar. 5, 1982, 12.

director, then succeeded her at WOC's office in Rochester, New York. Quixote's Ruth Fitzpatrick took a second job as WOC's Washington coordinator in 1977,[220] working out of a storefront office. Archbishop Jean Jadot,[221] apostolic delegate to the United States, attended "a WOC evening" of dialogue with "Christian feminists" in 1977 and exchanged letters "back and forth" with her that year, Fitzpatrick reports.[222]

While the NCCB was meeting in Chicago's Palmer House in May 1977, two members of WOC's first core commission, Rosalie Muschal-Reinhardt and Sister Donna Quinn, aided by Sister Delores Brooks, O.P., rounded up feminist activists to rally in front of the hotel and declare the formation of yet another organizational arm to harry the bishops.[223] The bishops were satisfactorily harried: the new organization, called "Women of the Church Coalition", functioned at first as an episcopal lobby for WOC. The coalition included WOC, CCW, NCAN, NARW, IWT, Quixote Center, Las Hermanas and also, for a time, LCWR, Chicago's Archdiocesan Council of Catholic Women, the Black Sisters' Conference, the Ladies Auxiliary of the Knights of St. Peter Claver and Center of Concern.[224]

During the November NCCB meeting the following year, members of the NCCB Liaison Committee with Religious and Laity, chaired by Bishop James Malone, conferred with thirty of the coalition's feminist leaders. Bishop Maurice Dingman then proposed to the NCCB general assembly that a dialogue be established "between the bishops' conference and the women of our church". Bishop Dingman said many women were feeling "increasing anger, alienation and pain" about their exclusion from "the life and ministry of the church".[225]

[220] Milhaven, "Fitzpatrick", in Milhaven, *Inside Stories*, 28.

[221] In Fitzpatrick's interview, he is repeatedly referred to as "Jardot".

[222] Milhaven, "Fitzpatrick", in Milhaven, *Inside Stories*, 37–38.

[223] Weaver, *New Catholic Women*, 132, 245, n. 82. See also Ruether, *Women-Church*, 66–67.

[224] Weaver, *New Catholic Women*, 245f., n. 84.

[225] "Dialogue on Women in the Church: Interim Report", *Origins*, n. 6

It is true that many Catholic women have been "marginalized" in the post-conciliar Church. Defective catechetics and irreverent liturgy have robbed their children of a basic understanding of the Faith, yet teachers, pastors and bishops refuse to hear their objections. It was not their anguish that Bishop Dingman had in mind, however, but that of WOC's Catholic feminists. With the approval of the NCCB, Archbishop John Quinn, president, directed the bishops' Ad Hoc Committee on the Role of Women in Society and the Church[226] to "explore the possibility" of a dialogue with WOC representatives.[227]

In 1978, nuns were lobbying Congress for an extension of the ERA time limit, teamed with secular feminists like Betty Friedan, Ellie Smeal and Gloria Steinem. Quixote's Maureen Fiedler was predicting confidently that women priests would be "acceptable" within ten years.[228] Infuriated by the Vatican declaration on women and priesthood,[229] some two thousand participants gathered in Baltimore for WOC's second major conference. There, Mary Hunt outlined the Church's "feminist future". Elisabeth Schussler Fiorenza called on women to challenge the ecclesiastical establishment. Sister Anne Carr spoke on the need to welcome the diversity of visions inevitable in the pluralist future. Father Richard McBrien talked about the Church as the "people of God". Sister Margaret Brennan, I.H.M., past president of LCWR, said the "shared faith experience of the Christian community" is "a source

(June 25, 1981): 81. See also National Conference of Catholic Bishops, *Partners in the Mystery of Redemption*, 2.

[226] The Committee on Women in the Church and in Society had been established in 1972 at the urging of women members of the Bishops' Advisory Council.

[227] *Origins*, June 25, 1981, 83.

[228] "Women Priests Acceptable by 1988", *National Catholic Reporter*, Nov. 10, 1978, 18. *NCR* reported the figure of 1,500 attendees at the WOC conference; Quixote Center claimed 2,000. See *Chronicles*: 1985, 3.

[229] Sacred Congregation for the Doctrine of the Faith, "Declaration on the Question of the Admission of Women to the Ministerial Priesthood" (*Inter Insigniores*); see *Origins* (1977): 517.

of continuing revelation".[230] That year marked the high tide of Catholic feminist optimism.

WOC's greatest success was the NCCB's agreement to engage in dialogue. The first organizational meeting was held in March 1979, and formal dialogue sessions were conducted between December 1979 and December 1981. In the first three sessions,[231] WOC participants were Sister Anne Carr, Ada Maria Isasi-Diaz, Rosemary Ruether, Sister Marjorie Tuite, Sister Jamie Phelps, O.P., and, incredibly, Barbara Zanotti,[232] with "staff assistance" from Rosalie Muschal-Reinhardt and Sister Joan Sobala, S.S.J. The NCCB representatives were Bishop Michael McAuliffe; Auxiliary Bishops George Evans, P. Francis Murphy and Amedee Proulx,[233] Sister Agnes Cunningham, S.S.C.M.,[234] and LeMay Bechtold, with staff assistance from Sister Mariella Frye, M.H.S.H. and Sister Rosalie Murphy, S.N.D. For the second triad of meetings,[235] Rita Bowen replaced Barbara Zanotti on WOC's team; Elisabeth Fiorenza presented a paper titled "Early Christian History in a Feminist Perspective" at one session; Francine Cardman served as a "resource person" at another. Sister Rosalie Murphy and Sister Mary Louise Lynch, M.M., acted as facilitators, and Sister Joan Sobala continued as WOC's staff assistant. The NCCB panel was unchanged except for the occasional attendance of Bishop Ernest Unterkoefler.[236] Fathers John Kselman and Joseph Komonchak appeared as "resource persons" at one session each.

[230] Weaver, *New Catholic Women*, 114–17. The proceedings were later published by WOC as *New Woman, New Church, New Priestly Ministry*, ed. Maureen Dwyer (Rochester, N.Y.: Kirkwood Press, 1980).

[231] Dec. 1979 to July 1980.

[232] See references in chap. 3 above.

[233] McAuliffe was ordinary of Jefferson City, Missouri. The auxiliary bishops represented Denver (Evans), Baltimore (Murphy) and Portland, Maine (Proulx).

[234] Past president of CTSA and a faculty member at Chicago's Mundelein Seminary.

[235] Dec. 1980 to Dec. 1981.

[236] Bishop of Charleston, S.C.

Mrs. Bechtold, mother of eleven, an editor at Liturgical Press,[237] and the sole dialogue participant representative of the majority of the nation's Catholic women, left the committee when her term on the NCCB Advisory Board expired at the end of 1980. She recalls Bishop McAuliffe and Bishop Unterkoefler as orthodox in faith, but generally silent before the feminists' arguments, in the belief that their role was to listen".

While WOC's representatives pitched their rhetoric somewhat less stridently than usual, they said what they always say: that (1) "women" suffer pain and anguish because they are excluded from priesthood although (2) Jesus neither founded a Church nor ordained priests; (3) in primitive Christianity, women shared equally in community leadership; (4) as the Church's hierarchical structure developed, it was arbitrarily patterned on Greek and Roman social structures; (5) "you never see 'yourself' up there on the altar." When the dialogue ended, the overmatched NCCB committee agreed with WOC's representatives that the Vatican's 1976 declaration on women's ordination had been written too hurriedly and lacked scholarly documentation. The bishops recommended magisterial review of that document "in the light of modern anthropology, sacramental theology and the practice and experience of women ministering in our American culture".[238] But WOC's feminists failed to win the symbolic victory they apparently expected: the bishops did not call outright for women's ordination.

Women-Church Converges

Muschal-Reinhardt's resignation from the WOC director's post was announced in 1980, along with changes on WOC's core commission. New members included Sister Barbara Ferraro, Sister Maureen Fiedler and ex-nun Marsie Silvestro. Among those

[237] Liturgical Press is headquartered at St. John's University, Collegeville, Minn.

[238] "Report on a Dialogue: The Future of Women in the Church", *Origins* 12, no. 1 (May 20, 1982): 7.

renamed were Sister Elizabeth Carroll and Elisabeth Schussler Fiorenza.[239]

At Center of Concern's 1981 "Women Moving Church" meeting, organized by Sister Maria Riley, an intense little group of feminist leaders heard Elisabeth Fiorenza propose the concept of "Women-Church" as the real center of a remodeled Church.[240] Diann Neu, who helped to coordinate the conference, said participants were to "see ourselves as the church". Sue Costa, representing a Massachusetts women's shelter, denounced not only "the exclusion of women from sacramental ministry, leadership and decision making in the church" but also "continual use of sexist language and an unwillingness to listen".[241]

Spurred by the "Women Moving Church" meeting, the Women of the Church Coalition scheduled its first major conference, "From Generation to Generation: Woman-Church Speaks", for November 1983 in Chicago. Bishops Murphy and Evans of the NCCB dialogue team, along with WOC's original NCCB champion, Bishop Dingman, and Bishops Charles Buswell,[242] Raymond Hunthausen[243] and Thomas Gumbleton,[244] publicly endorsed and contributed financially to the "Woman-Church Speaks" conference.[245]

When, before the conference date, Woman-Church coalition leaders decided to let CFFC and the incipient Conference for Catholic Lesbians participate, less extreme members withdrew. Chicago's Archdiocesan Council of Catholic Women, the Peter Claver Ladies, the Black Sisters' Conference, even LCWR and Center of Concern itself, apparently more fastidious about their

[239] "WOC Leaders Named", *National Catholic Reporter*, Oct. 10, 1980, 2.

[240] Fiorenza, *In Memory of Her*, 343–51. See also Milhaven, "Fiorenza", in Milhaven, *Inside Stories*, 61.

[241] Mary S. Gordon, "200 Catholic Feminists Meet in Washington", *National Catholic Reporter*, May 29, 1981, 5.

[242] Ordinary of Pueblo, Colorado.

[243] Archbishop of Seattle.

[244] Auxiliary bishop of Detroit.

[245] Ruether, *Women-Church*, 68f.

associations than the feminist bishops, resigned from the Women of the Church coalition. Thus the 1983 Woman-Church event, coordinated by NARW's Maureen Reiff,[246] was finally sponsored only by WOC, NARW, NCAN, CCW, Quixote Center, WATER, IWT and Las Hermanas.[247] Nevertheless, twelve hundred women attended. Sister Maureen Fiedler gave the keynote address. Elisabeth Fiorenza declared that "women are simply leaving the Church in growing numbers because it has become irrelevant to their lives".[248] Marjorie Maguire insisted that the ritual celebration was a "Eucharist". "I believe that the Real Presence of Christ was in that bread," she said, "as much as Christ is ever present in eucharistic bread."[249]

On January 1, 1984, the coalition was renamed "Women in the Church Convergence", and its membership was opened to other compatibly radical groups. Its evolution into Women-Church Convergence virtually complete,[250] the coalition had emerged as the most audible voice of Catholic feminism.

WOC, by contrast, went into abrupt decline. Its chief lobbying goal had been accomplished, however imperfectly, in the NCCB dialogue, and ambivalence about ordination had eroded member

[246] Conference program, *Women-Church*, 1987, 41.

[247] Weaver, *New Catholic Women*, 245, n. 84.

[248] Ibid., 132–33. See also Joan Turner Beifuss, "Amidst Laughter, Tears and Talks, Women Set Course", *National Catholic Reporter*, Nov. 25, 1983, 1.

[249] Quoted in Muggeridge, *Desolate City*, 140.

[250] Weaver, *New Catholic Women*, 133. By 1987, Women-Church Convergence listed twenty-five member groups: CFFC; CCW; NARW; NCAN; WOC; New Ways Ministry; Quixote Center; Grail Women's Task Force; IWT; Las Hermanas; WATER; Loretto Women's Network; BVM Network for Women's Issues (Chicago); Wheaton Franciscans Social Justice Team; Boston Catholic Women; Catholic Women for Reproductive Rights (Chicago); Community of the Anawim (Denver); Conference for Catholic Lesbians; Eighth Day Center for Justice (Chicago); Women in Spirit of Colorado (Denver); Feminist Action Coalition (Orange, N.J.); Sisters for Christian Community (SFCC, Chicago) and local Women-Church groups from Cincinnati, Louisville and Baltimore.

support. There seemed to be little WOC could do that Women-Church couldn't do better. WOC's tenth anniversary conference, held in St. Louis the weekend of October 24, 1985, attracted so little organizational support that two individuals, Father Andrew Greeley and CFFC board member Mary Gordon, joined Quixote Center, PFE and a handful of others as its co-sponsors.[251] Mary Hunt presided over a luncheon table reserved for lesbians. Mary Jo Weaver's keynote address urged women to claim a "self-activated" priesthood, participate in feminist "eucharists" and "call them sacraments".

Reflecting the view of religion as a psychological phenomenon, former WOC staff worker Sister Fidelis McDonough, R.S.M. said the women present "move in and out of what the Church believes about the Eucharist very comfortably. At times, they believe in transubstantiation, and at other times they believe it's chiefly symbolic and that Jesus is present in the community."

In her "reflection", Sister Theresa Kane called WOC a "significant structure" that had helped make feminism "the most volatile subject in the Vatican". Kane predicted "dramatic changes" in the Church within five years.

But only two hundred women attended, and some of them were admittedly dismayed by the meeting's bitter spirit and its "eucharistic" rituals. One weeping nun told a reporter, "Maybe I had to come to St. Louis to say to myself, 'No, this isn't my vision of the Church.' "[252]

By 1986, to cut expenses, Ruth Fitzpatrick moved WOC's main office to her home in Fairfax, Virginia. She complained then of the injustice of having only one person "largely responsible for the planning and execution" of the shrinking organization.[253] In 1987, WOC's bi-monthly newsletter reported the formal disbanding of the core commission, because "it has a paucity of members and

[251] Milhaven, "Fitzpatrick", in Milhaven, *Inside Stories*, 38–39.

[252] Charlotte Hays, " 'Patriarchal' Church Ripped by Women at WOC Gathering", *National Catholic Register*, Nov. 10, 1985, 1.

[253] "WOC Governing Structure Reconsidered", *New Women/New Church* (May/June 1987): 17.

is not functioning as it was originally intended". In its place, a "locally based board of directors" was named, and subscribers were urged to persuade "grass roots Communicators" from their own groups to "feed local WOC needs and suggestions to national WOC". Sister Theresa Kane, Rosemary Ruether and Elisabeth Fiorenza agreed to continue as a three-member "national advisory group".[254]

Over the years, WOC had presented awards to Theresa Kane, the Catholic Committee of Appalachia, Elisabeth Fiorenza, Rosemary Ruether, Quixote Center and Marjorie Tuite. Despite its shrunken state, WOC continued the practice in 1987, honoring seven at one blow at its annual dinner: Father Charles Curran; Sister Elizabeth Carroll; Sister Darlene Nicgorski, S.S.S.F.;[255] ex-nuns Barbara Ferraro and Patricia Hussey; WATER's Mary Hunt and Diann Neu.[256] Their acceptance speeches contained few surprises. Hunt warned against "infighting" and said, "I suggest we forsake ordination into this horrendous system in favor of ministry on our own terms." Of "priesthood as it exists today", Ferraro said, "I reject it outright." Curran admitted the "bad news" that Church "structures" have not changed much but claimed "we are getting great strides" anyway by educating "so many people" to "a changed theological understanding".[257]

By 1988, with Fitzpatrick still national coordinator, WOC's board was dominated by Quixote-complex personnel: Dolly Pomerleau, Maureen Fiedler, Jeannine Gramick, Barbara Cullom, Father Joe Dearborn and Georgia Fuller. Among the few others was WATER's Diann Neu.[258]

[254] "Minutes of Core Commissioners' Meeting", *New Women/New Church* (May/June 1987): 3.

[255] Nicgorski, best known for her activities with the "Sanctuary" movement, resigned from her order in the summer of 1990.

[256] *New Women/New Church* (May/June 1987), 1ff.

[257] Ibid., 7.

[258] *New Women/New Church* (Jan./Feb. 1988): 2.

Responding to Women's Concerns?

In 1981, nine years before his notorious "listening sessions" on abortion, Archbishop Rembert Weakland held "listening sessions" on the role of women in the Church. The first ten, held in parishes across his Milwaukee diocese, were open to all women. But then, apparently to ensure that no feminists were overlooked, he held seven "special interest" sessions for invited Church career women, members of Women's Ordination Conference, representatives of other women's groups, "young adults" and minorities. Though few minority representatives turned up, the archbishop was convinced that what he heard there was "reflective of the views" of most Catholic women.[259] His project became a model for the NCCB.

When the 1979–81 NCCB-WOC dialogue was over, the bishops' panel decided that the discontents of the feminists constituted "signs of the times".[260] In November 1983, the NCCB voted unanimously to write a letter about "women's concerns". Six bishops were named to a drafting committee headed by Bishop Joseph Imesch.[261] To prepare for their writing, they organized open "listening sessions" across the nation and several closed sessions of their own to hear from invited groups. Perhaps they could not have foreseen that the open sessions would be captured and controlled, as they were, by militant feminists. But no such naïveté can excuse their decisions about whom to consult in their own hearings. Among the twenty-one "national Catholic women's organizations"[262] chosen to testify before them were not only Leadership Conference of Women Religious but also Women's Ordination Conference, National Coalition of American Nuns, National Assembly of Religious Women, Grailville,

[259] Weaver, *New Catholic Women*, 60f.

[260] NCCB, *Partners*, 2.

[261] Bishop Imesch is the ordinary of Joliet, Illinois. Also on the committee were Archbishop William Levada, Portland, Oregon; Bishops Thomas Grady, of Orlando; and Matthew Clark of Rochester, New York; Auxiliary Bishops Amedee Proulx, Portland, Maine; and Alred Hughes, Boston.

[262] NCCB, *Partners*, 3.

Las Hermanas, St. Joan's Alliance[263] and the Association of Contemplative Sisters.

Most of the Catholic laity had been unaware of the theological and political maneuvering going on among Catholic feminists in the past twenty-five years. Not so the bishops, who had listened to their speeches, engaged them in formal dialogue and fretted about their grievances. Why did any bishops still think such declared enemies could tell them about the concerns of "Catholic women"? Attentive observers began to wonder about the bishops' distance from the faithful and their suitability for the role of shepherds.

On March 4, 1985, when the bishops' committee held its hearings, Sister Marjorie Tuite spoke for NARW. Far from avoiding the sore topic of CFFC's *New York Times* ad, she put it at the center of her testimony. "We bring to this event a basic assumption that reality is conflictual", she told them. "You have demanded we accept your symbols, your language, your ritual. . . . You have denied our right to dissent and stay within the institution. . . . You have elected a Bishop of Rome who refuses to dialogue with us. You have sent us letters that threaten dismissal. You have made laws about our bodies."

Why do women who deny the truth of Catholicism, who consider it "in its very roots" an oppressively institutionalized male symbol system, *want* to stay in the Church? "Because we are women of faith", Tuite explained. Faith in what? In "the unity of the personal and the political, the right to control our lives, including our bodies, the naming of our images and symbols".[264]

NARW board member Maureen Reiff, a lay signer of the first CFFC ad, followed Tuite at the microphone. She said she

[263] St. Joan's Alliance, founded in London in 1911 as the Catholic Women's Suffrage Society, became consciously feminist in 1959, focusing on "women's rights" in the Church. See Weaver, *New Catholic Women*, 240, n. 4.

[264] Marjorie Tuite, O.P., "The Weeping of Women Is All of Our Pain", NARW testimony of Mar. 4, 1985, to the National Conference of Catholic Bishops' Committee for the Pastoral Letter on Women, NARW, 1307 S. Wabash, Room 206, Chicago, IL 60605, 1–3.

spoke (1) for nuns who signed the ad, only to find themselves "in danger of dismissal because of the ways they have chosen to live out their commitment"; (2) for "women unable to choose an alternative to abortion" yet "condemned by a church who forbids birth control"; (3) for "the woman" [Sister Anne Carr] "forced to resign from this commission" simply because "her signature appeared on an ad regarding pluralism and abortion"; (4) for all Women's Ordination Conference and Women-Church participants. Abandon the projected pastoral letter, Reiff told the committee, unless "the ordination of women and reproduction are going to be intrinsic to the process".[265]

Testifying for the North American Conference of Separated and Divorced Catholics, midwest representative Marie Loy echoed the feminist line. "Women are not the problem", she said. "Patriarchy and sexism are the problems both in society and especially in the church. . . . You are men in a man's church writing out of men's culture and experience, about women."[266]

WATER's Diann Neu was among the witnesses for Women's Ordination Conference, who divided the bishops among them, one to one, and compelled them to listen to "their stories". After the closed hearing, one Duffi McDermott, identified as "national coordinator of WOC", told reporters, "We even have ten bishops who are 'secret' members."[267]

From the Top Down

Sorting out these feminist groups might seem a task unworthy of the trouble involved, like untangling a knot of vipers. What makes

[265] Ibid., 4–6.

[266] Marie Loy, "Is This Pastoral Letter Feasible?" Pastoral on Women Hearings, *Origins*, Oct. 3, 1985, 249.

[267] "Pastoral on Women Hearings, Presentation by the Women's Ordination Conference", *Origins*, Mar. 21, 1985, 658–61. Also testifying for WOC were M. Jeanne Steele, a grandmother and divinity student, and Dr. Catherine Stewart-Roche, a hospital "chaplain".

them important is the influence with which they continue to be endowed by Catholic media and Catholic bishops, who thus prolong the existence of a pathological movement, ultimately doomed but capable of wreaking enormous havoc during its death convulsions. Most bishops ignore even the grossest revolutionary deviations, saving their denunciations for "fundamentalists" internal and external. In the resulting confusion, growing numbers of unstable, doctrinally miseducated women with private grievances are drawn into sacrilegious anarchy, sure that no punitive consequences will follow. Scandalized, growing numbers of uninstructed Catholics depart for fundamentalism in the belief that they are fleeing to Jesus from a Church that seems to be collapsing around them.

It would be an error of optimism to suppose that WOC's decline signals a diminished feminist presence in the North American Church. While they fume and rage about a supposed persecution by the Vatican, Catholic feminists are not resigned to defeat. Instead, they have become increasingly bitter and aggressive toward the hierarchy. Canadian Catholic feminist Mary Malone, a leader in that nation's Ad Hoc Committee on the Role of Women in the Church, says Rosemary Ruether warned her, "Don't make the same mistake we did." According to Malone, Ruether believes WOC erred by settling for a dialogue with only six American bishops. "What they did was, they converted the six bishops to such an extent that they couldn't even talk to their fellow bishops", Malone reports. "And so they ended up with six or seven bishops, and that was all they accomplished." Ruether cautioned the Canadians to "work from the bottom up".[268]

Benefiting from the advice, Malone's Ad Hoc Committee marched through the full Canadian Conference of Catholic Bishops. Late in 1984, the CCCB not only approved distribution of the notorious "Green Kit" for the re-education of Catholic women

[268] E. Michael Jones, "Blueprint for a Revolution: The Canadian Bishops Issue Their Kit on Women", *Fidelity* (Apr. 1986): 23. In fact, of the bishops who endorsed Women-Church, only two were members of the dialogue committee.

in every parish[269] but also formally endorsed a package of twelve feminist policy resolutions. Among other things, it calls for revision of Church teaching on marriage and sexuality "in light of recent cultural developments"; elimination of "sexist" ecclesial language; diocesan scholarship funds for laywomen training for Church "ministries"; diocesan committees to study "ministries of women"; affirmative action appointments of women to Church committees at every level, including a permanent member on the CCCB Pastoral Team.[270] Catholic feminists in the United States continue striving toward the same ends—as steps on the way to even more radical ends. They do not walk alone.

Most of the errors of feminist theology are common in liberal theology. The notion that the community rather than the ordained priest confects the Eucharist, in which Jesus Christ is only symbolically present, is taught by male theologians and promoted in liberal Catholic media far more commonly than most "folk Catholics" know. For example, *National Catholic Reporter* ran an infuriating three-part series by ex-Jesuit Bernard J. Cooke in May 1990 on the "eucharistic crisis" facing the American Church in the priestless years ahead.[271] Animated by the provincial notion that in the United States humanity has at last come of age, the series declared "rigid central governance of liturgy" by Rome to be "obsolete". Cooke, who teaches sacramental theology at Holy Cross College in Worcester, Massachusetts, dismissed transubstantiation as a magical notion mistakenly understood in the past to be "the very essence of the Mass", which thus "could only be celebrated by the ordained". Now, says Cooke, that "physical/miraculous understanding of the bread become body" should be replaced with "a different explanation of Christ's eucharistic

[269] See chap. 3 above.

[270] Jones, "Blueprint", 22.

[271] Bernard J. Cooke, pt. 1, "Loss Takes the Heart from Salvation Process", *National Catholic Reporter*, May 11, 1990, 1; pt. 2, "Entire Faith Community Performs Eucharist", *National Catholic Reporter*, May 18, 1990, 14; pt. 3, "The People Must Be Enlisted to Meet Eucharistic Crisis", *National Catholic Reporter*, May 25, 1990, 12.

presence" as "a new depth of communicating power" in the "bread and wine",[272] that is, as a change in *meaning* rather than in *essence*. Far more casually than the disciples who walked away from Jesus in John 6, Cooke thus turns the Church's most sacred treasure, the very Bread of Life, into a cloverleaf bun at a neighborhood potluck supper. To what end? To justify replacing ordained priests with non-ordained "eucharistic celebrants" of either sex, married, single, or drawn from what he ambiguously terms "some of the groups that Rome does not approve".

If seminarians are being taught such "sacramental theology", the priest shortage is no mystery. Why sacrifice one's life to Christ, why accept celibacy and obedience, to perform a rite that can be done just as well by a divorced lesbian hair stylist on her day off? Why retain the Mass at all, if Christ's Presence is not *in* the Eucharist but only in the community? Why not just hold hands and sing? If religion is merely a human construct that can make no troublesome personal moral demands, if its function is simply to advocate the successive enthusiasms of the secular culture—from feminism to "reproductive freedom" to reproductive technology to environmentalism—why not hear about it all on television and avoid the collection basket? If religion is merely psychology, why not get it straight from the psychologist? What objection could there be to Women-Church rituals other than the esthetic, if the "Eucharist" is not truly Christ's Body and Blood but only a symbol of no intrinsic value?

Aided by such subversive propaganda, Women-Church is building on the constituency it inherited from WOC. Its national conferences are larger than WOC's were at their peak, and its local manifestations grow ever more demented, ever more blatant.

In Louisville, Kentucky, an October 1988 Women-Church meeting featuring Rosemary Ruether as keynoter was twice announced in the diocesan newspaper, *The Record*.[273] Potential reg-

[272] Cooke, "Faith Community", 14.

[273] For documentation about Louisville Women-Church, I am indebted to Vickie (Mrs. Paul) Sample of that city.

istrants were directed to call the Ursuline convent, for Sister Janet Marie Peterworth, O.S.U., who works with the archdiocesan Ministry Formation Program.[274] Suzanne Holland, a staff fund-raiser for the Sisters of Loretto,[275] introduced Dr. Ruether. During the requisite ritual, between verses of "This Little Light of Mine", members chanted obscenities against the Pope.

Another Women-Church "liturgy" publicized in the *Record* was held on January 21, 1989, in Louisville's St. William's Church (Father James E. Flynn, pastor).[276] Appropriately appalled, Vickie Sample, a fervent, Ursuline-educated Catholic who attended both events, photographed the ritual, concelebrated by Sister Helen Legeay, S.C.N., a staff member at the archdiocesan Peace and Justice commission, who wore a red pantsuit. (Holland and Sisters Peterworth and Legeay had all participated in the 1987 Women-Church Convergence.)[277] With two other women, Legeay "blessed" bread and wine on the parish altar. The congregation did a circle dance. There was a solo performance by liturgical dancer Irene Denton Schaefer, who announced that she was God. When it ended, Legeay tried to engage Mrs. Sample in theological debate about Schaefer's delusion. According to Sample's account:

> Sister Helen Legeay asked me what books I had read, and I said St. Teresa of Avila. Sister Helen said St. Teresa was a great mystic. I said yes, and St. Teresa knew from her ecstasies that she was St. Teresa and God was God.[278]

Scandalized, Mrs. Sample tried to persuade Archbishop Thomas Kelly, O.P., retired Auxiliary Bishop Charles Maloney and Sister Rosella McCormick, president of the Louisville Ursulines, that Women-Church should not be meeting in Catholic churches, and its members should not hold Church posts. According to

[274] See "Bulletin Board", *Record*, Sept. 18, 1988; Sept. 22, 1988; and Jan. 19, 1989.

[275] Conference program, *Women-Church: Claiming Our Power*, Women-Church Convergence, Oct. 9–11, 1987, 39.

[276] "Bulletin Board", *Record*, Jan. 19, 1989.

[277] Participants' list, *Women-Church*, 6–7.

[278] Vickie Sample, letter.

Sample, Sister Rosella threw her photographs into a wastebasket. Bishop Maloney said, "God bless you", but never contacted her again. Archbishop Kelly told her he couldn't interfere with an "ecumenical" group like Women-Church unless he had reason to believe its activities were "contrary to Catholic teaching."[279] He is not easily convinced, it seems. In the spring of 1990, when a Women-Church gathering was held on Louisville's Ursuline campus, the group's newsletter carried this word from Suzanne Holland:

> The Goddess of foremothers has spoken to men in these days, through your loving deeds of old and the Holy One says this: . . . I will tenderly gather their grief and I have felt the weight of their oppression. So I have sent valiant women to prophesy and proclaim my saving acts. . . . By the falseness and wickedness of their prosecutors' deeds . . . shall patriarchy be condemned and brought to ruin. It shall crumble as dried mud which the sun has baked . . . likewise shall their pride crumble before them. . . . I, the Holy One, the Goddess Within . . . have heard the anguish of my daughters and will permit their suffering no longer.[280]

St. Joan of Arc parish in the St. Paul/Minneapolis archdiocese is an avant-garde dream come true. When Father Harvey Egan became pastor in 1967, it was an ordinary, lower-middle-class parish in south Minneapolis. Egan swiftly turned it into a flamboyant carnival of revolutionary Catholicism run with an iron hand. A colleague once said of Egan that he had taken the vows of "poverty, chastity and publicity". Egan responded that he had never taken a vow of poverty.[281] He sneered at the traditional "stand pat" faithful; closed the parish school; signed a front-page newspaper

[279] Letter from Archbishop Kelly to Mrs. Sample, Mar. 22, 1989.

[280] Suzanne Holland, *New Visions* (newsletter of Louisville Women-Church) (Spring 1990).

[281] Harvey Egan, *Leaven: Canticle for a Changing Parish* (St. Cloud, Minn.: North Star Press, 1990), 79. Egan's small book details the evolution of the parish.

statement opposing *Humanae Vitae*;[282] drew his sermons from Edward Schillebeeckx, Hans Küng and Charles Curran; padded the Sunday Mass readings with selections from "non-biblical" sources; wrote his own illicit canons; urged everyone present at Mass to receive Communion. In 1973, he says, Teilhard de Chardin became the parish patron. Invited homilists, ranging from Catholic radicals like ex-priests Philip Berrigan and Anthony Padovano to Episcopalian priestess Jeanette Picard, "Gray Panther" leader Maggie Kuhn, leftist attorney William Kunstler and New Age poet Robert Bly, came and went without attracting much attention outside the parish. But local newspapers gave it lavish coverage, before and after the fact, when he invited Gloria Steinem to deliver a Sunday homily on September 17, 1978. Egan, who says he was a charter subscriber to *Ms* magazine and regarded Steinem as a "heroine",[283] recalls in his reminiscences that the parking lot filled an hour early with "well-orchestrated" pro-lifers, some of whom knelt in the gymnasium entrance and "shrilly" prayed the Rosary. Steinem "did not mention abortion", he says, but she pledged to "defend always" the "right to reproductive freedom".

Archbishop John Roach was always "eminently kind", says Egan, and had even said on one occasion that if "there were no contemporary parish a la St. Joan's, he would have to establish one".[284] However, "torn between institutional responsibilities, right-wing protesters and a genuine admiration for the Christian vitality of our parish", the archbishop apologized for the scandal in his diocesan paper, ordered Egan to submit weekly notice of scheduled homilists and delegated "four strait-laced pastors" to investigate the parish. Their report was submitted to the archbishop, who summoned Egan to "review" it. Egan asked for an advance copy of the report. The archbishop did not reply, so Egan decided not to show up for the review.

Nothing happened. Father Egan was permitted to retain his

[282] Ibid., 42–43. Of the 76 dissenters, exactly half later left the priesthood. One of those was Auxiliary Bishop James Shannon, who married a divorcee.

[283] Ibid., 74.

[284] Ibid., 76.

pastorate without further interference. In 1980, parish feminists established a "caucus" called "Christians United to Realize Equality". In 1985, inspired by visiting Father Edward Walsh, M.M., Egan wrote a rambling "creed" for his new religion using the pronoun "her" in reference to God.[285] The parish continued to attract radicals from throughout the area. Still undisturbed, Egan retired in 1987.

At St. Joan of Arc Church, on August 12, 1990, during the 9:00 A.M. Sunday Mass, "hostess" Katie Johnson, a public school teacher from St. Paul, joined visiting celebrant Father Roy Bourgeois, M.M., at the altar to "consecrate" the host and the wine. Joan Riebel, president-elect of the parish council, and Teresa Graham, lector, thought it was such a good idea that they repeated the act at the 11:00 A.M. Mass. When it ended, Graham said from the altar, "Thank you, God, for the most amazing day." Her statement drew a standing ovation from the congregation. She told reporters that the sacrilege had been the "spontaneous outgrowth" of an earlier conversation with Bourgeois.[286] Both Johnson and Graham told Religious News Service that they understood their action as "concelebration".[287]

Pastor William Murtaugh was away on vacation. Archbishop Roach was out of town. Jerry Klein, spokesman for the St. Paul/ Minneapolis archdiocese, at first sputtered incoherently when asked to comment. Women are on the altar every week, he said, "as lectors, acolytes. If the parish believes it's something worthy of our review, we would do it."[288] Father Bourgeois, who has a long history of "peace" activism in support of rebel forces in El Salvador, was a resident of Maryknoll House in Minneapolis.

Ex-Pastor Egan preached at St. Joan's—in favor of women's ordination—on Sunday, August 19. According to chancery officials,

[285] Ibid., 101–4.

[286] Jean Hopfensperger, "Women Celebrate Masses with Priest", *Minneapolis Star Tribune*, Aug. 18, 1990, 1.

[287] Willmar Thorkelson, "Priest Disciplined for Inviting Women to 'Concelebrate' Masses", *Wanderer*, Aug. 30, 1990, 6.

[288] Ibid.

he said nothing in his homily about why the women involved should not have attempted to consecrate the host, but he assured diocesan authorities that he would not have permitted it if he had still been pastor.[289]

Eight days after the incident, following a page-one report in the *Minneapolis Star Tribune*, Father Bourgeois officially lost his faculties in the archdiocese. He set off on "an assignment" to protest the training of Salvadoran army troops at Fort Benning, Georgia.[290] Father Murtaugh was still on vacation. I asked Roseanne Rogers, director of ministries at St. Joan of Arc, whether the archdiocese planned any disciplinary action against the parish. She said none was anticipated. I asked whether the parish itself would remove the women from their positions.

"Oh, no!" she told me. "That would just be feeding into that—well, about the hierarchy, I'm probably the wrong person to be talking to." Rogers asked whether I had read Bernard Cooke's series in *National Catholic Reporter*. "That was how Johnson saw what she was doing; she thought she was up there as a representative of the community. She didn't think she was doing anything wrong. We have women up on the altar all the time but just not saying the words. So lots of people didn't even realize it was a big deal until Graham made her speech at the end."[291]

Ten days after the incident, as calls poured into the chancery office, Archbishop Roach held a press conference about his "incredibly rare" action of suspending Bourgeois. He said he also intended to report him to Archbishop Agostino Cacciavillan, the new papal pro-nuncio. "For unordained persons to take on ritual activities which are clearly and identifiably reserved to priests is trivializing and manipulative", he said. "Contrary to the way some would characterize this, it is not an issue of women's ordination.

[289] Interview with Joan Bernet, archdiocesan information office, Aug. 23, 1990.

[290] Jean Hopfensperger, "Archbishop Disciplines Priest Who Allowed Women to Say Mass", *Minneapolis Star Tribune*, Aug. 21, 1990, 3B.

[291] Interview with Roseanne Rogers, director of ministries, St. Joan of Arc parish, Aug. 21, 1990.

It was gross impropriety and misuse of something very sacred." If investigation should prove that the women involved knowingly violated Church law and were aware of the penalties prescribed, they might even face excommunication, he said.[292] Consistent with local precedent, however, Roach announced just four days later that the women were clearly innocent dupes. Though the women indignantly denied to the press that Fr. Bourgeois had "manipulated" them, the archbishop ruled that no one but the maverick Maryknoller would be penalized.[293]

At the bishops' 1985 "listening session", NARW's Maureen Reiff warned that feminists would oppose any pastoral on women's concerns unless it recommended ordination and "reproductive freedom". As promised, the liberal feminist establishment rose as one against the second draft of the NCCB pastoral because it is much firmer than the first in its remarks about ordination and "reproductive issues". PFE launched a campaign against ratification; Center of Concern counseled against it; Archbishop Weakland wrote an acid column recommending that it be forgotten. Yet, except in those two areas, the second draft is still so replete with concessions that it alarmed the orthodox as well. It myopically refuses to see feminism and the condition of women's religious orders as they are. The suggestion that the diaconate be opened to women is not its most alarming proposal, since it is not one on which the American bishops could act independently of Rome. More alarming because more probable is the recommendation that women's commissions be established in every diocese.[294] One can predict with gloomy certainty that such commissions would be filled and staffed with Women-Church partisans bent on "conscientizing" laywomen, like those in Louisville and Minneapolis.

[292] Jean Hopfensperger, "Archdiocese Will Investigate Mass Conducted by Priest, Women", *Minneapolis Star Tribune*, Aug. 22, 1990, 3B.

[293] Church, "Women Who Helped with Mass Won't Be Punished", *St. Cloud Times*, Sept. 2, 1990.

[294] "One in Christ Jesus", *Origins*, April 5, 1990, 736, no. 18.

In the autumn of 1990, the Vatican cautioned the NCCB to defer approval of the second draft until American bishops had consulted with bishops from other nations. When, on September 13, president Archbishop Daniel Pilarczyk announced that the NCCB Administrative Board had indefinitely postponed a vote by the full bishops' conference on the draft, many faithful Catholic women were relieved. But in the long run, that decision may do little to slow the ongoing drive to radicalize American Catholic women.

Sister Mariella Frye, USCC staff assistant to the pastoral writing committee, told me that the USCC Secretariat for Laity and Family Life, directed by Delores Leckey, and the NCCB Committee on Women in Society and in the Church, currently chaired by Bishop Matthew Clark of Rochester, began organizing in 1988 to train leaders for women's commissions in the nation's dioceses. "Regional meetings" for that purpose were held in Miami, Florida, Elkins Park, Pennsylvania, and San Juan Bautista, California, in 1989.[295]

A "first national women's symposium", sponsored by the same NCCB/USCC offices, was held in Arlington, Virginia, from November 30 to December 2, 1990. According to Secretariat staff member Sheila Garcia, the purpose of the symposium was to "provide concrete assistance to new or developing women's commissions".[296] Garcia stressed that the meetings are an independent project, "*not* linked to the pastoral". Bishop Clark was the keynote speaker; other speakers included USCC staff members, employees of various ecclesiastical bureaucracies, and other representatives of the feminist/peace-and-justice elite within the American Church. Some two hundred selected participants were instructed about "inclusive" language, opening the permanent diaconate to women, "sexism" and "societal injustices that oppress women", "women's ministry" in the administration of priestless parishes, pro-life feminism, women's spirituality, etc. The meeting was open

[295] Interview with Sister Mariella Frye, Sept. 21, 1990.

[296] Interview with Sheila Garcia, Sept. 25, 1990.

to just two representatives from each diocese, chosen by their bishop. But inevitably, other Catholic women will feel its effects as diocesan women's commissions are established and strengthened everywhere. Helen Hull Hitchcock, president of Women for Faith and Family, has warned that "at a minimum" such commissions will "interpose yet another bureaucratic layer between the bishop and his people".[297] They will "further marginalize and alienate orthodox Catholic women and their families". They will provide unlimited opportunities for feminist infiltration and indoctrination, financially supported and officially sponsored by the Church, whether or not a pastoral draft is ever formally approved.

The bishops' inexplicable behavior seems to presume that ordinary lay Catholics will remain faithful no matter what theologians say or bishops do. That assumption is unwarranted; the state of the laity is increasingly desperate. As long as feminist organizations are allowed to claim a Catholic identity, however spurious, their influence continues to grow among religious professionals, and the devastation they effect on the faithful intensifies. Few young Catholics even know that the Church claims to be the unique possessor of Christ's truth and authority; a generation of misinterpreted "ecumenism" has convinced them that all denominations are equally valid. The mounting plague of scandals among clerics and religious further diminishes lay respect for the bishops. And Catholic feminists in schools, parishes and diocesan offices refer to the hierarchy with unconcealed contempt.

It is true that most of the faithful do not know what is happening in the theological establishment. What reaches them is a message of laxity in belief and in morality. Because they are fallen beings, many find the message agreeable. Others see no difference between lax Catholicism and the secular world. Thus many defectors to fundamentalism or schismatic traditionalism leave Christ's living Church behind with clear and peaceful consciences.

[297] Helen Hull Hitchcock, "Observations and Recommendations on the Draft Pastoral", statement from Women for Faith and Family, Sept. 1, 1990, 1.

Do the bishops care about the souls of lay men and women? Perhaps they need to be reminded of Cardinal Newman's observation: "The laity. Ah, yes. The Church would look quite ridiculous without them."

Chapter Seven

From the Catacombs

Catholic feminism is sweeping across the American Church like a prairie fire from hell. Whether or not any given feminist intends to serve the Prince of Lies, every progression more clearly reveals the cause itself as a demonic assault on God, on his creation, on the Church and on the family. Its first victims are women. Men who subscribe to it show their disregard for the Faith. They also display contempt for women as women and an eagerness to escape masculine responsibility.

To view the devastation all at once is almost overwhelming. The unvarnished reality is that the faithful remnant of believers are living in the catacombs of an American Church under the domination of revolutionaries within a decadent secular society. Where, we ask, are our shepherds? How could God let this happen? If the Church can fall into such disarray, is she after all the true Church? Is there hope for her restoration? How can we and our children survive as Catholics until order is restored?

Where Are the Shepherds?

The American Church is convulsed by a lack of courageous leadership. What can explain the episcopal impotence so widely apparent? Twinges of guilt for past condescension? Misplaced gallantry? Hope that feminism will subside unconfronted? Dread of public criticism by feminist partisans in the media? Are bishops overawed by assertive women with graduate degrees? Or, feeling helplessly swept along by a torrent they can neither understand nor control, do they choose to ignore blatant disorders in order to keep their burgeoning bureaucracies staffed? Any of those explanations would seem more humanly comprehensible than bias in favor of a revolution in which their own offices are prime targets. If they hope to appease the mutineers, they might well review the lesson of Mary Daly: appeasement feeds revolutionary rage and inflates revolutionary arrogance.

The North American bishops have shown in other circumstances that they are capable of brusqueness. However they justify it in their own consciences, during the past generation they have not only tolerated but enforced discrimination against the non-feminist majority of Catholic women, often poorly instructed but meaning to be faithful, trying to live their vocations against the stream of mounting feminist influence within the American Church. Orthodox laywomen, disturbed about aberrant liturgical practices, spiritual direction, catechetics and sex education, have been either ignored or reproved for divisiveness. Meanwhile, women involved in the most egregiously offensive Catholic feminist activities have been given approval, a respectful ear if they want one and promotion in the religious bureaucracy.

The bishops do see the problems that result when children are left to raise themselves because their mothers are employed away from home. They see the injustice of women and children abandoned to poverty after divorce. Yet their proposals, in two drafts of the pastoral letter on women's concerns as well as in the letter on economics, have been focused on band-aid remedies like day care. They have not unambiguously enunciated the principles required for the healthy restoration of family life. Their most immediate pastoral duty in that regard is to remove the revolutionary vipers being cherished in the bosom of Catholic bureaucracy and to ensure that the Catholic Faith is taught in its purity and fullness. They are responsible before God for the spiritual welfare of their flocks; the souls of the faithful cannot be sacrificed to placate the unfaithful.

If, in addition, the bishops are also determined to speak out on public policy matters, they could do more for the well-being of families by lobbying effectively for a family wage or for restoration of a dependent income tax exemption at the original 1948 level than by the measures proposed in all three pastoral letters. The family wage, traditionally favored in Catholic social teaching, would guarantee the family head—of either sex—an income sufficient to support a family decently. There is probably little prospect for achieving it today. Chances would be better for tax reform. If families could deduct approximately six thousand dollars per child rather than the current two thousand, parents with five children would pay no tax on the first thirty thousand dollars of income. Most problems of maternal neglect, latchkey children and day care would be solved at once because most mothers in the labor force could afford to stay at home.

At even closer hand, surely the American bishops must see the terrible effects of feminism on the Church, yet they seem unwilling to recognize its nature. "One in Christ Jesus", their second draft letter to women, restates the Church's reasoning on male priesthood, abortion and contraception far more competently than the first. But in neither draft do the writers attempt to analyze the errors of feminism, and in the second, they actually praise it. They note the decline in vocations but suggest no explanation for it and even claim to find the "contemplative dimension" of postconciliar renewal in women's orders "edifying",[1] of all things. In other, more general public statements, too, bishops prominent in the NCCB speak so glowingly of conditions in the American Church as to bewilder the faithful. Everything would be rosy, their comments suggest, if it weren't for those few troublesome lay and clerical "fundamentalists" in the ranks.

The bishops' behavior seems curiously self-destructive. If, as often claimed, their motive for doctrinal laxity has been an ecumenical hope that separated Christian churches could be reunited through broader theological "pluralism", they should by now have noticed that religion without doctrinal clarity produces only a unity

[1] "One in Christ Jesus", *Origins*, April 5, 1990, 731, no. 126.

of indifference. If their shift toward "social gospel" Christianity was motivated by a hope of attracting more converts or more young people, it should have expired years ago; far from attracting those groups, liberal Catholicism has repelled them, just as liberal Protestantism has. By the time the American bishops took to doctrinal liberalism, mainline Protestant churches were already emptying. Over the past twenty years, impressive denominational growth has been confined to the culturally despised "fundamentalist" churches that reject all explaining away of the meaning of Scripture or basic Christian doctrines. Historical-critical Scripture scholars notwithstanding, "modern man", Protestant and, regrettably, Catholic, continues to flock to them. The only visible Catholic vigor has been in small orthodox groups and institutions, the charismatic movement (which has bitterly disappointed revolutionaries by becoming increasingly orthodox and Marian) and the small but intense schismatic traditionalist groups. Genuine ecumenism, based not on indifference but on a common moral vision arising from faith, is found most strikingly in the pro-life movement, which continues to grow despite the tepidity of episcopal support, because even lay men and women uncertain about theological matters can see that killing babies is hideously wrong.

Have the bishops hoped for the esteem of the secular world, which approves culturally assimilated Catholics? Or do they still not see women's activities as matters of real consequence? Only God knows. Whatever their motives, the genuine spiritual welfare of the faithful cannot have been one of them. The consequences of their passivity demonstrate how compelling the need is for legitimate episcopal authority.

Why Did God Let This Happen?

In an immediate sense, the present disorders are not God's doing. They follow from the encounter between religious revolutionaries who reject authority and ecclesiastical leaders who decline to exercise it. As we have seen, Catholic feminism, a critical part of the revolutionary force, is the unexpected fruit of bad theology and cultural dislocation in the closed society of women religious. Because those designated to guard the truth have allowed error to spread unchecked, it has grown and metastasized to its present catastrophic proportions.

God let this happen only in the sense that he created man with free will. Although he knew that we would sin, he wanted those who chose to serve him to choose him freely. Sin is universal. Though we tend to expect better of clerics and religious professionals, we should not be surprised when anyone sins. Even God's first human children sinned in spite of their extraordinary gifts and their intimacy with him. Repudiation of the story of their Fall, a focus on the humanity of Jesus to the exclusion of his Divinity and his role as Divine Redeemer and the consequent denial of his Church's authority as divinely given, are the theoretical hinges of neo-modernism. The doctrine of original sin is especially pertinent today for the clarifying light it casts on feminist errors.

In the beginning as today, rejection of authority was the central problem. The particular roles of Eve and Adam seem to indicate the temptations to which each sex is most inclined. Genesis reveals that God created both man and woman in his own image, sharing one human nature, equal in dignity, intended for each other in a complementary relationship in the unity of marriage. When Eve steps forth from God's hands, Adam rejoices in her equality, exclaiming, "She now is bone of my bone and flesh of my flesh." They are delighted in each other, naked and innocent. Just as their human nature is made in the divine image, so their union in the faithful, fruitful, permanent covenant of marriage is an image of the inner life of the Blessed Trinity, loving and creative.

Cunning, the serpent draws Eve into dialogue. She knows the limits God has set, but she listens as the deceiving voice lures her with a promise of autonomy—the promise that she can be her own God. When she yields, her disobedience separates her from God and from Adam. Contemporary Catholic feminists are part of a vivid, and ruinous, re-enactment of that ancient tragedy. Their history strikingly recalls Eve's susceptibility to false promises, her rebellion against legitimate authority and her presumptuous ambition to make herself "as God". Women, it seems, are more prone than men to such fraudulent spiritual enthusiasms.

Men, in contrast, seem especially tempted to irresponsibility. Adam chooses to evade the very duties of leadership that Eve covets. He is not deceived by the serpent, but he eats the forbidden fruit anyway.[2] Perhaps he cannot bear to be separated from his bride by her sin. Perhaps he is intimidated by the prospect of confronting her. In either case, the head of the first family disobeys his Creator and betrays his patriarchal obligations with his eyes open. We can see parallels to Adam's sin in men who abdicate their legitimate authority and obligations in the family. Some use the slogans of feminism to seduce women into sexual relationships outside of marriage, then coerce them to abort their babies. Some deny their wives motherhood or deprive them of the right to live their maternal vocation with full attention by driving them into the labor force. Some welcome any excuse to remain immature and carefree boys by shunting their responsibilities onto their wives.

Many contemporary Catholic pastors and shepherds have similarly succumbed to the lure of irresponsibility. They have failed to teach with clarity and conviction, to defend the Church with courage or to protect their flocks from enemies internal or external, neo-modernist, feminist or atheist. Male support for women's ordination probably springs from the same root. Ultimately, feminists are less culpable than those in the hierarchy who permit them to desolate the American Church unopposed. It could not have happened if pastors and bishops had fulfilled their patriarchal obligations. Seeing them vacillate, one can understand at last how the collapse of St. John Fisher's episcopal brethren must have happened.

If there were no grain of truth beneath the psychopathology of feminism, it would have attracted no adherents. That grain is the charge that there is division between men and women where

[2] 1 Tim 2:13–14.

there should be harmony. Feminists are right in tracing it back to Genesis, though they utterly misinterpret the Fall. The division began there; nothing in the Genesis account is more poignantly recognizable than the sinners' immediate denial of guilt: Adam blames Eve, and she blames the serpent. Since then no culture has perfectly overcome it. But feminist theologians like Rosemary Ruether distort the Church's teaching about original sin to make it seem a direct affront to women. Of birth and baptism, Ruether says:

> The Christian Church teaches that birth is shameful, that from the sexual libido the corruption of the human race is passed from generation to generation. Only through the second birth of baptism . . . is the filth of mother's birth remedied and the offspring of the women's womb made fit to be a child of God.[3]

This is not the Catholic doctrine of original sin, as every Catholic child knew when Ruether was a child. One could just as well say that intellect and free will are consequences of sexual libido. The Church does not teach that sexual libido has anything to do with the transmission of original sin other than the biological fact that the act of sexual intercourse—a positive moral good within marriage—is the means by which human life, and thus human nature, is transmitted. All infants, born and unborn, are unique persons of eternal value and innocent of personal sin, even those conceived in actual sin: in fornication, adultery or even by rape. There is no "filth" in the mother's womb or her giving birth. Although feminists endlessly complain that the Church blames Eve for the Fall, it is in fact Adam whom Christian Tradition has held responsible for original sin and for its transmission.[4]

The effect of Adam's sin was the loss of something supernatural, something not intrinsic to human nature. It was sanctifying grace, God's gift to our first parents in their original innocence, which

[3] Ruether, *Sexism and God Talk*, 260.

[4] See Pope Paul VI, "Credo of the People of God", no. 16, in John A. Hardon, S.J., *Modern Catholic Dictionary* (Garden City, N.Y.: Doubleday, 1980), 581.

had raised them above what they were by nature to allow them to share in God's life as his children. When Adam and Eve turned away from his love in disobedience, they destroyed the supernatural life of grace in their own souls. And because Adam betrayed his patriarchal responsibility as head of the first family, Christians hold that it was he who deprived their posterity of the life of grace, leaving mankind in worse condition than if he had never had it. Not only was sanctifying grace no longer part of the human inheritance, as the Jones fortune would cease to be part of the Jones family inheritance if Grandpa Jones had gambled it away in Las Vegas, but the human family was left with a deficit it was incapable of ever making up—incomparably worse than if Grandpa Jones had saddled his family with the national debt.

In their original integrity, Adam and Eve also had other gifts that the Church calls *preternatural*: their intellects and passions were fully in harmony with their wills, and they were preserved from natural death. Those gifts, too, were lost to human nature by that first sin. Just as man's soul was no longer at one with God, so his soul and body were no longer at one with each other.

Because he was both God and Man, Christ's saving death restored mankind's oneness with God. His sacrifice gives man the opportunity to regain supernatural grace in Baptism, which does not make him "fit to be" a child of God, as Ruether puts it, but in fact *makes* him a child of God, reborn in God's life. But the damage to human nature was permanent. Created in God's image, Adam and Eve were still good and still yearned for God, but their minds were darkened, their wills weakened and they were no longer exempt from death. Mankind is not what it was before the Fall, a truth so painfully evident in each of us, and in the world around us, that those who deny the doctrine of original sin never cease looking for something else to blame for our condition: the stars, or ignorance or patriarchy. That is why knowledge of the good is no guarantee of good behavior. Only by cooperation with God's grace can man even hope to overcome the disorder in his nature that inclines him toward personal sin. The sacraments are the means of grace Christ gives us, through his Bride, the Church, to heal and sustain us in the internal struggle that continues as long as we live.

In the sacrament of Matrimony Christ restores the dignity of the spousal union. It is the clearest image of God's relationship with the Church; Sacred Scripture is full of marital imagery. Just as husband and wife cooperate in the procreation of a baby, so the Church as Bride receives, nurtures and returns life to God. And just as their distinct roles as husband and wife complement each other in marriage, so marriage and celibacy are complementary in the Church's life. Distinction of roles is the basis of relationship; the priestly role is distinct from but complementary to that of the laity. Priestly celibacy is another way to live the same consecration in charity, not with a human person but with God. And in celebrating Mass, every priest represents both Christ as Bridegroom and the Church as Bride.

Seeing the human failings that follow from original sin but rejecting the doctrine, feminists have blamed them on patriarchy in all its forms, beginning with the Eternal Father. The bitterest irony of this latest battle between the sexes is that it was not men who declared it but feminists. The primary target of secular feminism was the traditional family. Looking back on the cultural expectations prevailing when the "sexual revolution" began, one can concede that some men demeaned women's characteristic role. Every era has its own imperfections. But it was a far better society for women and children than the present chaotic one, and few women would not gladly trade their present state to restore it if they could. The feminists did not call on society to value women's distinctive contributions properly but instead attempted the impossible task of opposing human nature, denying the differences everywhere revealed in experience. Feminists won the battle, and women lost.

More than ever before in the Christian era, women now are expected to submit to sexual exploitation, contraception, abortion, pornography, divorce and permanent assignments in the labor force. Those determined to live as women have traditionally lived often feel they must apologize for, or at least explain, their eccentricity. Single mothers, discarded wives and their children make up the majority of the new poor in this country. A generation of latchkey children is growing up neglected, many of them emotionally and intellectually stunted victims of deficient mothering. At the same time, an indignant masculine backlash against irrational feminist accusations and litigation is emerging to erode further men's protective instincts toward women. Having seen its consequences, most women have abandoned organized feminism, but they still suffer its damaging effects in prevailing sexual permissiveness, employment expectations and marital instability. They are trying to raise their children in their spare time in a culture warped by perverted education, degraded media and widespread doctrinal and moral confusion.

Catholic feminism incorporates all the errors of secular feminism and others more profound. Its major target is the religious belief that underlies the traditional family and society. It has led ever further from Christian belief into alienation, dissent, rejection of all authority and denial of the sacredness of human life. Feminist theologians maintain that God was mistaken in creating two sexes. Their attack on Church doctrine is aimed directly at the roots of human existence. Consistent in their inability to recognize in embryo the identity of the full-grown organism, they deny both the divine origin of the Church and the human personhood of the fetus. The reason for Catholic feminism's otherwise puzzling zeal for abortion is its inherently gnostic intent, arising from liberation theology, to build a "new man", isolated from the mediating institution of the family. So long as the family stands between the naked individual and the power of the state, utopian totalitarianism cannot abolish all freedom. Since, as the Red Guard of the Catholic cultural revolution, feminists expect to be in control in the new order, they seek only what would benefit childless elitists in a collectivist utopia. They are enemies of God, of life, of nature, of the normal.

Under the feminist assault, patriarchy has come to be regarded as odious, even by patriarchs. Feminists denounce it as atavistic, inherently inequitable, irredeemably oppressive. But they misunderstand the nature of women's rights. Recovering those rights will require that patriarchy be reclaimed.

Selfishness, like pride, is gender neutral. So patriarchy has sometimes been abused by sinners to justify their selfishness. But the present agonies of the family, of secular society and of the Church all result from failure to meet patriarchal responsibilities, understood and lived as St. Paul outlined them.[5] The term *patriarchy* refers to the male-headed family form and social system expressed in Scripture and existing everywhere in human society. In the Church, it is a title referring to bishops who rank just below the Pope in jurisdiction, though Catholic feminists use the word to mean the male priesthood and the entire male hierarchy. In all cases, it is properly an office, not a declaration of qualitative superiority. As Lyman Stebbins liked to say, "St. Joseph was the least of the Holy Family, but its head."

Feminist mythology to the contrary, the Church did not inflict inequality on women. Catholicism in fact elevated women to a status they had never enjoyed in pre-Christian societies by venerating the Blessed Virgin Mary as the perfect model of human response to God, by consecrating marriage as a sacrament, by recognizing the family as the basic unit of society and by constantly teaching that sexual acts are the unique privilege of the married state. No less a feminist than Sidney Callahan recognizes the protection such a morality provides for women:

> While the ideal has never been universally obtained, a culturally dominant demand for monogamy, self-control, and emotionally bonded and committed sex works for women in every stage of their sexual life styles. When love, chastity, fidelity and commitment for better or worse are the ascendant cultural prerequisites for sexual functioning, young girls and women expect protection from rape and seduction, adult women justifiably demand male

[5] Eph 5:25–32.

support in childrearing, and older women are more protected from abandonment as their biological attractions wane.[6]

The Church teaches that creation exists to raise up souls to God. Woman's natural vocation is irreplaceably at the heart of that purpose, where human nature is most plainly seen to be neither simply animal nor purely spiritual but a mysterious combination of both. Mothers not only share in the procreation of new lives; they also bring them into being within their own bodies. In the "domestic Church" of the family, where the future Church is born, they are the ones most immediately responsible for the physical and spiritual formation of the new generation through the transmission of faith and culture. Their wisdom and generosity are essential in shaping the family as a holy and enduring center where each member is cherished not for what he does but because his immortal soul is of incalculable value. It is in the family that all mankind's labor is transmuted by love into the human and the personal.

Parenthood is a work of eternal significance in which both parents share, but by nature woman is the one most deeply engrossed. Her vocation is so much a part of herself that she becomes submerged in it; she is compelled by its demands always to be centered outside herself. Certainly motherhood is a demanding work, and it sometimes brings anguish as well as joy. When a woman's husband and children rise up and call her blessed,[7] she doubtless deserves their praise. Some who deserve it never receive it; there are heroines of holiness struggling at the brutally difficult task of raising and supporting their children alone. But even in the most painful circumstances, a mother usually finds that her baby awakens in her a previously unknown passion of protective love. To have a life work so absorbing that it makes us forget ourselves is a great human privilege.

[6] Sidney Callahan, "Abortion and the Sexual Agenda", *Commonweal*, Apr. 25, 1986, 237.

[7] Prov 31:28.

Fathers are called by that name because they reflect God's capacity to generate life outside himself, a high honor and an awesome responsibility. A father's role is of great importance; many women have lately discovered from painful experience how vital it is to family stability and the healthy psychological and moral development of children. But normally he must be engaged elsewhere much of the time, dealing with the world, providing for his family's material needs. Only a fortunate minority of men find a work significant in itself. For most, the knowledge that they are supporting their families is all that gives their labor meaning.

Patriarchy, properly interpreted, means men meeting their vocational obligations. When a husband fulfills his responsibilities as St. Paul prescribes, his role is not one of domination but of service. As husband and father he is to negotiate with the outside world, provide for and protect his family, guide and direct it in consultation with his wife. In normal human relationships, such consultation is broad; Germaine Greer was turned away from rabid feminism when she discovered how broad it is in Third World villages.[8] Sustained by her husband's loving care, a wife is freed to live her maternal vocation. She can accept a subordinate role in the chain of command as her part in their mutual subjection to Christ. Most women would be delighted with a restoration of the family in which duties were so divided that their husband's work could support them while they cared for children and home. When spouses give themselves to each other as a gift to create "the unity of the two",[9] both can happily fulfill the destiny for which they were created, and the family can flourish.

Both secular and religious feminists erred by adopting the faulty view that, as Lydwine Van Kersbergen put it, "identifies the human with the masculine".[10] Their program was never designed for the common good but for those few women determined that

[8] Germaine Greer, *Sex and Destiny: The Politics of Human Fertility* (New York: Harper Colophon Books, 1985).

[9] Pope John Paul II, *On the Dignity and Vocation of Women* (*Mulieris Dignitatem*) (Vatican City: Libreria Editrice Vaticana, 1988), 21.

[10] Kersbergen, *Woman*, 12.

biology should not control their lives. Feminism rages at the notion that sex is destiny. In fact, sex is not destiny in the sense of ultimate destination: it does not determine whether we will go to heaven or hell. But it is integral to identity. Our bodies, female or male, are part of our indivisible unity as persons and thus determine to a considerable extent how we will attain our eternal destiny. Wherever it takes us, we will still be men and women.

A family-centered perspective, with its exclusive emphasis on the mother's domestic role, seems unfairly confining not only to feminists but also to a good many other women these days. Of course, there are women who do not marry. Of course, single career women deserve justice. Nothing whatever in the teachings of the Church suggests that their sex should limit their career ambitions. They are free to pursue any for which they have the requisite gifts, to be lawyers or astronauts, brain surgeons or theologians. Those who marry, however, are not choosing a career but a vocation. If they become mothers, their children remain their most sacred responsibility until they are grown. Marriage is a sacrament because it is the ordinary state of life; the Church always emphasizes the common good. A society formed on Christian principles will hold the intact family as the norm. It will not permit discrimination against marriage or childbearing, or legitimize illicit or perverse sexual behavior, to ensure that the unmarried feel equitably treated. The importance of the family to its own children, to the wider society and to the future of the species requires that it be given special consideration.

Down the Christian centuries, other women have sacrificed the privileges of marriage and motherhood for lives of consecrated service as Brides of Christ. Pope John Paul II, in his 1988 letter on the role of women, *Mulieris Dignitatem*, restated the traditional view that even as consecrated virgins, they exercise in a spiritual way the maternity that is woman's natural vocation. That position, too, is rejected by feminists, including nuns, who see it as defining women by their relationship to others rather than as individuals. Whether or not women's religious communities will survive to debate the point is unclear. The minority of women's orders—those orthodox communities represented in Consortium Perfectae Caritatis and the Institute on Religious Life—still believe in consecration. They may continue to grow. But unless God sends some new St. Teresas to reform the major congregations in LCWR, they seem doomed to extinction.

In any case, justice for women must begin with recognition of the absolute importance of their maternal vocation. Because the Enemy recognizes it, he strikes first at women. Where the role of wives and mothers is respected as noble, demanding and essential, where husbands, children and society honor and support it as it deserves, feminism loses most of its seductive allure. Because the division of roles in the family is natural and universal, hope remains for the restoration of the family. Few of those who abjure the place of patriarchy will survive as families. But until Catholic authorities again honor patriarchy in the Church as well, there is little prospect for restoring a mature priesthood.

Is the Catholic Church Still the True Church?

In this life, we will probably never fully understand why the present disorders occurred; that judgment is between God and the consciences of those responsible. Nevertheless, persecuted, betrayed and abused though she is, the Catholic Church *is* Christ's true Church. Her children fail as individuals—we all fail in different ways—but she remains our Holy Mother. Knowing by faith that the sins and failings of individual Catholics cannot change her nature, we must remain confident that God will look after her, since she is his Bride. However dark things may appear—and they certainly do—the future of the Church is in his hands. We can trust him, knowing he brings good out of evil. His will for us is to become saints in a time of internal persecution, when his Church's beauty is often obscured by men and women beside whom the money changers in the temple look comparatively innocent. But

Christ's beauty and truth are still hers, and the supernatural graces he dispenses through her are still necessary for our salvation. To allow ourselves to be driven from her by anger and dismay at the sins of her abusers would render ironic tribute to Satan. As surely as Christians in earlier persecutions, we must pray for the conversion of those who abuse her while we remain steadfast in the Faith, defend the honor of the Church, avail ourselves of her sacraments, preserve and transmit her truth. We must also bring to our prayers and penitential acts for her, every day, all the fervor we would bring to prayers for our natural mother in a grave illness.

Hope of Restoration

Can we reasonably hope for the restoration of the American Church? Christ's promise that the gates of hell will not prevail against his Church, after all, made no mention of North America. Nevertheless, there is much to be hopeful about among American Catholics. Indeed, there are so many signs of a new spring that we could grow euphoric if we shut our eyes to the blight and looked only at the new enterprises springing up like green shoots around a storm-split willow.

First of all, it is apparent that Pope John Paul II and Cardinal Ratzinger recognize the need for reform. The Pope is attempting to tilt the balance within the national bishops' conferences away from schism by appointing papal loyalists as sees become vacant. So far, admittedly, few of the new men show the kind of counter-revolutionary militancy needed to extirpate the revolutionaries from the national bureaucracy or even from their own diocesan apparats. But when the orthodox become the controlling majority, the progressive faction is more likely to assume a low profile than to break from Rome entirely. Vatican initiatives have provoked a gratifying if unwarranted paranoia in Americanist ranks; *National Catholic Reporter*, for example, routinely writes as though the Church were undergoing a reign of terror.

Unsurprisingly, conversions have not recovered in raw numbers from the pit into which they dropped after the Council.

But against all natural expectations, their quality is superb. While a certain proportion are social converts who have learned little about the Faith during their RCIA season, others are adornments to the Church, luminous replacements provided by Divine Providence for the academic, clerical and religious defectors to neo-modernism. Among them are such names as Richard John Neuhaus, Father George Rutler, Helen Hull Hitchcock, Warren Carroll, Thomas Howard, Peter Kreeft, Ronda Chervin, Dale Vree, James Likoudis, Paul Vitz, Onalee McGraw, Charlotte Hays, Kenneth Whitehead, John Haas, Scott Hahn and Tom Bethell, to mention only a few. Convert Charles Wilson founded the St. Joseph Foundation to help beleaguered laymen seek the rights guaranteed them in canon law. Catholics United for the Faith, founded by another convert, the late Lyman Stebbins, provides catechetical research and brings together in local chapters some of the most apostolic, activist and enterprising laymen in the country, including delightful young families. Most other converts I know are young intellectuals who have read their way into the Faith independently, usually before they ever introduced themselves to a priest. The orthodoxy and piety of a surprising proportion of young priests, despite the prevalence of aggressive neo-modernism in their seminary educations, gives further unexpected evidence of God's mysterious Providence. Impressive numbers of young, and not-so-young, returnees to orthodoxy have been reconverted and beleaguered members of the faithful have been sustained through the charismatic movement, the Marian movement, the Apostolate for Family Consecration, Cardinal Mindzenty Foundation, the Communion and Liberation movement, Opus Dei, Women for Faith and Family, the pro life movement, the natural family planning movement and other instruments of Providence. Most young Catholics never knew the Catholicism of Gregorian chant, stained glass and self-confident doctrine. It attracts them, as beauty and truth always will. When they return, they are more interested in restoration than in continued religious minimalism.

Counter-revolutionary student groups are springing up in Catholic colleges where many faculty members no longer teach Catholicism with conviction. The *Observer* of Boston College is the flagship of a growing little fleet of their publications. Lay-directed Catholic Forums at St. Louis University and in New York and Washington, D.C., bring together and help sustain believers. The outspoken *Wanderer* is still the conservative journal of record of the post-conciliar decline, and *National Catholic Register* continues to record Catholic news from an orthodox perspective. Long-established *Homiletic and Pastoral Review*, though published chiefly for priests, provides sound and inspiring reading for laymen as well. But new Catholic publications and publishing companies have also been born. Ignatius Press produces higher-quality work than Sheed and Ward did even before it decomposed, and Ignatius' *30 Days* magazine has pioneered new territory as an international Catholic news magazine. Servant Books, Neumann Press, Christendom Press, Trinity Communications and Keep the Faith are among recent entrants to the publishing field. *Our Sunday Visitor* weekly newspaper is back on the Catholic track after a dismal period when CFFC collaborator James Castelli was its Washington correspondent. OSV also publishes popularly written orthodox books, as well as Father Peter Stravinskas' excellent *Catholic Answer* magazine. Sophia Institute Press reprints classic Catholic books in handsome new editions, most recently Dietrich von Hildebrand's *Transformation in Christ* and St. Thomas Aquinas' splendid commentaries on the Lord's Prayer, the Hail Mary and the Apostle's Creed, *The Three Greatest Prayers. Fidelity*, *Crisis*, *New Covenant*, *Twin Circle*, *St. Paul's Family Magazine*, *Faith and Reason*, *Catholic Eye*, *Social Justice Review* and *This Rock* are among the lively new Catholic journals with growing readerships.

In the scorched earth of Catholic education, new institutions are preparing a small but privileged core of intellectual leaders for tomorrow's Catholic world. Thomas Aquinas College in California, now in its twentieth year, is admired both for its Catholicity and for its academic excellence. St. Ignatius Institute continues to strike sparks in the general gloom of the Jesuit University of San Francisco. Christendom College, in Virginia, turns out increasing numbers of joyously Catholic graduates. Magdalen College, in New Hampshire, is building a new campus. Thomas More Institute, an even younger New Hampshire college, is adding new buildings. Orthodox seminaries, including those of the Legionaries of Christ, the Oblates of the Virgin Mary, the Toronto Oratorians and Holy Apostles Seminary for late vocations, are outgrowing their quarters. In Catholic colleges, philosophy is more likely than theology to have survived in recognizable condition. Sound Catholic philosophy departments survive in some long-established colleges, including St. Anselm's College in Manchester, New Hampshire, and St. Thomas College in St. Paul. Other enterprises prove that recovery is possible. The Franciscan University of Steubenville, Ohio, dramatically reformed by Father Michael Scanlan, is thriving. And under Father Richard Villano, religious education director John Sondag offers the best adult education programs I know of, at St. Helena's parish in Minneapolis, where ex-Bishop James Shannon was once pastor. Pontifical catechetical institutes offering orthodox certification and degree programs operate at St. John's University in New York, Notre Dame Catechetical Institute in Arlington, Virginia and Our Lady of Peace Institute in Beaverton, Oregon. More detailed information is available from the Catholic Center in Washington, which monitors Catholic educational institutions as one of its projects.[11]

On the level of secondary education the need is vast, but models like Trivium School in Massachusetts, Trinity Schools in South Bend and Minneapolis and Colorado Catholic Academy in Denver prove that adolescents are not ineducable, even today, if someone will teach them the truth. The broadest and perhaps most important new development is Catholic home schooling. Evangelical Protestants began building home schooling programs, publishing companies and support networks in the 1970s, years before most Catholic parents realized they could no longer depend on parochial schools to educate their children as Catholics. Alter-

[11] Contact: Michael Schwartz, Director, The Catholic Center, 721 Second Street N.E., Washington, DC 20002, (202) 546-3004.

native school programs need no defense on educational grounds. America's public school systems are drug-infested and often violent centers, apparently able to teach little but sexual permissiveness and moral relativism: at great expense, they have produced some twenty-seven million functional illiterates. Parochial schools are physically and academically much better, but for twenty-five years they have failed in their chief purpose, which is to teach the Catholic Faith. Few of their graduates know what the Church teaches about sin and grace, while most are falsely convinced that Catholics must be pacifists. They have seldom learned that Jesus Christ is both God and Man, that the Eucharist is his Real Body and Blood or that the Catholic Church has unique authority, but they are thoroughly indoctrinated with feminism, indignation against the government of El Salvador and anxiety about the rain forests. Though nuns are gone from most parochial schools, the neo-modernist bias saturates diocesan education offices, religious education offices, catechetical certification programs, Catholic education congresses and textbooks.

Back in the late 1960s, scattered groups of disenchanted Catholic parents began establishing small, independent academies, but between fund-raising difficulties, state regulations, administrative problems, mandated insurance expenses and internal disagreements, only the exceptional survived.

Over the decade of the 1980s, however, Catholic home schooling grew exponentially, from a few small ventures to a vigorous alternative system, educating, it is estimated, more than a million Catholic children from pre-school through senior high school.[12] Leading the field are Seton School, of Front Royal, Virginia; Our Lady of the Rosary, of Bardstown, Kentucky and Our Lady of Victory, of Mission Hills, California. Some parents enroll children for their full home study correspondence courses; others use their materials and testing services but plan their own classes and do their own grading. Others, still more confident, entirely design their own curricula. Their results are admirable. Almost always,

[12] Interview with Janet Smythe, Aug. 25, 1990.

home-taught children test several years ahead of classroom-taught contemporaries. Janet Smythe, founding president of Our Lady of the Rosary, reports an average 1990 SAT score of 1000 for their students. The most important result of home schooling, however, is that students learn the doctrines of the Catholic Faith. So do their parents, many of whom turned to this kind of education because they recognized the gaps in their own.

Unfortunately, these budding enterprises are in most cases still outside the mainstream, ignored or coolly tolerated by the Catholic bureaucracy. Few bishops seem to recognize that they are standing at a cultural crossroads in the United States, free to choose between restored orthodoxy and further decay. While they were still testing the water, the remarkable Mother Angelica forged ahead independently to build her successful Eternal Word Television Network. Their joint reaction seemed to be annoyance at her traditional convictions. Except for her, only a garnish of nuns is visible in the orthodox Catholic counter-culture. Few if any of the promising ventures mentioned here receive financial support—or even appreciable moral support—from the dioceses in which they operate. Most are staffed entirely by laymen, while much of the Church's former labor force is off at feminist spirituality conferences, plotting to destroy Catholicism from within. Nevertheless, among the tares, the wheat still grows. A healthy and vigorous sub-culture is thriving among believers, and millions of Americans are hungering for truth. The fields are still white with the harvest.

What Can We Do about the Feminist Revolution?

Anyone who supposes that Catholic feminism represents the thinking of "Catholic women" has not been paying attention. Phyllis Schlafly, the Catholic woman who led a host of other Catholic and Christian women in defeating the Equal Rights Amendment, is exceptionally gifted, but her views are far more typical of the majority than are those of any Catholic feminist. That is why she was able to succeed. Most Catholic women are spiritual descendants of the women of Jerusalem, who followed the way of the Cross and stood at Christ's feet while he died. It is such Catholic women who are leading battles against feminist spirituality, "creation spirituality", defective catechetics and relativistic sex education in every part of the country. As they know, it is necessary to distinguish between the problem of the feminists and the question of one's own children. A long view may be called for in dealing with feminist domination in one's parish or diocese, but matters regarding one's children demand a short view. They are not expendable; the safety of their immortal souls requires that they be protected from perverted doctrine. One cannot wait until they have lost the Faith to accept the fact that many Catholic institutions are corrupt and systematically corrupting. Parents have always tried to keep their children away from likely occasions of sin. Today, these quite possibly include parochial schools, CCD classes and retreat programs. Unless one knows beyond doubt that the directors, teachers and materials used in parish or diocesan programs are sound, it is prudent to assume they are not.

Hard as it is to believe there could be poison behind the gentle geniality of Catholic teachers, the evidence continues to mount. In Minnesota in 1989, just after she had garnered press attention as a defender of Matthew Fox, Sister Ramona Fallon, O.S.B., was promoted from the New Ulm diocesan chancery office to the post of director of education at Minnesota Catholic Conference. In New Orleans, at the August 1990 Catholic Educators' Convention, Fox adjutant Sister Jose Hobday said in her keynote address that Catholic teachers should "forget about any Church doctrine prior to twenty years ago". They must "cut the spiritual and emotional umbilical cord to the Church and start in a new direction", she said.[13] Even programs that once looked sound show signs of infiltration: at the 1988 national convention of Teens Encounter

[13] Paul Likoudis, "Keynote Speaker Tells Teachers to Forget about 'Old' Doctrines", *Wanderer*, Aug. 30, 1990, 1.

Christ, for example, Quixote Center veteran Sister Fran Ferder was listed as keynote speaker.[14] And even in parishes with good pastors, feminists are apt to control the school and the CCD programs.

Believing American Catholics can no longer look with confidence to Church institutions and agencies. By grim necessity, this is an age of the laity. Perhaps its unseen approach was the otherwise obscure purpose of the Holy Spirit at Vatican II: to prepare us with conciliar documents providing the theological framework and formal authorization for lay responsibilities.

Anguished by the condition of the Church and the disorders in the family that follow from it, lay Catholics must recognize the dimensions and limitations of their roles. The restoration of the Church, which is his Body, is in Christ's hands. All we can do is our duty, as we see it, where we are. We must fulfill the requirements of our own vocations in our own daily lives. The vocation of Catholic wives and mothers is centered in their homes and parishes. The role of the home as a "little Church" becomes more important than ever where the larger Church is unreliable. If our geographical parishes are dominated by revolutionaries, we can transfer to the best parish to be found in our area. It is antithetical to the essence of worship to be affronted constantly by illicit liturgical and homiletic innovations. Mass at many Catholic churches these days looks like a 1930s Busby Berkeley musical: a lone male celebrant surrounded by bevies of pastel-clad females. My husband and I have settled gratefully in a parish where two fine priests, a vital sacramental life and a congregation including many families with small children help compensate for a building that resembles a subway station or a catacomb.

Once you have found a parish in which you can worship without agony, it is possible to consider ways to combat the revolution. Some practical advice: be prepared for unpopularity and frequent defeat. As Father Paul Marx frequently says, God

[14] Registration brochure, "Bismarck, ND, Invites YOU to the 1988 National TEC Convention, May 27–30, 1988, University of Mary Campus".

will not ask whether you won, only whether you tried. If your parish, school, diocese, alma mater or an organization of which you are a member cooperates in presenting feminist or revolutionary speakers, register your complaint with your bishop and diocesan authorities and encourage other faithful Catholics to object as well. Document your objections if possible. This book is intended to be of assistance to doing so, though the multiplication of Women-Church groups and Matthew Fox collaborators makes it impossible to identify all those working subversively at the local level. Since most feminists condone abortion, you may be able to find records of their past anti-life positions.

Usually, though not always, the event will take place despite your protests. If it does, attend with at least one other witness and record the presentation or take photographs or notes. Evidence of any outrage to the Faith should be reported to the bishop, but don't send him your only copies. If he does not respond to your letter or dismisses your concerns, you might write a courteous but factual letter to the editor of the secular newspaper. Fear of hostile publicity has rendered many diocesan authorities supine before the feminists, so it may be wholesome to give them some orthodox counter-publicity to worry about.

When confronting an individual who seems to be violating Catholic teaching or practice, be calm, courteous and charitable but not apologetic; admonishing the sinner is a spiritual work of mercy. Follow the New Testament procedure:[15] first speak to him privately; if he does not correct his error, go to him again with another member of the Church. If he still persists in error, you may confront him publicly. When appealing to Church authorities on matters of policy or public scandal, however, you are not dealing with private matters. It is most strongly recommended that more than one person attend any meeting with an authority in such cases. Judge prudently whether a given matter is so grave as to require the bishop's attention. For example, concerns about bad publications in the parish magazine rack, while entirely valid—and

[15] Mt 18:15–18.

very common—are best handled within the parish by speaking to the pastor (who probably has not read them) or joining the relevant committee to try to influence decisions about which publications will be stocked. Liturgical abuses are more serious. If speaking to the pastor and joining the liturgy committee prove fruitless, report the matter to the bishop. If he has not responded within a month, it may be appropriate to write a brief, factual, documented report to the papal pro-nuncio, especially if the matter concerns abuses of the sacraments.[16] If you believe your rights to orthodox instruction or valid sacraments are being denied, you may call or write the St. Joseph Foundation for a consultation.[17]

Some Catholics, to ensure that their financial support to the Church is not squandered on abuses, have begun mailing their contributions directly to the Holy Father in Vatican City.[18] Parishes cannot survive without income, however, so prudence as well as justice would advise maintaining some level of local giving.

How Can We Survive as Catholics Until Order Is Restored?

The world has always opposed the demanding truth of Catholicism, to an extent varying with the degeneracy of the times. Today, more than ever, it is impossible to be at home in one's culture and still be a faithful Catholic. Survival demands that we be countercultural.

Next to giving them life, the primary obligation Catholic parents owe their children is to educate them so that they can save their souls. Parents would be wise to consider educating them at home. Most people considering home-schooling are initially daunted by fear that they don't know the secrets of teaching, but in fact there is

[16] Address: The Most Reverend Archbishop Agostino Cacciavillan, Apostolic Pro-Nuncio, 3339 Massachusetts Avenue NW, Washington, DC 20008.

[17] Address: Charles Wilson, Director, The St. Joseph Foundation, 4211 Gardendale, Suite A-100, San Antonio, TX 78229, (512) 690-8998.

[18] Mail to: Personal Funds, His Holiness, Pope John Paul II, Apostolic Palace, 00120 Vatican City, Europe (postage $.50 per half ounce).

little secret about it. It is a time-consuming task, but those whose vocation is motherhood could spend that time no better way. There are home-schooling groups in almost every community. If you don't know how to begin, look for Mary Pride's *Big Book of Home Learning*[19] at any Christian bookstore. She surveys most of the Catholic and non-sectarian materials available.

Most families find that home-taught children are not only better educated but also happier. They avoid the petty cruelties of the playground and the peer-group stratification that are routine at any school. They remain normal children while others their age are being turned into pathetic mainstream teenagers at the local junior high. No sceptical amateurs tamper with either their religious beliefs or their psychological attitudes. Their self-confidence is bolstered by the assurance that their parents love them enough to give them years of genuinely "quality" time. Home-taught children may benefit from community sports programs (track and swimming are commonly offered), dancing, art and music lessons; such activities provide opportunities to mix with other children without being swallowed up in a peer group. And because home education is a net bargain, parents can probably afford to pay for the extra programs. Further "socialization skills" are learned in play with their siblings. Home-schooling families frequently provide a lot of siblings.

After you have removed your children from institutions you believe to be destructive, there is still the problem of living as Catholics in the midst of scandalous disorder. Institutional decay is now so pervasive that it has become impossible to fight every objectionable phenomenon separately. How can one raise children as faithful Catholics and survive spiritually oneself when Church bureaucrats and institutions seem determined to prevent it?

Above all, faith must be nourished by prayer if it is to survive. Attend Mass daily if possible. Say the Rosary daily as a family. Mary is our Mother and our model in the following of Christ. We

[19] Mary Pride, *The Big Book of Home Learning* (Westchester, Ill.: Crossway Books, 1986).

must imitate her and pray for her intercession. Catholics devoted to Mary—laymen, religious, priests and bishops—tend to remain close to Christ and to grow into orthodoxy.

Participating in parish and diocesan organizations is a worthy effort, though its potential effectiveness depends on the degree to which they are already controlled by revolutionaries. Parish council, school board and pastoral council seats may be important locations. Most parish women's organizations, in my experience, are moribund. If you have allies, you could probably rise to office rapidly and perhaps bring them back to life. With pastoral support, you might be able to start a new program to draw together people hungry for substantial spiritual nourishment. However, one cannot neglect family life to attend an endless succession of meetings. Parish-wide efforts at restoration are probably hopeless, anyway. But small autonomous groups open to interested parishioners can be vitally important for awakening and sustaining the faith of their members. I have been astonished by the fruits observed over just two years in a local Communion and Liberation group, which has drawn young families into a transforming mutual effort to build Christian community. It is extremely important to find, or build, a small community of believers, especially where parish life is bleakest. You may find companions in faith through the pro-life movement or through any of the groups in the orthodox sub-cultural network.

Grim as it is, our trial does not leave us so bereft of spiritual support as the Japanese Catholics were when Catholic missionaries were expelled by the Emperor in 1616. Tens of thousands were martyred, and for two centuries every Japanese was directed by law to trample on the cross. No priests were permitted to enter the country until 1859. Yet when a Catholic Church at last reopened—in Nagasaki—more than fifty thousand Catholics came forward. They identified the true Church by three marks: a celibate clergy, loyalty to the Pope and veneration of the Virgin Mary.[20] Mary's

[20] François Ligneul, "Christianity in Japan: Catholicism", in *Catholic Encyclopedia* (New York: Robert Appleton, 1910), 307.

Rosary has been a school of doctrine as well as a source of spiritual comfort for persecuted Catholics in many times and places. In her apparitions in our own times, she has promised those who say it faithfully all the graces necessary to their state in life.

My own grandparents, like many others, raised eleven children in a little mission town where there was no resident pastor until my widowed grandmother was past seventy. While my mother was growing up, the family pumped a railroad handcar to the next town for Sunday Mass, a trip not far by automobile but a long way by handcar. Two of the girls grew up to be nuns, in the days when that seemed like a good thing. All the children remained faithful, life-long Catholics. It is not because of the pending scarcity of priests that today's young so often do not remain faithful, but because they do not know the essential doctrines of the Faith.

When feminism is defined as a movement to establish the equality of women, it sounds plausible. But its fruits betray its real nature. Even at its least destructive, it is a tactical falsehood, like the Emperor's new clothes. It attempts to establish equality between the sexes, which already exists in fact, by forcing everyone to pretend the sexes are identical. In the family, it would substitute performance contracts and pre-nuptial divorce agreements for the loving donation of all one's self and goods to a permanent common life. In commerce, it is a divisive form of reverse discrimination. In academia, as academics know, it is a cut-throat politics, unconcerned with fact or scholarly objectivity. In its ultimate manifestation, in religious feminism, it is an anarchic madness.

Most of secular society has moved past it to different enthusiasms, not necessarily wholesome. Even Gloria Steinem is talking more about the New Age "journey within" than about feminism these days. But in the Church, feminism is still at a fever peak. Catholic feminists are like Gadarene swine, plunging off a cliff into the sea. Eventually, like all religious revolutionaries, they will dash themselves to destruction against the rock of the Church. Even Elaine Pagels, fond though she had grown of gnosticism, admitted in the *Gnostic Gospels* that ancient gnosticism died and Catholicism lived because the Church's sacraments and moral teachings, affirming the goodness of the natural order, of marriage, procreation, childbirth and practical charity, are exactly what men need to make ordinary life sacred.[21] In the end, in his own time, God will restore his Church, writing straight with man's crooked lines. Until then, he has promised us the graces we need to be faithful. If it seems that we are exiled to the catacombs while we wait for the restoration of the American Church, we can be comforted with the knowledge that it is not an inappropriate place for Christians to begin rebuilding.

[21] Pagels, *Gnostic Gospels*, 175–76.

Abbreviations of Organizations

ACLN	American Catholic Lay Network
ACS	Association of Contemplative Sisters
ASCD	Association for Supervision and Curriculum Development
CCA	Chicago Call to Action
CCC	Coalition of Concerned Catholics
CCCB	Canadian Conference of Catholic Bishops
CCL	Conference for Catholic Lesbians
CCW	Chicago Catholic Women
CFFC	Catholics for a Free Choice
CIWPC	Committee for Incorporation of Women's Perspectives into Curriculum
CMSW	Congregation of Major Superiors of Women
COC	Center of Concern
CORPUS	Corps of Reserve Priests United for Service
CTSA	Catholic Theological Society of America
CUF	Catholics United for the Faith
CWU	Church Women United
ERA	Equal Rights Amendment
GTU	Graduate Theological Union

ICCS	Institute for Culture and Creation Spirituality
IWT	Institute of Women Today
IWY	International Women's Year
LCWR	Leadership Conference of Women Religious
NARW	National Assembly of Religious Women
NCAN	National Coalition of American Nuns
NCCB	National Conference of Catholic Bishops
NCCW	National Council of Catholic Women
NCEA	National Catholic Education Association
NOW	National Organization for Women
PFE	Priests for Equality
SBL	Society of Biblical Literature
SFCC	Sisters for Christian Community
SIECUS	Sex Information and Education Council of the United States
SIGMA	Sisters in Gay Ministry Associated
USCC	United States Catholic Conference
WATER	Women's Alliance for Theology, Ethics and Ritual
WOC	Women's Ordination Conference

Acknowledgments

Many people have contributed information and documentation for this book. I wish to thank especially those sane and faithful women religious and priests whose help has been invaluable but whose lives might become more difficult than they already are if their names were mentioned. Special thanks are due to Rita Marker, who first insisted I pay attention to the Catholic witches, and to LeMay Bechtold, who patiently answered my questions so many times; to Liz Stong, Peggy Cuddy, Carol Lloyd, Ann Vicinanzo, Laurene Connor, Patricia Hannie, Vickie Sample, Nancy Coughran, Kathleen Sullivan, Mary Jane Brix, Anne Marie Collopy, Fred Blonigen, Charles Wilson, William Lawton, Jerald Cooper and Jeff Ottle; to Elaine Zitzman, Delores Boyle and Darlene Gerber of the St. Paul/Minneapolis Archdiocesan Council of Catholic Women and to the many others who helped me with research all along the way. I am deeply indebted to Marcus Berquist, my son-in-law, who knew the answers to all my theological and philosophical questions and generously discussed them with me. I am most grateful to my patient husband, Roy, who encouraged and supported me through months of abstracted neglect. Finally, my most grateful thanks to Laura Berquist, Peggy O'Reilly and Ann Steichen, my beloved daughters and daughter-in-law, who read the work in progress, warned me when something wasn't clear, cheered me on with their interest and support and who give me constant joy and hope by so admirably living their vocations as Catholic wives and mothers.

Acknowledgments

Many people have contributed information and encouragement to [illegible]

Index